STATIUS
SILVAE IV

BCP Classic Commentaries on Latin and Greek Texts

Current and forthcoming titles:
Aristophanes: Ecclesiazusae, R. Ussher
Calpurnius Siculus: The Eclogues, C. Keene
Empedocles: The Extant Fragments, M. Wright
Euripides: Cyclops, R. Seaford
Euripides: Helen, A. Dale
Euripides: Iphigenia in Tauris, M. Platnauer
Euripides: Troades, K. Lee
Herodotus: Book II, W.G. Waddell
Nicander: Poems & Poetical Fragments, A. Gow & A. Scholfield
Persius: Satires, J. Conington & H. Nettleship
Plutarch: Alexander (commentary only), J. Hamilton
Seneca the Elder: Suasoriae, W. Edward
Statius: Silvae IV, K. Coleman
Tacitus: Dialogus, W. Peterson
Tacitus: Germania, J. Anderson
The Poems of Cicero, W. Ewbank
Virgil: Aeneid III, R. Williams

STATIUS
SILVAE IV

Edited with an English Translation,
Commentary and Bibliography by
K.M. Coleman

Bristol Classical Press

Cover illustration: Herakles Epitrapezios of Lysippus. Bronze (ht 0.75m).
Roman version of an original of the late 4th century BC.
Naples, Archaeological Museum.

First published by the Oxford University Press, 1988

This edition published in 1998 by
Bristol Classical Press
an imprint of
Gerald Duckworth & Co. Ltd
61 Frith Street
London W1D 3JL
e-mail: inquiries@duckworth-publishers.co.uk
Website: www.ducknet.co.uk

Reprinted, 2000, 2001

© K.M. Coleman 1988

All rights reserved. No part of this publication
may be reproduced, stored in a retrieval system, or
transmitted, in any form or by any means, electronic,
mechanical, photocopying, recording or otherwise,
without the prior permission of the publisher.

A catalogue record for this book is available
from the British Library

ISBN 1-85399-582-7

Offset from the Oxford University Press edition of
Statius: *Silvae* IV by K.M. Coleman.

EDITOR'S PREFACE

AMID the renewed attention which the *Siluae* are attracting, their topicality and a corrupt text still create obscurities and discouragement. Book 4, the most varied in content, metre, and genre, has not previously been edited on its own. A commentary submitted as a D.Phil. thesis in Oxford in 1979 has developed into this edition; I hope that the translation will elucidate both text and commentary.

An editor of the *Siluae* has a difficult task, but shortcomings in this edition are not for lack of constant assistance and encouragement. I owe the greatest possible gratitude to Professor F. R. D. Goodyear, Dr N. M. Horsfall, and Professor R. G. M. Nisbet, each of whom read the entire manuscript in its successive stages and gave me unstintingly of their time, their wisdom, and their scholarship. Mrs Miriam Griffin, who supervised the original thesis with Professor Nisbet, meticulously guided my prosopographical researches. For invaluable discussion on many points I am especially grateful to Professor E. Badian, Professor H. D. Jocelyn, Mr F. M. A. Jones, Professor D. A. Russell, and Sir Ronald Syme; and to Professor W. S. Watt for generously allowing me to print two conjectures which he is shortly to publish elsewhere. By courtesy of Professor Russell I was able to consult a copy of Vollmer's commentary, belonging to St John's College, Oxford, which was annotated by Housman. To the many other people who helped me with a wide range of queries I say *in omnes a uobis studiorum sinus ducor*; but where the arguments in this edition are simplistic, and the conclusions false, *ego sum quae traducor*.

The Ashmolean Library in Oxford, with its superb resources and its 'family' of librarians and readers, has made successive visits happy and productive. Research grants from the University of Cape Town and the Human Sciences Research Council have made research trips possible. Helen Murray scoured Campania with me in search of the Via Domitiana, Susan Abraham drew the plans and processed my photographs, and the British School at Rome gave me invaluable help in arranging accommodation and acquiring the photograph for Pl. 3. Glenda Muhl processed the manuscript on floppy disc with the utmost fortitude and accuracy, and the editors at the Oxford University Press have been unfailingly generous with their time and expertise; Dr L. A. Holford-Strevens in particular has assisted me far beyond an editor's conventional responsibility, alerting me to much evidence and scholarship of which I should otherwise have remained ignorant.

Cape Town
May 1986

KATHLEEN COLEMAN

CONTENTS

List of Illustrations	viii
Bibliography	ix
General Introduction	xv
Sigla	1
Text and translation	2
Commentary	53
Index	241

LIST OF ILLUSTRATIONS

Fig. 1. Plan of the imperial fora — 70
Fig. 2. Map of Northern Campania — 103
Fig. 3. Roman highway: stylized cross-section — 114
Fig. 4. Roman causeway: stylized cross-section — 117

Pl. 1. The *Via Domitiana* on the slope beneath the Arco Felice — 115
Pl. 2. The *Via Domitiana* on the slope beneath the Arco Felice: close-up of *gomphus* — 115
Pl. 3. Bust of the river-god Volturnus from the ampitheatre at Capua (now S. Maria Capua Vetere) — 121
Pl. 4. The Volturno near its mouth at Castel Volturno — 121

BIBLIOGRAPHY

THE list below consists of the core of works cited so often as to merit an abbreviated reference in the text: where different works by a single author need to be distinguished, books are referred to by abbreviated titles and articles by date.

(i) *SILVAE* EDITIONS, COMMENTARIES, AND TRANSLATIONS

This selection comprises the most accessible works. For an exhaustive list see van Dam, *Comm.* 509-11.

Politian: L. Cesarini Martinelli (ed.), *A. Poliziano. Commento inedito alle Selve di Stazio* (Florence, 1978)

Markland: J. Markland, *P. Papinii Statii libri quinque Silvarum* (London, 1728; edn.[2] Dresden-London, 1827) (text and commentary)

Baehrens: E. Baehrens, *P. Papinii Statii Silvae* (Leipzig, 1876) (Teubner)

Vollmer: F. Vollmer, *P. Papinius Statius, Silvarum libri* (Leipzig, 1898; repr. Hildesheim, 1971) (text and commentary)

Klotz: A. Klotz, *P. Papinii Statii Silvae* (Leipzig, 1900; edn.[2] Leipzig, 1911) (Teubner)

Phillimore: J. S. Phillimore, *P. Papini Stati Silvae* (Oxford, 1905; edn.[2] 1917, repr. 1967) (Oxford Classical Text)

Slater: D. A. Slater, *The Silvae of Statius Translated, with Introduction and Notes* (Oxford, 1908; repr. 1968)

Saenger: G. Saenger, *P. Papini Stati Silvae* (St Petersburg, 1909) (text)

Mozley: J. H. Mozley, *Statius I: Silvae, Thebaid I-IV* (New York-London, 1928) (Loeb Classical Library)

Frère: H. Frère (ed.) and H. J. Izaac (tr.), *Stace, Silves* (Paris, 1944, repr. 1961) (Coll. Budé)

Marastoni: A. Marastoni, *P. Papini Stati Silvae* (Leipzig, 1960; corr. edn. 1970) (Teubner)

Traglia: A. Traglia, *P. Papini Stati Silvae* (Turin, 1978) (Corpus Paravianum)

Traglia-Aricò: A. Traglia and G. Aricò, *Opere di Publio Papinio Stazio* (Turin, 1980) (Coll. classici Latini)

van Dam, *Comm.*: H.-J. van Dam, *P. Papinius Statius, Silvae Book II: A Commentary* (Leiden, 1984)

(ii) STANDARD REFERENCE WORKS

Blümner: H. Blümner, *Die römischen Privataltertümer* (Munich, 1911)

Broughton: T. R. S. Broughton, *The Magistrates of the Roman Republic* (New York, 1951-2)

CIL: *Corpus Inscriptionum Latinarum* (Berlin, 1862-)

BIBLIOGRAPHY

CLE: F. Bücheler and E. Lommatzch (eds.), *Carmina Epigraphica Latina* (Leipzig, 1895–1926)
Degrassi: A. Degrassi, *I fasti consolari dell'impero Romano* (Rome, 1952)
Dict. Geog.: W. Smith (ed.), *A Dictionary of Greek and Roman Geography*, 2 vols. (London, 1873)
D–S: C. Daremberg and E. Saglio, *Dictionnaire des antiquités grecques et romaines d'après les textes et les monuments*, 5 vols. (Paris, 1877–1919)
E–J: V. Ehrenberg and A. H. M. Jones (eds.), *Documents Illustrating the Reigns of Augustus and Tiberius*[2] (Oxford, 1955, repr. with addns. 1976)
Ernout–Meillet: A. Ernout and A. Meillet, *Dictionnaire étymologique de la langue latine* (Paris, 1951)
FIRA[2]: S. Riccobono, J. Baviera, C. Ferrini, J. Furlani, V. Arangio-Ruiz, *Fontes Iuris Romani Anteiustiniani*[2] i–iii (Rome, 1940–3)
Head: B. V. Head, *Historia Numorum: A Manual of Greek Numismatics*[2] (Oxford, 1911)
ILS: H. Dessau (ed.), *Inscriptiones Latinae Selectae* (Berlin, 1892–1916)
IRT: J. M. Reynolds and J. B. Ward-Perkins (eds.), *Inscriptions of Roman Tripolitania* (Rome, 1952)
Kaser: M. Kaser, *Das römische Privatrecht* i[2] (Munich, 1971), ii[2] (Munich, 1975)
Kl. P.: K. Ziegler and W. Sontheimer (eds.), *Der Kleine Pauly*, 5 vols. (Munich, 1975)
K–S: R. Kühner and C. Stegmann, *Ausführliche Grammatik der lateinischen Sprache*[3], rev. A. Thierfelder, 2 vols. (Leverkusen, 1955)
Latte: K. Latte, *Römische Religionsgeschichte* (Munich, 1960)
Lausberg: H. Lausberg, *Handbuch der literarischen Rhetorik* (Munich, 1960)
L–H–S: M. Leumann, J. B. Hofmann, and A. Szantyr, *Lateinische Syntax und Stilistik* ii (Munich, 1965)
Mattingly, *BMC*: H. Mattingly, *Coins of the Roman Empire in the British Museum*, i. *Augustus to Vitellius* (London, 1923; rev. 1976); ii. *Vespasian to Domitian* (London, 1930; repr. 1966)
Mattingly, *RIC*: H. Mattingly and E. A. Sydenham, *The Roman Imperial Coinage*, i. *Augustus to Vitellius* (London, 1923); ii. *Vespasian to Hadrian* (London, 1926)
McC–W: M. McCrum and A. G. Woodhead, *Select Documents of the Principates of the Flavian Emperors* (Cambridge, 1961)
N–W: F. Neue and C. Wagener, *Formenlehre der lateinischen Sprache*[3], 4 vols. (Leipzig, 1892–1905)
OCD: N. G. L. Hammond and H. H. Scullard (eds.), *The Oxford Classical Dictionary*[2] (Oxford, 1970)
OGIS: W. Dittenberger, *Orientis Graeci Inscriptiones Selectae* (Leipzig, 1903–5)
OLD: P. G. W. Glare (ed.), *Oxford Latin Dictionary* (Oxford, 1968–82)
Otto, *Sprichwörter*: A. Otto, *Die Sprichwörter und sprichwörtlichen Redensarten der Römer* (Leipzig, 1890; Hildesheim–New York, 1971)

BIBLIOGRAPHY   xi

PIR: *Prosopographia Imperii Romani*[1] (Berlin, 1897–8)
PIR[2]: *Prosopographia Imperii Romani*[2] (Berlin–Leipzig, 1933–)
Platner–Ashby: S. B. Platner and T. Ashby, *Topographical Dictionary of Ancient Rome* (Oxford, 1929)
RAC: *Reallexikon für Antike und Christentum* (Stuttgart, 1950–)
RE: *Real-Encyclopädie der classischen Altertumswissenschaft* (Stuttgart, 1893–)
Roscher: W. H. Roscher (ed.), *Ausführliches Lexicon der griechischen und römischen Mythologie*, 2 vols. (Leipzig, 1884–1937)
Schanz–Hosius: M. Schanz and C. Hosius, *Geschichte der römischen Literatur bis zum Gesetzgebungswerk des Kaisers Justinian*[4], 2 vols. (Munich, 1935)
SEG: J. J. E. Hondius and A. G. Woodhead, *Supplementum Epigraphicum Graecum* (Leiden, 1923–)
TLL: *Thesaurus Linguae Latinae* (Leipzig, 1900–)
Wissowa, *RKR*[2]: G. Wissowa, *Religion und Kultus der Römer*[2] (Munich, 1912)

(iii) OTHER WORKS

André, *Couleur*: J. André, *Études sur les termes de couleur dans la langue latine* (Paris, 1949)
André, *Alimentation*: J. André, *L'Alimentation et la cuisine à Rome* (Paris, 1961; edn.[2] 1981)
Axelson: B. Axelson, *Unpoetische Wörter: Ein Beitrag zur Kenntnis der lateinischen Dichtersprache* (Lund, 1945)
Beloch: K.-J. Beloch, *Campanien: Geschichte und Topographie des antiken Neapel und seiner Umgebung* (1879; edn.[2] Breslau, 1890)
Birt, *Buchwesen*: Th. Birt, *Das antike Buchwesen* (Berlin, 1882)
Birt, *Abriß*: Th. Birt, *Abriß des antiken Buchwesens* (Munich, 1913)
Bonjour: M. Bonjour, *Terre natale* (Paris, 1975)
Bright: D. F. Bright, *Elaborate Disarray: The Nature of Statius' Silvae* (Meisenheim, 1980)
Cancik, *ANRW*: H. Cancik, 'Statius, "Silvae": Ein Bericht über die Forschung seit Friedrich Vollmer (1898)', in W. Haase (ed.), *Aufstieg und Niedergang der römischen Welt*, ii. 32/5 (Berlin–New York, 1986), 2681–726
Cancik, *LK*: H. Cancik, *Untersuchungen zur lyrischen Kunst des P. Papinius Statius* (Hildesheim, 1965)
Chevallier: R. Chevallier, *Les Voies romaines* (Paris, 1972) = *Roman Roads*, tr. N. H. Field (London, 1976)
Citroni: M. Citroni, *M. Valerii Martialis Epigrammaton liber primus* (Florence, 1975)
Courtney: E. Courtney, *A Commentary on the Satires of Juvenal* (London, 1980)
Curtius: E. R. Curtius, tr. W. R. Trask, *European Literature and the Latin Middle Ages* (London–Henley, 1953)
van Dam, *ANRW*: H.-J. van Dam, 'Statius, "Silvae": Forschungsbericht 1974–1984', in W. Haase (ed.), *Aufstieg und Niedergang der römischen Welt*, ii. 32/5 (Berlin–New York, 1986), 2727–53

BIBLIOGRAPHY

D'Arcy Thompson, *Birds*: D'Arcy W. Thompson, *A Glossary of Greek Birds* (London–Oxford, 1936, repr. Hildesheim, 1966)

D'Arcy Thompson, *Fishes*: D'Arcy W. Thompson, *A Glossary of Greek Fishes* (London–Oxford, 1947)

D'Arms: J. H. D'Arms, *Romans on the Bay of Naples: A Social and Cultural Study of the Villas and their Owners from 150 BC to AD 400* (Cambridge, Mass., 1970)

Doblhofer: E. Doblhofer, *Die Augustuspanegyrik des Horaz in formalhistorischer Sicht* (Heidelberg, 1966)

Eck (1975): W. Eck, 'Die Laufbahn eines Ritters aus Apri in Thrakien', *Chiron* 5 (1975), 365–92

Eck, *Organisation*: W. Eck, *Die staatliche Organisation Italiens* (Munich, 1979)

Frederiksen: M. Frederiksen, *Campania*, ed. N. Purcell (British School at Rome, 1984)

Friedländer: L. Friedländer, tr. J. H. Freese and L. A. Magnus, *Roman Life and Manners under the Early Empire* (London, 1907–13, repr. New York, 1979)

Garzetti: A. Garzetti, tr. J. R. Foster, *From Tiberius to the Antonines: A History of the Roman Empire, AD 14–192* (London, 1974)

Håkanson: L. Håkanson, *Statius' Silvae: Critical and Exegetical Remarks with Some Notes on the Thebaid* (Lund, 1969)

Hardie: A. Hardie, *Statius and the* Silvae: *Poets, Patrons and Epideixis in the Graeco-Roman World* (Liverpool, 1983)

Härtel: W. Härtel, *Studia Statiana* (diss. Leipzig, 1900)

Housman, *Cl. Pap.*: J. Diggle and F. R. D. Goodyear (eds.), *The Classical Papers of A. E. Housman*, 3 vols. (Cambridge, 1972)

Janson: T. Janson, *Latin Prose Prefaces: Studies in Literary Conventions* (Stockholm, 1964)

Legras: L. Legras, 'Les dernières années de Stace', *REA* 9 (1907), 338–49 and 10 (1908), 34–70

Maiuri (1928): A. Maiuri, 'Cuma: Nuovi tratti messi in luce della "Via Domitiana"', *NSc* 1928, 181–5

Maiuri, *Passegiate campane*: A. Maiuri, *Passegiate campane*[3] (Florence, 1957)

Millar, *Emperor*: F. Millar, *The Emperor in the Roman World (31 BC–AD 337)* (London, 1977)

Newmyer: S. T. Newmyer, *The Silvae of Statius: Structure and Theme* (Leiden, 1979)

N–H: R. G. M. Nisbet and Margaret Hubbard, *A Commentary on Horace, Odes: Book 1* (Oxford, 1970), *Book 2* (Oxford, 1978)

Pavlovskis: Z. Pavlovskis, *Man in an Artificial Landscape* (Leiden, 1973)

Robertson: C. M. Robertson, *A History of Greek Art*, 2 vols. (Cambridge, 1975)

Sauter: F. Sauter, *Der römische Kaiserkult bei Martial und Statius* (Stuttgart–Berlin, 1934)

Scott: K. Scott, *The Imperial Cult under the Flavians* (Stuttgart–Berlin, 1936)
Sherwin-White: A. N. Sherwin-White, *The Letters of Pliny: A Historical and Social Commentary* (Oxford, 1966)
Syme, *Arval Brethren*: R. Syme, *Some Arval Brethren* (Oxford, 1980)
Syme, *RR*: R. Syme, *The Roman Revolution* (Oxford, 1939)
Syme, *Rom. Pap.*: R. Syme, *Roman Papers* i–ii, ed. E. Badian (Oxford, 1979); iii, ed. A. R. Birley (Oxford, 1984)
Syme, *Tacitus*: R. Syme, *Tacitus*, 2 vols. (Oxford, 1958)
Vessey, *ANRW*: D. W. T. C. Vessey, 'Transience Preserved: Style and Theme in Statius' "Silvae"', in W. Haase (ed.), *Aufstieg und Niedergang der römischen Welt*, ii. 32/5 (Berlin–New York, 1986), 2754–802
Vessey, *CHCL* ii: D. W. T. C. Vessey 'Flavian Epic', in E. J. Kenney (ed.), *The Cambridge History of Classical Literature* ii (Cambridge, 1982)
Vessey, *Statius and the Thebaid*: D. Vessey, *Statius and the Thebaid* (Cambridge, 1973)
Weinstock: S. Weinstock, *Divus Julius* (Oxford, 1971)
White (1973a): P. White, 'Notes on Two Statian ΠΡΟΣΩΠΑ', *CPh* 68 (1973), 279–84
White (1973b): P. White, 'Vibius Maximus, the Friend of Statius', *Hist.* 22 (1973), 295–301
White (1974): P. White, 'The Presentation and Dedication of the *Silvae* and the *Epigrams*', *JRS* 64 (1974), 40–61
White (1975): P. White, 'The Friends of Martial, Statius, and Pliny, and the Dispersal of Patronage', *HSCPh* 79 (1975), 265–300
White (1978): P. White, '*Amicitia* and the Profession of Poetry in Early Imperial Rome', *JRS* 68 (1978), 74–92
White, *Technology*: K. D. White, *Greek and Roman Technology* (London, 1984)

GENERAL INTRODUCTION

1. STATIUS' CAREER

ALMOST all the evidence we possess for St.'s career is derived from his own poetry, especially two autobiographical passages: *S.* 3. 5. 22–42, 5. 3. 209–45. But these passages are relevant only for St.'s competitive entries and his epics, and it is generic principles and not chronology which govern the order in which he cites these compositions. External evidence is provided by Juv. 7. 82–7, and four lines of the lost work *De Bello Germanico* are quoted by Valla on Juv. 4. 94.[1]

St.'s background and origins are of considerable importance in understanding the type of poetry contained in the *Siluae*. His father was born at Velia in S. Italy (5. 3. 126 f.). His family had perhaps lost equestrian status through failure to meet the census requirement (5. 3. 117 f.). He won several prizes in poetry and perhaps also oratory at the Augustalia, world-famous games which were held every four years at Naples (5. 3. 134 ff.), and at the Pythian, Nemean, and Isthmian Games (5. 3. 141 ff.).[2] He taught in Naples (5. 3. 146 ff.), where his son was born (3. 5. 12 f., 4. 7. 17 ff.), and thereafter in Rome (5. 3. 176 ff.). His Neapolitan curriculum comprised a recondite selection of Greek poets (5. 3. 148 ff.); he also tutored Domitian in religious lore.[3] His son's estate at Alba Longa, equipped by Domitian with a water-supply (3. 1. 61–4), may have originally been granted (perhaps by Vespasian) to the elder Papinius.[4]

St. thus spent his youth in a highly cultured environment; from his father, who was both a professional poet and a teacher, he learnt the art of composing poetry (5. 3. 209–14). His first recitations were at Rome in front of his father and a senatorial

[1] 'lumina, Nestorei mitis prudentia Crispi / et Fabius Veiento: potentem signat utrumque / purpura, ter memores impleurunt nomina fastos; / et prope Caesareae confinis Acilius aulae.'
[2] On the Augustalia see R. M. Geer, *TAPhA* 66 (1935), 208–21. For the elder Papinius in Greece see K. Clinton, *TAPhA* 103 (1972), 79–82, and see Hardie, 6 ff., for a full account of his career.
[3] Deduced by G. Curcio, *Studio su P. Papinio Stazio* (Catania, 1893), 8, from *S.* 5. 3. 178 ff. 'sub te Dardanius facis explorator opertae, / qui Diomedei celat penetralia furti, / creuit et inde sacrum didicit puer'. See Hardie, 11 and ch. 1 n. 68.
[4] On the elder Papinius' associations with the Alban estate see Hardie, 13.

audience (5. 3. 215 f.). In his father's lifetime he won at the Augustalia, like his father before him (5. 3. 225).[5] He composed the libretto for a mime, *Agaue*, to be performed by the pantomime Paris (Juv. 7. 87).[6] This must date from before 83, when Domitian had Paris executed (Plin. *Pan*. 46. 1 ff.). The extant fragment of the *DBG* suggests that it dealt with Domitian's campaigns of AD 82/3 against the Chatti and may have been intended for his triumph in 83.[7] In Rome St. ('florentibus annis', 3. 5. 23) married Claudia, a widow with one daughter (3. 5. 35 f., 56–67);[8] no children were born of this marriage (5. 5. 79 f.). Despite Vollmer, 17 n. 7, the slave whose death he mourns is not an adopted son: cf. 5. 5. 10 f. 'non de stirpe quidem nec qui mea nomina ferret / oraque'.

The reconstruction of the major part of St.'s career depends upon four disputed dates: the publication of *S*. 1–3; St.'s victory at the Alban Games; his defeat in the Capitoline Games; his father's death. Three factors suggest that *S*. 1–3 were published simultaneously:[9] (i) in the *Praefatio* to Book 4 St. answers criticism of the first three books *en bloc* (4 *Pr*. 24 ff.); (ii) he claims that no *opusculum* of his has begun 'aliter quam inuocato numine maximi imperatoris' (4 *Pr*. 2 f.), and since only 1. 1 meets this criterion Books 1–3 must therefore be conceived of as a single *opusculum* (see further ad loc.); (iii) the *Praefatio* to Book 1, written when the *Thebaid* was complete (1 *Pr*. 6 f.), post-dates the completion of the *propempticon* to Maecius Celer, written when the *Thebaid* was still unfinished (3. 2. 142 f.). The *Thebaid* was also unfinished when 1. 5 was written to Claudius Etruscus; Mart. 6. 42, also to Etruscus, was published between 89 and 90.[10] St. probably published the

---

[5] Hardie, 58 f.

[6] On Juvenal's picture of St. prostituting his talent see V. Tandoi, *Maia* 21 (1969), 103–22, G. B. Townend, *JRS* 63 (1973), 151 f., F. Jones, *CQ* NS 32 (1982), 478 f. For the special popularity of pantomime in Campania see Hardie, 60.

[7] See J. G. Griffith, *G&R*² 16 (1969), 137 ff., Hardie, 61.

[8] Claudia's anxiety that her daughter is not yet married, and St.'s confident prediction that Naples will supply her with a son-in-law (3. 5. 60 ff.), suggest that the girl was in her late teens by 93, i.e. Claudia was probably born c.60; since it was very unusual for a man to marry an older woman, even when it was her second marriage, this is additional evidence that St. was born in the fifties. For the average age of Roman girls at their first marriage see on 4. 8. 60.

[9] See Vollmer, 12 n. 4, Newmyer, 46 ff., Bright, 53 f.; separate publication, at approximately yearly intervals, is postulated by Frère, p. xxi, Vessey, *Statius and the Thebaid*, 15, *CHCL* ii. 561, van Dam, *Comm*. 3, *ANRW* 2748.

[10] But it does not follow that the *Thebaid* was finished in 90/1: so B. Kytzler, *Hermes* 88 (1960), 344.

Thebaid before January 93, when Domitian defeated the Sarmatae, because the proem mentions only Domitian's first two Danubian expeditions (*Theb.* 1. 19) and not the Sarmatian campaign. The defeat of the Sarmatae is mentioned at 3. 3. 170 f.; hence *S.* 1-3 were published after January 93.

S. 3. 5. 31-3 refers to St.'s defeat in the Capitoline Games, established by Domitian in 86 and held every four years.[11] The month is not known, but presumably they were not held in winter. St.'s defeat occurred after he had won the Alban Games (3. 5. 28-33, 5. 3. 227-32).[12] They were celebrated by Domitian annually (Suet. *Dom.* 4. 4) or almost annually (Dio 67. 1) for the Quinquatrus (19-23 March), a festival in honour of Minerva (Ov. *F.* 3. 809-34). St.'s subject was *Germanas acies* and *Daca ... proelia* (4. 2. 66 f.), i.e. he celebrated Domitian's triumphs of 89: see note ad loc.[13] Hence, as with the proem to the *Thebaid*, no mention is made of the defeat of the Sarmatae in 93, and St.'s victory in the Alban Games must therefore have occurred between 90 and 92. Thus St.'s defeat cannot have occurred at the first celebration of the Capitoline Games in 86. If the Alban victory was in March 90, the Capitoline defeat could have occurred later in 90 or in 94; but if the Alban victory was in 91 or 92 the Capitoline defeat must have been in 94. This difficulty may be resolved by the interpretation of 5. 3. 233 ff. (to St.'s father, deceased) 'te nostra magistro / Thebais urgebat priscorum exordia uatum; / tu cantus stimulare meos, tu pandere facta / heroum bellique modos positusque locorum / monstrabas. labat incerto mihi limite cursus / te sine, et orbatae caligant uela carinae'. If the epic which St. is struggling with ('labat ... carinae') is still the *Thebaid*, to be completed by 92, then the Alban victory and Capitoline defeat which St. has just mentioned (5. 3. 227-33) must both be dated to 90: cf. St.'s assertion to his wife that she alone saw him through the completion of the *Thebaid* (3. 5. 35 f.) 'longi tu sola laboris / conscia, cumque tuis creuit mea Thebais

---

[11] Suet. *Dom.* 4. 4, Censorin. 18. 15; see *RE* iii. 1527-30 (Wissowa).
[12] At 3. 5. 28 *ter* (M) should read *tu* (Politian), i.e. St. won the Alban Games not three times but once.
[13] St. cannot have entered the *De Bello Germanico* for this competition, as suggested by Härtel, 17, since that does not include *Daca proelia*, and a full-scale epic sustaining the detail displayed in the surviving fragment would have been too long for entry in a competition: see Hardie, 61. Perhaps St.'s entry consisted of extracts from the German epic alongside a poem about Domitian's campaigns in Dacia.

annis'. This argument is not absolutely conclusive, since 5. 3. 237 f. might refer to the *Achilleid*, or even to the projected epic about Domitian (4. 4. 99 f.) or the *De Bello Germanico*; but it seems reasonable to infer that St. means the *Thebaid*.

Finally: the date of the elder Papinius' death. The *Thebaid* took twelve years to write (*Theb*. 12. 811 'o mihi bis senos multum uigilata per annos / Thebai'), i.e. St. must have begun it *c*.80. At his death, St.'s father was composing a poem about the eruption of Vesuvius in 79 (5. 3. 205 ff. 'iamque et flere pio Vesuuina incendia cantu / mens erat et gemitum patriis impendere damnis, / cum pater exemptum terris ad sidera montem / sustulit et late miseras deiecit in urbes'); hence Legras, 338, assumes that he died soon after the eruption. The *cum* clause seems to suggest that the poem was at least planned soon after the event. But although the elder Papinius composed a poem about the fall of the Capitol in 69 immediately after it happened, there was a political motive for speed here (i.e. alignment with the Flavian cause); no such motive required an instantaneous composition about the eruption: see Hardie, 13. St.'s father was, however, dead when St. composed his *epicedion* on the death of Atedius Melior's favourite, Glaucias (2. 1. 33 f.); since Mart. 6. 28 and 29, on the same theme, were published for the Saturnalia of 90, St.'s poem can also be dated to 90. St. mourned three months without writing anything (5. 3. 29 ff. 'nam me ter relegens caelo terque ora retexens / luna uidet residem nullaque Heliconide tristis / solantem curas'). Since he does not mention his father's death in 2. 2, written after the Neapolitan Games in August 90,[14] Hardie, 14, assumes that he died in late August or early September. But St.'s father was surely dead and not merely absent when St. won the Alban Games in March 90 (5. 3. 227 ff.) 'qualem te Dardanus Albae / aspexisset [*Håkanson*: uix cepisset *M*] ager, si per me serta tulisses / Caesarea donata manu'. Hence St.'s father's death must have occurred before March 90. His assertion that his wife witnessed the completion of the *Thebaid* 'longi ... sola laboris / conscia' (3. 5. 35 f., cit. above) may also suggest that the father, who had helped in the initial stages, was long dead. He died aged sixty-five (5. 3. 235 f.) and must therefore have been born between AD 15 and 25. Since St.'s *epicedion* alludes to the subsequent Alban victory and

---

[14] See Frère, p. xviii.

GENERAL INTRODUCTION xix

Capitoline defeat (5. 3. 227 ff.), and yet claims to be written immediately after three months' mourning (5. 3. 29 ff.), the inescapable conclusion is that these two passages are irreconcilable: either 29 ff. are not true,[15] or else 225–33 are a later accretion.[16] Since Book 5 is a posthumous collection (see below), it is reasonable to suppose that two or more poems (or parts thereof) have been put together to form what is the longest poem in the *Siluae*.[17]

The date of publication of Book 4 of the *Siluae* is one of the few certainties. It is dedicated to Vitorius Marcellus and contains a poem which Marcellus had not yet seen (4 *Pr.* 8 f.) and which was written in the year of Marcellus' praetorship when he had been designated *curator Viae Latinae* for the following year (4. 4. 59 f.). The arguments for this date, which are fully documented in the introduction to Poem 4, can be summarized as follows: Marcellus was consul in 105; as a *nouus homo* he would have had to wait at least ten years between praetorship and consulship; St. is to send his poem to Marcellus along the Via Domitiana, which was completed in the year of Flauius Clemens' death (Dio 67. 14. 1), i.e. during 95.[18] Hence we must postulate the minimum gap between Marcellus' praetorship and consulship: in 95 he was praetor, 4. 4 was written, and Book 4 was published. 4. 4 was composed at Naples (4 *Pr.* 9, 4. 4. 1 ff.); hence it is at Naples that the poems of Book 4 were made up into a collection, where St. had proposed to spend his latter years (3. 5. 12 f.) 'Euboicos fessus remeare penatis / auguror et patria senium componere terra'. This remark, anticipating his *senium*, need not mean that St. was more than middle-aged: see on 4. 4. 70. The decision to leave Rome is commonly attributed to ill-health[19] (3. 5. 37 ff.) and sometimes also to St.'s disappointment over his Capitoline defeat.[20] But St. was clearly well enough both physically and emotionally to compile and publish Book 3, let alone Book 4. It is misleading to regard his return to Naples as 'retirement'. Naples

---

[15] Vollmer, 9 n. 10.   [16] Traglia–Aricò, 25.   [17] Härtel, 47 ff.
[18] To reconcile the statement of Dio 67. 14. 1 that Clemens died ὑπατεύοντα with that of Suet. *Dom.* 15. 1 'tantum non in ipso eius consulatu interemit', it must be assumed that he died in the year of his consulship but after he had been replaced by a suffect on 1 May (*Fast. Ost.*); confusion between ὕπατος and ὑπατικός is common.
[19] Vollmer, 18. Attempts (e.g. by Frère, p. xix) to interpret the poem to Sleep (5. 4) as evidence of illness are fanciful.
[20] Frère, p. xix.

xx GENERAL INTRODUCTION

was a cultural centre to rival Rome, and along its bay St. already had a circle of wealthy *amici*.²¹ If St. was middle-aged in the mid nineties, and his father was born between AD 15 and 25, St. himself was probably born *c*.50. How long he lived after the publication of Book 4 cannot be ascertained; he is assumed to have died *c*.96.

2. THE CHRONOLOGY AND ARRANGEMENT OF THE POEMS IN BOOK 4

It has been established above that St. wrote 4. 4 and the *Praefatio* at Naples in summer 95 to accompany the publication of Book 4. But few of the poems were written there (see below). The announcement in 3. 5 of St.'s impending departure from Rome may in turn have prompted commissions from *amici* there before he left; St. may indeed have visited his estate at Alba from Naples since, even allowing for the detour via Capua, an ordinary traveller with pack-animals could have covered the distance in three to four days, and so mobility between Rome and Campania must have been common.²²

4. 1 celebrates the inauguration of Domitian's seventeenth consulship (4 *Pr.* 5) on 1 January 95 (*Fast. Ost.*), and was presumably composed in readiness at the end of 94. 4. 2 thanks Domitian for a dinner which St. attended in the Domus Domitiana (4. 2. 18 ff.). It must have been written after the first three books were published, otherwise it would surely appear there.²³ 4. 3 celebrates the completion of the Via Domitiana in 95: see above. Since St. claims that the fastest journey between Rome and Puteoli can now be accomplished between sunrise and sunset (4. 3. 112 f.), which would be impossible in the shorter daylight hours of late winter, 4. 3 must have been written in early summer, before

---

²¹ See Hardie, 59 f.   ²² See Friedländer, i. 282.
²³ See Frère, p. xix. Cancik, *LK* 82 f., suggests that the occasion was the *cena aditialis* for Domitian's inauguration as consul; but, if so, St. might be expected to allude to Domitian's consular role. Legras, 345, compares Mart. 9. 91, datable to late 94, in which Martial hopes for an invitation from Domitian; this coincidence could suggest either that Martial subsequently attended a party to which St. was also invited, or that St. had already attended a dinner for which Martial did not receive an invitation. But verbal and thematic correspondences between 4. 1 and 2 (1. 2 ~ 2. 60 f., 1. 17 ff. ~ 2. 61) indicate that they were written within months of each other; probably the brief allusions in 4. 2 echo the fuller treatment of the same motifs in 4. 1.

GENERAL INTRODUCTION   xxi

the *Praefatio* and 4. 4.[24] The poem begins from the standpoint of someone within earshot of the building operations, to accommodate a series of questions; this is a technique of priamel and is no evidence that St. visited the site. The poem ends beneath the acropolis at Cumae (114 ff.), to introduce a prophecy by the Sibyl. St.'s imaginary progression along the route (106 ff.) gives no hint of where he wrote this poem.

4. 5 is written in spring from Alba (4. 5. 1-12) and traditionally dated to 95. The only chronological clue is that St. has already won the Alban Games. As this victory was probably in 90 (see above), 4. 5 may have been written before 95. 4. 6 is set in Rome in winter (4. 6. 13). The same theme (Vindex' statuette of Hercules) is treated at Mart. 9. 43 and 44, published in 94. Assuming that these publications were nearly contemporaneous, before the theme became stale, 4. 6 can be dated to winter 94/5. When St. addressed 4. 7 to Vibius Maximus he had finished the *Thebaid*, begun the *Achilleid*, and run into difficulties with it (4. 7. 23 ff.). He writes from Rome (or Alba): cf. 4. 7. 17-20 and n. This poem may be written some while before summer 95, when the *Achilleid* is apparently proceeding smoothly (4. 4. 94), since in *S*. 5. 2, composed before Domitian's death in September 96 (cf. 5. 2. 177), St. is contemplating recitations at Rome of at least part of the *Achilleid* (5. 2. 163). 4. 7 was probably written in 94 between spring and early autumn, when regular sea-crossings were made, because St. implies that Vibius could return from Dalmatia at once if he so wished (4 *Pr*. 17, 4. 7. 13 f., 29 f.).

4. 8 is composed at Alba, where the news of the birth of Menecrates' third child has reached St. *uulgari . . . fama* (4. 8. 34): cf. l. 39 'Albanoque cadum sordentem promere fumo'. *S*. 3. 1, written one year after 2. 2 (3. 1. 1 ff., 136 ff., 2. 2. 6 ff.), i.e. in 91, mentions only two grandchildren of Pollius Felix (3. 1. 176). Hence 4. 8 must date from 92 or later. 4. 9 was written for the Saturnalia. St.'s promise to send a *dignius opusculum* (4. *Pr*. 21) to make up for it suggests that 4. 9 was written recently, i.e. at the Saturnalia in 94. It was probably written in Rome, since St. says that it would be improper (and hence not actually impossible) for Grypus to visit his house for the *salutatio* (4. 9. 48 ff.).

[24] For seasonal variation in the division of daylight into hours see the table at Courtney, 59, derived from J. Marquardt, *Das Privatleben der Römer* (edn.[2] A. Mau) (Leipzig, 1886).

Thus only 4. 4 and the *Praefatio* were certainly written at Naples. 4. 1, 3, 4, 6, 7, 9 can be dated after the publication of Books 1–3; 2, 5, and 8 were written at the same time as the other poems in Book 4, or perhaps earlier. Hence St. used largely (if not completely) fresh material in compiling Book 4 as an answer to the critics of the first three books (see on 4 *Pr.* 24 ff.). As only the most recent poem (4. 4) and the *Praefatio* were certainly written at Naples, we must conclude either that St.'s promise of moving there was not fulfilled until 95 or else that, after he had moved, he still spent time in Latium.

The poems in Book 4 are arranged to display thematic and metrical correspondences and contrasts.[25] The first three poems, on imperial themes, constitute a unit. This initial cycle of three, ending with a hendecasyllabic poem, is matched by the hendecasyllables of the last poem. 4, 6, 8 are in hexameters, 5 and 7 in lyric metres.

3. THE TITLE *SILVAE*

St. gives these books of poems the collective title *Siluae*: see 3 *Pr.* 7 f. 'securus itaque tertius hic siluarum nostrarum liber ad te mittitur', 4 *Pr.* 24 'quare ergo plura in quarto siluarum quam in prioribus'. He never refers to an individual poem as a *silua*[26] but instead uses generic designations or defines a poem by its subject-matter and addressee: see below, on the authenticity of the *tituli*. Lucan is the only poet before St. to whom the title *Siluae* is attributed (*Vit. Vacc.* 'extant eius conplures et alii ut . . . Siluarum X'). St.'s esteem for Lucan, attested in the *genethliacon* (2. 7), suggests that he may have derived the title at least from Lucan's work.

silua can be used metaphorically in various contexts to represent ὕλη, 'matter', for which the normal Latin word was *materies*: (i) in the sense of unspecific substance: cf. *Aetna* 446 (Etna supplying

---

[25] For a diagram illustrating the relationships see Vessey, *CHCL* ii. 567. In the diagram by Bright, 71, the correspondence between 4. 2 and 6 ('dinner parties') is distorted, since the *cena* is the subject of 4. 2 but supplies only the context in 4. 6. Poems 4. 3 and 6 correspond in so far as each contains an *ecphrasis*; to imply that 'nature altered' is a major theme of both (Bright, 71) is to exaggerate its importance.

[26] Likewise the plural *Bucolica* is the title for Virgil's collection, but an individual poem within it is not designated by the singular form: see N. M. Horsfall, *BICS* 28 (1981), 108.

GENERAL INTRODUCTION	xxiii

Stromboli with fuel) 'materiam siluamque suam'; (ii) in philosophical contexts: cf. Cic. *Inu.* 1. 34 'quandam siluam atque materiam uniuersam ante permixtim et confuse exponere omnium argumentationum'; (iii) in rhetorical contexts, denoting raw material derived, for example, from philosophers: cf. Cic. *Orat.* 12 'omnis enim ubertas et quasi silua dicendi ducta ab illis [philosophorum disputationibus] est', and Kroll's note; sometimes the emphasis is on further elaboration and revision of this source-material: cf. Quint. 10. 3. 17 'primo decurrere per materiam stilo quam uel uolunt, et sequentes calorem atque impetum ex tempore scribunt: hanc siluam uocant. repetunt deinde et componunt quae effuderant: sed uerba emendantur et numeri, manet in rebus temere congestis quae fuit leuitas'.

Sometimes instead of raw material the metaphor emphasizes the profusion and variety of a wood; *silua* can denote undergrowth as well as trees: cf. Virg. *E..* 1. 152 f. 'intereunt segetes, subit aspera silua / lappaeque tribolique', *OLD* s.v. *silua* 2.[27] Hence *silua*, like ὕλη, comes to refer to a collection: cf. Gell. *NA Pr.* 5–6 '[scriptores] quia uariam et miscellam et quasi confusaneam doctrinam conquisiuerant, eo titulos quoque ad eam sententiam exquisitissimos indiderunt. namque alii "Musarum" inscripserunt, alii "Siluarum"', Jerome, *Rufin.* 3. 39 'de tanta librorum silua unum fruticem ac surculum proferre non possum', Hippolyt. *Refut.* 1. 10. 1 πολλὴν ... ὕλην βιβλίων.[28] *Hyle* (ὕλη) describes the encyclopaedic *commentarii* of L. Ateius Praetextatus (Philologus) in 800 books (Suet. *Gramm.* 10 = *GRF* 136–7 Funaioli) 'de [commentariorum] tamen copia sic altera ad eundem Hermam epistula significat: "Hylen nostram aliis memento commendare, quam omnis generis coegimus uti scis, octingentos in libros."' *Hyle* here may even be a title.[29] This notion of miscellany and variety dominates in St.'s title, as the plural *Siluae* shows: St. is advertising his versatility.

[27] Although *silua* is sometimes used of a man-made landscape (cf. Vitr. 6. 5. 2 'siluae ambulationesque laxiores ad decorem maiestatis perfectae'), a context is required to define this usage, and despite M. Gothein, *RhM* 63 (1908), 475 f., the title *Siluae* does not denote a shrubbery where the reader can relax. The danger of overemphasizing the notion of 'marvels of civilization' in the *Siluae* is illustrated by the belief of Bright, 42, that the title is meant to convey both a disordered wilderness and the imposition of order upon nature by man.
[28] See J. H. Waszink on Tert. *De Anima* 2. 6.
[29] See K.-E. Henriksson, *Griechische Büchertitel in der römischen Literatur* (Helsinki, 1956), 122.

Book-titles drawn from the natural world were common: cf. Plin. *NH Pr.* 24 'inscriptionis apud Graecos mira felicitas: κηρίον inscripsere, quod uolebant intellegi fauom . . . alii . . . iam ἴα . . . λειμών', Gell. *NA Pr.* 6 'alius κηρία, partim λειμῶνας'. Cicero wrote a poem entitled Λειμών (Suet. *Vit. Ter.* 7, p. 9. 2 W).[30]

St.'s titulature has been imitated in English: Ben Jonson published *The Forrest* in 1616, a miscellaneous collection of fifteen short poems, odes, epistles, and songs, and in 1640 another miscellaneous collection, *Underwoods*, a title borrowed subsequently by Robert Louis Stevenson.

4. THE NATURE OF THE COLLECTION

The poems of the *Siluae*, for the most part, profess to celebrate particular occasions. The first poem of the fourth book commemorates Domitian's seventeenth consulate; the second describes a dinner at his palace (again preferring the particular occasion to more general eulogy);[31] the third is written for the opening of the Via Domitiana. There is the same tendency in many of the addresses to *priuati*: the sixth poem describes a statuette belonging to Vindex which St. claims to have seen at a dinner-party; the eighth poem celebrates the birth of a third child to Julius Menecrates, the ninth is written in response to a gift from Plotius Grypus at the Saturnalia. The other poems of the book are tied to less specific events, but 4 to Vitorius Marcellus takes the form of a letter, while the direct allocutions of the two lyric poems (5 to Septimius Seuerus and 7 to Vibius Maximus) imitate the immediacy of a Horatian ode.

The *Siluae* derive many characteristics from the fact that they are addressed to individuals; *Somnus* (5. 4) is the only exception. Such poems will sometimes have been commissioned, but when they are addressed to *priuati* this is not obtrusive. St. addresses his friends not as an equal but as an *amicus inferior*.[32] Patronage was

---

[30] If *Pratum* (or *Prata*), the title of a prose work ascribed to Suetonius, were authentic, it would be analogous, the collective singular being the original title, subsequently used to denote one of the component sections while the plural described the entire work: see Schanz–Hosius, iii. 63 ff. But doubts have been cast by G. Brugnoli, *Studi suetoniani* (Lecce, 1968), 137–84.

[31] General eulogy very conveniently arises from particular occasions: cf. Pliny's *Panegyricus* or Claudian's poems on Honorius.

[32] R. P. Saller's phrase, *CQ* NS 33 (1983), 256.

an aspect of the *amicitia* between wealthy, cultivated persons and those of lesser status. Hence there was no special word for this sort of patron, and the relationship was described in the terminology of friendship.[33] St.'s tone in addressing these *amici* combines just the right degrees of familiarity and deference: in the epistle to Vitorius Marcellus he names a mutual friend, Gallus, and teasingly remarks that Gallus and Marcellus are probably chatting about St. at that very moment; but later in the poem panegyric elements predominate, based on the distinction between Marcellus' public service and St.'s essentially passive role. A teasing tone demonstrating general affability may underpin a whole poem, as in the *hendecasyllabi iocosi* to Plotius Grypus (9). Throughout, St., like Horace, tries to match the content and style of his poetry to the standing and tastes of the individual addressee: lyric metre is appropriate to address Septimius Seuerus, himself a composer of lyrics; the congratulations to Julius Menecrates include a subtle compliment to his father-in-law, Pollius Felix, himself one of St.'s richest patrons.

Court poetry, directed to the emperor, is harder for modern readers to understand. St. is working in the same tradition as Theocritus' stylized adulation of Ptolemy, or Virgil's extravagant praise of Augustus in *Georgics* 3. The deserts of the *laudandus* were less relevant than the virtuosity of the *laudator*, duly rewarded by his small share in the glory of the court. The emperor is an august figure, but the emphasis is on his *ciuilitas* and beneficence: he is the modest and reluctant consul (4. 1. 34), his excellence shines in his countenance despite his self-effacing behaviour (4. 2. 43 f.), his wise counsel prevails over the rebellious nature of Campania's largest river (4. 3. 82). Speeches of homage by personages mythical or divine add a touch of exuberant fantasy not permitted to orators, even in panegyric.[34]

The Augustans had composed verse panegyrics, but by St.'s time a much more formal structure is apparent and certain topics are conventionally included. Verse has by now taken over and handled in its own way some of the themes of prose. Speeches for consular inaugurations must have been regular (see introduction to 4. 1); one would conjecture also speeches at opening ceremonies for a newly-completed construction. The use in the prefaces of

[33] See White (1978), 78 ff.   [34] See introduction to 4. 1.

Greek titles to designate individual poems (see below) reflects jargon which properly belongs to prose. The *rhetor* taught composition in prose, not in verse. But in celebrating (for example) the birth of a son to an *amicus*, a poet composed verses which reflected something of the structure and topoi of a prose *genethliacon*; his poem might also fuse elements from other genres, without any notion of 'breaking rules'.[35]

A framework of stock topics, and guidelines for their arrangement and presentation, were part of the equipment of an epideictic poet competing in festivals. He was taught to improvise, to 'think on his feet' (to borrow Michael Winterbottom's phrase about declamation[36]). This quality of hasty improvisation was the hallmark, too, of the *Siluae*, since topicality was of the essence when the poems were first delivered; in the published collections St., displaying the feigned modesty usual in prefaces (e.g. Gell. *NA Pr.* 10), confesses to an unorthodox lack of *limae labor*: cf. 1 *Pr.* 1 ff. 'diu multumque dubitaui ... an hos libellos, qui mihi subito calore et quadam festinandi uoluptate fluxerunt, cum singuli de sinu meo prodierunt, congregatos ipse dimitterem'. As the phrase 'quadam festinandi uoluptate fluxerunt' suggests, this poetry was composed with spectacular fluency and confidence. It does not profess to display the profundity which is sometimes born of painstaking πόνος. This speed of composition constitutes the *audacia* on St.'s part which unnerved his cultured friend Pollius Felix (3 *Pr.* 4).[37] When St. apologizes for this feature of the *Siluae*, there is deliberate irony in the self-advertisement: cf. 1 *Pr.* 14 ff. 'nullum enim ex illis biduo longius tractum, quaedam et in singulis diebus effusa. quam timeo ne uerum istuc uersus quoque ipsi de se probent!'

The fluency of the *Siluae*, combined with richness of ornament,[38] avoids the ponderousness of much ceremonial poetry. *Ecphrasis* in particular conveys a vivid visual element, as in the description of Domitian's palace (4. 2. 18 ff.), where different varieties of marble vie with each other as decoration and the

---

[35] Successful commissions depended on sensitivity to the occasion rather than allegiance to the rule-book, as noted by D. A. Russell and N. G. Wilson, *Menander Rhetor* (Oxford, 1981), p. xix.
[36] *Roman Declamation* (Bristol, 1980), p. v.
[37] *audacia* here does not refer to 'strained' Latin usage, as implied by D. W. T. C. Vessey, *CPh* 66 (1971), 274 (review of Håkanson).
[38] Well illustrated by Vessey, *CHCL* ii, 567–71, in an analysis of *S.* 1. 2.

interior opens up vistas as wide as a landscape. Hyperbolic conceits which are both flattering and witty characterize St.'s encomiastic approach, especially to the emperor: the vistas of the palace are dwarfed only by the person of Domitian himself (4. 2. 26). Yet these conceits are judiciously deployed, avoiding the worst Neronian excesses of fatiguing heaps of *sententiae*. Much in the *Siluae* derives from Ovid, especially the rational treatment of fantasy, but with his encomiastic purpose St. cannot display Ovid's lightness of touch: St. puts into Janus' mouth an explicit and obsequious tribute to Domitian (4. 1. 17 ff.); Ovid's complacent Janus remarks obliquely that even Jupiter is beholden to him (*F.* 1. 126) 'it, redit officio Iuppiter ipse meo'. St.'s epic model was Virgil (*S.* 4. 4. 54 f., *Theb.* 12. 816 f.); in *Siluae* 4 he can adopt the style of Horace (5 and 7) or Catullus (9); he shares themes with Martial (see especially on 6 and 9) and even acknowledges affinities with epigram (2 *Pr.* 16 f.) 'in arborem ... et psittacum scis a me leues libellos quasi epigrammatis loco scriptos'.

One of the most striking features of the *Siluae* is St.'s love of antithesis and paradox, ranging from verbal collocations (4. 4. 14 'ardua iam *densae rarescunt* moenia Romae') to an innate incongruity pervading an entire scene, as with the deferential and obsequious behaviour of a naturally tempestuous river (4. 3. 72 ff.). Extravagant hyperbole suits the unnatural and unexpected domestic features which St. celebrates for his *amici*: Vopiscus' villa, built on opposite banks of the Anio, is undisturbed by the passage of water in its midst (1. 3. 24 ff.); seventy-seven lines of aetiological mythologizing explain the contorted shape of a tree on Melior's estate (2. 3). The titles of some recent books about St. reflect this atmosphere of paradox: *Man in an Artificial Landscape* (Pavlovskis), *Elaborate Disarray: the Nature of Statius' Silvae* (Bright).

E. R. Curtius's concept of 'mannerism' has been widely adopted to define the nature of the *Siluae*: Curtius meant 'all literary tendencies which are opposed to Classicism', 'the artificial and the affected [preferred] to the natural'.[39] Vessey[40] empha-

---

[39] Curtius, 273, 282.
[40] Vessey, *Statius and the Thebaid*, 8 f. Vessey's most recent publication on the *Siluae* (Vessey, *ANRW*), a very wordy stucturalist reading, recognizes the constituents of 'Wit' in the *Siluae* and offers some perspective analyses of selected passages: for example, in his discussion of *S.* 2. 1 (pp. 2769–83), Vessey demonstrates that St.'s debts to his predecessors go beyond verbal echoes, so that often a contextual reminiscence imbues whole passages with the atmosphere of a predecessor's style. But his attempt to

sizes that these characteristics usually arise out of *imitatio* of classical models whose judiciously used effects are reproduced to excess. Hence 'mannerism' can be seen to be a very broad concept, unhelpful in defining the specific characteristics of the *Siluae*. The term 'baroque',[41] rejected by Curtius because it implies a chronological progression, is perhaps of some value, since it conveys a post-classical trend of virtuosity, facility, overblown realism, and rejection of classical ideals of taste. But while St. can display the superfluity of decoration which is usually associated with baroque art and architecture, he paradoxically combines this with strict economy of expression: cf. the subtlety of his description of Dalmatia (4. 7. 14 ff.) 'ubi Dite uiso / pallidus fossor redit erutoque / concolor auro', or the remarkable brevity and precision of the description of road-building at 4. 3. 40–8. This very economy and ingenuity may sometimes have led to the corruptions which lie behind some apparently obscure and tortuous passages.

5. THE AUTHENTICITY OF THE *TITVLI*

In M each poem is headed by a short *titulus*. Since St.'s *praefationes* to the first four books specify the order of the poems and also the subject and addressee of each, the *tituli* seems largely superfluous. They are, however, the sole source for the *cognomen* of Pollius (Felix) and the *nomina* of five addressees: 2. 1, 3 (Atedius) Melior, 2. 6 (Flauius) Vrsus, 3. 4 (Flauius) Earinus, 4. 4 (Vitorius) Marcellus, 4. 6 (Nouius) Vindex. It is likely that the full nomenclature derives from a contemporary source, if not from St. himself.

It does not seem to have been an ancient custom to give titles to individual poems, at least not when they belonged to a homogeneous collection. Hence individual poems are referred to by number or by their *incipit*. The headings to the epigrams in Martial 13 and 14 (*Xenia* and *Apophoreta*) are in a different category, because they are usually vital to the sense: the epigrams

---

defend 'mannerism' as the essential quality of the *Siluae* leads him to ignore textual corruption as the source of much bizarre or even meaningless expression (e.g. M's reading at 4. 1. 24–5, accepted by Vessey on p. 2800 without comment, discussed in the commentary below).

[41] Advocated by H. Bardon, *Lat.* 21 (1962), 732–48.

are supposed to accompany gifts, but when they form part of a collection instead of being attached to the relevant items the identity of the gifts must be given: cf. Mart. 14. 61 *Lanterna cornua* (paired with 14. 62 *Lanterna de uesica*) 'dux lanterna uiae clusis feror aurea flammis, / et tuta est gremio parua lucerna meo'. Before poems were made up into a collection, they appear to have been presented to their addressee with a covering letter (cf. the epistle to accompany *S.* 5. 1 which is now affixed to the whole book) and thus probably had no title (nor needed one).

The following points may tell against the authenticity of the *tituli* in the *Siluae*.

(i) Many of the *tituli* for the poems in Books 1-4 simply paraphrase or quote the descriptions in the *praefationes*: cf. 4. 1 'Septimus Decimus Consulatus Imp. Aug. Germanici' ~ 4 *Pr.* 5 f. 'septimum decimum Germanici nostri consulatum adoraui', 4. 9 'Hendecasyllabi Iocosi ad Plotium Grypum' ~ 4 *Pr.* 20 ff. 'Plotio Grypo . . . hendecasyllabos quos Saturnalibus una risimus huic uolumini inserui'.

(ii) The emperor's titulature is never complete, and the titles used are in an unusual order. The basic formula was *Imperator Caesar Domitianus Augustus*. The *tituli* of poems in the *Siluae* which incorporate the emperor's name are: 1. 1 'Equus Maximus Domitiani Imperatoris', 4. 1 'Septimus Decimus Consulatus Imp. Aug. Germanici', 4. 2 'Eucharisticon ad Imp. Aug. Germ. Domitianum'. The abbreviated form on inscriptions and coins often attests the variant order *Imp. Dom. Caes. Aug.*; occasionally *Caes.* or *Dom.* is omitted, or the order varied further: cf. *CIL* ii. 1963 'Imp. Caes. Aug. Dom.' Honorific titles were appended: from the summer of 83 *Germanicus* was added, and the nomenclature is further expanded in the salutation to the epistle prefacing Martial, Book 8: 'Imperatori Domitiano Caesari Augusto Germanico Dacico Valerius Martialis s.' On Greek inscriptions the choice and order of titles is very flexible, including the formula Καῖσαρ Σεβαστὸς Γερμανικὸς Δομιτιανός.[42] Hence, while it is hardly credible that a formal *titulus* would incorporate the abbreviated nomenclature whereby St. refers to the emperor in the *praefationes* (cf. 1 *Pr.* 18 ff. 'centum hos uersus . . . indulgentissimo imperatori . . . tradere iussus sum'), it is wrong to assume

---

[42] See S. Gsell, *Essai sur le règne de l'empereur Domitien* (Paris, 1893), 44 n. 3.

that Domitian's names could not have been cited in an unorthodox order by St., who in any case attests the widespread contemporary practice of inverting the names of private individuals: cf. 4 *Pr.* 14 f. 'Maximum Vibium' and n. It is also a mistake to demand consistency: of the four instances in the *Strategemata* where Frontinus quotes Domitian's titles, only two are identical: 2. 3. 23, 11. 7 (cf. 1. 1. 8, 3. 10). Yet it is also possible that at 4. 2 St. wrote 'Eucharisticon ad Imp. Aug. Germ.' (cf. 4. 1 'Septimus Decimus Consulatus Imp. Aug. Germanici') and that *Domitianum* was a later gloss which became incorporated with the *titulus*.

(iii) Some of the generic terms in the *tituli* are used by St. himself in the *praefationes*: cf. 1. 2 'Epithalamion' ~ 1 *Pr.* 22 'epithalamium tuum', 2. 6 'Consolatio' ~ 2 *Pr.* 21 f. 'scriptam de amisso puero consolationem', 2. 7 'Genethliacon' ~ 2 *Pr.* 23 f. 'cludit uolumen Genethliacon Lucani', 3. 5 'Ecloga' ~ 3 *Pr.* 21 'summa est ecloga', 4. 4 'Epistula' ~ 4 *Pr.* 8 f. 'epistulam meam'. Others are clearly derived from the prefatory descriptions: cf. 3. 3 'Consolatio' ~ 3 *Pr.* 15 f. 'merebatur et Claudi Etrusci mei pietas aliquod . . . solatium', 4. 8 'Gratulatio' ~ 4 *Pr.* 18 f. 'Iulium Menecraten . . . gratulor.' The term *epicedion*, which St. uses to describe 2. 1 at 2 *Pr.* 8, does not recur in the *titulus* to 2. 1 but does occur in the *tituli* to 5. 3 and 5. The generic terms in the *tituli* which are not attested elsewhere in St. are *propempticon* (3. 1), *eucharisticon* (4. 2), *ode* (4. 5, 7).[43] Since *epithalamion* is attested also at Quint. 9. 3. 16 'Catullus in epithalamio', as well as both *epithalamion* and *epicedion* in St.'s *praefationes*, it is not impossible that the Greek borrowings *propempticon* and *eucharisticon* should also be contemporary, although their first authenticated appearances are later: cf. Paul. Pell. *Pr.* p. 289, 17 '[ut] eucharisticon . . . opusculum . . . contexerem', *TLL* v. 1004. 77 ff., Char. *GL* i. 124. 5 Keil 'Cinna in propemptico Pollionis', Sid. *Carm.* 24 (*tit.*) *Propempticon ad libellum*; note especially Char. *GL* i. 134. 12 Keil 'Iulius Hyginus in Cinnae propemptico', which may imply that Hyginus in the Augustan era already knew the work as a *propempticon*. The term used by grammarians for an individual

---

[43] In the *titulus* to 1. 4, 'Soteria Rutili Gallici', *soteria* (though apparently singular, the counterpart to *epicedion* etc., hence assimilated to the first declension) parallels *soteria* neut. pl. 'gifts upon recovery', Mart. 12. 56. 3 'quotiens surgis, soteria poscis amicos': the *titulus* will mean 'a gift upon the recovery of Rutilius Gallicus'. Thus to explain *soteria* in this *titulus* it is unnecessary to suppose with van Dam, *Comm.* 71, that 'later philologists' gave the word a technical sense as a generic term.

lyric poem was *ode* (*lyrica*): cf. Serv. *GL* iv. 468. 13 Keil, Apthon. *GL* vi. 168. 15 Keil. There is no reason to suppose that St. could not have called 4. 5 or 4. 7 'ode lyrica'. He was not, like Horace, writing a homogeneous collection of *carmina*.[44] To call 4. 5 or 4. 7 'carmen' would not distinguish them from the rest of the *Siluae*. But *ode lyrica* could equally well be a designation given later by a grammarian, and the same holds for the rest of the *tituli*.

Having established that St. could have referred to the individual poems of the *Siluae* by the generic designations included in the *tituli*, it remains to decide whether he would have included these designations at the head of each poem in the published collections. This is unlikely because: (i) the *praefatio* to each book functions as a table of contents; (ii) poems within a collection appear to have been separated from each other by a space or a symbol, with an enlarged initial at the beginning of each poem;[45] (iii) such a *titulus* as 'Psittacus Eiusdem' (2. 4) clearly belongs to a series, since to make sense it must follow 2. 3 'Arbor Atedi Melioris'.

Book 5 has no *praefatio*. Hence there is nothing to define the content of the poems other than the *tituli*. *Tituli* could prima facie have been affixed to the individual poems by St. and transferred by the editor *en bloc* to the collection. But would St. have called 5. 3 'Epicedion in Patrem Suum' or 5. 5 'Epicedion in Puerum Suum'? Hence the *tituli* to Book 5 were perhaps affixed by the original editor to compensate for the absence of a *praefatio*; the lack of a preface, the preponderance of *epicedia* in the book, and the unusual lengths of the poems (Book 5 contains both the longest and the shortest in the *Siluae*) all argue for a posthumous collection of miscellaneous pieces. Book 5 may be our earliest evidence for entitling individual poems within a collection. We do not know when the five books were collected together, but at this stage *tituli* may have been provided for the first four books by analogy with the fifth book. This probably happened within

[44] But Horace's odes also acquired individual *tituli* in some of the manuscripts (cited in the apparatus of Klingner's Teubner edition).
[45] In the Gallus papyrus, the twin symbols resembling the letter 'H' probably mark off different poems: see R. D. Anderson, P. J. Parsons, and R. G. M. Nisbet, *JRS* 69 (1979), 131; if, however, Gallus is to combine all his *Leitmotive* in one poem, then the marks must distinguish stanzas: see A. G. Lee, *LCM* 5 (1980), 45 f. For examples of punctuation to separate lines within verse see E. Otha Wingo, *Latin Punctuation in the Classical Age* (Paris, 1972), 147 ff.

decades of St.'s death, since the full names of the addressees were still known (see above).

Vollmer, 207 f., tries to reconstruct *tituli* which St. might have used. M's *tituli* he relegates to the apparatus. Although I believe that St. would not have included *tituli* in his published collections, I have retained M's *tituli* in the text for the convenience of the reader, since the poems are commonly known by these designations.

6. THE TEXTUAL TRADITION

Echoes of the *Siluae* are numerous in late antiquity, especially in the works of Ausonius, Claudian, and Sidonius;[46] after Charlemagne, whose court correspondence contains a pastiche of 4. 4. 1 (see ad loc.), there is no trace of the *Siluae* until the Renaissance, except for a tenth-century manuscript (L) containing 2. 7 (*Genethliacon Lucani*) amongst a miscellany of pieces.[47] In 1417, near Lake Constance, Poggio found a manuscript (now lost) containing both the *Siluae* and the works of Manilius and Silius. He had a copy made which he sent to Francesco Barbaro in Venice, lamenting its imperfections,[48] with instructions to convey it to Nicolò Niccoli in Florence. Apart from the works of Silius, the rest of the copy survives, annotated by Poggio and Niccoli. It was discovered in the Biblioteca Nacional at Madrid in 1879 by G. Loewe, and hence is known as the Matritensis or M (= M. 3678, formerly M. 31). It was identified as Poggio's copy by A. C. Clark.[49]

The Laurentine manuscript and the Matritensis probably share a common source.[50] After Poggio settled in Florence in 1453 at least five copies of M were made.[51] The *editio princeps* was published at Venice in 1472 from a very poor copy of M.

[46] See Vollmer, 32–3, Cancik, *ANRW* 2705.
[47] Florence, Laur. 29. 32, known to Politian, rediscovered by Heinsius, and finally documented by Baehrens: see Klotz, pp. lii–liii.
[48] Poggio's famous indictment of the scribe, 'ignorantissimus omnium uiuentium fuit', refers not to the scribe's own errors but to his failure to correct obvious mistakes in his *Vorlage* ('diuinare oportet, non legere'): see Th. Stangl, *BPhW* 33 (1913), 1180–4, 1211–5.   [49] *CR* 13 (1899), 119–30.
[50] Perhaps a manuscript entitled 'Ouidii Metamorfoseon Sili et Stacii uolumen I' catalogued in s. IX^2 at a library near Lake Constance: see M. D. Reeve, in L. D. Reynolds, *Texts and Transmissions* (Oxford, 1983), 398 (the definitive synopsis of the textual tradition of the *Siluae*).
[51] See M. D. Reeve, *CQ* NS 21 (1977), 202–25.

Lectures on the *Siluae* were delivered c.1470–3 by Calderini;[52] his edition was published at Rome in 1475. Politian lectured on the *Siluae* in 1480–1, drafted a commentary,[53] and recorded in his copy of the *editio princeps*[54] both his own conjectures and also readings from what he described as 'exemplar ... quod ex Gallia Poggius Gallica scriptum manu in Italiam attulerat' and 'codex uetustissimus'. Politian's annotations are now almost illegible, but eighty have been identified as readings which he attributed to the *liber Poggii*, seventy-four of which are attested in M.[55] The most serious discrepancies are that Politian (i) claims that S. 1. 4. 86a, which is in M, was not in the *liber Poggii*, and (ii) says of S. 5. 5. 24–7 'codex uetustissimus intercisos habet hos uersus'; but A. J. Dunston has argued convincingly that 'intercisos ... uersus' refers to the way in which 5. 5. 24–7 appear in M with a gap in the middle of each line, as though copied from an exemplar with a blot or stain on it, and thus Politian is no longer believed to have seen some other manuscript with a hole in it.[56] The remaining problem concerning S. 1. 4. 86a is not adequate to justify continued insistence (e.g. by Marastoni) that Politian did not see M.[57]

Of the frequent editions of the *Siluae* since the fifteenth century, the most important is by Markland (London, 1728). Vollmer's commentary (Leipzig, 1898), frequently cited as authoritative in modern times, was condemned by Housman (e.g. *CR* 22 [1908], 88–9 = *Cl. Pap.* ii. 771). The Teubner text by Klotz (edn.² Leipzig, 1911) is useful for its extensive record of conjectures, whereas the apparatus of its successor by Marastoni (rev. Leipzig, 1970) is meagre. The slender annotations by Frère (Budé, 1961)

[52] See A. J. Dunston, *Ital. med. e uman.* 11 (1968), 74 f.
[53] Politian's collation is dated before his lectures and his commentary by Lucia Cesarini Martinelli, *RIFC* 47 (1975), 130–74. The commentary, hitherto unpublished, is now available in her edition: L. Cesarini Martinelli, *Angelo Poliziano: commento inedito alle Selve di Stazio* (Florence, 1978).
[54] Cors. 50 F. 37, commonly referred to as the *exemplar Corsinianum*.
[55] Clark, *CR* 13 (1899), 128. [56] *BICS* 14 (1967), 96–101 and pl. IX.
[57] In his review of Klotz (1911) in *CR* 26 (1912), 261–3, H. W. Garrod incredibly concluded that Politian lied about what he found in M, i.e. claimed to have seen a *codex uetustissimus* in order to add weight to his corrections of Calderini's text. Van Dam's solution (*ARW* 2730–1, based on Traglia, 21 n. 99) is that Politian saw a copy of M made in Florence before 1453 (when Poggio, having settled there, could resume possession of his MS), but on his own admission (p. 2731 n. 13) this does not explain 'Gallica scriptum manu'. For a refutation of the argument that Politian did not see M, see M. D. Reeve, *SIFC* 49 (1977), 285–6.

are often illuminating. A substantial commentary on Book 2 by van Dam (Leiden, 1984) is based on a modified version of Marastoni's text.

7. METHODS OF CITATION

(i) I have generally used the *Oxford Classical Dictionary*[2] as a model in abbreviating the names and works of ancient authors, and *L'Année philologique* in citing modern journals (expanding any obscure acronyms).

(ii) In abbreviated references, usually either the author alone is cited or an acronym of the title; but where different works by a single author need to be distinguished, books are referred to by abbreviated titles and articles by date.

(iii) I have not quoted in the commentary the published source for those emendations by nineteenth- and early twentieth-century scholars which are included in the apparatus criticus, since comprehensive lists appear in the Teubner editions by Klotz and Marastoni.

(iv) Line-numbering for the *praefationes* in the *Siluae* differs between editions. In the commentary I cite the numbering in this edition for the *Praefatio* to Book 4, and the numbering of the Oxford Classical Text for the rest.

(v) In measurements of distance, 1 Roman mile = 1.4785 km.

SIGLA

M   codex Matritensis Bibl. Nation. 3678 (olim 31)
M¹   ipsius librarii manus
M²   Poggii manus correctrix
a   editio princeps 1472
b   editio Parmensis 1473
c   editio Domitii Calderini 1475
A*   lectiones quas Politianus in exemplar Corsinianum post inspectum M intulit
A   Politiani ipsius adnotationes
ς   doctorum Italorum coniecturae nullo nomine editae, pleraeque ante annum 1500

P. PAPINI STATI
SILVARVM
LIBER QVARTVS

PRAEFATIO

STATIVS MARCELLO SVO SALVTEM

INVENI librum, Marcelle carissime, quem pietati tuae dedicarem. reor equidem aliter quam inuocato numine maximi imperatoris nullum opusculum meum coepisse, sed hic liber tres habet ⟨...⟩ se quam quod quarta ad honorem tuum pertinet.
5 primo autem septimum decimum Germanici nostri consulatum adoraui; secundo gratias egi sacratissimis eius epulis honoratus; tertio uiam Domitianam miratus sum, qua grauissimam harenarum moram exemit, cuius beneficio tu quoque maturius epistulam meam accipies, quam tibi in hoc libro a Neapoli scribo. proximum
10 est lyricum carmen ad Septimium Seuerum, iuuenem, uti scis, inter ornatissimos secundi ordinis, tuum quidem et condiscipulum sed mihi citra hoc quoque ius artissime carum. nam Vindicis nostri Herculem Epitrapezion secundum honorem quem de me et de ipsis studiis meretur, imputare etiam tibi possum. Maximum
15 Vibium et dignitatis et eloquentiae nomine a nobis diligi satis eram testatus epistula quam ad illum de editione Thebaidos meae publicaui; sed nunc quoque eum reuerti maturius ex Dalmatia rogo. iuncta est ecloga ad municipem meum Iulium Menecraten, splendidum iuuenem et Polli mei generum, cui gratulor quod
20 Neapolim nostram numero liberorum honestauerit. Plotio Grypo, maioris gradus iuueni, dignius opusculum reddam, sed interim hendecasyllabos quos Saturnalibus una risimus huic uolumini inserui.

3 meum *M*: me *Frère*   4 *lac. Hahn*: se quam quod (quad *ab ipso librario correctum*) quarta *M*: sequitur quarta quae *ς*   6 epulis *ς*: epistolis *M*   8 quoque *M*²: quo *M*   9 meam *M*: eam *Markland*   10 Septimium *M*²: Septimum *M*   12 citra *Nohl*: contra *M*   15 Vibium *Nohl*: uiuium *A*: niuium *M*²: uinium *M*¹
22 risimus *M*: lusimus *Phillimore*

P. PAPINIUS STATIUS

SILVAE
BOOK FOUR

PREFACE

GREETINGS FROM STATIUS TO MARCELLUS

I HAVE contrived a book, my dearest Marcellus, that I could dedicate to your caring affection. I do not actually think any of my pieces has begun without invoking the sacred majesty of our most excellent emperor, but this book has three ... than the fact that the fourth reflects my respect for you. First, I have paid homage to the seventeenth consulship of our emperor Germanicus; secondly, I have returned thanks for the privilege of attending his august banquet; thirdly, I have expressed my admiration for the Via Domitiana, whereby he removed the tedious obstacle of the sand-dunes; thanks to his munificence you too will receive all the sooner this letter of mine, which I am writing to you in this book from Naples. Following this is a lyric poem to Septimius Seuerus, a young man who, as you know, is among the most distinguished of the equestrian rank; while he is also a schoolfellow of yours, he is, quite apart from this additional claim, a very close friend of mine. As for the 'Hercules Epitrapezios' of our friend Vindex, I can also charge that to your account in accordance with the honour which he deserves for his services to me and to literature in general. That Maximus Vibius is dear to us on the score of both his social distinction and his literary skill I had amply testified in the letter to him which I published about the production of my *Thebaid*; but now in particular I am asking him to return from Dalmatia in good time. Next is a select piece to my fellow townsman Julius Menecrates, an excellent young man and son-in-law of my friend Pollius, whom I am congratulating for having done honour to our city of Naples by the number of his children. To Plotius Grypus, a young man of elevated rank, I shall send another piece more worthy of him, but in the meantime I have included in this volume the hendecasyllables which we laughed about together at the Saturnalia.

PRAEFATIO

quare ergo plura in quarto Siluarum quam in prioribus? ne se
putent aliquid egisse qui reprehenderunt, ut audio, quod hoc stili
genus edidissem. primum superuacuum est dissuadere rem fac-
tam. deinde multa ex illis iam domino Caesari dederam. et
quanto hoc plus est quam edere! exerceri autem ioco non licet?
'secreto' inquit. sed et sphaeromachia spectantes et palaris lusio
admittit. nouissime: quisquis ex meis inuitus aliquid legit, statim
se profitetur aduersum. ita quare consilio eius accedam? in
summam: nempe ego sum qui traducor; taceat et gaudeat. hunc
tamen librum tu, Marcelle, defendes, si uidetur, hactenus; sin
minus, reprehendemur. uale.

I

SEPTIMVS DECIMVS CONSVLATVS IMP. AVG. GERMANICI

LAETA bis octonis accedit purpura fastis
Caesaris insignemque aperit Germanicus annum
atque oritur cum sole nouo, cum grandibus astris
clarius ipse nitens et primo maior Eoo.
exsultent leges Latiae, gaudete, curules,   5
et septemgemino iactantior aethera pulset
Roma iugo, plusque ante alias Euandrius arces
collis ouet: subiere noui Palatia fasces
et rediit bis saeptus honos precibusque receptis
curia Caesareum gaudet uicisse pudorem.   10
ipse etiam immensi reparator maximus aeui
attollit uultus, et utroque a limine grates
Ianus agit, quem tu uicina Pace ligatum
omnia iussisti componere bella nouique
in leges iurare fori. leuat ecce supinas   15

27 et *M*: at *Markland*   28 exerceri *in commentario Vollmer*: exercere *M*   ioco *M*: iocos *c*: ⟨artem⟩ ioco *Phillimore*   29 sphaeromachia spectantes *Phillimore*: sphaeromachias spectamus *M*   palaris *M*: pilaris ⲋ   30 admittit *M*: admittitur ⲋ   inuitus *M*: inuidus *Markland*   31 profitetur *Aldina*: profiteatur *M*   ita *M*: itaque *Baehrens*   32–3 hunc... defendes *post* hactenus *Vollmer*   33 defendes *M*: defende *Madvig*: defendas *Frère*   si *Goodyear*: et si *M*: sed si *Madvig, Vollmer*: haec si *Phillimore*   *lac. post* hactenus *Saenger*   33–4 sin minus *M*: si nimis *Madvig*   reprehendemur *M*: reprehendamur *Markland*

I 5 gaudete M^2: gaudere *M*   9 rediit *Markland* (rediens *Courtney*) ... saeptus *Saenger* (sanctus *Nisbet*): requiem (regimen *Cruceus*) ... sextus (senus *Stange*) *M*

So why then more poems in the fourth book of *Siluae* than in the earlier ones? So that the people who have criticized me, so I hear, for publishing this sort of writing won't think they have achieved anything. First, it is pointless to argue against a *fait accompli*. Next, I had already presented many of them to our lord Caesar, and how much more this means than publication! But isn't it permissible to do exercises for fun? 'In private' comes the reply. But the sphaeromachia and trial fencing let in spectators. Finally: whoever reads anything of mine who doesn't want to immediately declares himself hostile: very well, why should I accede to his opinion? In short: surely I am the one who is being put on show; let him keep quiet and enjoy himself. In spite of everything you, Marcellus, will defend this book, if you see fit, up to this point; if not, we shall stand rebuked. Farewell.

I

THE SEVENTEENTH CONSULSHIP OF THE EMPEROR
AUGUSTUS GERMANICUS

JOYOUSLY the purple accrues to Caesar's twice eight consulships and Germanicus opens an illustrious year and rises with the new sun and with the great constellations, shining more brightly himself and mightier than the early morning star. Let the laws of Latium exult, rejoice ye curule seats, and let Rome with rising pride beat on the heavens with her sevenfold summits, and more than the other heights let Evander's hill rejoice: anew the fasces have entered the Palace, and our doublyguarded privilege has returned, and the senate-house, its supplications accepted, rejoices to have prevailed over the modesty of Caesar. Even the mighty renewer of immeasurable ages raises his faces and from both his thresholds gives thanks, Janus himself, whom, under the constraint of his neighbour Peace, you have bidden to settle all wars and swear obedience to the laws of the new forum. Look, on this

ECLOGA PRIMA

hinc atque inde manus geminaque haec uoce profatur:
'salue, magne parens mundi, qui saecula mecum
instaurare paras, talem te cernere semper
mense meo tua Roma cupit; sic tempora nasci,
sic annos intrare decet. da gaudia fastis   20
continua; hos umeros multo sinus ambiat ostro
et properata tuae manibus praetexta Mineruae.
aspicis ut templis alius nitor, altior aris
ignis, et ipsa meae tepeant tibi sidera brumae
moribus aequa tuis? gaudent turmaeque tribusque   25
purpureique patres, lucemque a consule ducit
omnis honos. quid tale precor prior annus habebat?
dic age, Roma potens, et mecum, longa Vetustas,
dinumera fastos, nec parua exempla recense
sed quae sola meus dignetur uincere Caesar.   30
ter Latios deciesque tulit labentibus annis
Augustus fasces, sed coepit sero mereri:
tu iuuenis praegressus auos. et quanta recusas,
quanta uetas! flectere tamen precibusque senatus
permittes hunc saepe diem. manet insuper ordo   35
longior, et totidem felix tibi Roma curules
terque quaterque dabit. mecum altera saecula condes,
et tibi longaeui renouabitur ara Tarenti.
mille tropaea feres—tantum permitte triumphos.
restat Bactra nouis, restat Babylona tributis   40
frenari; nondum in gremio Iouis Indica laurus,
nondum Arabes Seresque rogant, nondum omnis honorem
annus habet, cupiuntque decem tua nomina menses.'
   Sic Ianus, clausoque libens se poste recepit.
tunc omnes stupuere dei laetoque dederunt   45
signa polo, longamque tibi, rex magne, iuuentam
annuit atque suos promisit Iuppiter annos.

17 *comma post* parens *Bentley*   23 aris *M*: astris *M¹ in margine*   25 moribus aequa *Bursian*: moribus atque *M*: lauribus aequa *Polster*: fascibus ecce *Markland*   31 Latios *Gronovius*: Latio *M*   32 fasces *ς*: faces *M*   sed *M*: et *Krohn*   sero mereri *M*: sero uereri *Stange*: serus amari *Phillimore*   35 permittes *A*: promittitis *M*: promittes *ς*   38 longaeui *M*: longaeuo *Bishop*   Tarenti *Turnebus*: parentis *M*   39 permitte *ς*: promitte *M*   41 in *add. Livineius*   42 rogant *M*: togam *Stange*   45 stupuere *Watt*: patuere *M*: fauere *Baehrens*: omen plausere fores *Markland*   46 rex *M*: dux *Markland*   *comma post* rex *Leo*

side and that he raises his hands, palms upwards, and with twin voices he pronounces as follows: 'Hail, great father of the world, who are preparing to inaugurate centuries with me, your city of Rome longs to see you always thus in this month of mine; thus should eras be born, thus should the years make their entry. Give continual rejoicing to the calendar; let the folds of the toga of office which the hands of your Minerva eagerly made for you swathe these shoulders in repeated purple. Do you see how the temples have a new glitter and the altars a taller flame, and even my midwinter stars grow warm to match you and your virtues? The knights and common people and empurpled senators rejoice, and every magistrate draws his light from the consul. What of such a kind did the previous year afford, I pray? Speak, mighty Rome, and, venerable Antiquity, count up the annals with me, and do not review trivial examples but only such as my emperor condescends to surpass. Thrice and ten times as the years glided by did Augustus wield the Latin fasces, but it was late that he began to deserve them: you in early manhood surpassed your ancestors. And how great are the honours you refuse, how great those you forbid! Yet you will be swayed and often concede this day's repetition in answer to the Senate's prayers. A longer sequence yet awaits you, and thrice and four times as often will fortunate Rome grant you curule office. You will found another age with me and inaugurate afresh the altar of the venerable Tarentum. You will carry off a thousand trophies—only allow the triumphs. Bactra remains to be curbed with unfamiliar tribute, Babylon too remains; not yet do the laurels of India rest in Jupiter's lap, nor yet do the Arabs and Chinese file petitions, nor yet is the whole year honoured, and ten months desire a name from you.'

So spake Janus, and willingly withdrew within his closed gate. Then all the gods were amazed and gave signs in the exultant sky, and Jupiter granted you enduring youth, great king, and promised you years equal to his own.

II

EVCHARISTICON AD IMP. AVG. GERM. DOMITIANVM

REGIA Sidoniae conuiuia laudat Elissae
qui magnum Aenean Laurentibus intulit aruis
Alcinoique dapes mansuro carmine monstrat
aequore qui multo reducem consumpsit Vlixem:
ast ego cui sacrae Caesar noua gaudia cenae   5
nunc primum dominamque dedit contingere mensam,
qua celebrem mea uota lyra, quas soluere gratis
sufficiam? non si pariter mihi uertice laeto
nectat adoratas et Smyrna et Mantua lauros,
digna loquar. mediis uideor discumbere in astris   10
cum Ioue et Iliaca porrectum sumere dextra
immortale merum! sterilis transmisimus annos:
haec aeui mihi prima dies, hic limina uitae!
tene ego, regnator terrarum orbisque subacti
magne parens, te, spes hominum, te, cura deorum,   15
cerno iacens? datur haec iuxta, datur ora tueri
uina inter mensasque, et non assurgere fas est?
   Tectum augustum, ingens, non centum insigne columnis
sed quantae superos caelumque Atlante remisso
sustentare queant. stupet hoc uicina Tonantis   20
regia teque pari laetantur sede locatum
numina (nec magnum properes escendere caelum):
tanta patet moles effusaeque impetus aulae
liberior campi multumque amplexus operti
aetheros et tantum domino minor: ille penatis   25
implet et ingenti genio grauat. aemulus illic
mons Libys Iliacusque nitet, simul atra Syene
et Chios et glaucae certantia Doridi saxa,
Lunaque portandis tantum suffecta columnis.

II 6 dominamque ... mensam *Waller*: dominaque ... mensa *M*   contingere *Waller*: consurgere *M*: considere *Markland*: non surgere *Ellis*   7 quas *M*: qua *Vollmer*   9 adoratas *ς*: odoratas *M*   13 hic *M*: haec *ς*   15 cura *A*: curam *M*   22 nec *M*: ne *ς*: ne in *Lundström*   escendere *Gronovius*: excedere *M*: conscendere *Saenger*   24 campi *M*: campo *A*   operti *M*: aperti *ς*   26 grauat *Schwartz*: iuuat *M*   27 simul atra *Watt*: multa *M*: *post* nitet *lac. indic.* $M^1 A^c$: maculata *Nisbet*: coniuncta *Delz*: cumulata *Phillimore*: hic multa *Baehrens*: Nilaea *Slater*   28 Chios *ς*: duos *M*   Doridi *A*: Doride *M*

2

A THANK-OFFERING TO THE EMPEROR AUGUSTUS GERMANICUS DOMITIANUS

HE who brought great Aeneas to the Laurentian lands extols the regal banquets of Tyrian Dido, and he who wore out returning Ulysses with a great deal of sea displays Alcinous' feasts in lasting song: but I, to whom Caesar has granted the novel delights of his sacred repast and to reach my lord's table now for the first time, with what instrument am I to hymn my praise, what thanks shall I be able to pay in return? Not if both Smyrna and Mantua together were to entwine my exultant head with holy bay would my words be worthy. I think I am reclining with Jupiter amid the stars and receiving the immortal draught proffered by the hand of Ganymede! The barren years I have put behind me: this is the first day of my allotted span, here the threshold of my life! Is it you, ruler of the nations, great father of the subject world, is it you, hope of mankind and concern of the gods, whom I behold as I recline? Is it granted me to look upon this face beside mine amid the drinking and feasting, and is it no sacrilege not to stand?

Awesome and vast is the edifice, distinguished not by a hundred columns but by as many as could shoulder the gods and the sky if Atlas were let off. The Thunderer's palace next door gapes at it and the gods rejoice that you are lodged in a like abode (do not hurry to mount high heaven yet): so great extends the structure and the sweep of the far-flung hall, more expansive than that of an open plain, embracing much enclosed sky and lesser only than its master: he fills the house and weighs it down with his mighty spirit. The mountains of Libya and Troy glitter there in rivalry, with dark Syene and Chios and the rock that vies with the grey-green sea, and Luna deputed to carry the columns. Far above

longa supra species: fessis uix culmina prendas 30
uisibus auratique putes laquearia caeli.
  Hic cum Romuleos proceres trabeataque Caesar
agmina mille simul iussit discumbere mensis,
ipsa sinus accincta Ceres Bacchusque laborat
sufficere. aetherii felix sic orbita fluxit 35
Triptolemi, sic uuifero sub palmite nudos
umbrauit collis et sobria rura Lyaeus.
  Sed mihi non epulas Indisque innixa columnis
robora Maurorum famulasque ex ordine turmas,
ipsum, ipsum cupido tantum spectare uacauit 40
tranquillum uultus et maiestate serena
mulcentem radios summittentemque modeste
fortunae uexilla suae; tamen ore nitebat
dissimulatus honos. talem quoque barbarus hostis
posset et ignotae conspectum agnoscere gentes. 45
non aliter gelida Rhodopes in ualle recumbit
dimissis Gradiuus equis; sic lubrica ponit
membra Therapnaea resolutus gymnade Pollux,
sic iacet ad Gangen Indis ululantibus Euhan,
sic grauis Alcides post horrida iussa reuersus 50
gaudebat strato latus acclinare leoni.
parua loquor necdum aequo tuos, Germanice, †uultus:
talis, ubi Oceani finem mensasque reuisit
Aethiopum sacro diffusus nectare uultus,
dux superum secreta iubet dare carmina Musas 55
et Pallenaeos Phoebum laudare triumphos.
  Di tibi (namque animas saepe exaudire minores
dicuntur) patriae bis terque exire senectae
annuerint finis! rata numina miseris astris,
templaque des habitesque domos! saepe annua pandas 60
limina, saepe nouo Ianum lictore salutes,
saepe coronatis iteres quinquennia lustris!
qua mihi felicis epulas mensaeque dedisti
sacra tuae, talis longo post tempore uenit

---

36 uuifero *Krohn*: uitifero *M*   41 uultus et *A*: uultu sed *M*   50 reuersus *M*:
nouercae *Markland*   52 uultus *M*: cultus *Nisbet*: uisus *Markland*: (tuum) sidus
Saenger   54 sacro *M*: sacros ς   uultus *M*: uultum *Goodyear*: uittas *Phillimore*
55 secreta *M*: secura *Schwartz*   60 habitesque *M*: habilesque *Barth*   61 limina *c*: lumina *M*

extends the vista: you could scarcely take in the roof with your tired gaze and you would think it the ceiling of the gilded heaven.

Here when Caesar has commanded the leaders of the people and the columns of robed knights to recline together at a thousand tables, Ceres herself with hitched-up skirts toils with Bacchus to provide for them. With such bounty slid the tracks of air-boring Triptolemus, even so with the grape-bearing vine Lyaeus overshadowed the naked hills and sober countryside.

But not on the feast, not on Moorish wood propped on Indian supports, not on fleets of servants in serried ranks: on him, on him alone had I leisure avidly to gaze, tranquil in his expression, with serene majesty tempering his radiance, and modestly dipping the standards of his eminence; yet the splendour that he tried to hide shone in his countenance. Such a man even a foreign foe and strange tribes could have recognized if they had seen him. Not otherwise does Gradiuus relax in Rhodope's cool valley, his horses unharnessed; just so does Pollux lay down his oily limbs, at ease from the boxing-ring at Therapnae, so Euhan lies by the Ganges while Indians yowl, so grim Alcides, returning after his dread instructions, delighted to prop his flank upon the out-stretched lionskin. I speak of small things and cannot yet match your face, Germanicus: such is the leader of the gods when, his face suffused with sacred nectar, he visits once more the limits of Ocean and the tables of the Ethiopians, and bids the Muses sing songs undivulged and Phoebus celebrate the triumph of Pallene.

May the gods grant you (for they are said to listen often to lesser souls) to outlast twice and three times the limits of your father's old age! Let it suffice to have sent authentic deities to the stars; grant temples, but remain in human dwelling-places! May you often open the gates of the year, often greet Janus with your new lictors, often renew the quinquennial festival with garlanded ceremonies. The day when you granted me the blessings of your banquet and the sacred hospitality of your table shone as brightly

lux mihi, Troianae qualis sub collibus Albae   65
cum modo Germanas acies modo Daca sonantem
proelia Palladio tua me manus induit auro.

III

VIA DOMITIANA

Qvis duri silicis grauisque ferri
immanis sonus aequori propinquum
saxosae latus Appiae repleuit?
certe non Libycae sonant cateruae,
nec dux aduena peierante bello   5
Campanos quatit inquietus agros,
nec frangit uada montibusque caesis
inducit Nero sordidas paludes.
sed qui limina bellicosa Iani
iustis legibus et foro coronat,   10
qui castae Cereri diu negata
reddit iugera sobriasque terras,
qui fortem uetat interire sexum
et censor prohibet mares adultos
pulchrae supplicium timere formae,   15
qui reddit Capitolio Tonantem
et Pacem propria domo reponit,
qui genti patriae futura semper
sancit limina Flauiumque caelum;
hic segnis populi uias grauatus   20
et campos iter omne detinentis
longos eximit ambitus nouoque
iniectu solidat grauis harenas,
gaudens Euboicae domum Sibyllae
Gauranosque sinus et aestuantis   25
septem montibus admouere Baias.
  Hic quondam piger axe uectus uno

III 2 aequori ς: aequoris M   11 qui c: quis M   13 qui c: quis M
19 limina ς: lumina M: numina Bücheler   caelum Turnebus: caluum M: culmen
Aldina: cliuum Slater: clauum Ellis   20 segnis ς: senis M: caenis Gronovius   gra-
uatus Heinsius: grauatas M   23 graues M: putres Clericus: cauas Phillimore
27 uno M: udo Heinsius

after many years as when, beneath the hills of Trojan Alba, I sang now of German wars, now of Dacian battles, and your hand crowned me with Minerva's own wreath of gold.

3

THE VIA DOMITIANA

WHAT monstrous sound of hard flint and heavy iron has filled the side of the paved Appia that comes close to the sea? It is certainly not Libyan hordes thundering, nor is a foreign commander who cannot keep at peace making the lands of Campania quake with perfidious warfare, nor is Nero breaking the lagoons and channelling the mire of marshes through cloven mountains. No, it is he who encircles Janus' warlike threshold with just laws and a forum; he who returns to chaste Ceres acres long denied her and temperate fields; he who forbids virility to be destroyed and, as censor, stops adult males fearing the penalty of good looks; he who restores the Thunderer to the Capitol and puts Peace back in her own home; he who consecrates for his father's family a temple which will last for ever and a Flavian heaven; he, resenting the people's weary travels and the plains that held up every journey, is removing the long detours and stabilizing the heavy sand with a new dumping of earth, delighting to bring the Euboean Sibyl's home, the inlets of Gaurus, and steaming Baiae closer to the seven hills.

Here once the sluggish traveller, borne along on a single axle,

ECLOGA TERTIA

  nutabat cruce pendula uiator,
sorbebatque rotas maligna tellus,
et plebs in mediis Latina campis   30
horrebat mala nauigationis;
nec cursus agiles sed impeditum
tardabant iter orbitae tenaces,
dum pondus nimium querens sub alta
repit languida quadrupes statera.   35
at nunc quae solidum diem terebat
horarum uia facta uix duarum.
non tensae uolucrum per astra pennae,
nec uelocius ibitis, carinae.
  Hic primus labor incohare sulcos   40
et rescindere limites et alto
egestu penitus cauare terras;
mox haustas aliter replere fossas
et summo gremium parare dorso,
ne nutent sola, ne maligna sedes   45
det pressis dubium cubile saxis;
tunc umbonibus hinc et hinc coactis
et crebris iter alligare gomphis.
o quantae pariter manus laborant!
hi caedunt nemus exuuntque montis,   50
hi ferro scolopas trabesque leuant;
illi saxa ligant opusque texunt
cocto puluere sordidoque tofo;
hi siccant bibulas manu lacunas
et longe fluuios agunt minores.   55
hae possent et Athon cauare dextrae
et maestum pelagus gementis Helles
intercludere ponte non natanti.
his paruus, nisi †deuiae† uetarent,
Inous freta miscuisset Isthmos.   60
  Feruent litora mobilesque siluae,

---

33 tenaces *Davies*: tacentes *M*: iacentes *Markland*   35 repit ς (*M*¹ *in margine ad u.* 79): reperit *M*   36 at *A*: ac *M*   43 fossas ς: fossos *M*   46 det *Heinsius*: et *M*   51 scolopas *Nisbet*: scopulos *M*: corylos *Horsfall*   53 sordidoque *M*: torridoque *Heinsius*   topho *M*   59 paruus *M*: laurus *Constantius Fanensis*   deuiae *uel* cleuiae *M*: Deliae *Constantius Fanensis*: di uiam *Barth*: di uia *Macnaghten*: cliuiae *Is. Vossius*

used to sway on a precarious cross, while the spiteful earth sucked down his wheels, and the people of Latium in the middle of the land shivered at the miseries of a sea-voyage; their progress was not nimble—instead, the sticky furrow encumbered their course and slowed it down, while their enfeebled beast, complaining of its excessive load, crept along under the towering yoke. What used to waste a whole day is now a journey of scarcely two hours. Ships will not go faster, nor the outstretched wings of birds through the heavens.

Here the first task is to start with the furrows, cut back the edges and hollow out the earth far down with deep excavation; next, to refill the scooped-out trenches with other material and prepare a bed for the topmost camber, so that the earth shall not wobble nor the spiteful ground provide a treacherous bed for the weight of slabs; then to bind the road with blocks rammed in on both sides and numerous pegs. How many hands labour together! Some cut down groves and strip mountains, some smooth stakes and beams with iron; others bind together the slabs and interweave the work with baked dust and dirty tufa; some dry up thirsty pools by hand and divert lesser streams far away. These hands could tunnel through Athos and shut off moaning Helle's sad sea with a bridge that did not float. Ino's Isthmus, a trifle for these labourers, would have mingled the waters if . . . did not forbid it.

The shores and moving woods are astir, the noise travels far and

16 ECLOGA TERTIA

it longus medias fragor per urbes
atque echon simul hinc et inde fractam
Gauro Massicus uuifer remittit.
miratur sonitum quieta Cyme 65
et Literna palus pigerque Sauo.
At flauum caput umidumque late
crinem mollibus impeditus uluis
Volturnus leuat ora maximoque
pontis Caesarei reclinis arcu 70
raucis talia faucibus redundat:
'camporum bone conditor meorum,
qui me uallibus auiis refusum
et ripas habitare nescientem
recti legibus aluei ligasti, 75
en nunc ille ego turbidus minaxque,
uix passus dubias prius carinas,
iam pontem fero peruiusque calcor;
qui terras rapere et rotare siluas
assueram (pudet!), amnis esse coepi. 80
sed gratis ago seruitusque tanti est
quod sub te duce, te iubente, cessi,
quod tu maximus arbiter meaeque
uictor perpetuus legere ripae.
et nunc limite me colis beato 85
nec sordere sinis malumque late
deterges sterilis soli pudorem
ne me puluereum grauemque caeno
Tyrrheni sinus adluat profundi
(qualis Cinyphios tacente ripa 90
Poenus Bagrada serpit inter agros)
sed talis ferar ut nitente cursu
tranquillum mare proximumque possim
puro gurgite prouocare Lirim.'
Haec amnis: pariterque se leuarat 95

62 it *A*: et *M* fragror *M* 63 ethon *M* 66 Sauo *c*: Sason *M* 73 qui
ç: quis *M* 74 et *ç*: it *M* 75 *sign. interr. post* ligasti *Phillimore* 76 en
Turnebus: et *M* 81 seruitusque *A*•: scruitusque *M* 84 uictor *M*: uinctor
Heinsius: uindex *Saenger* 88 caeno *ç*: caelo *M* 89 adluat *Coleman*: obluat *M*:
obruat *ç*: abluat *Baehrens*: abnuat *Stange* 89 *post* 91 *Brandes* 90–1 Cinyphios . . .
Poenus *Coleman*: Cinyphius . . . Poenos *M* 95 leuarat *M*: leuabat *ç*

wide through the intervening cities, and grape-bearing Massicus returns to Gaurus the echo splintered on this side and on that. Peaceful Cumae is amazed at the sound—so are the pond at Liternum and the lazy Savo.

But Volturnus, his yellow head and wet hair all entangled with pliant weed, raises his face and, leaning on the enormous arch of Caesar's bridge, pours out this speech from his hoarse throat: 'Gracious organizer of my fields who, while I flooded my pathless valleys in ignorance of how to live within banks, bound me with the laws of a strict channel, look at me, once turbulent and threatening, scarcely tolerating hesitant craft: now I carry a bridge and am trampled by those who cross over; I who (shame on me!) used to snatch up the lands and whirl away forests have begun to be a river. But I owe you thanks and my servitude is worthwhile because under your guidance and at your command I have yielded, and your name will be read as mighty controller and everlasting conqueror of my bank. And now you honour me with a magnificent embankment and do not let me get dirty, and far and wide you wipe away the dreadful stain of barren soil so that the bay of the Tyrrhenian deep does not wash against me in a dirty state and laden with mud (like the Punic Bagradas snaking with its silent stream among the Cinyphian fields), but such shall I flow that with my sparkling current I can challenge the calm sea and my neighbour the Liris with my pure flood.'

So spoke the river: and in the mean time a strip of marble had

ingenti plaga marmorata dorso.
huius ianua prosperumque limen
arcus, belligeris ducis tropaeis
et totis Ligurum nitens metallis,
quantus nubila quo coronat Iris.   100
illic flectit iter citus uiator,
illic Appia se dolet relinqui.
tunc uelocior acriorque cursus,
tunc ipsos iuuat impetus iugalis,
ceu fessis ubi remigum lacertis   105
primae carbasa uentilatis, aurae.   106
qui primo Tiberim relinquit ortu,   112
primo uespere nauiget Lucrinum.   113
nil obstat cupidis, nihil moratur: 111
ergo omnes, age, quae sub axe primo   107
Romani colitis fidem Parentis,
prono limite commeate gentes,
Eoae citius uenite laurus.   110
   Sed quam fine uiae recentis imo,
qua monstrat ueteres Apollo Cumas,   115
albam crinibus infulisque cerno?
uisu fallimur? an sacris ab antris
profert Chalcidicas Sibylla laurus?
cedamus; chely, iam repone cantus:
uates sanctior incipit, tacendum est.   120
en! et colla rotat nouisque late
bacchatur spatiis uiamque replet.
tunc sic uirgineo profatur ore:
'dicebam, ueniet (manete campi
atque amnis), ueniet fauente caelo,   125
qui foedum nemus et putris arenas
celsis pontibus et uia leuabit.
en! hic est deus, hunc iubet beatis
pro se Iuppiter imperare terris,
quo non dignior has subit habenas   130
ex quo me duce praescios Auerni

---

98 belligeris *M*: belligeri *Avantius*   100 quo *Heinsius*: qui *M*   Iris *Heinsius*: imbri *M*: iri ς   101 flectit iter citus *Cartault*: flectitur excitus *M*   104 ipsos ς: ipso *M*   112–13 *post* 106 *Köstlin: del. Markland*   111 *post* 113 *Coleman*   114 imo *a*: uno *M*   118 profest *M*   125 fauente ς: fauete *M*   127 leuabit *M*: ligabit *Saenger*

raised itself with a mighty ridge. Its gateway and auspicious threshold was an arch gleaming with our leader's trophies of war and all the quarries of the Ligures, as great as that with which Iris crowns the clouds. There the hastening traveller bends his path, there the Appia grieves at being abandoned. Then swifter and more eager is the journey, even the draught-animals delight in the speed, just as when, O breezes, the sailors' arms are weary and you begin to fan the sails. He who leaves the Tiber at early dawn can sail on the Lucrine when twilight falls. Nothing hinders the eager, there is no delay: so come, all you peoples beneath the oriental sky who owe allegiance to our Father in Rome, flock hither by an easy route, and, you laurels of the east, come faster.

But whom do I see, white-haired and white-filleted, at the far end of the new road, where Apollo points out ancient Cumae? Does my sight deceive me, or is the Sibyl bringing out the Chalcidian bay from her hallowed grotto? Let us withdraw; lyre, set aside your music: a more venerable bard is beginning, we must be silent. Look, she is rolling her head, roaming in a frenzy all over the new course and occupying the width of the road. Then from her chaste lips she speaks: 'I used to say, one will come (be patient, you fields and river), one will come with heaven's favour who will raise on lofty bridges and a highway the rank forest and the crumbling sands. See! a god is he, him Jupiter commands to rule the happy earth in his stead; none worthier than he has taken up these reins since under my guidance Aeneas, hungry to know the future, both penetrated the prescient groves of Avernus and

ECLOGA TERTIA

  Aeneas auide futura quaerens
lucos et penetrauit et reliquit.
hic paci bonus, hic timendus armis.
natura melior potentiorque   135
hic si flammigeros teneret axis,
largis, India, nubibus maderes,
undaret Libye, teperet Haemus.
  Salue, dux hominum et parens deorum,
prouisum mihi cognitumque numen,   140
nec iam putribus euoluta chartis
sollemni prece Quindecim Virorum
perlustra mea dicta, sed canentem
ipsam comminus ut mereris audi.
uidi quam seriem imminentis aeui   145
pronectant tibi candidae Sorores:
magnus te manet ordo saeculorum,
natis longior abnepotibusque
annos perpetua geres iuuenta
quos fertur placidos adisse Nestor,   150
quos Tithonia computat senectus
et quantos ego Delium poposci.
iurauit tibi iam niualis Arctos,
nunc magnos Oriens dabit triumphos.
ibis qua uagus Hercules et Euhan   155
ultra sidera flammeumque solem
et Nili caput et niues Atlantis,
et laudum cumulo beatus omni
scandes belliger abnuesque currus,
donec Troicus ignis et renatae   160
Tarpeius pater intonabit aulae,
haec donec uia te regente terras
annosa magis Appia senescet.'

135 *post* 136 *Russell*   138 undaret *M*: umbraret *Postgate*: fronderet *Phillimore* 140 cognitumque ς: conditumque *M*   145 uidi *M*: audi *Heinsius*   seriem ς: series *M*   imminentis *Polster*: merentis *M*: manentis *Phillimore*: uirentis *Heinsius*: uigentis *Saenger*: recentis *Krohn*   150 quos *M*: quot *Markland*   placidos *M*: placidus *Heinsius*   adisse *M*: obisse *c*: subisse *Heinsius*   157 et[1] *M*: ad *Brandes*   159 scandes ς: sandes *M*: frondes *Slater*: laudes *uel* uades *Phillimore*   162 regente ς: gerente *M* 163 senescet *Heinsius*: senescat *M*

left them again. He is a friend to peace and formidable in arms. If, better and more powerful than nature, he were to drive the sun's fiery chariot, you, India, would be drenched with generous clouds, Libya would be awash, the Haemus would thaw.

Hail, leader of men and father of deities, whose godhead I foresaw and recognized; no longer scan my words as they are unrolled on rotting papyrus with the ritual liturgy of the Priesthood of Fifteen, but, as you deserve, listen to me delivering my prophecy in person. I have seen what a series of forthcoming years the shining Sisters are weaving for you: a great cycle of ages awaits you; outliving your children and grandchildren you will enjoy in eternal youth the peaceful years which Nestor is said to have reached, the years which Tithonus' old age counts up and the number which I once demanded from Delian Apollo. Already the snowy north has sworn allegiance to you, soon the Orient will afford you great triumphs. Where roving Hercules went, and Bacchus, will you go, beyond the stars and the flaming sun, the source of the Nile and the snows of Atlas, and, blessed with every increment of honour, you will mount some chariots as warlord and decline others, as long as the Trojan fire burns and the Tarpeian god thunders in his resurrected palace, until, under your rule upon earth, this road outlives the ancient Appian Way.'

IV

EPISTVLA AD VITORIVM MARCELLVM

CVRRE per Euboicos non segnis, epistula, campos,
hac ingressa uias qua nobilis Appia crescit
in latus et mollis solidus premit agger harenas;
atque ubi Romuleas uelox penetraueris arces,
continuo dextras flaui pete Thybridis oras, 5
Lydia qua penitus Stagnum Nauale coercet
ripa suburbanisque uadum praetexitur hortis.
illic egregium formaque animisque uidebis
Marcellum et celso praesignem uertice nosces.
cui primam solito uulgi de more salutem, 10
mox inclusa modis haec reddere uerba memento:
   'iam terras uolucremque polum fuga ueris aquosi
lassat et Icariis caelum latratibus urit;
ardua iam densae rarescunt moenia Romae.
hos Praeneste sacrum, nemus hos glaciale Dianae, 15
Algidus aut horrens aut Tuscula protegit umbra;
Tiburis hi lucos Anienaque frigora captant.
te quoque clamosae quae iam plaga mitior Vrbi
subtrahit? aestiuos quo decipis aere soles?
quid tuus ante omnis, tua cura potissima, Gallus, 20
nec non noster amor (dubium morumne probandus
ingeniine bonis)? Latiis aestiuat in oris
anne metalliferae repetit iam moenia Lunae
Tyrrhenasque domos? quod si tibi proximus haeret,
non ego nunc uestro procul a sermone recedo: 25
certum est, inde sonus geminas mihi circumit auris.
sed tu, dum nimio possessa Hyperione flagrat
torua Cleonaei iuba sideris, exue curis
pectus et assiduo temet furare labori.
et sontis operit pharetras arcumque retendit 30
Parthus, et Eleos auriga laboribus actis

IV VITORIVM *Nohl*: VICTORIVM *M*   MARCELLVM *A*: MARCILLVM *M*   2 uias *M*: uia *Vollmer*   8 illic *ς*: ille *M*: illac *Krohn*   10 primam *M*: primum *ς*   13 lassat *Nisbet*: laxat *M*   17 Anienaque *ς*: amenaque *M*   18 quae iam *Otto*: quaenam *M*   22 ingeniine *ς*: ingeniiue *M*   Latiis *M*: Latiisne *Otto*   26 circumit *vulg.*: cirumit *M*: circuit *Vollmer*   27 fraglat *M*   30 operit *ς*: aperit *M*   31 Eleos *Markland*: Eleis *M*   actis *Markland*: actos *M*

4

LETTER TO VITORIUS MARCELLUS

RUN over the Euboean plains without delay, letter, starting the journey here, where the venerable Appian Way bulges sideways and its close-packed embankment presses down the soft sand. Then when you have penetrated swiftly within the citadels of Romulus, straight away make for the right side of the yellow Tiber where the Lydian bank holds in the Naval Lake deep down and the water is fringed by the gardens on the outskirts of the city. There you will see Marcellus, outstanding in both body and mind, and you will recognize him, conspicuous for his lofty stature. Remember to give him the initial greeting in the customary popular fashion, and then this message framed in verse:

'Now the flight of the moist spring is enervating the land and the whirling sky, and scorches the air while the dog-star barks; now the tall buildings of crowded Rome are thinning out. Holy Praeneste shelters some people, Diana's ice-cool grove or shivering Algidus or Tusculum's shade protect others, while others again make for the groves of Tibur and the cool of the Anio. And you now? What more temperate clime takes you away from the noisy city? Under what sky are you cheating summer's sun? What of your friend Gallus, your greatest concern beyond everyone else, and dear to me too (who is to say whether he is praiseworthy more for the distinction of his character or his intellect?)? Is he spending the summer on the shores of Latium, or is he once again making for the walls of Luna, rich in marble, and the palaces of Tuscany? If he stays close beside you then I don't fade out of your conversation for long: that is certain, which is why a sound is buzzing in both my ears. As for you, as long as the horrid mane of Cleone's star blazes under the sway of a scorching sun, shrug off cares from your heart and snatch yourself away from ceaseless duties. The Parthian covers his guilty quiver and relaxes his bow, and the charioteer refreshes his Olympic steeds in the Alpheus

ECLOGA QVARTA

Alpheo permulcet equos, et nostra fatiscit
laxaturque chelys. uires instigat alitque
tempestiua quies: maior post otia uirtus.
talis cantata Briseide venit Achilles   35
acrior et positis erupit in Hectora plectris.
te quoque flammabit tacite repetita parumper
desidia et solitos nouus exsultabis in actus.
certe iam Latiae non miscent iurgia leges
et pacem piger annus habet messesque reuersae   40
dimisere forum: nec iam tibi turba reorum
uestibulo querulique rogant exire clientes;
cessat centeni moderatrix iudicis hasta,
qua tibi sublimi iam nunc celeberrima fama
eminet et iuuenis facundia praeterit annos.   45
felix curarum cui non Heliconia cordi
serta nec imbelles Parnasi e uertice laurus
sed uiget ingenium et magnos accinctus in usus
fert animus quascumque uices! nos otia uitae
solamur cantu uentosaque gaudia famae   50
quaerimus. en egomet somnum et geniale secutus
litus ubi Ausonio se condidit hospita portu
Parthenope, tenuis ignauo pollice chordas
pulso Maroneique sedens in margine templi
sumo animum et magni tumulis accanto magistri.   55
at tu si longi cursum dabit Atropos aeui
(detque precor) Latiique ducis sic numina pergent,
quem tibi posthabito studium est coluisse Tonante
quique tuos alio subtexit munere fascis
et spatia obliquae mandat renouare Latinae,   60
forsitan Ausonias ibis frenare cohortes:
aut Rheni populos aut nigrae litora Thules
aut Histrum seruare datur metuendaque Portae
limina Caspiacae. nec enim tibi sola potentis
eloquii uirtus: sunt membra accommoda bellis,   65
quique grauem †tarde† subeant thoraca lacerti:

32 Alpheo ς: Alpheos *M*   36 positis ς: postis *M*   37 tacite ς: tacitae *M*
38 solitos ς: solidos *M*   40 habet ς: labet *M*   42 rogant *M*: negant *Burman*
48 usus *M*: ausus *Cornelissen, Grasberg*: actus *Baehrens*   57 pergent *Markland*:
pergant *M*   60 obliquae *M*: antiquae *c*   63 datur *A*: datus *M*: latus *c*
66 tarde *M*: haud tarde *Barth*: ualidi *Markland*: ingentes *Coleman*: artandi *Phillimore*: *del.*
O. Müller, Goodyear   subeant *M*: subeant arte *O. Müller*: subeant apte *Goodyear*

after their labours are over, and my lyre grows tired and slack. Timely rest stimulates and nourishes one's strength: action is more vigorous after leisure. Just so, when he had sung about Briseis, Achilles came forth more fiercely and, abandoning his music, sallied out to fight Hector. Rest in silence for a while: you too will be inflamed and will leap like a new man into your accustomed activity. The laws of Latium are certainly not causing contention now, peace and quiet comes with the lazy season, the return of the harvest has emptied the forum: a crowd of litigants no longer throngs your entrance and importunate clients do not ask you to come out; the spear that governs the Centumviral judge is at rest but, when raised, it already elevates your reputation to heights of renown and your eloquence outstrips your youthful years. Happy in his concerns is the man whose passion is not the garlands of Helicon nor the civilian wreath from the peak of Parnassus but whose talents flourish and whose spirit, equipped for heroic undertakings, bears whatever chance decrees! By singing I console myself for my life of inactivity and I seek my reward in the vagaries of fame.

Behold, here am I, clinging to slumber and that genial shore where Parthenope, a refugee, hid herself in an Ausonian harbour; with my idle thumb I pluck the slender strings and, sitting in the precinct of Maro's shrine, I summon up my courage and sing beside the great master's tomb. But you, if Atropos grants you a long course of years (and I pray she will) and if the spirit of our Latin leader confirms it—whom you love to worship before Jupiter and who has woven on to your rods another commission, to renovate the whole length of the slanting Latin way—perhaps you will go and command the Ausonian cohorts: there are commissions to protect the peoples of the Rhine or murky Thule's shores or the Danube and the daunting portals of the Caspian Gates.

For powerful speech is not your only strength: you have the physique for warfare and arms ... able to shoulder a weighty

seu campo pedes ire pares, est agmina supra
nutaturus apex; seu frena sonantia flectes,
seruiet asper equus. nos facta aliena canendo
uergimus in senium: propriis tu pulcher in armis   70
ipse canenda geres paruoque exempla parabis
magna Getae, dignos quem iam nunc belliger actus
poscit auus praestatque domi nouisse triumphos.
surge, agedum, iuuenemque puer deprende parentem,
stemmate materno felix, uirtute paterna.   75
iam te blanda sinu Tyrio sibi Gloria felix
educat et cunctas gaudet spondere curulis.
    Haec ego Chalcidicis ad te, Marcelle, sonabam
litoribus, fractas ubi Vesuius egerit iras,
aemula Trinacriis uoluens incendia flammis.   80
mira fides! credetne uirum uentura propago,
cum segetes iterum, cum iam haec deserta uirebunt,
infra urbes populosque premi proauitaque tanto
rura abiisse mari? necdum letale minari
cessat apex. procul ista tuo sint fata Teate   85
nec Marrucinos agat haec insania montis.
    Nunc si forte meis quae sint exordia musis
scire petis, iam Sidonios emensa labores
Thebais optato collegit carbasa portu,
Parnasique iugis siluaque Heliconide festis   90
tura dedit flammis et uirginis exta iuuencae
uotiferaque meas suspendit ab arbore uittas.
nunc uacuos crinis alio subit infula nexu:
Troia quidem magnusque mihi temptatur Achilles
sed uocat arcitenens alio pater armaque monstrat   95
Ausonii maiora ducis. trahit impetus illo
iam pridem retrahitque timor. stabuntne sub illa
mole umeri an magno uincetur pondere ceruix?
dic, Marcelle, feram? fluctus an sueta minores
nosse ratis nondum Ioniis credenda periclis?   100

---

68 nutaturus ς: nittaurus *M*   70 uergimus *Coleman*: uergimur *M*   71 ipse ς:
ipsa *M*   paruoque ς: paruaque *M*   73 auus *A*: auos *M*   prestatque *M*:
perstatque *Peyrared*   76 gloria *M*: curia *Markland*   79 Vesuius ς: ue suus
M   egerit *Avantius*: eriget *M*: erigit ς   83 tanto *Marastoni*: toto *M*: fato *Slater*:
tosto *Vollmer*: cocto *Krohn*: tofo *Saenger*: taetro *Phillimore*   84 mari *M*: pari *Slater*:
graui *Saenger*   85 tuo sint *b*: tuos in *M*: tibi sint *Markland*

breastplate. If you should make ready to brave the field on foot, your helmet's peak will nod above the ranks; if you jerk the jingling reins, your spirited horse will obey. I am approaching old age, singing of other people's exploits, while you, a fine figure in the armour which is your proper gear, perform deeds to be celebrated in song and provide great examples to tiny Geta; his veteran grandparent, already expecting from him worthy performance, enables him to learn of triumphs while still at home. Up, boy, come on, overtake your young father, blessed in your mother's lineage and the prowess of your sire. Already Glory, happy and smiling, clasps you on her sumptuous lap, brings you up to be her favourite and delights in reserving for you every magisterial office.

So sing I to you, Marcellus, on the Cumaean shores where Vesuvius spews out its wrath, part assuaged, whirling firebrands to rival Etna's flames. It is very hard to credit! Will the coming generation of men believe—when the crops return, when these deserts have turned green—that cities and people are crushed underneath and that our ancestors' fields have disappeared in such a great inundation? The peak has not yet ceased to threaten destruction. Let that fate stay far from your Teate and this madness not afflict the mountains of the Marrucini.

Now, if by chance you seek to know what my Muses are undertaking, my *Thebaid* has now fulfilled the measure of its Tyrian labours and furled its sails in its longed-for harbour, and on the peaks of Parnassus and in the grove of Helicon it has consecrated incense and the entrails of a virgin heifer on the festive flames and hung up my chaplet on a tree of dedication. Now a head-dress with a different knot covers my bare hair: it is Troy and heroic Achilles whom I am undertaking, but the archer god summons me elsewhere and brings before me the still greater campaigns of our Ausonian lord. For a long time now my inclination has dragged me in that direction and fear has dragged me away again. Will my shoulders sustain that burden or will my neck be crushed under the enormous weight? Tell me, Marcellus, shall I bear it? Or should my craft, accustomed to lesser waves, not yet be entrusted to the dangers of the Ionian sea?

Iamque uale et penitus uoti tibi uatis amorem
corde exire ueta. nec enim
* * * * *
                       Tirynthius almae
pectus amicitiae, cedet tibi gloria fidi
Theseos et lacerum qui circa moenia Troiae
Priamiden caeso solatia traxit amico.'   105

V

ODE LYRICA AD SEPTIMIVM SEVERVM

PARVI beatus ruris honoribus
  qua prisca Teucros Alba colit lares,
    fortem atque facundum Seuerum
      non solitis fidibus saluto.

iam trux ad Arctos Parrhasias hiems   5
  concessit altis obruta solibus,
    iam pontus ac tellus renident
      ad Zephyros Aquilone fracto.

nunc cuncta uernans frondibus annuis
  crinitur arbos, nunc uolucrum noui   10
    questus inexpertumque carmen
      quod tacita siluere bruma.

nos parca tellus peruigil et focus
  culmenque multo lumine sordidum
    solantur exemptusque testa   15
      qua modo ferbuerat Lyaeus.

---

101 uoti *M*: noti *s*   amorem *c*: honorem *M*   102 *lac. post* enim *Coleman (post* Tirynthius *iam Markland)*: tirynthius *M*: te mitius *A*: seruantius *Saenger*: tibi uinctius *Otto: locus uarie temptatus*   103 pectus *M*: parcus *Slater*
V 8 ad Zephyros Aquilone fracto *Coleman*: iam zephiros aquilone fractos *M*: iam Zephyris Aquilo refractus *Markland*: in Zephyros Aquilone fracto *Bücheler, Krohn*
9 uernans *Markland*: ueris *M*: ueri *Baehrens*: ruri *Polster*   10 crinitur *s*: crinitus *M*
12 siluere *Owen*: statuere *M*: tacuere *Phillimore*: studuere *Clark*   13 nos *s*: hos *M*
16 qua *s*: quo *M*: qui *c*   ferbuerat *s*: fer uerat *M*: feruuerat *Frère*

Now farewell and don't let affection for a poet who is deeply attached to you disappear from your heart. For ... Hercules ... not ... a heart of life-giving friendship. The fame of faithful Theseus will be eclipsed by you, as will the hero who dragged Priam's mutilated offspring round the walls of Troy as reparation for his slaughtered friend.'

5

LYRIC ODE TO SEPTIMIUS SEVERUS

RICH in the adornments of my small estate where ancient Alba worships her Trojan household-gods, I greet the brave and eloquent Seuerus on an unaccustomed lyre. Now the grim winter, overcome by the mounting sun, has retreated to the Parrhasian north; now sea and earth smile at the Zephyrs, the north wind shattered; now every burgeoning tree is being tressed with annual foliage; now the birds have new plaints and an unpractised song which they kept hushed in the soundless winter. I am comforted by a parsimonious plot, an all-night fire, and a roof dirtied by many a light, and also wine drawn from the jar where but now it

non mille balant lanigeri greges
nec uacca dulci mugit adultero,
    unique siquando canenti
        mutus ager domino reclamat.   20

sed terra primis post patriam mihi
dilecta curis; hic mea carmina
    regina bellorum uirago
        Caesareo redimiuit auro,

cum tu sodalis dulce periculum   25
conisus omni pectore tolleres,
    ut Castor ad cunctos tremebat
        Bebryciae strepitus harenae.

tene in remotis Syrtibus auia
Lepcis creauit? iam feret Indicas   30
    messis odoratisque rara
        cinnama praeripiet Sabaeis.

quis non in omni uertice Romuli
reptasse dulcem Septimium putet?
    quis fonte Iuturnae relictis   35
        uberibus neget esse pastum?

nec mira uirtus: protinus Ausonum
portus uadosae nescius Africae
    intras adoptatusque Tuscis
        gurgitibus puer innatasti.   40

hinc paruus inter pignora curiae
contentus ⟨artae⟩ lumine purpurae
    crescis, sed immensos labores
        indole patricia secutus.

---

17 balant ς: lauant *M*   lanigeri ς: lapigeri *M*: iapigeri *a*   22 hic *Heinsius*: hinc *M*   24 redimiuit *Baehrens*: peramauit *M*: reparauit *Cruceus*: decorauit *Markland*: perarauit ς   26 tolleres *M*: pelleres *Heinsius*: falleres *Saenger*   28 strepitus harenae *M*: crepitus habenae *Schrader*   30 Lepcis *scripsi*: Leptis *M*   34 reptasse ς: raptasse *M*   38 nescius *Avantius*: nesciet *M*   42 *suppl. Burman*: arcto *Turnebus*

had been fermenting. A thousand wool-clad flocks do not bleat, no cow lows to her dear paramour, and only to the owner if he ever sings do the voiceless fields re-echo. But after my home country this land is cherished with especial love; here the maiden queen of warfare crowned my poetry with the emperor's gold while you strove with all your might to relieve your friend's delightful ordeal, just as Castor shuddered at every shout of the Bebrycian arena. Were you born of trackless Lepcis in its remote Syrtes? Soon she will produce an Indian crop and pre-empt the scarce cinnamon of the scented Arabs. Who would not think that dear little Septimius had crawled on Romulus' summit? Who would deny that he left his mother's breast to be fed from Juturna's spring? Nor are your powers surprising: unacquainted with African shallows you forthwith entered Ausonia's harbours and swam in Etruscan waters as an adopted child. Then as a small boy you grew up among the sons of the senate-house, content with the blaze of narrow purple but pursuing boundless tasks with

non sermo Poenus, non habitus tibi, 45
externa non mens: Italus, Italus.
   sunt Vrbe Romanisque turmis
      qui Libyam deceant alumni.

est et frementi uox hilaris foro;
uenale sed non eloquium tibi, 50
   ensisque uagina quiescit
      stringere ni iubeant amici.

sed rura cordi saepius et quies,
nunc in paternis sedibus et solo
   Veiente, nunc frondosa supra 55
      Hernica, nunc Curibus uetustis.

hic plura pones uocibus et modis
passu solutis, sed memor interim
   nostri uerecundo latentem
      barbiton ingemina sub antro. 60

VI

HERCVLES EPITRAPEZIOS NOVI VINDICIS

FORTE remittentem curas Phoeboque leuatum
pectora, cum patulis tererem uagus otia Saeptis
iam moriente die, rapuit me cena benigni
Vindicis. haec imos animi perlapsa recessus
inconsumpta manet: neque enim ludibria uentris 5
hausimus aut epulas diuerso a sole petitas
uinaque perpetuis aeuo certantia fastis.
a miseri, quos nosse iuuat quid Phasidis ales
distet ab hiberna Rhodopes grue, quis magis anser
exta †ferat†, cur Tuscus aper generosior Vmbro, 10
lubrica qua recubent conchylia mollius alga.

---

47 Vrbe ς: turbae M   49 hilaris M: habilis Markland   52 ni ς: ne M
54 in ς: et in M   58 passu Markland: passum M: passim ς   60 ingemina Gronovius: ingeminas M
   VI 5 manet ς: manent M   6 a M: e ς   10 exta M: esca Slater   ferat M: ferax Phillimore: satur Postgate

inborn nobility. Your speech is not Punic, nor your bearing; your outlook is not foreign: Italian you are, Italian. In the City and among Roman knights there are foster-children to do Libya credit. Yours is a cheerful voice in the buzzing forum; but your eloquence is not for sale, and your sword rests in the sheath unless friends should bid you draw it. But more often the country and seclusion beguile you, now in your father's seat on Veii's soil, now above leafy Hernica, now at ancient Cures. There you will set down more themes in diction and rhythms free from metre, but between whiles remember me and in a bashful grotto sound once more your retiring lyre.

6

THE HERCULES STATUETTE OF NOVIUS VINDEX

ONE day, as I set aside my preoccupations and my heart was lightened of Apollo, I was spending my leisure in drifting round the open Enclosure now that daylight was fading, when I was whisked off to dinner with generous Vindex. The memory has sunk into the deepest corners of my heart and abides there undiminished: for we did not gulp down playthings of the stomach or courses imported from far-off suns and wines old enough to challenge the Annual Register. Unhappy are they who delight in knowing how the bird of the Phasis differs from the winter crane of Rhodope, which goose ... its entrails more, why a boar from Tuscany is nobler than one from Umbria, on what seaweed

ECLOGA SEXTA

  nobis uerus amor medioque Helicone petitus
sermo hilaresque ioci brumalem absumere noctem
suaserunt mollemque oculis expellere somnum,
donec ab Elysiis prospexit sedibus alter   15
Castor et hesternas risit Tithonia mensas.
  O bona nox iunctaque utinam Tirynthia luna!
nox et Erythraeae Thetidis signanda lapillis
et memoranda diu geniumque habitura perennem!
mille ibi tunc species aerisque eborisque uetusti   20
atque locuturas mentito corpore ceras
edidici. quis namque oculis certauerit usquam
Vindicis artificum ueteres agnoscere ductus
et non inscriptis auctorem reddere signis?
hic tibi quae docto multum uigilata Myroni   25
aera, laboriferi uiuant quae marmora caelo
Praxitelis, quod ebur Pisaeo pollice rasum,
quod Polycleteis iussum spirare caminis,
linea quae ueterem longe fateatur Apellen
monstrabit: namque haec, quotiens chelyn exuit, illi   30
desidia est, hic Aoniis amor auocat antris.
  Haec inter castae genius tutelaque mensae
Amphitryoniades multo mea cepit amore
pectora nec longo satiaui lumina uisu:
tantus honos operi finisque inclusa per artos   35
maiestas! deus ille, deus! seseque tuendum
indulsit, Lysippe, tibi, paruusque uideri
sentirique ingens, et cum mirabilis intra
stet mensura pedem, tamen exclamare libebit,
si uisus per membra feres: 'hoc pectore pressus   40
uastator Nemees, haec exitiale ferebant
robur et Argoos frangebant bracchia remos
†ac† spatium
          *   *   *   *   *
          tam magna breui mendacia formae.
  quis modus in dextra, quanta experientia docti

18 Erythraeae *Markland*: Erythraeis *M*   19 habitura *Avantius*: habitumque *M*
25 hic *ς*: haec *M*   26 caelo *Avantius*: caeli *M*   29 ueterem *M*: uerum *Markland*
30 monstrabit *Geuaert*: monstrauit *M*   illi *Geuaert*: ille *M*   34 satiaui *Phillimore*:
satiauit *M*   35 finesque *M*: tenuesque *Bursian*   artos *ς*: artus *M*   36 tuendum *Schrader*: uidendum *M*   39 pedem *A*: pedum *M*   43 ac *M*: hae *Russell*:
hoc *A*: an *ς*: nec *Phillimore*   spatium *M*: spatio *c*   *post* spatium *lac. Housman*

slippery shell-fish lie more softly. But, as for ourselves, true affection, conversation drawn from the recesses of Helicon, and joyful merriment encouraged us to use up the winter's night and banish soft sleep from our eyes, until the second Castor looked out from his Elysian abode and Aurora laughed at yesterday's banquet.

Oh blessed night! If only it had been Herculean, with moon added to moon! It is a night to be marked with stones from Erythraean Thetis and to be recalled for a long time, and its festive spirit will endure! There on that occasion I learnt about a thousand beauties in ancient ivory and bronze, and wax images that with counterfeited form seemed likely to speak. For who could anywhere rival the eye of Vindex in recognizing the stamp of the old masters and ascribing an artist to untitled statues? He will show you which bronzes skilled Myron spent sleepless hours fashioning, which marbles have come alive through painstaking Praxiteles' chisel, which ivory was smoothed by an Olympic thumb, what statuary was bidden draw breath in Polycleitus' furnace, which outline betrays from afar Apelles of old: for whenever he doffs the lyre this is his idleness, this is the passion that calls him away from Aonian grottoes.

Amongst these, as spirit and guardian of his temperate table, was Amphitryon's son. He captured my heart with great desire and I could not satisfy my eyes however long I looked: such was the distinction of the work and the majesty encompassed within narrow limits. A god he is, a god, and he granted you the privilege of gazing upon him, Lysippus, small in appearance and mighty in impression, and although his measure stands miraculously within a foot, nevertheless when you carry your gaze over his limbs you will want to exclaim: 'By this stout breast the scourge of Nemea was crushed, these arms wielded the destructive wood and smashed Argo's oars . . . so great is the deception of that tiny form. What precision of touch, what enterprise in the skilled artist, at

ECLOGA SEXTA

    artificis, curis pariter gestamina mensae   45
fingere et ingentis animo uersare colossos!
tale nec Idaeis quicquam Telchines in antris
nec stolidus Brontes nec qui polit arma deorum
Lemnius exigua potuisset ludere massa.
nec torua effigies epulisque aliena remissis,   50
sed qualem parci domus admirata Molorchi
aut Aleae lucis uidit Tegeaea sacerdos;
qualis et Oetaeis emissus in astra fauillis
nectar adhuc torua laetus Iunone bibebat:
sic mitis uultus ueluti de pectore gaudens   55
hortatur mensas. tenet haec marcentia fratris
pocula, at haec clauae meminit manus: aspera sedis
sustinet et cultum Nemeaeo tegmine saxum.
    Digna operi fortuna sacro. Pellaeus habebat
regnator laetis numen uenerabile mensis   60
et comitem occasu secum portabat et ortu
prensabatque libens modo qua diademata dextra
abstulerat dederatque et magnas uerterat urbes.
semper ab hoc animos in crastina bella petebat,
huic acies semper uictor narrabat opimas,   65
siue catenatos Bromio detraxerat Indos
seu clusam magna Babylona refregerat hasta
seu Pelopis terras libertatemque Pelasgam
obruerat bello, magnoque ex agmine laudum
fertur Thebanos tantum excusasse triumphos.   70
ille etiam, magnos fatis rumpentibus actus,
cum traheret letale merum, iam mortis opaca
nube grauis uultus alios in numine caro
aeraque supremis timuit sudantia mensis.

45 curis *M*: ceris *Brandes*: cuiuis *Saenger*: curtae *Markland*: tenuis *Waller*: paruae *Courtney*: cui ius *uel* cuius *Phillimore*: cursim *Baehrens*   48 stolidus (solidus ς: ualidus *Hand*: Siculus *Baehrens*: solitus *Otto*) Brontes nec *M*: Brontes Steropesue et *Saenger*   50 torua *M*: tetrica *Saenger*   51 parci ς: parti *M*   52 Aleae *Hermolaus Barbarus*: taleae *M*   Tegeaea ς: tegea *M*   55 uultus *M*: uultu *Hand*: uultum *Baehrens*   57 clauae *Markland*: leuae *M*   sedis *M*: sedes *Markland*   58 et cultum *M*: occultum *Hand*: effultum *Polster*   59 Pellaeus ς: polleus *M*   60 laetis *M*: lautis *Heinsius*   61 occasu . . . et ortu *Heinsius*: occasus . . . et ortus *M*: casus . . . in omnes *Markland*   62 prensabat *c*: praestabat *M*   64 ab M^1, *c*: ad *M*   65 acies ς: acie *M*   narrabat *M*: referebat *Markland*   opimas ς: opinas *M*   66 detraxerat *M*: deuicerat *Markland*   67 clusam magna *M*: clusam multa *Baehrens*: Susa ac magna *Saenger*: densa Macetum *Korsch*   69 magno *M*: longo *Markland*   74 timuit *M*: tenuit *Markland*

the same time to fashion by his pains a table ornament and to revolve in his mind a great colossus! The Telchines in their caves under Mount Ida could not have produced such a *jeu d'esprit* out of a tiny mass of metal, neither could brutish Brontes nor the Lemnian who burnishes the armour of the gods. No glowering likeness this, unsuited to a relaxed banquet, but in the mood which thrifty Molorchus' household was amazed at or the priestess of Tegea saw in the groves of Alea; just as when, sent up to the stars from the ashes on Oeta, he drank nectar and rejoiced despite Juno's continued frown: with so benign a countenance, as if rejoicing from his heart, he cheers on the feast. One hand holds his brother's languorous cup; the other remembers the club: a rough seat supports him, and a rock embellished with the Nemean covering.

Worthy has been the fate of the sacred artefact. The Macedonian ruler possessed it as a deity to be revered at his joyous banquets and he carried it with him as his companion at both the setting and the rising of the sun, and he willingly clutched it with the hand with which he had taken away and bestowed crowns and overthrown great cities. Always from it he sought courage for the morrow's battle; to it, victorious, he always recounted the glorious fight, whether he had wrested the fettered Indians from Bromius or broken into embattled Babylon with his mighty spear, or whether he had crushed in war the lands of Pelops and the freedom of the Greeks, and out of this great procession of achievements he is said to have apologized only for his triumph over Thebes. And when fate snapped off his great exploits and he was draining the fatal wine, while engulfed in the dark cloud of death, he felt fear at the changed look in his beloved deity and at the omen of the bronze sweating at that last banquet.

ECLOGA SEXTA

  Mox Nasamoniaco decus admirabile regi   75
possessum, fortique deo libauit honores
semper atrox dextra periuroque ense superbus
Hannibal. Italicae perfusum sanguine gentis
diraque Romuleis portantem incendia tectis
oderat, et cum epulas et cum Lenaea dicaret   80
dona, deus castris maerens comes ire nefandis,
praecipue cum sacrilega face miscuit arces
ipsius immeritaeque domos ac templa Sagunti
polluit et populis furias immisit honestas.
  Nec post Sidonii letum ducis aere potita   85
egregio plebeia domus: conuiuia Sullae
ornabat semper claros intrare penatis
assuetum et felix dominorum stemmate signum.
  Nunc quoque, si mores humanaque pectora curae
nosse deis, non aula quidem, Tirynthie, nec te   90
regius ambit honos, sed casta ignaraque culpae
mens domini cui prisca fides coeptaeque perenne
foedus amicitiae. scit adhuc florente sub aeuo
par magnis Vestinus auis, quem nocte dieque
spirat et in carae uiuit complexibus umbrae.   95
hic igitur tibi laeta quies, fortissime diuum
Alcide, nec bella uides pugnasque ferocis,
sed chelyn et uittas et amantis tempora laurus.
hic tibi sollemni memorabit carmine quantus
Iliacas Geticasque domos quantusque niualem   100
Stymphalon quantusque iugis Erymanthon aquosis
terrueris, quem te pecoris possessor Hiberi,
quem tulerit saeuae Mareoticus arbiter arae;
hic penetrata tibi spoliataque limina mortis
concinet et flentis Libyae Scythiaeque puellas.   105
nec te regnator Macetum nec barbarus umquam
Hannibal aut saeui posset uox horrida Sullae
his celebrare modis. certe tu, muneris auctor,
non aliis malles oculis, Lysippe, probari.

78 Italicae ς: italiae *M*   79 portantem ς: portentem *M*   80 dicaret *M*: dicarat *Otto*   81 comes ς: .comis *M*   82 sacrilega *Gronovius*: sacrilegas *M*   arces ς: artes *M*   83 immeritaeque ς: meritaeque *M*   Sagunti ς: sgunti *M*   85 aere *A*: aera *M*   86 egregio ς: egregia *M*   Sullae *c*: sibullae *M*¹: sibullae *M*   89 si *M*: sic *Schraeder*   90 Tirynthie *A*: tirintia *M*   91 casta ς: castra *M*   94 auis *Auantius*: aquis *M*   96 diuum *M*¹: diuumque *M*   98 tempora *Markland*: carmina *M*: stamina *Waller*: limina *Otto*: numina *Saenger*   101 Stymphalon *A*: Strymphalon *M*   105 Libyae ς: libre *M*

Next the marvellous treasure became the possession of the Nasamonian king, and Hannibal, who was always ruthless in battle and exulted in his perfidious sword, poured libations to the strong god. Yet this god hated the man who, drenched with the blood of the Italian nation, carried the dread flames to Roman buildings, and even when he dedicated to him feasts and the gifts of Lenaeus he grieved to accompany his cursed camp, above all when he wrecked his own shrine with sacrilegious flames and defiled the houses and temples of blameless Saguntum and roused an honourable frenzy in the peoples.

After the death of the Tyrian leader no plebeian household gained possession of this extraordinary bronze: the statue adorned Sulla's table, accustomed always to enter famous homes and fortunate in its owners' pedigree.

And now, if it is the gods' concern to know men's character and hearts, it is not indeed a palace, Tirynthian hero, nor royal rank that surrounds you, but the pure and innocent outlook of a master of old-fashioned loyalty, whose pact of friendship once begun is eternal. Vestinus knows this, who was equal to his great ancestry even in the flower of his youth, for Vindex breathes his spirit night and day, and lives in the embrace of his beloved shade. So here, Alcides, bravest of the gods, you can enjoy welcome peace and look not on wars and fierce battles, but on lyre and chaplet and the bay clinging to the brow. He will recount to you in a solemn chant with what might you struck terror into the homes of the Trojans and the Getae and snowy Stymphalus and the streaming ridges of Erymanthus, how the owner of the Iberian herd and the Mareotic guardian of the cruel shrine met your approach; he will sing of how you crossed and robbed the threshold of death, and the weeping maidens of Africa and Scythia. Neither the ruler of Macedon nor barbaric Hannibal or cruel Sulla's harsh voice could ever have celebrated you in such strains. Certainly you, Lysippus, the author of this work, would prefer to be approved by no other eyes.

VII

ODE LYRICA AD VIBIVM MAXIMVM

Iam diu lato spatiata campo
fortis heroos, Erato, labores
differ atque ingens opus in minores
    contrahe gyros,

tuque, regnator lyricae cohortis,
da noui paulum mihi iura plectri,
si tuas cantu Latio sacraui,
    Pindare, Thebas:

Maximo carmen tenuare tempto;
nunc ab intonsa capienda myrto
serta, nunc maior sitit et bibendus
    castior amnis.

quando te dulci Latio remittent
Dalmatae montes, ubi Dite uiso
pallidus fossor redit erutoque
    concolor auro?

ecce me natum propiore terra
non tamen portu retinent amoeno
desides Baiae liticenue notus
    Hectoris armis.

torpor est nostris sine te Camenis,
tardius sueto uenit ipse Thymbrae
rector et primis meus ecce metis
    haeret Achilles.

quippe te fido monitore nostra
Thebais multa cruciata lima
temptat audaci fide Mantuanae
    gaudia famae.

VII VIBIVM *Nohl*: VIVIVM *M*   1 spatiata *ς*: sociata *M*: satiata *ς*   2 heroos *ς*: herois *M*   3 opus *M*: epos *Heinsius*   11 nunc *M*: nec *Markland*   maior *M*: Mauors *Saenger*   sitit *Saenger*: sitis *M*   15 fossor *ς*: fessor *M*   19–20 liticenue notus Hectoris armis *b*: laticemue motus Hectoris amnis *M*   23 ecce *M*: ille *Saenger*   28 gaudia *M*: grandia *Postgate*

7

LYRIC ODE TO VIBIUS MAXIMUS

Now that you have ranged the broad plain for a long time, bold Erato, postpone the labours of heroes and confine your huge enterprise to a narrower circuit. And do you, monarch of the lyric band, grant me rights awhile over a novel plectrum, if, Pindar, I have sanctified your Thebes with Latian song: I am venturing to fine down a poem for Maximus; now I must take my garland from untrimmed myrtle, now the greater source is running dry and I must drink from a purer stream. When will you be restored to dear Latium by the mountains of Dalmatia, where the miner returns pallid after a glimpse of Dis and the same colour as the gold he has unearthed? I was born in a nearer land, yet lazy Baiae does not hold me in its delightful haven, nor does the trumpeter distinguished by Hector's weapons. My Muses are sluggish without you, the lord of Thymbra himself comes more slowly than usual and, look, my Achilles is stuck at the first turn, for under your faithful guidance my *Thebaid*, tortured by many an application of the file, essays with bold lyre the joys of Mantuan fame.

sed damus lento ueniam quod alma
prole fundasti uacuos penatis.
o diem laetum! uenit ecce nobis
    Maximus alter.

orbitas omni fugienda nisu
quam premit uotis inimicus heres
optimo poscens (pudet heu) propinquum
    funus amico.

orbitas nullo tumulata fletu:
stat domo capta cupidus superstes
imminens leti spoliis et ipsum
    computat ignem.

duret in longum generosus infans,
perque non multis iter expeditum
crescat in mores patrios auumque
    prouocet actis!

tu tuos paruo memorabis ensis
quos ad Eoum tuleris Oronten
signa frenatae moderatus alae
    Castore dextro;

ille ut inuicti rapidum secutus
Caesaris fulmen refugis amaram
Sarmatis legem dederit, sub uno
    uiuere caelo.

sed tuas artes puer ante discat,
omne quis mundi senium remensus
orsa Sallusti breuis et Timaui
    reddis alumnum.

---

35 optimo *M*: optimi *Håkanson*   propinquum ς: propinquo *M*: propinqui *Postgate*   36 amico ς: amici *M*: amice *Krohn, Klotz*   42 expeditum *M*: expetitum *Baehrens*   46 Eoum ς: eum *M*   tuleris *Avantius*: tuleras *M*   Oronten *Housman*: Orontem *M*

But I do excuse your slowness, because with your sustaining progeny you have put your empty home on firm foundations. Oh joyous day! Look, we see coming another Maximus. We should make every effort to avoid the childlessness which a hostile heir besets with his prayers, demanding for his admirable friend—shame on him!—that death will come soon. The childless are entombed without tears: once he has captured the household the eager heir stands hovering over the spoils of death and counts the cost even of the pyre. May your highborn baby live a long life, and along a road where few have forged a track may he grow into his father's ways, and may he challenge his grandfather in his exploits! *You* will tell the little boy about the weapons you wielded at the Orontes in the east, commanding the standards of a mounted division with Castor behind you; *he* will tell how, following invincible Caesar's swift thunderbolt, he imposed bitter terms on the retreating Sarmatae: to live under a single sky. But first let the boy learn the arts by which you retraced all the long history of the world, reproducing the enterprise of terse Sallust and the scion of the Timavus.

VIII

GRATVLATIO AD IVLIVM MENECRATEN

PANDE foris superum uittataque templa Sabaeis
nubibus et pecudum fibris spirantibus imple,
Parthenope; clari genus ecce Menecratis auget
tertia iam suboles, procerum tibi nobile uulgus
crescit et insani solatur damna Vesaeui.   5
nec solum festas secreta Neapolis aras
ambiat, et socii portus dilectaque miti
terra Dicarcheo nec non plaga cara madenti
Surrentina deo sertis altaria cingat,
materni qua litus aui, quem turba nepotum   10
circumit et similis contendit reddere uultus.
gaudeat et Libyca praesignis auunculus hasta,
quaeque sibi genitos putat attollitque benigno
Polla sinu. macte, o iuuenis, qui tanta merenti
lumina das patriae. dulci strepit ecce tumultu 15
tot dominis clamata domus. procul atra recedat
Inuidia atque alio liuentia lumina flectat:
his senium longaeque decus uirtutis et alba
Atropos et patrius lauro promisit Apollo.
Ergo quod Ausoniae pater augustissimus urbis   20
ius tibi tergeminae dederat laetabile prolis,
omen erat. uenit totiens Lucina piumque
intrauit repetita larem. sic fertilis oro
stet domus et donis numquam mutata sacratis.
macte, quod et proles tibi saepius aucta uirili 25
robore, sed iuueni laetanda et uirgo parenti!
aptior his uirtus, citius dabit illa nepotes,
qualis maternis Helene iam digna palaestris
inter Amyclaeos reptabat candida fratres;

VIII 1 pandere (re *del. rubr.*) sorores (*corr. M*¹)   3 Menecratis *s*: Menecrates *M*
6 secreta *M*: secrata *a*: cretata *Rothstein*: recreata *Otto*   8 Dicarcheo *Baehrens*:
dicachen *M*: dicarchei *s*: Dicaearcho *Krohn*   11 similes ... uultus *M*: simili ...
uultu *Heinsius*   15 dulci *c*: dulcis *M*   strepit *Baehrens*: tremit *M*: fremit *Heinsius*
tumultu *c*: tumultus *M*   17 lumina *Markland*: pectora *M*   18 et alba *M*:
alebat *Phillimore*   19 lauro *M*: lauros *s*: laurus *Krohn*   24 mutata *M*: nudata
Markland: immutata *Otto*   26 sed *M*: sic *Heinsius*: se *A*   laetanda et *Saenger*: letam
dat *M*: laetandast *Baehrens*: laeta addita *Owen*   27 *del. Markland*

8

CONGRATULATIONS TO JULIUS MENECRATES

FLING open the gods' doors, Parthenope, and fill the festooned temples with clouds of Arabian incense and victims' throbbing entrails; behold, now a third offspring augments the illustrious Menecrates' line, a noble crowd of aristocrats is growing for you, giving comfort for the losses from crazed Vesuvius. Let not only secluded Naples throng the festive altars; let also the neighbouring harbours and the land beloved of gentle Dicarcheus deck the altars with garlands, and likewise the Surrentine coast dear to the wine-soaked god, where is the shore of their maternal grandfather who is surrounded by a throng of grandchildren, competing to reflect his likeness in their features. Let their uncle too rejoice, distinguished by his Libyan spear, and Polla who counts them as born to herself and lifts them on to her kindly lap.

Bravo young man, who bestow such ornaments on the country to which you owe so much. Look, the house shakes with sweet confusion, ringing with the shouts of so many masters. Let black Envy retreat afar and divert elsewhere her malicious gaze: both white Atropos and their family's friend Apollo, with his bay, have promised them old age and the distinction of a long and meritorious life. So it was an omen, the fact that the most revered father of the Ausonian city had granted you the joyful privilege earned by triple offspring. Three times has Lucina come and been invited back to enter your god-fearing home again. I pray that your house should endure likewise in fruitfulness and never be stripped of its hallowed gifts. Bravo, in that your stock has been more than once increased by sturdy males, while you also have a girl to delight her young father! Courage befits the former more, the latter will give you grandchildren sooner, just as Helen, already worthy of her mother's wrestling-floors, crawled radiantly

uel qualis caeli facies ubi nocte serena 30
admouere iubar mediae duo sidera lunae.
　Sed queror haud facilis, iuuenum rarissime, questus
irascorque etiam, quantum irascuntur amantes.
tantane me decuit uulgari gaudia fama
noscere? cumque tibi uagiret tertius infans, 35
protinus ingenti non uenit nuntia cursu
littera quae festos cumulare altaribus ignis
et redimire chelyn postisque ornare iuberet
Albanoque cadum sordentem promere fumo
et creta signare diem? si tardus inersque 40
nunc demum mea uota cano, tua culpa tuusque
hic pudor. ulterius sed enim producere questus
non licet: en hilaris circumstat turba tuorum
defensatque patrem. quem non hoc agmine uincas?
　Di patrii, quos auguriis super aequora magnis 45
litus ad Ausonium deuexit Abantia classis,
tu, ductor populi longe migrantis, Apollo,
cuius adhuc uolucrem laeua ceruice sedentem
respiciens blande felix Eumelus adorat,
tuque, Actaea Ceres, cursu cui semper anhelo 50
uotiuam taciti quassamus lampada mystae,
et uos, Tyndaridae, quos non horrenda Lycurgi
Taygeta umbrosaeque magis coluere Therapnae:
hos cum plebe sua patriae seruate penates.
sint qui fessam aeuo crebrisque laboribus urbem 55
uoce opibusque iuuent uiridique in nomine seruent.
his placidos genitor mores largumque nitorem
monstret auus, pulchrae studium uirtutis uterque.
quippe et opes et origo sinunt hanc lampade prima
patricias intrare foris, hos pube sub ipsa, 60
si modo prona bonis inuicti Caesaris adsint
numina, Romulei limen pulsare senatus.

---

32 rarissime *M*: carissime *ς*　　38 chelyn *M*: comam *Polster*　　39 Albanoque *M*:
Albanique *Krohn*　　40 creta *Bentley*: cantu *M*　　signare *M*: insignire *Goodyear*:
sacrare *Polster*　si *Brandes*: sed *M*: sic *Baehrens*　　46 Abantia *ς*: abanxia *M*
49 Eumelus *Housman*: eumeliss *M*: Eumelis *uulg.*　　　50 Actaea *c*: acea *M*
54 patriae *Gronovius*: patrii *M*　　55 fessam *ς*: fossam *M*　　57 his placidos *ς*: his
placidus *M*: hos placidus *Sudhaus*　　59 hanc *b*: hac *M*

between her Spartan brothers, or like the appearance of the sky when, on a calm night, two stars have brought their light close to the moon between them.

But the complaints I have to make are not trivial, most uncommon young man, and I am angry too, as far as people who love one another can be angry. Was it appropriate for me to hear of such great joy from common rumour, and when your third baby was wailing did a letter of announcement fail to come forth with immense speed bidding me heap festal fires on the altars and garland my lyre and decorate the doorposts, and bring out the cask sooty with Alban smoke and mark the date with chalk? If I fulfil my vows only now, slowly and ineptly, yours is the responsibility, and yours this shame. But I may not spin out my complaints any further: behold, your cheerful troop is standing round you defending their father. Whom would you not conquer with this array?

Gods of my homeland, whom the fleet of Abas with portentous omens brought over the sea to the Ausonian shore, and you, Apollo, guide of your seafaring people, on whose left shoulder still perches the bird that is worshipped by fortunate Eumelus as he looks back at it affectionately, and you, Ceres of Attica, for whom we silent initiates cease not to shake the votive torch in our breathless course, and you, sons of Tyndarus, whom Lycurgus' awe-inspiring Taygetus and shady Therapnae have not worshipped more: keep this household with its people safe for their fatherland. Let there be those who, by their eloquence and wealth, may support this city, which is wearied by age and repeated troubles, and let them keep its fame fresh. Let their father show his sons gentle ways, their grandfather bountiful splendour, and both of them the love of beauteous virtue. Indeed both wealth and lineage enable your daughter to enter a noble household when she is initiated in marriage, and her brothers while still in their youth—if only the godhead of invincible Caesar, which favours the righteous, attends them—to knock at the door of the senate of Romulus.

IX

HENDECASYLLABI IOCOSI AD PLOTIVM GRYPVM

Est sane iocus iste quod libellum
misisti mihi, Grype, pro libello.
urbanum tamen hoc potest uideri
si post hoc aliquid mihi remittas;
nam si ludere, Grype, perseueras,   5
non ludis. licet ecce computemus:
noster purpureus nouusque charta
et binis decoratus umbilicis
praeter me mihi constitit decussis:
tu rosum tineis situque putrem,   10
quales aut Libycis madent oliuis
aut tus Niliacum piperue seruant
aut Byzantiacos cocunt lacertos,
nec saltem tua dicta continentem
quae trino iuuenis foro tonabas   15
aut centum prope iudices, priusquam
te Germanicus arbitrum sequenti
annonae dedit omniumque late
praefecit stationibus uiarum,
sed Bruti senis oscitationes   20
de capsa miseri libellionis,
emptum plus minus asse Gaiano,
donas. usque adeone defuerunt
scissis pillea suta de lacernis
uel mantelia luridaeue mappae,   25
chartae, Thebaicaeue Caricaeue?
nusquam turbine conditus ruenti
prunorum globus atque cottanorum?
non enlychnia sicca, non replictae
bulborum tunicae, nec oua †tantum†,   30

IX ADPLOTIV̄M: AD PLOCIV̄A   GRYPVM M: GRIPPV̄A   4 si post hoc aliquid mih (mihi M² *in margine*) remittas M: si posthac aliud mihi remittes *Heinsius*   8 umbilicis ς: umbilicus M   9 decussis M: decussi *Turnebus*   12 miliacum M   13 cocunt *Thomson*: colunt M: olent *Heinsius*   21 libellionis ς: libelliones M   24 scissis *Heinsius*: caesis M: crassis *Waller*: cassis *Polster*   suta ς: sicta *uel* sicca *uel* suta M: secta *Polster*   26 Carthae M   28 cottanorum ς: cattanorum M   29 enlychnia *Klotz*: eulychnia M   30 bulborum ς: bullorum M   tantum M: tandem *Markland*: tota *Turnebus*: —quantum!— *Postgate*

9

HENDECASYLLABLES IN JEST TO PLOTIUS GRYPUS

To be sure it is only your fun, Grypus, to have sent me a slim volume in exchange for a slim volume. All the same even this can seem sophisticated, if only after this you send me something significant in return. For if you are unremitting in your game, Grypus, it is no game. Look, let's do the sums. Mine, in scarlet, of new papyrus and embellished with twin knobs, cost me (apart from my personal contribution) ten asses; you send me one nibbled by bookworms and mouldy from lying around, like the paper that drips with Libyan olives, or wraps incense from the Nile or pepper, or cooks tunny-fish from Byzantium, and you don't even offer me one containing the speeches which you thundered as a young man in the three forums or in front of the hundred judges before Germanicus appointed you as controller of the co-operative corn-supply and put you in charge of the stopping-stages on all the roads far and wide: instead, your present is the yawnings of old Brutus, bought from a miserable book-pedlar's box for more or less one of Gaius' pennies.

Was there such a scarcity of caps sewn out of cut-up cloaks, or cloths, or yellowing napkins, papyrus rolls, Theban dates, or Carian figs? Was there nowhere to be found a mass of plums or figs packed in a collapsing cone, no dry wicks, no peeled onion-

nec lenes alicae, nec asperum far?
nusquam Cinyphiis uagata campis
curuarum domus uda coclearum?
non lardum graue debilisue perna,
non Lucanica, non breues falisci?　35
non sal oxyporumue caseusue
aut panes uiridantis aphronitri
uel passum psithiis suis recoctum,
dulci defruta uel lutosa caeno?
quantum uel dare cereos olentis,　40
cultellum, tenuisue codicillos?
ollaris, rogo, non licebat uuas,
Cumano patinas uel orbe tortas,
aut unam dare synthesin (quid horres?)
alborum calicum atque caccaborum?　45

　Sed certa uelut aequus in statera
nil mutas, sed idem mihi rependis.
quid si cum bene mane semicrudus
inflatam tibi dixero salutem,
et tu me uicibus domi salutes?　50
aut cum me dape iuueris opima,
exspectes similis et ipse cenas?
irascor tibi, Grype. sed ualebis;
tantum ne mihi, quo soles lepore,
et nunc hendecasyllabos remittas.　55

31 lenes *Heinsius*: leues *M*　34 graue *M*: breue *Markland*　35 breues *Coleman*: graues *M*　36 oxyporumue *Aldina*: oxyforumue *M*　37 aphronitri ς: afronitri *M*　38 suis *Avantius*: uuis *uel* unis *M*　39 defruta ς: defructa *M*　40 uel *A*: nec *M*　41 cultellum ς: cutellum *M*: scutellam *Slater*　43 uel *Heinsius*: in *M*: sub *Saenger*　45 alborum *M*: obbarum *Heinsius*: rubrorum *Coleman*　49 inflatam *Otto*: inlatam *M*: inlotam *Turnebus*: inlaesam *uel* intactam *Cornelissen*: inuitam *Phillimore*　dixero ς: dixere *M*　54 ne ς: me *M*　quo ς: quod *M*　lepore *c*: lepori *M*
55 P· PAPINI· STACII· SILVARVM· LIBER/IIII· EXPLICIT· INCIP· LIB· V *M*

sleeves, nor [even] eggs? No smooth-tasting groats or rough flour? Was there nowhere the moist home of curling snails that had trailed over the Cinyphian plains, no lump of bacon or flabby ham, no Lucanian sausages or short Faliscan ones? Was there no salt or salad-dressing or cheese or cakes of green soda or wine boiled up again with its own skins, or dessert-wine clouded with its sweet sludge? What sort of behaviour was it not even to give me any smelly candles, a knife, or slender notebooks? I ask you, couldn't you send preserved grapes, or plates turned on a Cumaean wheel, or a table-set (why are you shuddering?) of plain white mugs and dishes?

But like a fair dealer with an accurate scale you change nothing, but you weigh me out the same amount. Well? If, somewhat flatulent, I have uttered my windy respects to you very early in the morning, would you also in turn greet me at my house? Or, when you have regaled me with a splendid repast, would you in your turn look forward to similar meals? I am angry with you, Grypus, but good luck to you; only don't do the same thing again and with your usual humour send me back hendecasyllables.

COMMENTARY

PREFACE

INTRODUCTION

EACH of the first four books of the *Siluae* is preceded by a prose dedication in epistolary style. The epistle affixed to Book 5 is different: it refers solely to the first poem and was presumably affixed to the book when it was edited after St.'s death (see General Introduction).

Prose prefaces are attested for prose works in Greek from the fourth-century rhetoricians onwards, and the epistolary form emerges in the Hellenistic period (e.g. Archimedes): see Janson, 16 ff., 20 ff. The introductory sections to single works of poetry such as epic are contained within the poem itself: cf. Hom. *Il.* 1. 1–7, Virg. *A.* 1. 1–11. In a collection the opening poem can serve as an introduction: cf. *Anth. Pal.* 4. 1–3, i.e. the poems of the anthologies of Meleager, Philip, and Agathias; Meleager and Philip mention by name a sample of the contributors to their *Garlands*, equating each with a flower or vegetable, and Agathias describes the contents of his *Garland* by categories. Frequently the introductory poem which now heads a collection was originally intended for a smaller selection: cf. Cat. 1, and see on l. 27 below.

Sometimes a poem was preceded by a verse preface in a less grand style:[1] cf. Cat. 65–6, 67–8, Persius' prologue in scazons, the elegiac preface to Claudian's *De Raptu Proserpinae*, T. Viljamaa, *Studies in Greek Encomiastic Poetry of the Early Byzantine Period* (Helsinki, 1968), 68 ff., Alan Cameron, *CQ* NS 20 (1970), 119–29.

Martial and St. are the first extant Latin poets to affix epistolary prose prefaces to collections of poetry. 'Occasional' verse like the *Siluae*, consisting of heterogeneous pieces intended for delivery on various occasions in the past, required a general introduction to defend its publication as an anthology. In this respect the *praefationes* to the *Siluae* contain a propagandistic (and sometimes polemical) aspect akin to the prologues of Plautus and Terence. Martial's addressee Decianus, objecting to prefatory letters before collections of epigrams, concedes a preface to drama, which is restricted by plot and dialogue (Mart. 2 *Pr.*): 'uideo quare tragoedia atque comoedia epistolam accipiant, quibus pro se loqui non licet'. This remark may be relevant to the tragedies of Seneca and Pomponius, which included debate on style: cf. Quint. 8. 3. 31 'nam memini iuuenis admodum inter Pomponium et Senecam etiam praefationibus esse tractatum an "gradus eliminat" in tragoedia dici oportuisset'. Vessey, *Statius and the Thebaid*, 40, claims that St. wrote prose prefaces because he 'could not make his defence in verse, for material of such a kind could not have been integrated with the other poems

---

[1] Agathias' preface begins in iambic trimeters but changes to hexameters at l. 47 for the section in praise of Justinian.

that are included in the *Siluae*'. But this reasoning is false: cf. the collected fables of Phaedrus, where each book is preceded by a verse prologue containing literary polemic and *apologia*.[2] St. may have written his prefaces in prose because poems to the emperor had to have pride of place at the beginning of a book (see below on 2), but if the prefatory material had been in verse it would have had to usurp first position in Books 1 and 4; hence the pattern was sustained with prose prefaces for Books 2 and 3.

Vollmer, 11 n. 1, suggests that Lucan may have written a prose preface for his *Siluae*: cf. Suet. *Vit. Luc.* 'ciuile bellum, quod a Pompeio et Caesare gestum est, recitauit ⟨lacunam Ritterscheid⟩ ut praefatione quadam aetatem et initia sua cum Vergilio conparans ausus sit dicere: "et quantum mihi restat ad Culicem."' But without Ritterscheid's lacuna the text can be taken naturally to refer to introductory remarks before a recitation of the epic.[3]

Prose *epistulae* are affixed to Books 1, 2, 8, 9, and 12 of Martial's *Epigrams*. 1 *Pr.* and 9 *Pr.* both quote a sample epigram. At 9 *Pr.* the letter does not introduce the book which follows but refers solely to the epigram which it contains and which is described as 'extra ordinem paginarum'.[4] Of Martial's prefaces only 1 *Pr.* is directed to the anonymous public, but it is still described as an *epistula* despite the absence of an epistolary form (but may not have been written to introduce Book 1 as we now have it: see Citroni, 5); only 8 *Pr.* is a dedication (to Domitian). The dominant theme is *apologia*: for apparently damaging and risqué verse (1 *Pr.*, 8 *Pr.*) or hasty composition (12 *Pr.*). White (1974), 45 f., has demonstrated that the *praefatio* to Book 12 originally accompanied a small selection for Priscus in the form of a *libellus* (cf. 'studui paucissimis diebus', which could not describe the total compilation of Book 12). It was customary to send a covering letter when a *libellus* was submitted to a friend for criticism before revision and publication: cf. Plin. *Epist.* 1. 2, 8, 3. 10, 13, 4. 14, 5. 12, 7. 12, 8. 19, 9. 29. Hence the epistolary preface develops as a vehicle to dedicate the work: see Janson, 112, H. Peter, *Der Brief in der römischen Literatur* (Leipzig, 1901, repr. Hildesheim, 1965), 246. None of Martial's prefaces specifies the contents of the book as St.'s do, since it would be absurd to enumerate the contents of a hundred or more epigrams, many of them extremely short. Furthermore, the credit accruing to the individual addressees of the *Siluae* is enhanced by flattering notice in a *praefatio*. Pliny is strongly critical of *praefationes* (especially long ones: *Epist.* 4. 14. 8), believing

---

[2] Phaedrus claims to be heir to Aesop (1 *Pr.* 1 f.), justifies his own additions on the grounds of *uarietas* (2 *Pr.* 9 ff.), asks his addressee to read the *neniae* which will delight posterity (3 *Pr.* 10, 31 f.), warns against plagiarism (4 *Pr.* 16), and defends himself against *Inuidia mordax* (5 *Pr.* 8 f.).

[3] Z. Pavlovskis believes that Lucan's preface was in verse, detecting a metrical pattern in 'restat ad Culicem' (*RIL* 10 [1967], 537 n. 11), but this rhythm is entirely normal, simply cretic and spondee with resolution.

[4] Birt, *Buchwesen*, 142, infers from this phrase that the *praefationes* of Martial and St. were written on the outside of the papyrus roll. But in any case the papyrus could only be read if the *uolumen* was taken out of its wrapper and unrolled, and since the average length of a papyrus roll could easily accommodate the *praefatio* as well as a book of the *Epigrams* or the *Siluae*, it is difficult to see any practical advantage in copying the *praefatio* on to the outside of the roll.

that their information should be inferred from the *tituli* and from the works themselves (*Epist.* 5. 12. 3). But the *praefatio* to a published edition clearly serves various purposes: each of the *praefationes* to *S.* 1–4 is addressed to the dedicatee and conveys the dedication; since each book also contains poems addressed to others, St. provides a list of the contents with the ostensible aim of justifying their inclusion in a book for this particular dedicatee; but this information is so superficial that the dedicatee probably knew it already through the operation of *amicitia*, and the list of contents really advertises the nature of the poems and the patrons to whom they are addressed, and establishes the order. The end of the *praefatio* to Book 1 is lost, but the *praefationes* to Books 2–4 both end with a plea for the dedicatee to support the publication. For the anticipation of criticism in 1 *Pr.* and St.'s refutation of his critics in 4 *Pr.* see on ll. 24 ff. Clearly the *praefationes*, ostensibly addressed to the dedicatee, are for the general reader. The pretence is dropped by Ausonius, whose epistolary prefaces are addressed to the *lector*: see Z. Pavlovskis, *RIL* 10 (1967), 546.

1. Inueni librum: not the writing of the poems themselves, which were composed within a day or two of the occasion which prompted each (1 *Pr.* 13), but the editorial process of selection and arrangement. St. is here using a technical term from rhetoric, denoting creation rather than discovery: cf. Sen. *Contr.* 9. 6. 11 'non inuenit illam [rem], sed conrupit', *TLL* vii. 2. 150. 16 ff.

Marcelle carissime: this single phrase of salutation matches the brevity of the entire opening sentence; St. adopts a new and businesslike tone after the effusive openings of the first three books, where each salutation is expressed by two superlatives and a predicate: 1 *Pr.* 1 f. 'Stella iuuenis optime et in studiis nostris eminentissime qua parte et uoluisti', 2 *Pr.* 1 ff. 'Melior, uir optime nec minus in iudicio litterarum quam in omni uitae colore tersissime', 3 *Pr.* 1 f. 'Polli dulcissime et hac cui tam fideliter inhaeres quiete dignissime'.

pietati tuae: 'your caring affection' (reciprocating *carissime*); *pius* and *pietas* do not necessarily imply the attitude of a subordinate, and *pietas* is part of a sense of responsibility towards one's dependants: cf. medieval Latin ('mercy'), Old French *pitiét* ('pity' as well as 'piety'), and see U. Knoche in *Festschrift Bruno Snell* (Munich, 1956), 89–100. White (1973), 279 and n. 3, sees a reference to Marcellus' loyalty to Domitian, which would explain his readiness to accept fourth place in the book; but if that were the meaning, the connection with the following sentence would be indicated more explicitly. The expression with an abstract noun shows the type of phrase which led ultimately to formulae like *maiestas uestra*: see J. Svennung, *Anredeformen* (Lund, 1958), 68 ff. But there is no reason to suppose that *pius* is a standing epithet of Marcellus.

1–2. dedicarem: for bibliography on literary dedication see White (1974), 51 ff.

2. reor equidem . . .: St. is arguing that while all his previous *opuscula* began with an invocation of the emperor's *numen*, this book has three such poems (i.e. *S.* 4. 1–3). The difficulty is that while Book 1 of the *Siluae* begins with the poem about Domitian's equestrian statue, the place of honour in Books 2 and 3 is given to private citizens; this suggests that Books 1–3, like the *Odes* of Horace, were published together (Vollmer, 12 and n. 4). The other *opuscula* are hardly epics like the *Thebaid*, but presumably lost minor works like the mime *Agaue*. Elsewhere *opusculum* is used of single poems (*S.* 2 *Pr.* 3 ff., 4 *Pr.* 21), but St.'s terminology is clearly inconsistent: see on 4. 9. 9 (*libellus*). Frère supposed that a formulaic invocation of the emperor was recited before every poem (*Mélanges P. Thomas* [Bruges, 1930], 300–11), but this would have no relevance to what follows ('sed hic liber ...').

3. opusculum meum coepisse: in view of the unusual clausula Frère proposed *me coepisse* (*Mélanges Thomas*, 308). One might also try *coepisse opusculum*. But certainty is impossible, especially as the sentence is not yet complete; we find at 3 *Pr.* 20 (admittedly at a slighter pause) 'Asclepium mittebat'.

3–4. sed ... pertinet: the general drift here may be supplied by the following kind of supplement (an abbreviated version of Vollmer's): 'sed hic liber tres habet ⟨eclogas in laudem eius in fronte praepositas; uides igitur te magis honorari non potuis⟩se quam quod quarta ad honorem tuum pertinet'. That is to say, the book begins with no fewer than three poems to Domitian, but this makes it all the more honorific to Marcellus that he is addressed in the fourth poem. *ecloga*, 'chosen piece', is the word for one poem within a collection: see N. M. Horsfall, *BICS* 28 (1981), 108 f.; hence *eclogae* is supplied here to provide a feminine noun to which *quarta* may refer. Unless *quarta* is corrupt, *primo, secundo, tertio* must be adverbs.

6. adoraui: this verb attributes to a secular act of celebration an attitude of religious fervour: cf. 3 *Pr.* 9 ff. 'nam primum limen eius Hercules Surrentinus aperit, quem in litore tuo consecratum, statim ut uideram, his uersibus adoraui', Mart. 4. 49. 9 'illa [scripta] tamen laudant omnes, mirantur, adorant', *Pan. Lat..* 8(5). 5. 1 'adoratae sint igitur mihi Sarmaticae expeditiones'.

sacratissimis ... epulis: *sacer* originally conveyed the notion of divine protection, and it is this basic concept of inviolability which becomes associated with the emperor. *sacer* first denotes 'imperial' in Ovid: 'sacra ... domo' (*F.* 6. 810), 'sacrae ... domus' (*Pont.* 4. 6. 20). Tiberius would not allow this epithet to be used of him (Suet. *Tib.* 27) 'alium dicentem sacras eius occupationes ... verba mutare et ... pro sacris laboriosas dicere coegit'; cf. Tac. *Ann.* 2. 87. In St. and Martial it commonly denotes things associated with the emperor: Martial applies *sacer* to the *munus* (games) of Titus (*Lib. Spect.* 24. 2) and to his *numen* and *potestas* (30. 7). Of Domitian it is used to denote features as various as *cena* (*S.* 4. 2. 5), *domus* (5. 1. 85), *pectus* (Mart. 7. 1. 4), *nomen* (8 *Pr.* 15). Once only it is used of Domitian himself: 'sacer ... Germanicus' (*S.* 5. 2. 177). As an epithet for the emperor, *sacratissimus* first appears in literature to describe Domitian (*S.* 2 *Pr.* 19, 3 *Pr.* 13), although *sacratissimus princeps* is attested in an inscription dated to AD 66 under Nero (*CIL* vi. 2044). It must be noted, however, that *sacratissimus* is not restricted to the emperor himself; like *sacer* it is also used to describe items associated with him, as here. Similarly *diuinus* is already attested of the imperial household under Augustus and

Tiberius: cf. E–J 98 = *OGIS* 458 = *SEG* 4. 490 (of Augustus) 'diuina merita' (lacking an equivalent for *diuina* in the Greek text), E–J 137 = *CIL* xiii. 4635 (under Tiberius) 'pro perpetua salute diuinae domus', Vitr. 1 *Pr.* 1, Val. Max. 4. 33, Goodyear on Tac. *Ann.* 2. 87.

7–8. harenarum moram: delay caused by the sandy conditions along the coastal route from Sinuessa to Puteoli: see on 4. 3. 23, 4. 3.

8–9. cuius beneficio tu quoque maturius epistulam meam accipies, quam tibi in hoc libro a Neapoli scribo: Markland objected that *meam* pre-empts the relative clause. But St. is concerned to demonstrate the miracle of communication effected by the Via Domitiana, and so *tu* and *meam* are deliberately contrasted, representing addressee and author at either end of the route; the relative clause then supplies explanatory detail. The future tense *accipies* implies that Marcellus has not received the *epistula* (Poem 4) in advance (cf. the specific location *in hoc libro*). It is obviously unusual for St. to include cross-references in his poems, since they were delivered independently to their addressees, and so the reference to the Via Domitiana at 4. 4. 1–3 reinforces the impression that 4. 4, which does not mark any event, was written to create an occasion for dedicating to Vitorius Marcellus the book which St. had put together.

12. citra hoc quoque ius: the basic meaning of *citra*, 'short of', develops into a synonym for *sine* from the Augustan period onwards: cf. Ov. *Tr.* 5. 8. 23 'peccaui citra scelus', Quint. 12. 2. 1 'quando igitur orator est uir bonus, is autem citra uirtutem intellegi non potest' with Austin's n.

artissime carum: *artus* commonly describes the ties of friendship: cf. Val. Max. 2. 9. 6 'artissimo ... amicitiae foedere', *TLL* ii. 721. 38 ff. The superlative adverb commonly modifies a past participle: cf. Sen. *Epist.* 95. 2 'historiam ... minutissime scriptam, artissime plictam', Plin. *NH* 29. 38 'cauda ... quam artissime praeligata'. Sometimes it has the force of a general intensifier: cf. Plin. *Epist.* 6. 8. 1 'hunc ego non ut multi, sed artissime diligo', *TLL* ii. 725. 19 ff.

nam: White (1974), 61, criticizes St. for the 'pretext' which he gives to include 4. 6. The thought is, however, coherent: Septimius Seuerus is a friend of Marcellus, but this is not St.'s only reason for including a poem to him ('sed ... carum'); as for Nouius Vindex, although he is not an acquaintance of Marcellus, his poem still deserves inclusion in Book 4 because he and St. have literary interests in common (cf. 4. 6. 12 ff.), and a person who has secured St.'s *amicitia* thereby qualifies for Marcellus' approval; hence St. can charge 4. 6 to Marcellus' account. *nam* is used as a sequential conjunction in transitions to another topic, particularly when a new name is introduced: cf. 1 *Pr.* 30 'nam Claudi Etrusci testimonium est', Pease on Cic. *ND* 1. 27 with bibliography.

14. imputare: the image from bookkeeping implies that the dedicatee (or recipient) of the poem incurs a reciprocal debt towards St. according to the conventions of *amicitia*: cf. 2 *Pr.* 23 ff. 'cludit uolumen Genethliacon Lucani quod Polla Argentaria ... imputari sibi uoluit'. The elder Pliny uses the same image in requesting Vespasian to take the responsibility for Pliny's presumption in dedicating the *Natural History* to the emperor (*NH Pr.* 4) 'itaque cum ceteris in uenerationem tui pateant omnia illa, nobis ad colendum te familiarius audacia sola superest: hanc igitur tibi imputabis et in nostra culpa tibi ignosces'. See Mayor on Juv. 5. 14, Housman on Luc. 7. 322–5.

14–15. Maximum Vibium: the inversion of *nomen* and *cognomen* is well attested from the Republic onwards. Both the conventional order and the inversion (cf. 2 *Pr.* 23 ff. cit. in previous n.) are common in first-century prose: see Shackleton Bailey on Cic. *Att.* 2. 24. 3. This technique can emphasize the *cognomen* (see N–H on Hor. *O.* 2. 2. 3 'Crispe Sallusti'); while Vibius' *cognomen* may seem too common to merit prominence, St. does play on it in composing his poem: see on 4. 7. 9, 32.

16–17. epistula quam ad illum de editione Thebaidos meae publicaui: it was common to send a covering letter (in prose) requesting a friend to cast a critical eye over an enclosed manuscript: see introduction. The introductory epistle to *S.* 5 may be comparable to the letter to Vibius: it describes only the first poem, but its availability to the posthumous editor suggests public circulation. The *Institutio Oratoria* is preceded by Quintilian's letter to Trypho, clearly because Quintilian's remarks to his editor must be kept separate from the dedication to Vitorius Marcellus in the *praefatio*. Similarly St. may have included personal details in a letter to Vibius Maximus for circulation with the *Thebaid*.

22–3. huic uolumini inserui: *uolumen* = the papyrus-roll comprising Book 4. *insero* is the *uox propria* for including material in a literary work: cf. 2 *Pr.* 22 'consolationem... huic libro libenter inserui', Plin. *Epist.* 7. 33. 1, 9. 11. 1, *TLL* vii. 1. 1873. 10 ff.

24 ff. The style in the last section of the *Praefatio* alters abruptly to shorter sentences phrased as questions and answers, reflecting the change from description to informal and jocular polemic: cf. Hor. *Sat.* 2. 1, *S.* 1 *Pr.* 5–15. The earliest examples in Latin of this use of a preface to answer criticism of earlier work are the prologues of Terence and the Plautine revivals. For jocular *apologiae* in brisk facetious style see especially Martial's prefaces. St. chooses not to attack his critics directly (as the elder Pliny does, *NH Pr.* 28 ff.) but confines himself to *apologia* culminating in his request for Marcellus to sponsor the work. The main issues which St. concentrates on in the *praefatio* to Book 1 are: the propriety of an epic poet publishing occasional verse; the loss of topicality; and the extempore nature of their composition. It is only the first point (i.e. the most general) to which St. reverts in the *praefatio* to Book 4.

There has been much speculation as to who St.'s critics were. He presents them as traditionalists. Clearly the feature most antipathetic to our taste, flattery of Domitian, is that least likely to be criticized openly by contemporaries, *pace* F. Delarue, *RPh* 48 (1974), 285 f. Delarue suggests also that the Epicurean tone of the *Siluae* aroused criticism, but the criticism anticipated in 1 *Pr.* is literary not philosophical, i.e. the publication of lightweight works which were composed in haste. Quintilian has been suggested as a critic of St., on the basis of his objections to orators who publish extempore compositions (10. 3. 17, shown above in the General Introduction to belong to a rhetorical context, unrelated to criticism of the *Siluae*): see Vollmer, *Rh. Mus.* 26 (1891), 343–5. H. T.

Karsten, *Mnem.*² 27 (1899), 365 ff., noting similarities in vocabulary between Quint. 10. 3. 17 and the *praefationes* to *S.* 1–3, deduces that Quintilian was criticizing St. in his own words; but G. Giri, *RFIC* 35 (1907), 253, demonstrates that *effundo* (*S.* 1 *Pr.* 15) is the only truly parallel term. If St.'s antagonistic tone towards his critics was directed at Quintilian, he would not have dedicated this book to the man whom Quintilian also chose as dedicatee: see F. Delarue, *Lat.* 33 (1974), 547 (although his idea that St. wanted Marcellus to enlist Quintilian's support is putting it too strongly). Delarue elsewhere identifies St.'s critics with the *Catones* whose censure Martial anticipates (Mart. 1 *Pr.* 8, 11. 2. 1 ff.): see *RPh* 48 (1974), 285 ff. But the licentiousness which the strait-laced would disapprove of in Martial is entirely absent from St.; furthermore, St.'s mockery of the speeches of Brutus (see on 4. 9. 20), which Delarue interprets as a modern and anti-classicist attitude, must reflect general consensus of opinion if St. intends it to show up Plotius Grypus' lack of taste. There is perhaps some evidence that Pliny disapproved of features which are found in the *Siluae* (e.g. the *praefationes*: see introduction above), but Pliny's silence about St. is probably fortuitous: he could hardly mention everyone.

Grounds for enmity between St. and Martial are catalogued by H. Heuvel, *Mnem.*³ 4 (1936–7), 229–330. He goes too far in interpreting the flattery of Domitian in *S.* 4. 1–3 as an attempt to outdo Martial's flattery in Book 8 of the *Epigrams* (published in 93): the same impulse from the emperor is likely to account for the attitudes of both authors. Delarue, *Lat.* 33 (1974), 539 ff., argues that it is perfectly natural that St., primarily an epic poet, should not be mentioned in Martial's epigrams, and thus this is no proof of enmity. But although the *Siluae* are largely different from the *Epigrams* in style and genre, they are prompted by similar circumstances of patronage, and Martial could have considered that St., in publishing them, was poaching Martial's own public. Juvenal too was in poetic circles in Rome by 92: cf. Mart. 7. 24, 91, R. Syme, *CPh* 74 (1979), 11 (= *Rom. Pap.* iii. 1130). Although he probably published nothing until two decades after St.'s (presumed) death, he parodies the type of political panegyric exemplified in the *DBG* (*Sat.* 4. 94), observes that the *Thebaid* was a financial failure despite its popular success (*Sat.* 7. 82–7), and attacks the imperial monopoly of literary patronage (*Sat.* 7: cf. l. 27 below); these attitudes suggest not that the young Juvenal opposed the publication of the *Siluae* but that during their period of neglect under Hadrian he noted the irony of their former popularity.

24. in prioribus: Book 4 contains more poems than each of the preceding books; but the fact that St. does not allude to criticism of any of the first three books until now supports the argument that the first three were published together.

25. ut audio: a parenthesis comprising *ut* and a verb of sense-perception is a colloquial phrase: cf. Ter. *Phorm.* 483 'nam per eius unam, ut audio, aut uiuam aut moriar sententiam', Cic. *Att.* 14. 9. 2 'hic turba magna est eritque, ut audio, maior'.

25–6. hoc stili genus edidissem: the metaphorical use of *stilus* to mean 'composition' is first attested at Ter. *Andria* 12 '[fabulae] dissimili oratione sunt factae et stilo'.

26–7. superuacuum est dissuadere rem factam: a proverbial sentiment: cf. Plaut. *Aul.* 741 'factum est illud: fiere infectum non potest', *Truc.* 730 'stultus es qui facta infecta facere uerbis postules', Otto, *Sprichwörter*, no. 627. *rem factam* sounds like a colloquialism: cf. Mart. 1. 27. 4 'tu factam tibi rem statim putasti', 2. 26. 3 'iam te rem factam, Bithynice, credis habere?', 6. 61(60). 1 'rem factam Pompullus habet, Faustine'.

27. multa ex illis iam domino Caesari dederam: *dominus* became fashionable as a mode of address from the Augustan age onwards. Its use to refer to a third person is first found in Sen. *Epist.* 104. 1 'domini mei Gallionis', and from Gaius onwards ([Aur. Vict.] *Epit.* 3. 8) individual emperors admitted it as a mode of address: see J. Svennung, *Anredeformen* (Lund, 1958), 338 ff. There could be direct communication between emperor and author about the author's current project: cf. Augustus' letters of request to Virgil (Suet. *Vit. Verg.* 31) 'ut sibi de *Aeneide*... uel prima carminis ὑπογραφή uel quodlibet κῶλον mitteretur'. Only three poems in *S.* 1–3 concern Domitian (1. 1, 1. 6, 2. 5). Hence the preview selection ('multa ex illis') must have included some of the poems to *priuati*. White (1974), 46 ff., documents a similar procedure in Martial, corresponding to the intermediate stage between composition and publication, in which a *libellus* containing a selection of poems was sent to a patron (including, sometimes, the emperor) for inspection: cf. 2. 91 (to Domitian) 'si festinatis totiens tibi lecta libellis / detinuere oculos carmina nostra tuos', 5. 6 (to accompany a *charta* sent to Domitian), 5. 15 (where the assumption that his *liber* contains only complimentary verse is true of only half the poems in the book, i.e. a selection which could have comprised a *libellus*), 8 *Epist.* 14–15 'pars libri et maior et melior ad maiestatem sacri nominis tui alligata', 12. 4 (describing a *libellus* sent to Nerva). St. claims that this is a more rigorous test of the poetry's worth than publication itself ('quanto hoc plus est quam edere!'). Martial seems habitually to have submitted samples of his poetry to whoever was in power: cf. Mart. 1. 101. 1 ff. 'illa manus quondam studiorum fida meorum / et felix domino notaque Caesaribus / destituit primos uiridis Demetrius annos' (where White [1974], 47, observes that the plural *Caesaribus* implies more than one emperor), and the passages cited above relating to Domitian and Nerva. Hence St. is probably arguing simply that, if his poems gain the approval of the emperor, they merit publication.

28. exerceri autem ioco: paradoxical, and appropriate to the following illustrations from training routines (29–30). *exercere* (M) in a medio-passive sense is limited to the present participle and gerund: see *TLL* v. 1370. 50 ff. The single apparent exception, Var. *Men.* 237 Bücheler, is easily changed to 'exercebam ⟨me⟩ ambulando': see Lindsay's apparatus criticus to Nonius. No convincing parallels for *exercere ioco* can be found in the intransitive uses in Late Latin which are cited by L. Feltenius, *Intransitivizations in Latin* (Uppsala, 1977), 89 f.

29. inquit: for the generalizing singular of unspecified interlocutors (= *aiunt*) see *TLL* vii. 1. 1779. 74 ff.

29–30. sed et sphaeromachia spectantes et palaris lusio admittit: training sessions attract an audience, so why should not occasional poetry have a public? Cf. St.'s defence for publishing the *Siluae* after the *Thebaid* (1 *Pr.* 7 ff.) 'sed et Culicem legimus et Batrachomachiam etiam agnoscimus; nec quisquam est illustrium poetarum qui non aliquid operibus suis stilo remissiore praeluserit', Plin. *Epist.* 7. 9. 10 (recommending that orators write poetry) 'lusus uocantur: sed hi lusus non minorem interdum gloriam quam seria consequuntur'. 'sphaeromachiam spectamus' (M) leaves *admittit* without an explicit object. For the absolute use of *admittere* where the object can be supplied from the context cf. Prop. 3. 21. 7 '[puella] uix ... aut semel admittit, cum saepe negauit', *TLL* i. 755. 26 ff. But since (i) the stress in St.'s example is on the existence of an audience, and (ii) *spectamus ... admittit* creates a rather clumsy change of subject, *sphaeromachia spectantes* (Phillimore) seems right, and the distribution of object and verb between the two cola is typical of St.'s style: cf. 4. 2. 16.

The meaning of *sphaeromachia* is difficult to determine. I shall start from *palaris lusio*, which is clearer. Gladiators, like soldiers, practised with *arma lusoria*, mock weapons of basketry and wood, against a *palus* representing the human opponent: cf. Veg. *Mil.* 1. 11 'palorum enim usus non solum militibus sed etiam gladiatoribus plurimum prodest ... contra illum palum tamquam contra aduersarium tiro cum crate illa et claua uelut cum gladio se exercebat et scuto', 2. 23, Sen. *Epist.* 18. 8, Mart. 7. 32. 8, Juv. 6. 247. Hence *sphaeromachia* should likewise be a form of combat involving harmless imitations of weapons. A σφαῖρα can be the protective button or knob which was fixed to the point of a spear or javelin during practice-sessions (i.e. a foil): cf. Xen. *Eq.* 8. 10 ἐσφαιρωμένα ἀκόντια, Polyb. 10. 20. 3 (ἐκέλευσε) τοὺς μὲν μαχαιρομαχεῖν ξυλίναις ἐσκυτωμέναις μετ' ἐπισφαιρῶν μαχαίραις, τοὺς δὲ τοῖς ἐσφαιρωμένοις γρόσφοις ἀκοντίζειν, Clem. Al. *Strom.* 2. 60. 5 (= *GCS* ii. 145) ὁ ταῖς ἐσφαιρωμέναις λόγχαις γυμναζόμενος καὶ ἀποκτείνας τινὰ τοῦ δόρατος ἀποβαλόντος τὴν σφαῖραν. For the equation ἐπίσφαιραι (as above) = σφαῖραι see M. Poliakoff, *Studies in the Terminology of the Greek Combat Sports* (Hain, 1982), 96. Hence a fencing session with these harmless weapons, i.e. blunted by the (ἐπί)σφαιραι, would match the *palaris lusio*, in which substitute weapons were wielded against a stake. In view of these parallels for foils there is nothing to be said for the view that soft gloves are meant (cf. Plato, *Laws* 830 B, Plut. *Mor.* 825 E, and see H. A. Harris, *Greek Athletes and Athletics* [London, 1964], 98, Poliakoff, 92), nor for Frère's idea that St. and Seneca (*Epist.* 80. 1) are referring to a sparring-match in the gymnasium at Naples (*Mélanges ... Ernout* [Paris, 1940], 141–58).

31. profitetur: *nouissime* (30) introduces the final point which St. musters in answer to his critics: cf. *primum, deinde*. This is an observation, not a challenge: people who don't want to read the *Siluae* (because they consider it improper for St. to publish them) criticize them as soon as they have read them, and so their criticism, being inevitable, is of no account. *inuitus*, implying compulsion, is odd. Presumably, however, it implies anyone who was prejudiced against the *Siluae* in advance but read them because they were newly published. *inuidus* (Markland) accords with the traditional envy displayed by practitioners of the same skill, but *inuitus* is perhaps less limiting, implying any reluctant reader among the public at large.

32. traducor: a metaphor derived from the custom of parading prisoners in triumphal processions, i.e. 'on show', hence 'exposed to ridicule': cf. Liv. 2. 38. 3 'an non sensistis triumphatum hodie de uobis esse? ... uestras coniuges, uestros liberos traductos per ora hominum?', Mart. 1. 53. 1 ff. 'una est in nostris tua, Fidentine, libellis / pagina ... quae tua traducit manifesto carmina furto', and see Courtney on Juv. 8. 17.

32–4. hunc tamen librum tu, Marcelle, defendes, si uidetur, hactenus; sin minus, reprehendemur: *hunc* is emphatic, contrasting the fourth book of the *Siluae* with previous books: cf. above 'quare ergo plura in quarto Siluarum quam in prioribus?' *tu* is also emphatic: Marcellus at any rate will defend the book because of his special position in it. The future tense is a polite formula for requests: cf. Cat. 13. 1 'cenabis bene, mi Fabulle, apud me', L–H–S 311. St.'s book relies on Marcellus as counsel for the defence, just like his *amici* (4. 4. 41 ff.); a dedicatee is obliged to promote the work dedicated to him: cf. 2 *Pr.* 28 ff. 'haec qualiacumque sunt, Melior carissime, si tibi non displicuerint, a te publicum accipiant; sin minus, ad me reuertantur'. *si uidetur* is a polite formula meaning 'if you agree' (i.e. to defend the book): see *OLD* s.v. *uideo* 24e. *hactenus* is usually interpreted as 'enough said', and taken as the elliptical apodosis of the condition. But Professor Goodyear has suggested to me that if *si uidetur, hactenus* is attached to *defendes*, deleting *et* (M) (which is otiose on any interpretation), *hactenus* must modify *defendes*, i.e. Marcellus will defend the book as far as St.'s arguments have gone: for this sense of *hactenus*, summarizing what has preceded, see *TLL* vi. 3. 2750. 51 ff. This solution, involving only one minimal change, seems preferable to Vollmer's proposal 'sed, si uidetur, hactenus. hunc tamen librum tu, Marcelle, defendes', whereby *si uidetur hactenus* introduces the appeal to Marcellus in a rather summary fashion. *minus* is an urbanely mild negative, used particularly in conditions (*OLD* s.v. *minus* 4b): cf. Phaedr. 4 *Pr.* 29 ff. 'librum exarabo tertium Aesopi stilo, / honori et meritis dedicans illum tuis. / quem si leges laetabor; sin autem minus, / habebunt certe quo se oblectent posteri', and *sin minus* (= 'si displicuerint') in St.'s parallel preface cited above.

I

INTRODUCTION

This poem celebrates the inauguration of Domitian as consul for the seventeenth time on 1 January 95; he was replaced by L. Neratius Marcellus as suffect on the Ides (*Fast. Ost.*). Few of his consulships were longer than this, and none extended beyond 1 May (Suet. *Dom.* 13. 3).[1] Domitian's

---

[1] Pliny criticized twelve-day consulships as an insult to the office (*Pan.* 65) 'quam diuersum consuetudine illorum qui pauculis diebus gestum consulatum, immo non gestum, abiciebant per edictum!'

consular colleague in 95 was his cousin, Flauius Clemens, whose sons he had adopted as his heirs; as Domitian had not been consul since 92, it looks as if he was using the occasion to introduce the boys (now aged fifteen and fourteen) to public life. In the same way Augustus had used his last two consulships in 5 and 2 BC to introduce his adopted heirs, Gaius and Lucius Caesar.[2] The simultaneous appointment of Flauius Clemens seems to confirm Domitian's aim.[3]

Panegyric of rulers must have been a common type of oratory in the Hellenistic world; the pattern had been set in the late fourth century by Isocrates' encomium *Euagoras* on the recently deceased ruler of Cypriot Salamis. The topics were analysed in due course by the rhetorical theorists: these analyses vary in details, but a core of topoi emerges.[4] At the same time the poets praised rulers in a briefer and less schematic manner. Usually poetic eulogies were general rather than devoted to specific occasions: cf. the eulogies of the Ptolemies by Callimachus (*H.* 1) and Theocritus (especially *Id.* 17). But there are exceptions: Pindar, *Nem.* 11 in honour of Aristagoras of Tenedos on his election as πρύτανις and *Pyth.* 1 to celebrate Hieron's assumption of the title Αἰτναῖος,[5] the paean to Demetrius Poliorcetes on his entry into Athens (perhaps in 290 BC), attributed to Hermocles of Cyzicus (Athen. 7. 253 = *Coll. Alex.* 173 f. Powell).

Roman panegyrics were often joined to recurring ceremonies in the Roman calendar. Formal words of congratulation were no doubt spoken at the installation of a consul;[6] private congratulations (usually conveying a petition) are certainly recorded: cf. Cic. *Fam.* 15. 7–13. It can be assumed that under the empire ceremonies on 1 January became much more honorific. Pliny's *Panegyric*, delivered on 1 September 100, marked a mere suffect consulship, as did Fronto's speech to Antoninus Pius delivered in the senate on 13 August 143; such speeches were avowedly encomiastic: hence Fronto conceives of his speech as both *actio gratiarum* (156. 18 van den Hout) and *laudatio* (110. 1, 24. 23 f.).[7] Later panegyrics were frequently delivered upon ceremonial occasions, including imperial consulships or other anniversaries: cf. Symm. *Or.* 2 (= 323 ff. Seeck) (Valentinian I's third consulship in 370), *Pan. Lat.* 5(8) (the fifth anniversary of Constantine's accession), 4(10) (Constantine's fifteenth anniversary). A national victory might be celebrated by the emperor's assumption of the consulship, and the double occasion

---

[2] Hardie, 192, citing Suet. *Aug.* 26. 2.
[3] B. W. Jones, *Domitian and the Senatorial Order* (= Memoirs of the American Philosophical Society 132) (Philadelphia, 1979), 40.
[4] See Lester B. Struthers, *HSCPh* 30 (1919), 50 ff., D. A. Russell and N. G. Wilson (eds.), *Menander Rhetor* (Oxford, 1981), pp. xxvi ff.
[5] Cited by I. M. Le M. Du Quesnay in *Papers of the Liverpool Latin Seminar 1976*, ed. F. Cairns (Liverpool, 1977), 44, analysing Virg. *Ecl.* 4 within the tradition of poetic celebrations of assumption of office.
[6] Cic. *Phil.* 5, delivered on 1 Jan. 43 BC, was part of the four-day senatorial debate following the inaugural speeches of the consuls Hirtius and Pansa.
[7] For the date see Fronto, *Epist.* 24. 10 f. van den Hout. The main cast of Fronto's speech is pieced together by Edward Champlin, *Fronto and Antonine Rome* (Cambridge, Mass. and London, 1980), 83–6.

commemorated in panegyric: cf. Claud. *VI Cons. Hon.* (Honorius' sixth consulship, assumed after the defeat of the Goths in 403).[8] Naturally, when an emperor was also consul, the first day of the year provided a special occasion for celebration; here the consul does not pay the honours but receives them.

So too Roman poets praised rulers.[9] Horace drew on the tradition of panegyric to praise Augustus,[10] sometimes on the particular occasion of an *aduentus*: cf. *O.* 3. 14, on Augustus' return from Spain in 25 BC, and 4. 5, looking forward to his return from Gaul in 13 BC. Such was the importance of entry to the consulship that Ovid used this occasion to file petitions: cf. *Pont.* 4. 4 (for Sextus Pompeius, consul AD 14), 4. 9 (for Pomponius Graecinus, suffect consul AD 16, and his brother L. Pomponius Flaccus, consul designate AD 17). St.'s poem is the forerunner of the poems of Claudian and Sidonius eulogizing the entry of the emperor to consular office and transferring into verse the conventional prose eulogy.

The date of consular inauguration (1 January) and the annual duration of the consulship determine a range of topoi:[11] the sun ushering in the new year (*S.* 4. 1. 3, Claud. *Prob. et Olyb.* 1-3, *III Cons. Hon.* 9), the mention of Janus (Ov. *Pont.* 4. 4. 23, 9. 60: cf. *S.* 4. 1. 13 ff., and see below), the advent of peace, usually associated with the closing of Janus' temple (*S.* 4. 1. 13 ff., Claud. *IV Cons. Hon.* 6 ff.), predictions of a happy year ahead (Ov. *Pont.* 4. 4. 18, 9. 55 ff., *S.* 4. 1. 1 ff., Claud. *Prob. et Olyb.* 266 f., *VI Cons. Hon.* 12 ff.), good omens (*S.* 4. 1. 23 f., Claud. *Prob. et Olyb.* 206 ff., *VI Cons. Hon.* 12 ff.). inaugural ceremonies (Ov. *Pont.* 4. 4. 24 ff., 9. 23 ff., *S.* 4. 1. 1 ff., Sid. *Carm.* 2. 544 ff., Claud. *IV Cons. Hon.* 1-17), national rejoicing (Ov. *Pont.* 4. 9. 17 ff., *S.* 4. 1. 5 ff., Claud. *Prob. et Olyb.* 226 ff., *Theod.* 270 ff., *Stil.* 2. 376 ff., 3. 202 ff., *VI Cons. Hon.* 611 ff.). Some of these topoi, especially omens, the advent of peace, and national rejoicing, belong to general prescriptions for a λόγος βασιλικός (cf. *Rhet. Gr.* iii. 375. 5 ff., 377. 24 ff. Sp.), but St.'s treatment is much less schematic than a real prose speech, let alone a theoretical prescription.[12] Certain themes would be inappropriate for extended treatment in prose: prosopopoeia is of course a feature of public oratory in Cicero, as when the *patria* is made to speak (*Cat.* 1. 18, 27); it is treated at length by Quintilian (9. 2. 29 ff.), but his admission of divine impersonation seems grudging (9. 2. 31) 'quin deducere deos in hoc genere dicendi ... concessum

---

[8] For occasions for panegyric in late antiquity see Sabine MacCormack in T. A. Dorey (ed.), *Empire and Aftermath: Silver Latin II* (Greek and Latin Studies. Classical Literature and its Influence, London, 1975), 154 ff.

[9] Even youthful entry into minor office might occasion congratulations: cf. *S.* 5. 2, on Crispinus' appointment as military tribune.

[10] See Doblhofer.

[11] My list is a modification of Du Quesnay's, art. cit. (n. 5), 45 ff.

[12] Even in prose a certain flexibility was acknowledged: Pliny, advising Vettenius Seuerus, consul designate, on his *actio gratiarum*, warns him that the individual circumstances must determine the content of the encomium (*Epist.* 6. 27). In general, the Latin prose panegyrics can be shown to share topics in common with Menander's precepts for the βασιλικὸς λόγος while owing little allegiance to his arrangement of material: see Russell and Wilson, op. cit. (n. 4), 271.

est'. St.'s introduction of Janus, however, owes more to Ovid: cf. Janus' speech at Ov. *F.* 1. 101–44.[13] The use of Janus as spokesman, appropriate for a ceremony on the day of his festival, accords with St.'s technique of attributing encomiastic remarks to a superior authority associated with either the site or the occasion: cf. 1. 1. 74–83 (Curtius to Domitian, the equestrian statue having been erected beside the Lacus Curtius), 2. 7. 41–104 (the muse Calliope to Lucan), 3. 1. 91–116, 160–83 (Hercules to Pollius, who has built him a shrine), 4. 32–45 (Venus to Earinus), 95–7 (Cupid to Earinus), 4. 3. 72–94 (River Volturnus, chief obstacle along the route of the Via Domitiana, to Domitian), 124–36 (Sibyl of Cumae to Domitian, at the southern end of the Via Domitiana). This technique gives the poet an opportunity to indulge his exuberant imagination, while its clearly fictitious character makes the flattery less blatant than in prose eulogy: see the discussion of this poem by Vessey, *ANRW* 2799–801.

1. **Laeta ... purpura:** by metonymy *purpura* represents the purple-edged consular toga: cf. Ov. *Pont.* 4. 4. 25 'purpura Pompeium summi uelabit honoris', and see André, *Couleur*, 91; the use of personification in conjunction with this type of metonymy is a natural device in the description of a consular inauguration: cf. *Laus Pisonis* 70 (in the context of Piso's *gratiarum actio* on his assumption of the consulship) 'cum tua bis senos numeraret purpura fasces', Mart. 8. 8. 3–4 (to Janus) 'te primum pia tura rogent, te uota salutent, / purpura te felix, te colat omnis honos'. Like Martial's 'purpura ... felix', so *laeta* contributes to the personification of the emblem of office. As first word in the poem, *laeta* sets the tone of exuberant celebration: cf. *exsultent, gaudete* (5), *iactantior* (6), *gaudet* (10), *gaudent* (25), *laeto ... polo* (45). With the position of emphasis compare *insignem* (2): it is a distinguished year which the emperor inaugurates.

   bis octonis ... fastis: up to AD 92 Domitian had held sixteen consulships (*Fast. Ost.* 92). Numerals are generally avoided in poetry, especially at this period: see Axelson, 96 f. In cases where a cardinal needs to be expressed but is metrically intractable, it is replaced by a multiplicative periphrasis. B. Löfstedt, *Eranos* 56 (1958), 92, compares in tabular form the frequency of multiplicative numerals formed from a numerical adverb with a cardinal numeral with those formed from a numerical adverb with a distributive; after Ovid the combination with a distributive becomes far more common. Since the *fasti* contained a consular record of each year, by metonymy *fasti* came to denote the consulship; hence Valerius Maximus' phrase (4. 4. 1) 'fastorum illud columen' refers to the recording of Valerius Publicola's three consulships: cf. *S.* 1. 4. 82 (to Rutilius Gallicus, consul designate) 'reuocant fasti maiorque curulis', Aus. *Grat. Act. Gratian.* 6 (= 220. 140 Prete) (of Domitian's seventeen consulships) 'pagina fastorum suorum'. For similarity of thought and diction cf. Luc. 5. 384 (Pompey) 'laetos fecit se consule fastos'. St.'s line appears to be

---

[13] But in *F.* 1 the ensuing dialogue between Ovid and Janus undercuts the dignity of this motif, whereas St. *in propria persona* never enters into dialogue with his spokesmen.

echoed at Aus. *Epig.* 62 (a lament for a boy, Glaucias, who died just before he turned sixteen) 'laeta bis octono tibi iam sub consule pubes / cingebat teneras, Glaucia adulte, genas'.

2. aperit ... annum: the *consules ordinarii* took up office on 1 January, the festival of Janus. The month of January, and associated persons or events, was commonly said to open the coming year: cf. Ov. *Pont.* 4. 4. 23 'ergo ubi, Iane biceps, longum reseraueris annum'; conversely, December closed off the year that was past: cf. the incomplete fragment at *Carm. de mens.* 3. 23 f. 'argumenta tibi mensis concedo Decemb⟨ris⟩ (*Housman*: December), / qui squamis (*Housman*: quae sis quam uis) annum claudere piscis ⟨amas⟩ (*Housman*: possis)', and see Housman, *Cl. Pap.* iii. 1192–3. The motif of the consul opening the year recurs at Plin. *Pan.* 58. 3 'contigit ergo priuatis aperire annum fastosque reserare', Claud. *VI cons. Hon.* 640 'iamque nouum fastis aperit felicibus annum', *Carm. ad Theodos.* 2. 7 (= *PLM* v. 84 Baehrens) 'ter quinis aperit cum fascibus annum'. The phrase *annum aperire* appears to have been used as a technical term referring to the cycle of the planets: cf. Virg. *G.* 1. 217 'candidus auratis aperit cum cornibus annum / Taurus'. The astronomical overtones here serve to introduce the astronomical imagery of ll. 3–4.

Germanicus: the *cognomen* 'Germanicus' was assumed by Domitian in AD 83: cf. Suet. *Dom.* 13. 3; for the date see R. A. Holder, *LCM* 2 (1977), 151: Holder describes an *aureus* (*Hunter Coin Collection* 1, Dom. 13, pl. 49) on which Domitian is entitled Germanicus after he had assumed the *tribunicia potestas* for the third time (14 September 83) and before the end of the year (*cos. IX des. X*).

3. Astronomical imagery was a feature of encomium in the Hellenistic tradition of epigram: see Alan Cameron, *CQ* NS 20 (1970), 125; cf. (e.g.) Hermocles, *Hymn Dem.* 11 f. (= *Coll. Alex.* 174. 11 f. Powell), where Demetrius' entourage is likened to the stars, and Demetrius himself to the sun (4. 8. 31 n.). Comparison with the sun is a topos which Menander recommends for praising a ruler (*Rhet. Gr.* iii. 378. 10 Sp.). Horace satirizes it as the bald, hackneyed stuff of *laudatio* (*Sat.* 1. 7. 23–6) 'laudat Brutum laudatque cohortem: / solem Asiae Brutum appellat, stellasque salubris / appellat comites, excepto Rege; canem illum / inuisum agricolis sidus uenisse'. But this topos appears in the *Odes*: see Doblhofer, 90. At *O.* 4. 2. 46–7 Horace, standing among the commons, uses their language and their metre: 'o sol pulcher, o laudande' is the first half of a *uersus quadratus*, fitted into the sapphic. At *O.* 4. 5. 5–8 Horace visualizes Augustus' return from the provinces as a light which will cause natural sources to reciprocate by shining more brightly; St.'s context is similar: Domitian once again takes up the leading magistracy. But while Horace claims that Augustus stimulates brilliance in nature, St. gives a more autocratic slant to the topos: Domitian outshines the stars.

sole nouo: dawn on 1 January starts a new year as well as a new day: cf. Ovid's epigram at *F.* 1. 163 f. (where by poetic licence *bruma*, strictly the winter solstice, represents the pivot between the old year and the new) 'bruma noui prima est ueterisque nouissima solis, / principium capiunt Phoebus et annus idem'. Domitian's assumption of office is likened to daylight breaking over the earth; Seneca uses the analogy of the sun to remind Nero that he is always in full view of his nation (*Clem.* 1. 8. 4) 'omnium in istam [lucem] conuersi oculi sunt; prodire te putes? oriris. loqui non potes, nisi ut uocem tuam, quae ubique sunt, gentes excipiant; irasci non potes, nisi ut quidquid circa fuerit quatiatur'. Nero's own reason for identifying himself with the sun was different (Suet. *Nero* 53) 'quia ... Solem aurigando aequiperare existimaretur'. For the importance of the sun in Neronian propaganda see P. Grimal, *REL* 49 (1971), 205–17. The Flavians continue the association with the sun; but for St.'s encomiastic purposes any moralizing is out of place.

4. clarius ... Eoo: the planet Venus, as the morning star, was known as Eous, Phosphorus, or Lucifer: see *RE* viiiA 1. 888 (Gundel). In antiquity it was recognized as the largest and brightest of the heavenly bodies, apart from sun and moon: cf. Plin. *NH* 2. 36 f. 'infra solem ambit ingens sidus appellatum Veneris ... iam magnitudine extra cuncta alia sidera est, claritatis quidem tantae ut huius stellae radiis umbrae reddantur'. St. says that Domitian outshines the morning star when it first appears (*primo*), i.e. before the dawn causes it to fade.

5. exsultent leges Latiae: oxymoron: *exsultare* (from the root of *salire*) denotes vigorous rejoicing, whereas legal contexts are usually solemn. *Latiae* goes more naturally with *leges* than with *curules*; *leges Latiae* forms an alliterative unit before the interjection *gaudete*. To take *Latiae* ἀπὸ κοινοῦ (Vollmer) is untidy: the two halves of the exhortation receive balanced emphasis if each begins with a verb (*exsultent ... gaudete*).

curules: used as a substantive (= *sella curulis*) to denote consular office: cf. Mart. 11. 98. 18, *S.* 3. 3. 115, 5. 2. 167, Plin. *Pan.* 59. 2, 61. 7.

6–7. septemgemino ... iugo: it would be normal for echoes of applause to hit the sky: cf. Virg. *A.* 5. 150 'uocem ... uolutant litora, pulsati colles clamore resultant'. There is a hint of this notion here, while St. is primarily adapting a proverbial expression for rejoicing (Otto, *Sprichwörter*, no. 289): cf. Mart. 8. 36. 11, Hor. *O.* 1. 1. 35–6 'quodsi me lyricis uatibus inseres, / sublimi feriam sidera uertice' with N–H. Rome personified indulges in a public display of pride (*iactantior*). St. is fond of amplifying a reference to the city by alluding to Rome's seven hills: cf. 1. 2. 191 'septemgeminae ... moenia Romae', 2. 7. 45 'septem iuga', 4. 5. 33 'in omni uertice Romuli'. Here the allusion affords him an unexpected twist: *iugo* replaces an anatomical feature which would be normal with *pulsare*: cf. Hor. *O.* 1. 37. 1–2 (a parallel occasion of celebration) 'nunc pede libero / pulsanda tellus'.

7–8. Euandrius ... collis: from the seven hills, St. focuses on the Palatine, where, according to legend, Evander established the first Roman settlement: Liv. 1. 7. 3, Virg. *A.* 8. 51–4. The Palatine was the site of the Domus Augustana which was burnt down in Nero's reign and restored by Vespasian, Titus, and Domitian as the Domus Flavia: Suet. *Dom.* 15, Platner–Ashby, 158. The periphrasis thus imbues Domitian's palace with associations of venerable antiquity.

9. et rediit bis saeptus honos: the paradosis would have to mean that Domitian took a rest from the consulship while there were other men to hold it, and the lictors were delighted that this period of rest had been finally terminated, i.e. *honos*, by metonymy, means 'magistrate': cf. *S.* 1. 2. 233 'omnis honos, cuncti ueniunt ad limina fasces', *TLL* vi. 3. 2931. 3 ff, and see on 26–7 below. Stange proposed replacing the ordinal *sextus* with the distributive *senus* (functioning as a multiplicative). But, in any case, twelve is the wrong number, because Domitian had twenty-four lictors (Dio 67. 4. 3). *saeptus* (Saenger), 'doublyguarded', gives the right sense, but this by itself will not solve the problem because the co-ordination, making *honos* and *requiem* parallel to *curia* and *pudorem*, is unbalanced beside *subiere* . . . *fasces*. This awkwardness is removed by *rediens* (E. Courtney, *BICS* 15 [1968], 56) or, better still, *rediit* (Markland), which forms a tricolon with *subiere* and *gaudet*. Between *fasces* and *curia*, however, a personification is required in *honos*: thus, by the *ab urbe condita* construction, *rediit bis saeptus honos* means not 'the doubly-guarded magistrate returns' but 'the circumstance of the magistrate's being doublyguarded returns'. Likewise *bis sanctus* (participle from *sancire*), suggested to me by Professor Nisbet, would mean that the consulship is doubly ratified by the double complement of lictors. *saeptus* seems preferable on palaeographic grounds, unless thought tactless as reflecting Domitian's concern with security.

10. curia . . . gaudet: the attribution of emotions to buildings is a type of pathetic fallacy first found in Latin at Plaut. *Asin.* 207 'tum me aedes quoque arridebant'. This personification is useful as a flattering device in encomiastic contexts, e.g. Plin. *Pan.* 50. 4 (the buildings themselves appreciate Trajan's policy of economic rehabilitation) 'muta quidem illa [tecta] et anima carentia sentire tamen et laetari uidentur', *Pan. Lat.* 11(3). 11. 3. Cicero's description of his return from exile affords a parallel for the curia's pleasure at seeing Domitian's consular procession: Cic. *Pis.* 52 '[Roma] me ita accepit ut . . . moenia ipsa uiderentur et tecta urbis ac templa laetari'. See Fraenkel, *Kl. Beit.* ii. 594 on the necrologue of the temple of Iuppiter Optimus Maximus at Tac. *Hist.* 3. 72, in which Tacitus reviews the role which the temple played in Rome's glorious past.

pudorem: *pudor* is a standard excuse in *recusationes*: for literary contexts cf. Hor. *O.* 1. 6. 9, *Epod.* 11. 18, *Epist.* 1. 9. 12, 2. 1. 259. The refusal of political office is a gesture which was variously practised by all the Roman emperors to sustain the illusion of ruling in accordance with democratic and republican principles: see J. Béranger, *Recherches sur l'aspect idéologique du principat* (Basle, 1953), 149 ff. A feigned reluctance to accept honours is not found among Hellenistic rulers: see A. Wallace-Hadrill, *JRS* 72 (1982), 36. The first consular *recusatio* was Augustus' refusal to accept a permanent consulship (*RG* 5. 3). The imperial family did not monopolize the ordinary consulships until the reign of the Flavians; from 71 to 88 at least one ordinary consulship every year was held by Vespasian, Titus, or Domitian: see M. Hammond, *The Antonine Monarchy* (Rome, 1959), 80. The Flavian practice may have aroused considerable resentment amongst senators, for it was not maintained by Trajan and the Antonines, who reverted to less frequent patterns of tenure (Hammond, 85). St.'s assertion that the senate prevailed upon Domitian to assume the consulship in 95, although he had demurred, matches the fiction of the reluctant ruler submitting to the nation's wishes.

POEM ONE 69

11. immensi reparator maximus aeui: Janus is *reparator aeui* because he ensures the continuity of time by presiding over the beginning of each year: cf. Plin. *NH* 34. 33 'temporis et aeui deum'. *reparare*, 'to restore', is used in the case of (e.g.) buildings which have become dilapidated: cf. Hor. *O*. 3. 3. 60 'ne ... tecta uelint reparare Troiae', Suet. *Dom.* 20 'quanquam bibliothecas incendio absumptas ... reparare curasset'. So to call someone a *reparator* of time itself is a very extravagant notion, implying here that without Janus to preside over each successive year the machinery of time would wear out. The association of Janus with beginnings causes him to be referred to as the most ancient of the gods (Juv. 6. 393 'antiquissime diuom': cf. the implication at Herodian, *Hist.* 1. 16. 1); so too his cult is said to have been founded by Romulus (Varro, *RD* fr. 35 Cardauns). But there is no evidence in theology or cult to suggest that the worship of Janus pre-dates that of any other deity in Italy; furthermore, the identification of Janus with Aion, the Alexandrian god of time (Lyd. *De. mens.* 4. 1), is judged to be a late rationalization (see L. R. Taylor and L. A. Holland, *CPh* 47 [1952], 142 n. 21).

12. attollit uultus: this phrase is particularly used to describe a gesture which symbolizes a recovery of spirit, e.g. Ov. *Met.* 4. 144 (Thisbe to Pyramus) 'exaudi uultusque attolle iacentes!', Sen. *Phaedr.* 587 (the nurse to Phaedra, who has fainted) 'attolle uultus, dimoue uocis moras!', Sil. 10. 632 'deiectum attollere uultum ... pigebat'. At *S.* 1. 1. 47 the sculpted horse shows spirit 'sonipes ... acrius attollit uultus'. Unless Janus is raising his head merely to make his voice carry, this gesture seems to imply that Domitian's presence raised Janus' hopes for the future. In Ovidian style, the apparently 'poetic' plural is here a true one.

utroque a limine: where is Janus speaking from? For the following discussion see plan of the imperial fora (Fig. 1). Evidence is supplied by *uicina Pace* (13), which refers to the Templum Pacis, begun by Vespasian (Suet. *Vesp.* 9. 1) and altered by Domitian (see on 4. 3. 17). It was on the south-east side of the Forum Transitorium (sometimes called Forum Peruium). This forum was built along the Argiletum by Domitian to connect the Forum Romanum and the other imperial fora; it was completed by Nerva, and is thus also known as the Forum Neruae (Suet. *Dom.* 5). By December 95, when Martial published Book 10 of the *Epigrams* (Friedländer, App. 56), Domitian had erected a temple to Janus Quadrifrons in the new forum: cf. Mart. 10. 28. 5–6 'nunc tua Caesareis cinguntur limina donis / et fora tot numeras, Iane, quot ora geris'. This was an improvement upon Janus' confined premises in the shrine of Janus Geminus: Mart. 10. 28. 3–4 'peruius exiguos habitabas ante penates / plurima qua medium Roma terebat iter'. The Janus Geminus was situated at the end of the Argiletum, where it entered the Forum Romanum between the Curia and the Basilica Aemilia: see Liv. 1. 19. 2, Ov. *F.* 1. 257 f., Sen. *Apocol.* 9, Dio 83. 13. The shrine had two entrances, fore and aft, and double doors at each end: Procop. *BG* 1. 25. 22 θύραι τε χαλκαῖ ἐφ' ἑκατέρωι προσώπωι εἰσίν. In effect it formed a corridor between the Forum Romanum and the Forum Iulium: see L. Richardson, Jr., *MDAI(R)* 85 (1978), 367. For Neronian coins depicting the Janus Geminus with closed

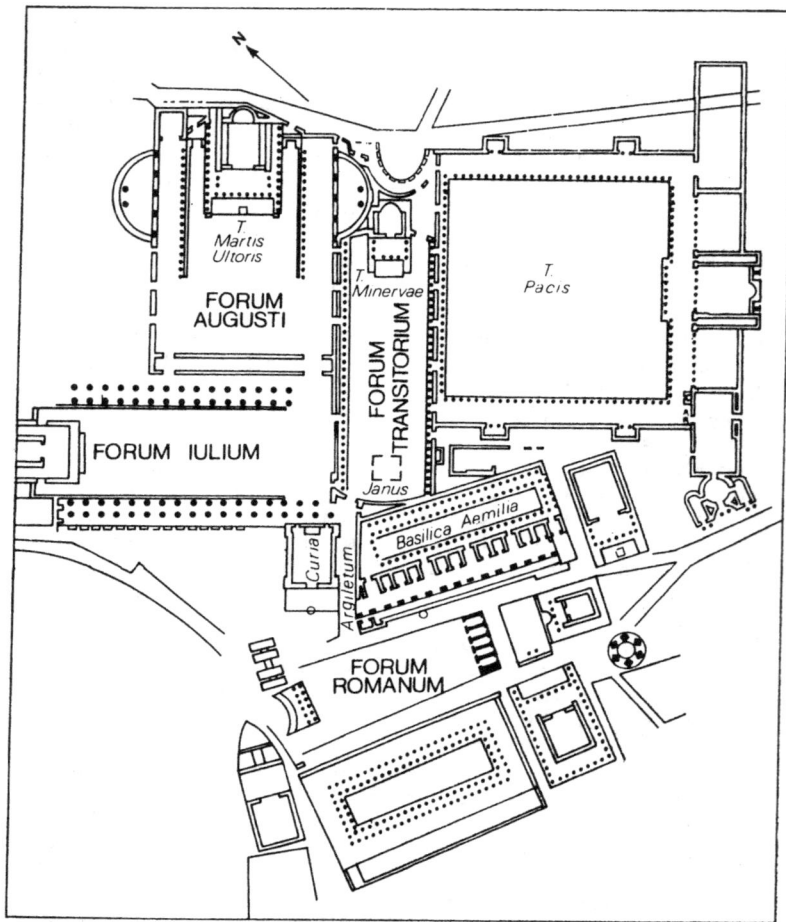

Fig. 1. Plan of the imperial fora. Drawing: S. L. Abraham

doors see C. H. V. Sutherland and R. A. G. Carson (eds.), *Roman Imperial Coinage*, i *From 31 B.C. to A.D. 69* (London, 1984), 140–1.

The site of this shrine is believed to have disappeared beneath the new Curia which Domitian built in AD 94 (Jerome, Olymp. 217): see Richardson, art. cit. 368. The site of the new Janus Quadrifrons in the Forum Transitorium has been identified at the south-west end, but the design is disputed. The archaeological remains have been interpreted as evidence for a conventional temple design, with pronaos and cella, by H. Bauer in two articles, *MDAI(R)* 84 (1977), 301–29 (especially figs. 1 and 2), and

*RPAA*³ 49 (1976–7), 117–48 (especially figs. 18 and 19). But this design has no relevance to the symbolism of Janus, and Bauer's interpretation of the archaeological evidence has been disputed by J. C. Anderson, *The Historical Topography of the Imperial Fora* (Brussels, 1984), 137 n. 58. Anderson, following Richardson, art. cit. 319, postulates a quadrifrontal arch, with a quadrifrontal statue inside (Lyd. *De Mens.* 4. 1), which marked the route of the Cloaca flowing beneath the Forum Transitorium.

But St.'s language here suits the Geminus rather than the Quadrifrons: a double herm with two faces would raise a pair of hands on each side ('levat ecce supinas / hinc atque inde manus', 15–16) and speak with two voices ('gemina ... uoce', 16, clearly alluding to the title 'Geminus'). *utroque a limine* suits a shrine with two entrances, not four. Yet *uicina Pace* suggests the site of the Quadrifrons. Even if the shrine of the Janus Geminus had to make way for Domitian's new Curia, it must have been preserved and kept in use until the Janus Quadrifrons was completed during 95. Hence it appears that Janus addresses Domitian on 1 January 95 from his shrine as Janus Geminus outside the Curia, and in what is virtually a parenthesis (*quem ... fori*) St. alludes to the new monument of the Quadrifrons which is to replace the shrine of Janus Geminus later in the year.

13. uicina Pace: the temple of Peace adjoining the Forum Transitorium: see on 4. 3. 17. Hence Peace is visualized as a neighbour of Janus: cf. Plaut. *Rud.* 849 'nescioquis senex, uicinus Veneris'. An association with peace was one of Janus' dominant characteristics, and so *uicina* carries also a nuance of spiritual kinship: cf. Sen. *Dial.* 12. 5. 2 'me ... in uicinum deo perductum praedicarem'; see *OLD* s.v. *uicinus* 5a. Janus was traditionally the custodian of peace: cf. Hor. *Epist.* 2. 1. 255, Ov. *F.* 1. 253, 281, Mart. 8. 66. 11.

14. omnia iussisti componere bella: *bellum componere* is the *uox propria* for establishing peace: *OLD* s.v. *componere* 15a. St. implies that the proximity of the Janus Quadrifrons to the Templum Pacis enjoins upon Janus a particular responsibility to exercise his authority in initiating peace. This was usually symbolized by the practice of closing the doors of the shrine of Janus Geminus: on the origins of this ritual see K. Latte, *RR* 132 n. 3, *Kl. Schr.* 845 ff., S. Weinstock, *JRS* 50 (1960), 48. There seems to be no direct allusion to this ritual here; it is rather Janus' general associations with peace which are evoked: for a specific allusion see l. 44. Domitian, issuing instructions to Janus (*iussisti*), fulfils the role of εἰρηνοποιός; for this encomiastic topos see Hermocles, *Hymn Dem.* 21 f. (= *Coll. Alex.* 174. 21 f. Powell). The implication that Domitian surpasses a god in authority is a technique of flattery which St. uses elsewhere; cf. the subservience of the River Volturnus at 4. 3. 67 ff.

14–15. nouique / in leges iurare fori: St. continues to exploit the locale of the Janus Quadrifrons: he envisages orders from Domitian that Janus is to abide by the rule of law administered by the civic authorities. The diction recalls the oath which the consul swore on taking up office, guaranteeing to abide by the law (*in leges iurare*); theoretically the oath could be taken within the first five days of office (*CIL* ii. 1963), but it had to be sworn before the senate could be convened; in practice it was taken on 1 January:

Dio 47. 18. 3, *RE* iv. 1116 (Kübler). The unexpected reversal here, whereby the consul instructs a god to swear the oath, contributes to St.'s presentation of Domitian as superhuman. To obtain and enforce *pax Romana* was one of the propagandist aims advertised by Domitian, as by other emperors: cf. 4. 7. 50–1 n.

15–16. supinas ... manus: outstretched arms was the gesture which usually accompanied prayer: see G. Appel, *De Romanorum precationibus* (Giessen, 1909), 194 ff.; hence the implication of Domitian's divinity is enhanced. In particular, upturned palms constituted a gesture of supplication: cf. Virg. *A.* 4. 205 'dicitur ... multa Iouem manibus supplex orasse supinis': see C. Sittl, *Die Gebärden der Griechen und Römer* (Leipzig, 1890), 174 and n. 2. Janus addresses to Domitian a series of requests conveying his prophecy. The concept of a divinity supplicating the emperor reinforces the impression that the emperor is superhuman.

17. parens mundi: Bentley punctuated with a comma after *parens*, taking *mundi* with *saecula*. But *parens mundi* is a variant of the honorific title *pater* (or *parens*) *patriae*; for *pater patriae*, first used (of Marius) at Cic. *Rab. perd.* 27, see. A. Alföldi, *MusHel* 9 (1952), 204–43; 10 (1953), 103–24; 11 (1954), 133–69. For the expanding sphere of influence implied in Domitian's titulature cf. Mart. 7. 7. 5 'summe mundi rector et parens orbis', 9. 5. 1 'summe Rheni domitor et parens orbis', *S.* 3. 4. 48 'pater inclitus orbis', 4. 2. 14 f. 'regnator terrarum orbisque subacti / magne parens', and the thought at 4. 3. 128 f. 'hunc iubet beatis / pro se Iuppiter imperare terris': see Sauter, 29 f. A comma after *parens* would also distort the natural phrasing of the salutation, which echoes the structure of a hymn; *magne parens mundi* combines the initial vocative and the phrase describing a characteristic of the god, and *qui* introduces the customary relative clause: see E. Norden, *Agnostos Theos* (Leipzig, 1913), 168 ff. The religious phrasing accords with Domitian's opinion of his own divinity, and it also achieves the paradox of a god pronouncing a religious salutation. The tribute is the greater because Janus, god of beginnings and hence himself addressed as 'sator ... mundi' (Mart. 10. 28. 1), acknowledges that Domitian is superior by calling him *parens mundi*. Implicit is the assimilation of Domitian to Jupiter: cf. 4. 3. 129, and see Sauter, 54–78.

17–18. saecula mecum / instaurare paras: is St. referring to a specific ceremony connected with the Ludi Saeculares? They were celebrated by Domitian in 88 (*S.* 1. 4. 17 f.). Vollmer remarks that the age which was thus inaugurated can still be extolled seven years after it began, and he infers that just as the stability of society is guaranteed by Janus as god of time, so it is by Domitian as legislator. But *instaurare* implies an act of renewal rather than the continued implementation of the status quo. And yet it is nearly a century too early to prepare for the next Ludi Saeculares; according to Augustus' reckoning of a *saeculum* as 110 years, they were next due in AD 198. For a table setting out in parallel columns the dates of the Ludi Saeculares according to the Valerian and Augustan reckoning see *RE* iA. 1699–1700 (Nilsson).

So a more general reference is required. A notion of annual renewal, observable in the cycle of the seasons (see l. 3), is formally attested by the renewal of *uota* each year. It is regarded as fitting that Domitian should be in office at the beginning of each year, just as Janus presides over the start of each annual cycle: 'sic tempora nasci, / sic annos intrare decet' (19 f.). Cf., of Janus, Plin. *NH* 34. 33 'temporis et aeui deum', Mart. 10. 28. 1 'annorum nitidique sator pulcherrime mundi', Nemes. *Cyneg.* 104 'cum Ianus, temporis auctor, pandit in occiduum bis senis mensibus aeuum'. Thus the emperor's assumption of the consulship is regarded as heralding a new age (i.e. a turn of affairs for the better): cf. Mart. 8. 8. 1 f. to Janus in January 93 (i.e. upon the completion of Domitian's Sarmatian campaign) 'licet . . . renoues uoltu saecula longa tuo', where *saecula* denotes the immediate but unlimited future. Instead of merely renewing the annual cycle, Janus and Domitian work together on a grand time-scale of *saecula*.

instaurare is the technical term for the ritual resumption of an activity (often after an ill-omened interruption), especially in the context of the games: see *TLL* vii. 1975. 72–81, F. Ritschl, *Parergon Plautinorum Terentianorumque*, i (Leipzig, 1845), 306–19. It is also attested of a secular activity which is repeated annually: cf. Colum. 4. 17. 2 (of pruning) 'hoc enim opus numquam intermittendum est, quin omnibus instauretur annis'. Thus *saecula instaurare* here, with overtones perhaps of the ceremonies connected with the *ludi*, alludes to the consular inauguration at the beginning of the year, and St. varies the topos of longevity by expressing the hope that Domitian will survive to conduct the inauguration ceremonies in ages to come. For the *processus consularis*, the consular procession to the Capitol culminating in sacrifice to Jupiter and an oath of allegiance to the state, see D–S i. 1470 f. (G. Bloch).

19. tua Roma: emperor and people are mutually devoted. Cf. the same phrase used of the relationship between Pompey and Rome at Luc. 7. 29 and 'mea Roma' said by Caesar at Petr. 122. 166.

tempora nasci: *nascor* is a natural verb to describe temporal beginnings: cf. Virg. *E.* 4. 5 'magnus ab integro saeclorum nascitur ordo'. With the inauguration of each consul a new period is born; Janus, wishing Domitian to be consul at the beginning of each year, begs him to hold successive consulships. *gaudia . . . continua* is a compressed expression for *gaudia propter consulatus continuos*: cf. Liv. 2. 42. 8 'post tres continuos consulatus'. As Janus specifies no time-limit, we must assume that he wants Domitian to be consul *in perpetuum*. This expedient had not been adopted by any of Domitian's predecessors, nor had it been necessary. St. exploits the republican façade, whereby the emperor occupies the consulship only intermittently (and nominally), in order to express an apparently spontaneous desire on the part of the state for the emperor's authority to be ratified as permanent and absolute.

hos . . . (22) Mineruae: the request 'da gaudia fastis / continua' is expressed hyperbolically in terms of the pageantry and ceremonial which had become associated with the emperor's person.

sinus = the curve formed by letting the upper edge of the toga fall from one shoulder behind the arm, to be gathered across the body and draped over the opposite shoulder so that the surplus material hung down behind:

see Lillian M. Wilson, *The Roman Toga* (Baltimore, 1924), figs. 30–2. It was the emperor's privilege to wear an all-purple toga, but here St. appears to envisage a consular toga woven specially for the occasion and by Minerva herself: this would be the purple-bordered *toga praetexta*. The purple border lies along the edge of the *sinus*, and thus extends from one shoulder, across the body, and over the other shoulder to hang down behind (*multo . . . ostro*). Cf. the *toga praetexta* worn by the chorus of boys at the Ludi Saeculares in 88 (*S.* 1. 4. 96–7) 'neque enim frustra mihi nuper honora / carmina patricio pueri sonuistis in ostro'.

22. properata tuae manibus praetexta Mineruae: St. pictures Minerva making Domitian's consular toga: cf. his speculation about the equestrian statue (1. 1. 5–6) 'an te Palladiae talem, Germanice, nobis / exegere manus'. Equipment constructed by deities for favoured mortals is a feature of epic (cf. *Il.* 18. 428 ff.: Achilles' shield), here taken over as an encomiastic theme. *properata* suggests bustling domestic activity: cf. Plin. *NH* 35. 138 (of women spinning) 'properant omnium mulierum pensa'; it is often used in instructing servants: *OLD* s.v. *propero* 2a, b. Domitian inherited the cult of Minerva from Vespasian and Titus, and he pursued it with particular devotion. The palladium symbolized the continuity of *imperium*: see Scott, 186; Domitian issued coinage which depicted him holding it: cf. Mattingly, *BMC* ii, pl. 68. 9. Minerva herself appeared very frequently on his coins; of special iconographical subtlety are coins which depict a herald holding a shield with a bust of Minerva decorating it: cf. Mattingly, *BMC* ii, pl. 63. 18, 64. 2. Domitian claimed to be Minerva's son (Philostr. *VA* 7. 24). Shortly before his death he had a nightmare in which Minerva deserted him (Suet. *Dom.* 15. 3). She was considered his *familiare numen* (Quint. 10. 1. 91); this was natural for an emperor keenly interested in literary creativity: see Sauter, 92. He celebrated her annual festival, the Quinquatrus, with great devotion (Dio 67. 1), and instituted a *collegium flaminum* in her honour (Suet. *Dom.* 4. 4). He founded the Legio I Flauia Mineruia, probably in 83 for the Chattan War: see M. Bös, *BJb* 158 (1958), 30, *RE* xii. 1276 (Ritterling); he added to its titulature the epithets *pia fidelis*, probably after his victory over the Chatti in 89. The connection between Domitian and Minerva is a recurrent theme in Martial, e.g. 5. 2. 6–8, 6. 10. 9–12, 7. 1. 1–2, 8. 1. 4, 9. 3. 10; at 14. 179 Martial alludes to Domitian's appropriation of Minerva's aegis as his emblem: see also Scott, 170. Domitian built at least two temples to Minerva: the Temple of Minerva Chalcidica (Dio 67. 5. 22), between the Iseum and the Pantheon, and the Templum Mineruae in the Forum Transitorium.

23. alius nitor: the temples with their marble façade would gleam naturally: cf. *Theb.* 1. 145 'montibus aut alte Grais effulta nitebant atria', *S.* 4. 2. 27 (varieties of marble) 'mons Libys Iliacusque nitet', 3. 99 (the archway where the Via Domitiana starts) 'totis Ligurum nitens metallis'. Janus claims that when Domitian takes up the consulship the temples gleam with a special brightness. St. seems to be using a type of artificial (as opposed to pathetic) fallacy, i.e. the inanimate world reflects the emotions of the population. Behind this image there is also the general notion that radiance streams from the emperor's person (cf. on 3 f., 26 f., 4. 2. 42 f.), and St. may conceive of this brilliance as reflected in the marble and thus making it gleam even more brightly.

24–5. ipsa ... tuis: there is insuperable difficulty with the phrase *moribus atque tuis* (M): (i) it makes no sense; (ii) *atque* is very rarely postponed to second place: there is only one example in Virgil (*E.* 6. 37 f.): see Norden, comm. on *Aen.* 6, app. III, 402 n. 3; M. Platnauer, *Latin Elegiac Verse* (Cambridge, 1951), 94, cites only two examples from elegy: Prop. 3. 13. 39, Ov. *Ars* 3. 282; (iii) *atque* is normally elided, although St. permits it before a consonant over twice as often in the *Siluae* as in the epics: 12 non-elisions out of 199 instances in the epics; 12 out of 72 in the *Siluae*, including another instance before an inflected form of *tuus* (5. 2. 171 'atque tuos implet, Crispine, penatis').

The context of ll. 23–4 consists of the natural omens presaging the nation's good fortune, and at 25–6 it is the general rejoicing at all levels in society, culminating in 'lucemque a consule ducit / omnis honos'. Punctuation after *brumae* (by Vollmer with a question-mark, and by Klotz with a comma) to connect *moribus atque tuis* to what follows is clearly wrong since it would be inappropriate for Roman society to revel on account of Domitian's *mores*, and in any case the expression admits the derogatory interpretation that Domitian's *mores* might not necessarily be a cause for rejoicing. Postgate punctuates after *tuis*, so that *moribus atque tuis* gives the reason for the climatic change ('tepeant ... sidera brumae'), which surely requires explanation; but the emperor's *mores* seem a strange and imprecise factor to mitigate the winter climate. With Bursian's emendation of *atque* to *aequa*, the phrase describes what is happening to the *sidera* and conveys a twofold compliment to Domitian by implying that he has a warm and beneficent personality and that his charisma even influences the weather: cf. 2. 2. 28 f. (to Pollius Felix about the environment of his villa) 'nulloque tumultu / stagna modesta iacent dominique imitantia mores', and see Håkanson, 104 f. The punctuation should thus be a question-mark after *tuis*, conveying the rhetorical question implied by *aspicis ut* (see *TLL* ii. 834. 33 ff.). 'gaudent ... omnis honos' is then punctuated as a statement.

25. turmaeque tribusque: for *Romanae turmae* as the official designation of the *equites* see A. Stein, *Der römische Ritterstand* (Munich, 1927), 61 ff. *tribus* denotes the common populace: cf. Plin. *NH* 19. 54 (condemning high prices which deprive the lower classes of even the humblest foods) 'in his quoque aliqua sibi nasci tribus negant, caule in tantum saginato ut pauperis mensa non capiat'.

26–7. lucemque ... honos: St. picks up the imagery of ll. 3–4. The beneficent ruler shedding light is a topos of encomium: cf. Hor. *O.* 4. 5. 5 'lucem redde tuae, dux bone, patriae'. For the idea in *lucem ducere* cf. Man. 1. 378 f. (of lands in the southern hemisphere) 'regna / commune ex uno lumen ducentia sole'. If *honos* here meant 'rank' (Mozley), this phrase would repeat the idea in 'gaudent ... patres' (25–6). Hence *honos*, in the sense of 'magistracy', is used here as metonymy for 'magistrate': see on 9 above. The more distinguished the consul, the more prestigious it is to hold curule office in his consular year. The image approaches the concept of 'reflected glory'.

28. Roma potens: Markland objected that *potens* intrudes upon the theme of the past which is expressed by *prior annus* and *longa Vetustas*; hence he suggested *parens* to convey the notion that Rome, by virtue of her age, is qualified to cite examples from the past. But *Roma potens* is a natural phrase: cf. Hor. *Epist.* 2. 1. 61–3 'hos ediscit et hos arto stipata theatro / spectat Roma potens; habet hos numeratque poetas / ad nostrum tempus Liui scriptoris ab aeuo.'

longa Vetustas: it is natural for Janus, associated with the past as well as the future, to appeal to antiquity; a long memory is one of his attributes: cf. Ov. *F.* 1. 103 f. 'me Chaos antiqui—nam sum res prisca—uocabant, / aspice, quam longi temporis acta canam'. At *S.* 1. 6. 39–42 St. makes a similar appeal to Vetustas in the context of a comparison between the Golden Age and the present, to Domitian's advantage: 'i nunc saecula compara, Vetustas, / antiqui Iouis aureumque tempus: / non sic libera uina tunc fluebant / nec tardum seges occupabat annum'.

29. dinumera ... nec ... recense: two imperatives joined by *nec* is a colloquial idiom found in prose only at Cic. *Att.* 12. 22. 3 and Sen. *Epist.* 59. 1, but quite frequently in poetry, especially Ovid (48 instances): see E. B. Lease, *AJPh* 34 (1913), 261 f. *recense* is an image from taking the census and reviewing the troops; the military flavour is sustained in *uincere* (30).

31–2. Markland criticizes St. for inconsistency because after his appeal to Vetustas he cites only one example of multiple consulships, and that from the recent past. But Janus has expressly forbidden Vetustas to waste time on *parua exempla* (29). The implication is that only Augustus, founder of the principate, is worthy of being compared with Domitian, and even he is found wanting.

31. Latios: *Latio* (M) or *Latios* (Gronovius)? Since Augustus held consulships *in absentia*, *Latio* is inaccurate as well as oddly specific. *Latii fasces* is a natural phrase; it occurs in a similar context of multiple consulships at Sil. 14. 112 'tertia ... Latios renouarat purpura fasces'. Stylistically, too, *Latios* is preferable, since the enclosing word-order *Latios ... fasces* binds the sentence together.

32. coepit sero mereri: Augustus, born in 63, held thirteen consulships: in 43, 33, 31–23, 5, and 2 BC: see Syme, *RR* 525–9. His constitutional 'settlements' were in 27 and 23 BC. By *sero mereri* St. must mean that only in his later years did Augustus show that he deserved so many consulships. Justification for this view could be derived from the establishment of peace after the civil wars, the ending of proscriptions, and Augustus' programme of restoration, including legislation and rebuilding. Domitian, too, held his first consulship at nineteen (AD 71). He outdoes Augustus because he has deserved his consulships throughout his *iuuentus*: cf. *tu iuuenis praegressus auos*. 'Thrice and ten times in the gliding years did Augustus wield the axes, but he entered late on his career of service' (Slater) is wrong; the point is that Augustus began his career as consul very young, but only latterly did he rule beneficently. For the view that Augustus' career was not above reproach cf. Sen. *Clem.* 1. 9, [Sen.] *Oct.* 251, Plin. *NH* 7. 147–50, Tac. *Ann.* 1. 9. 3, Dio 56. 37. 3, 38. 1, 44. 1, and for the concession that the principate was overall a credit to him cf. Sen. *Clem.* 1. 11, Tac. *Ann.* 1. 9. 5,

Dio 56. 35–41, 43. 4–44. 4. Thus Seneca, the author of the *Octauia*, the elder Pliny, and St. are dissenting voices, evidence that during the last forty years of the first century criticism was indeed voiced against Augustus, who was otherwise 'secure against attack and the model for all emperors' (M. P. Charlesworth, *JRS* 27 [1937], 56).

33. recusas: for the *recusatio* see on l. 10 *pudorem*.

35. permittes: *precibus senatus* is the equivalent of *senatui precanti*. Both promises and concessions are valid responses to a prayer, but here *permittes* is preferable for the magnanimous tone.

36. felix: this belongs to the diction of μακαρισμός, as does also the formula *terque quaterque*: cf. Hom. *Od.* 5. 306 τρὶς μάκαρες Δαναοὶ καὶ τετράκις, Prop. 3. 12. 15 'ter quater in casta felix, o Postume, Galla', Virg. *A.* 1. 94 'o terque quaterque beati', *TLL* vi. 1. 444. 48 ff.

37. mecum ... condes: the formula *condere saecla* is a Lucretian phrase (3. 1090) taken over by Virgil at *A.* 6. 792 f. 'aurea condet / saecula' to convey Augustus' role as a second *conditor urbis* (Suet. *Aug.* 7. 2): see Norden ad loc. The impression that Domitian is a second Romulus is strengthened by the partnership which St. imagines between Janus and the emperor.

38. et ... Tarenti: this clause is co-ordinate with 'mecum altera saecula condes' and so should be a logical extension of it. The interpretation depends upon the meaning of *saecula*: as at l. 17, does it refer to periods of time in general or does it refer specifically to the era which is to be inaugurated by the next Ludi Saeculares, in AD 198? Håkanson, 108, notes that *altera saecula* does not mean the same as *alia saecula*, i.e. the phrase is not an indefinite reference to the future but a specific prophecy about the Ludi Saeculares. The μακαρισμός formula, whereby St. envisages Domitian's seventeen consulships tripled or quadrupled (see on l. 37), leads him to the climactic prophecy of an event scheduled 103 years hence. What has the restoration of the *ara parentis* (M) to do with that? It would have to be either an altar of Jupiter (so Vollmer and Frère) or of Vespasian (Mozley, Scott), specifically the Templum Gentis Flauiae (H. Erkell, *Eranos* 56 [1958], 179). But it would be tactless for St. to imply that Domitian would let his father's shrine fall into disrepair. Further, adjectives expressing longevity are only applied to divine beings when the context makes the meiosis clear: cf. Aesch. *Sept.* 523–4 ἐχθρὸν εἴκασμα βροτοῖς τε καὶ / δαροβίοισι θεοῖσιν, Soph. *OT* 1099 τίς σ' ἔτικτε τᾶν μακραιώνων, [Sen.] *Oct.* 14–15 'utinam ante manu grandaeua sua / mea rupisset stamina Clotho'. Hence *longaeuus* would be inept for either the deified Vespasian or Jupiter: cf. Gell. 2. 16. 10 'neque dii "longaeui" appellantur, sed "inmortales"', J. H. Bishop, *CR* NS 4 (1954), 96. Turnebus proposed an emendation for *parentis* which would sustain a reference to the Ludi Saeculares: *Tarenti*. The Tarentum in the Campus Martius next to the Tiber was the site of sacrifices to Dis and Proserpine at the Ludi Saeculares: see Latte, *RR* 246. The Sibylline books decreed that the Ludi Tarentini of 249 BC be celebrated every hundred years, i.e. as the Ludi Saeculares: see *RE* ivA. 2313 (Weinstock). Cf. St.'s reference to the Ludi Saeculares of 88 at 1. 4. 17 f. (of Rutilius Gallicus' almost fatal illness) 'nec tantum induerint fatis noua saecula crimen / aut instaurati peccauerit ara Tarenti'. Vollmer tries to justify the association with the Tarentum while retaining *parentis* on the grounds that Jupiter received the first sacrifice at the *ara Tarenti*; but in any case there is no evidence that he did: see H. Wagenvoort, *Studies in Roman Literature, Culture and Religion* (Leiden, 1956), 193 ff. Thus 'et tibi longaeui renouabitur ara Tarenti' looks forward to the reinauguration of the rites at the *ara Tarenti* on the occasion of the next Ludi Saeculares in 198, the arcane reference presumably having led to the corruption. Håkanson, 109, justifies *mecum* as an allusion to Janus' role as god of beginnings and hence in charge of fresh undertakings: cf. 17 f. 'saecula mecum / instaurare paras'. Bishop, 96, followed by Erkell, 177, proposed *longaeuo* for *longaeui*, in order to read a direct allusion to the hope for Domitian's longevity: *tibi longaeuo*. But Håkanson, 110, points out that *longaeui ... ara Tarenti* is hypallage for *longaeua ara*, and even Bishop, *CR* NS 10 (1960), 8, admits that the word-order *longaeui ... Tarenti* is common in St.: adjective in second position in the line, agreeing with noun at the end.

39. permitte triumphos: St. is alluding to the circumstances of January 93, when Domitian refused a triumph after the eight-month campaign against the Sarmatae. This gesture of *recusatio* was in contrast to his triumphs after the campaigns against the Chatti and the Dacians, and was thus interpreted as a snub to the enemy: cf. *S.* 3. 3. 167–71 'haud mirum, ductor placidissime, quando / haec est quae uictis parcentia foedera Cattis, / quaeque suum Dacis donat clementia montem, / quae modo Marcomanos post horrida bella uagosque / Sauromatas Latio non est dignata triumpho'. Instead of a regular triumph Domitian merely conducted the ceremony of depositing the emblems of victory in the lap of the statue of Jupiter Capitolinus: cf. l. 41 below, Mart. 8. 15. 5, Suet. *Dom.* 6. 1 'de Chattis Dacisque post uaria proelia duplicem triumphum egit; de Sarmatis lauream modo Capitolino Ioui rettulit'.

St. urges Domitian to celebrate triumphs for which he will have ample booty (*mille tropaea feres*), i.e. he anticipates the necessity to forestall another *recusatio*; contrast 4. 3. 159, where a *recusatio* is predicted. Hence *permitte* (*ς*), corrected for *promitte* (M), suitably flatters Domitian by implying that if he celebrates a triumph it will be a gesture of concession to popular favour: cf. l. 35 above. But Suet. *Dom.* 13. 2 records public resentment at the numerous triumphal archways which Domitian erected. A request for more triumphs, however, whether or not it accords with general opinion, is obviously a compliment to the emperor.

A comma between *feres* and *tantum* (so Vollmer) implies that the imperative *permitte* replaces the protasis of a conditional clause, but actually there is a mild anacoluthon: there is ellipse of the protasis, and the thought jumps straight to the command which would naturally follow it, i.e. *mille tropaea feres [si permiseris ...]: permitte.* Hence I punctuate with a dash, to set off and emphasize the command, i.e. the climax.

40–1. restat Bactra nouis, restat Babylona tributis / frenari: for the word-order whereby anaphora of the verb distributes the predicate between both clauses cf. 4. 2. 16 'datur haec iuxta, datur ora tueri'. The anaphora conveys emphatic and repeated encouragement to Domitian to undertake an eastern expedition. The cities Bactra and Babylon together represent Parthia in Pompey's speech advocating a Parthian expedition (Luc. 8. 298–300) 'primi Pellaeas arcu fregere sarisas / Bactraque, Medorum sedem, murisque superbam / Assyrias Babylona domos'. The names of the chief cities commonly denote the satrapies, Bactria and Babylonia, which lay at opposite ends of the Parthian desert. For Bactria on the R. Oxus along the northern boundary of modern Afghanistan see W. W. Tarn, *The Greeks in Bactria and India* (Cambridge, 1938), 102 ff.; for Babylonia on the Euphrates in modern Iraq see Tarn, 56 ff. These areas figured prominently in Alexander's campaigns: for his triumphal entry into Babylon see Curt. 5. 1. 20; from Bactra he launched his mission eastwards in spring 327, and it was the site of his celebrated attempt to introduce προσκύνησις towards himself (Curt. 8. 5. 9–24). Thus by exhorting Domitian to conquer these territories St. is prophesying for him the role of a second Alexander. The prediction of Roman expansion into the east (cf. 4. 3. 154 ff.) had been a theme of Augustan encomium (e.g. Hor. *O.* 1. 2. 22, 35. 38 ff.); likewise comparison with Alexander: see Doblhofer, 129 ff. St. represents the subjugation of Rome's enemies as obedience to the civilizing discipline of law and taxation: cf. 4. 7. 50–1.

41. nondum in gremio Iouis Indica laurus: the climax of Janus' speech is a reminder to Domitian of fresh fields to conquer. This is not inconsistent with Janus' associations with peace (see on l. 13). Peace at home and campaigns abroad are compatible in imperial propaganda: see R. Syme, *JRS* 28 (1938), 218 (= *Rom. Pap.* i. 77) on Plin. *Pan.* 16. 2 ff. The bay decorating the *fasces* of victorious generals was laid *in gremio Iouis* after a victory: cf. Plin. *NH* 15. 134, and n. to l. 39 above. The plain ablative *gremio* without a preposition is very bald in conjunction with the ellipse of the verb; preferable is Livineius' *in gremio*.

42. Arabes Seresque: two semi-fabulous peoples whose annexation would bring glory to the emperor. Arabia was legendary for her riches: cf. Plin. *NH* 12. 51 'Arabiae diuitias ... causasque quae cognomen illi felicis ac beatae dedere'. Her epithet *Felix* was properly applied to the kingdom of Saba in the south of the Arabian peninsula, rich in the trade of spice and incense, which had evaded Roman grasp ever since the abortive expedition of Aelius Gallus *c*.26 BC. St. implies a hope which was to be partially fulfilled when the northern area, Arabia Nabataea, became a Roman province under Trajan in 106: see *RE* ii. 359 (v. Rohden), G. W. Bowersock, *Roman Arabia* (Cambridge, Mass. and London, 1983), 2, 76–89. The Seres, who gave their name to silk (σηρικόν), were the Chinese. Silk, which was coveted 'ut in publico matrona traluceat' (Sen. *Ben.* 7. 9) and is mentioned at least nine times by Martial, reached a peak of fashion in the nineties once the silk-route was made secure with the annexation of Turkestan by China *c*.AD 90: see J. Thorley, *G&R*² 18 (1971), 71–80. The Romans were vague about the exact location of the Chinese, whom they frequently mention in association with the peoples of India. At 5. 1. 60–3 the association (as here) of Babylon, Indians, Arabs, and Chinese (and Lydians) epitomizes wealth that Priscilla would have had the will-power to resist.

rogant: Stange proposed *togam*, to avoid the elliptical *rogant*. But the notion of defeated peoples becoming suppliants does not require an object to be stated for *rogant*: cf. the elliptical use of *rogare* at Sen. *Suas.* 6. 2 'M. Cato... mori maluit quam rogare'. *rogant* conveys a perfectly appropriate thought, i.e. that Rome's former enemies send delegations to plead for the benefits of Roman rule: cf. Hor. *CS* 55 f., Aug. *RG* 31-2, *S.* 3. 4. 61-3, *Pan. Lat.* 4(10). 38. 3. *togam* would be inappropriate, because it is the dress of Roman citizens and thus represents citizenship, and St. cannot be suggesting that the Arabs and Chinese are suing for citizenship.

43. cupiuntque decem tua nomina menses: with remarkable humility, Janus implies that he is willing for even January to relinquish its name so that every month may derive its title from the emperor's. His wish was eventually fulfilled by Commodus (Dio 72. 15). The Hellenistic practice of renaming months began under Demetrius Poliorcetes, when the Athenians renamed Munychion in honour of him: Plut. *Demetr.* 12. 2, schol. Pind. *Nem.* 3. 4. Weinstock, 155, sees this as a tribute to Demetrius for having liberated Athens from tyranny, but K. Scott, *YCS* 2 (1931), 202, interprets it as a divine honour since it is classified by Plutarch among other honours which accorded divinity to the recipient. But Plutarch may be reflecting a late interpretation rather than the original intention of the Athenians. At Mytilene a month was probably named after Pompey (*IG* 12. 2. 59. 18): see Scott, art. cit. 206. Julius Caesar was the first Roman after whom a month definitely was named: this gesture was classed as a divine honour by Suet. *Jul.* 76, Dio 44. 5, 45. 7, App. *BC* 2. 106, Flor. *Epit.* 2. 13. 91. Hence the Roman practice apparently was conceived as a tribute suitable for a deity. Under the empire, since July and August continued to be called after Caesar and Augustus, later emperors and flatterers generally favoured giving imperial nomenclature to September and October, to continue the sequence: Tiberius vetoed the naming of September 'Tiberius' and October 'Liuius' (Suet. *Tib.* 26); Caligula named September 'Germanicus' (Suet. *Gaius* 15. 4). Nero departed from the trend by turning his attention to the three months preceding July, which he called 'Neroneus', 'Claudius', and 'Germanicus'. Domitian renamed September 'Germanicus' and October 'Domitianus' because he became *princeps* on 14 September 81 and was born on 24 October 51 (Suet. *Dom.* 13. 3, recording Domitian's divine honours). The original names were restored in accordance with the *damnatio memoriae* after Domitian's death: Macr. *Sat.* 1. 36-7, Plut. *Numa* 19. 4; Pliny cites Domitian's honorific months to illustrate his lust for excessive honours (*Pan.* 54). Domitian may also have extended his cult of Minerva (see l. 22 n.) by naming a month after her: Eusebius, in the Armenian version of the *Chronicle* of Jerome under *a. Abr.* 2102 (i.e. 85/6), claims that Domitian called October 'Parthenicus', which is an error (see Suet. *Dom.* 13. 3), but Scott, art. cit. 234, suggests that this may indicate that another month was earmarked for this title. Hardie, 194, points out that in another sense the whole year took the name of Domitian as *consul ordinarius*.

44. clausoque libens se poste recepit: having encouraged Domitian to undertake an eastern campaign in the future, Janus withdraws from the limelight, closing the double doors of his shrine behind him: Domitian's seventeenth consulship begins in a time of peace. The role of Janus as guardian of peace at home during Domitian's consulship is similar to his role in the Golden Age: cf. Ov. *F.* 1. 253 f. 'nil mihi cum bello, pacem postesque tuebar / et clauam ostendens, "haec" ait "arma gero."' For the symbolism in closing the gates see l. 14 n. *libens* in the religious context conveys divine beneficence, like *uolens*: cf. Hor. *O.* 3. 30. 15 f. 'mihi Delphica / lauro cinge uolens, Melpomene, comam'. Fraenkel, on Aesch. *Ag.* 664, identifies *uolens* [*propitius*] with the ritual term θέλων, which is used both in prayers and (as *libens* here) in narrative.

45–6. tunc... polo: are the gods in their temples or in heaven? *patuere* (M) requires an epiphany, presumably manifested by the atmospheric phenomena (*signa*), i.e. thunder and lightning. Håkanson, 110 f., explains St.'s phrasing as an unsuccessful reminiscence of Luc. 2. 1 f. 'iamque irae patuere deum manifestaque belli / signa dedit mundus'. But Professor W. S. Watt's conjecture ⟨s⟩*tupuere* (*WJA* ns 14 [1988], forthcoming), which he has kindly communicated to me, is an easy correction (loss of initial letter by haplography, and inversion of *p* and *t*), and the resulting picture of the gods' initial stunned reaction is far more lively than mere approval (*fauere*, Baehrens) or instant applause (*plausere*, Markland): cf. *Ach.* 1. 14 f. (the attitude of the world towards the emperor) 'quem longe primum stupet Itala uirtus / Graiaque', *S.* 4. 2. 20 ff. (where, as here, astonishment is followed by divine rejoicing) 'stupet hoc uicina Tonantis / regia teque pari laetantur sede locatum / numina', Gell. 5. 1. 5 'praeterea dicebat magnam laudem non abesse ab admiratione, admirationem autem, quae maxima est, non uerba parere, sed silentium'. For *stupere* of joyful emotion cf. Caelius fr. 18 Malcovati 'stupere gaudio Graecus'.

46. rex magne: Leo, *Anal. Plaut.* i. 22, believing *rex* to be an exclusively pejorative term, proposed punctuating *rex, magne*, so that *rex* is in apposition to *Iuppiter* and Domitian is addressed by the bare epithet *magne*. But to divorce *rex* from *magne* is very artificial, and a Roman reading a text without any punctuation would surely not have separated them: cf. the arguments for the punctuation of *magne parens mundi* (17). Another expedient, proposed by Markland and adopted by Håkanson, 112, is to change *rex* to *dux*. But is *rex* necessarily pejorative? The early kings of Rome, apart from Tarquin the Proud, are approved of even in republican sources: see Elizabeth Rawson, *JRS* 65 (1975), 152. The republican attitude towards Hellenistic kings was ambivalent, combining scorn with admiration (Rawson, ibid.), and so J. H. Bishop's equation *rex* = βασιλεύς, *CR* ns 4 (1954), 152, is probably too simplistic. There are, however, philosophical contexts where *rex* is a term of approbation, especially in the collocation *rex et princeps*, as used by Seneca with reference to Nero, e.g. *Clem.* 1. 3. 3, 4. 3, 2. 5. 2, where *rex* is the equivalent of βασιλεύς and the antithesis of τύραννος: see Miriam Griffin, *Seneca: a Philosopher in Politics* (Oxford, 1976), 141–8. There are twenty-eight instances of *rex* in the *De Clementia*, and thirty-one of *princeps*, and in no case is any distinction made between them: see B. Mortureux, *Recherches sur le 'De clementia' de Sénèque* (Brussels, 1973), 41 n. 2. There are, however, two qualifications regarding Seneca's use of *rex*: he never addresses Nero directly as *rex*, and elsewhere he expresses the traditional Roman odium of *regnum*, e.g. at *Ben.* 5. 16. 6. But it is clear from the *De Clementia* that there were circumstances in which *rex* could denote benevolent absolutism. Domitian made no attempt to disguise his autocracy. Pliny flatters Trajan by saying that he has protected Rome from a *regnum*: *Pan.* 55. 7 'hic [Traianus] regnum ipsum ... arcet ac summouet sedemque obtinet principis, ne sit domino locus'. Here Pliny condemns the appellation *dominus* which Domitian demanded (Suet. *Dom.* 13. 1 f.); he may also imply that Domitian actually regarded his rule as a *regnum* and expected to be acknowledged as *rex*, although if this is the case it is surprising that Suetonius does not say so. At ll. 46–7 St. has constructed an imaginary situation which allows him to use the term *rex* as the apogee of flattery: Jupiter, *rex deorum*, grants Domitian longevity to equal his own (*suos annos*), i.e. immortality; hence Domitian will live for ever on earth as its ruler, equivalent to Jupiter in heaven: cf. 4. 3. 128 f., where the Sibyl describes Domitian as Jupiter's vicegerent.

2

INTRODUCTION

THIS poem is a tribute to Domitian in a less formal context than the consular inauguration of 4. 1. It conveys an impression of a relaxed and accessible emperor, in contrast to the dignity and solemnity of 4. 1 and the programme of diligent action and achievements stressed in 4. 3. It is conceived as an expression of thanks to Domitian for a dinner which St. had attended (4 *Pr.* 6) 'gratias egi sacratissimis eius epulis honoratus'. For an analysis of this poem as St.'s interpretation of Domitian's self-image see D. W. T. C. Vessey, *AC* 52 (1983), 206–20.

On the authenticity of *eucharisticon* in the *titulus*, derived from εὐχαριστικὸς λόγος, see General Introduction. The Latin equivalent, *gratiarum actio*, is attested as a *titulus* for a prose work: cf. Ausonius, *Gratiarum actio ad Gratianum imperatorem pro consulatu*, Pan. Lat. 3(11) *Cl. Mamertini gratiarum actio de consulatu suo Iuliano Imp.*, 5(8) *Incerti gratiarum actio Constantino Augusto*. K.-E. Henriksson, *Griechische Büchertitel in der römischen Literatur* (Helsinki, 1956), 97, suggests that a Greek title was felt to be more appropriate to the elevated style of poetry.

The *gratiarum actio*, integral to Roman social relations, was frequently used as a vehicle whereby a writer might address his patron. In the rhetorical schools, a *gratiarum actio* was considered to require an elevated delivery: cf. Quint. 11. 3. 153 'in laudationibus, nisi si funebres erunt, gratiarum actione, exhortatione, similibus laeta et magnifica et sublimis est actio'. In poetry, the tone reflects the degree of intimacy shared by the writer and his addressee; for example, the intimacy between Horace and Maecenas allows Horace in *Epode* 3 to affect displeasure at the menu which Maecenas has offered him. The elevated style of *S.* 4. 2 suits an imperial addressee. It may be that Domitian expected a proliferation of private *gratiarum actiones*, and that this became a burden, since Trajan restricted the practice, allowing votes of thanks to be delivered to him only upon the assumption of a consulship: see Plin. *Pan.* 4. 2 'parens noster [Traianus] priuatas actiones cohibet et comprimit, intercessurus etiam publicis, si permitteret sibi uetare quod senatus iuberet'.

The occasion of the banquet which St. attended cannot be ascertained. Cancik, *LK* 82 f., suggests that it was the *cena aditialis* for Domitian's inauguration as consul in January 95, but the absence of references to consular duties and distinction tells against this. *cenae* were a feature of Domitian's domestic policy: to limit public expenditure, Nero had reduced *cenae publicae* in favour of distributions of *sportulae* (Suet. *Nero* 16. 2), but Domitian reversed the process: Suet. *Dom.* 7. 1 'sportulas publicas sustulit, reuocata rectarum cenarum consuetudine'. In hosting *cenae* the emperor plays the role of patron *par excellence*: the *cena* was an important feature of Roman social patronage. Epictetus (*Diss.* 4. 1. 47 f.) bears witness that differential treatment for less important guests, which could be very humiliating, was a hazard at an imperial *cena*, as at any other. Clients who were poets were favoured recipients of dinner-invitations as a form of *beneficium* because they could provide entertainment: cf. Mart. 9. 97. 2, 9 f. 'quod me Roma legit, rumpitur inuidia . . . quod sum iucundus amicis, / quod conuiua frequens'. St. mentions attending dinners hosted by several of his addressees: Claudius Etruscus (1. 5. 10), Atedius Melior (2. 4. 4), Nouius Vindex (4. 6. 3), Plotius Grypus (4. 9. 51). During Claudius Etruscus' *cena* St. delivered *S.* 1. 5 about Etruscus' new baths: 1 *Pr.* 31 'balneolum a me suum intra moram cenae recepit'.

It is surely unnecessary to suppose that *S.* 4. 2 was formally commissioned in return for the invitation. St. says that many of his poems were presented to the emperor before they were recited in public (4 *Pr.* 27) 'multa ex illis iam domino Caesari dederam'. Augustus had been a sympathetic listener (Suet. *Aug.* 89. 3 'recitantis et benigne et patienter audiit'): see N. M. Horsfall, *Anc. Soc.* (Macquarie) 13 (1983), 164. Domitian would surely have assumed that a poet, especially one whose work was well-known to him, would celebrate in verse such clear evidence of the emperor's favour.

It is less certain whether 4. 2 was written after the event which it purports to be reflecting upon (note the tense of *uacauit* [40], *nitebat* [43]), or written in advance and delivered immediately after the function, or perhaps even recited towards the end of the proceedings. It was symposiastic etiquette for the guest to praise his host's house and belongings: cf. Athen. 5. 179 B. Hence the *ecphrasis* of Domitian's palace (18–31) accords with that symposiastic tradition, for St. describes lavishly the lavish surroundings in which Domitian lived. On architectural detail as a vehicle for panegyric in this poem see Cancik, *LK* 65–89. There is no detail in the poem which St. could not have acquired by hearsay; circumstantial evidence (e.g. the menu) is omitted. So it is possible that he composed this poem in advance and delivered it at the banquet. Under Trajan, even the dinners for the emperor's working-parties of officials included entertainment: see Plin. *Epist.* 6. 31. 13 'adhibebamur cotidie cenae; erat modica, si principem cogitares. interdum acroamata audiebamus, interdum iucundissimis sermonibus nox ducebatur'. The reference to poetry-recitals in the σύγκρισις with Jupiter (53–6) may indicate that St. recited the poem at the banquet. However, the comparison is traditional (see nn. ad loc.), and perhaps the details are not meant to reflect this particular banquet.

Although St. stresses that he composed the *Siluae* spontaneously, he is evasive in meeting the charge of prior preparation. For example, he anticipates, but does not expressly deny, the charge that he had seen the equestrian statue of Domitian before it was dedicated (1 *Pr.* 20 f.) and hence, by implication, had prepared in advance the poem which he delivered the following day. Again, he ostensibly meets such objections by appealing to Stella as witness that he composed the epithalamium for him within two days. This evasiveness suggests that St. did prepare poems for Domitian in advance of the events which they celebrated. If indeed, towards the end of the banquet, St. recited a poem of thanks to the emperor which was cast in the form of recollection after the event, that would have been a *tour de force* that must have appealed to the recipient.

1 ff. St. begins this poem with an allusion to banquet-scenes in Virgil and Homer. He implies that Domitian's banquet is worthy of treatment in the most elevated literary genre and that he will not be able to do it justice (7–10). Cf. 5. 3. 61 ff., where he claims that a eulogy worthy of his father's memory would rival the poetry of Homer and Virgil.

1. Regia: the first word sets the tone of imperial dignity and splendour. St. claims as a precedent Virgil's description of the banquet with which Dido welcomed the Trojans (*A.* 1. 699 ff.).

2. qui ... intulit: periphrases of the form [*is*] *qui* or the like, as at the opening of the *Odyssey*, became a signal feature of the epic proem: cf. Hom. *Od.* 1. 1 f. Ἄνδρα μοι ἔννεπε, Μοῦσα, πολύτροπον, ὃς μάλα πολλά / πλάγχθη, Ap. Rhod. *Arg.* 1. 1–4 Ἀρχόμενος σέο, Φοῖβε, παλαιγενέων κλέα φωτῶν / μνήσομαι, οἳ... ἤλασαν Ἀργώ, Virg. *A.* 1. 1 f. 'Arma uirumque cano, Troiae qui primus ab oris / Italiam ... uenit', Val. Fl. 1. 1–4 'Prima deum magnis canimus freta peruia natis / fatidicamque ratem, Scythici quae Phasidis oras / ausa sequi ... consedit Olympo', Sil. 1. 1–2 'Ordior arma, quibus caelo se gloria tollit / Aeneadum'. By a sophisticated technique of allusion, in contexts which refer to the writing of epic this formula is seen to be used of the epic authors themselves: cf. *Laus Pisonis* 230–2 (where Virgil is claimed to rival Homer) 'ipse per Ausonias Aeneia carmina gentes / qui sonat, ingenti qui nomine pulsat Olympum / Maeoniumque senem Romano prouocat ore', *S.* 2. 7. 77 f. (with reference to Varro of Atax and Ovid's *Metamorphoses*) 'et qui per freta duxit Argonautas, / et qui corpora prima transfigurat'. For the figure whereby the poet's description of the action is identified with the action itself cf. Virg. *E.* 6. 45 f. (of Silenus) 'et fortunatam, si numquam armenta fuissent, / Pasiphaen niuei solatur amore iuuenci', Hor. *Sat.* 1. 10. 36 'turgidus Alpinus iugulat dum Memnona', 2. 5. 41 'Furius hibernas cana niue conspuet Alpis', Prop. 2. 1. 18 'ut possem heroas ducere in arma manus', *Aetna* 80 ff., *S.* 2. 7. 77 f. (quoted above). In Greek, see e.g. Eur. *Hec.* 466, [Plut.] *Mor.* 105 D. See F. Leo, *Ausgewählte kleine Schriften* (Rome, 1960), ii.

39 and n. 2, and the full treatment by G. Lieberg, *Poeta Creator* (Amsterdam, 1982).

magnum: the traditional heroic epithet (*TLL* viii. 138. 67 ff.) contributes to the atmosphere of grandeur and epic proportions: cf. *multo* (4) and the highly mannered diction *mansuro* (3), *ast* (5).

intulit: St. again recalls the diction of the proem of the *Aeneid* describing Aeneas' mission (Virg. *A.* 1. 5 f.) 'dum conderet urbem / inferretque deos Latio'.

4. **aequore ... consumpsit:** the banquet of Alcinous (*Od.* 8. 59 ff.) renewed Odysseus' strength after his storm-tossed voyage upon leaving Calypso's island on his way back to Ithaca. Homer is said to 'wear out' his hero with the element (*aequore*) which provides the setting for his lengthy adventures (hence *multo*). *consumere*, 'exhaust' (*TLL* iv. 610. 69 ff.), can refer specifically to the completion of a literary work: cf. Macr. *Sat.* 1. 1. 5 '[Socrates] dialogum habita cum Timaeo disputatione consumpsit', *TLL* iv. 616. 37. There is a *double entendre* here whereby *aequore multo* both refers to Odysseus' νόστος and evokes the comparison of epic to the sea. Cf. Apollo's injunction to Horace contemplating epic themes (*O.* 4. 15. 2 f.) 'increpuit ... ne parua Tyrrhenum per aequor / uela darem'. There is some antithesis between *mansuro carmine*, denoting the immortality of poetry, and *consumpsit*, which conveys the precarious and ephemeral nature of human life.

5. **sacrae ... noua gaudia cenae:** *noua* and *nunc primum* (6) appear tautologous; but St. is not a flabby poet. Hence *noua* must mean 'new' not to St. specifically but in a more general sense, i.e. St. here appears to be referring to the custom of the *cena recta* (formal dinner), which had been reintroduced by Domitian (Suet. *Dom.* 7. 1) after Nero had removed it in favour of the *sportula* (Suet. *Nero* 16. 2): see introduction above.

6. **dominam ... mensam:** Domitian, as host and head of the imperial household, plays the role of *dominus*. He also expected to be referred to as *dominus et deus* (Suet. *Dom.* 13. 2). So here the adjective *domina*, describing Domitian's dinner-table, signifies its imperial ownership: cf. Mart. 1. 4. 2 (where the meaning of *dominum* is amplified by the defining genitive *terrarum*) 'Caesar ... terrarum dominum pone supercilium', and see *TLL* v. 1941. 31–55.

contingere: the privilege consists of reclining at dinner with the emperor: cf. *uideor discumbere* (10). St. was impressed by the apparent breach of etiquette: cf. 17 'et non assurgere fas est?' Hence *consurgere* (M) seems contradictory: to stand in the presence of another was a mark of deference and respect; thus Tiberius, observing the proprieties (unlike Caesar: Suet. *Jul.* 78. 1–2), rose to greet the senate (Suet. *Tib.* 17. 2). Vollmer understands *consurgere* in the transferred sense of 'to be exalted': cf. Ov. *Pont.* 3. 3. 31 f. (claiming that Love thwarted his ambitions to write lyric) 'nec me Maeonio consurgere carmine ... passus es', *S.* 1. 2. 262 f. (of Arruntius Stella's home-town Naples) 'nitidum consurgat ad aethera tellus / Eubois'; but in the context of a dinner-party it would be obvious to take *consurgere* literally and not metaphorically. *non surgere* (Ellis) pre-empts the climax at l. 17. *considere* (Markland) describes the wrong posture. Waller's suggestion *dominamque dedit contingere mensam* could have produced *domina ... mensa* through simple failure to note two supralinear strokes; thence followed change from *contingere* to *consurgere*, to restore syntax. *TLL* iv. 715. 44–74 lists examples of *contingere* meaning 'to reach' a place; a close parallel for Waller's conjecture is Sil. 13. 292 'adit omnia iamque / concilia ac mensas contingit et, abdita nube, / accumbitque toris epulaturque improba Erinys'. The diction combines something of the flavour of the English phrase 'attain to', conveying the notion of an exalted and desirable goal, and the idea of sacred contact established by the suppliant who touches the altar (see C. Sittl, *Die Gebärden der Griechen und Römer* [Leipzig, 1890], 318 and n. 2). The metaphor of touch is used to describe the approach to Jupiter's throne: cf. Hor. *Epist.* 1. 17. 34 'attingit solium Iouis et caelestia temptat', Petr. *Sat.* 51. 5 'hoc facto putabat se solium Iouis tenere', *S.* 3. 1. 25 f. 'tui solium Iouis ... tenes'. After the *exempla* of the journeys of Aeneas and Odysseus, a verb implying motion to attain a goal is appropriate: St. has 'made it' to Domitian's dinner-table.

7. quas: Vollmer prints *qua* for *quas* on the grounds that *sufficiam* needs a reference to means to fulfil the sense. But Håkanson, 113, shows that *quas grates (per)soluere* is a natural expression, quoting Val. Fl. *Arg.* 4. 629 f. '"quaenam tibi praemia," dixit / "quas, decus o Boreae, possim persoluere grates?"' In both St. and Valerius *quas ... gratis* is heavily emphatic; for the qualitative notion in the interrogative adjective and pronoun *qui* see K–S i. 655.

8. non si: equivalent to οὐδ' εἰ introducing a hyperbolic hypothesis. The thought is first expressed by Homer, embarking on the catalogue of the ships (*Il.* 2. 489) οὐδ' εἴ μοι δέκα μὲν γλῶσσαι, δέκα δὲ στόματ' εἶεν, adapted by Virgil (*G.* 2. 42–4) 'non ego cuncta meis amplecti uersibus opto, / non mihi si linguae centum sint oraque centum, / ferrea uox'. P. Courcelle, *REL* 33 (1955), 231–40, points out that this expression is a type of adynaton particularly suited to panegyric themes. Menander recommends this type of expression for all epideictic subjects and especially for the proem to a βασιλικὸς λόγος (*Rhet. Gr.* iii. 368. 22–369. 2 Sp.) εἰ λέγοιμεν ... βασιλέως εὐφημίαν λόγωι περιλαβεῖν οὐ ῥάιδιον. The topos of inability points up the poetic excellence which is (claimed to be) demanded by an imperial theme. Compare St.'s reluctance to embark on an epic about Domitian (4. 4. 95–100).

9. adoratas: the epithet *odoratus* (M) is odd because bay has no distinctive scent. Håkanson, 113, supports *adoratas* (ς), appealing to the analogy of *Theb.* 10. 254 '[Thiodamas] ponit adoratas Phoebea insignia frondes'. This use would be parallel to the use of *laudatus* for *laudabilis*, for which Håkanson, 165, cites *S.* 3. 3. 7, 4. 6. The inspiring properties of bay prompt Thiodamas to venerate the prophetic wreath (*Theb.* 8. 284) 'oblatas frondes submissus adorat'. St. uses the same term in instructing the *Thebaid* to pay homage to its Virgilian predecessor (*Theb.* 12. 816 f.) 'nec tu diuinam Aeneida tempta, / sed longe sequere et uestigia semper adora'. St. says that even if he were to receive the holy wreath of inspiration from Homer and Virgil he would not be able to do justice to his theme.

Smyrna: this was the educated spelling in the first century AD. A sibilant was voiced before a nasal: see W. S. Allen, *Vox Graeca*² (Cambridge, 1974), 44. This contaminated the spelling: the form with Z, widely attested on inscriptions, is faulted at Prisc. *GL* ii. 42 Keil 'in semiuocalibus similiter aut aliae praepositae aliis semiuocalibus in eadem syllaba, ut . . . s . . . sequente m, ut "Smyrna", "smaragdus": nam uitium faciunt qui zm scribunt; numquam enim duplex in capite syllabae posita potest cum alia iungi consonante'. Priscian quotes the end of the hexameter at Luc. 10. 121 'distincta smaragdo'. See W. S. Allen, *Vox Latina*² (Cambridge, 1978), 46 and cf. Sext. Emp. *Adu. gramm.* 169, Schol. Lond. 'Dion. Thr.' 504. 14–15 Hilgard (also Ael. Dion. fr. 187 Schwabe). Smyrna vies with Chios (and other less popular candidates) as the traditional birthplace of Homer: see *RE* viii. 2166 (Rzach). It is a common mannerism to refer to a poet's birthplace instead of naming him: cf. *S.* 4. 7. 27, Juv. 1. 20 (Lucilius) 'Auruncae . . . alumnus', 51 (Horace) 'haec ego non credam Venusina digna lucerna'.

11. Iliaca ... dextra: periphrasis for the Olympian cupbearer, Ganymede, i.e. Domitian is compared to Jupiter.

12. immortale merum: in the exalted atmosphere of Domitian's banquet the wine tastes like 'wine of the gods', i.e. nectar. Compare St.'s description of vine-covered slopes at Surrentum (*S.* 2. 2. 99) 'madidas Baccheo nectare rupis'. The subsidiary notion of a vintage so fine that it is ageless is a link in St.'s chain of thought leading him to regard his own past, by comparison, as a waste of time (*sterilis . . . annos*). St.'s metaphor of a heavenly banquet matches the details in an epigram by Martial published in 93 in which he claims that before Domitian built his palace on the Palatine there was no venue suitable for such exalted banquets: see 8. 39. 3 f. 'hic haurire decet sacrum, Germanice, nectar / et Ganymedea pocula mixta manu'; he also expresses the conventional wish that Domitian will not leave earth for heaven just yet (8. 39. 5: cf. on l. 22 below), and he invites Jupiter to attend Domitian's banquet instead (8. 39. 6: cf. l. 11 above).

sterilis ... annos: M. A. H. Maestre Yenes, *Emerita* 39 (1971), 435–53, interprets *sterilis . . . annos* as a period in which St. has been out of Domitian's favour, which he dates from the cluster of poems in Books 1–3 that can be assigned to the period around AD 90. It would, however, be tactless for St. to refer to any period when he was out of Domitian's favour. The point of *sterilis . . . annos* is to introduce the imagery of rebirth, 'haec aeui mihi prima dies, hic limina uitae'. Similarly in the *soteria* to Rutilius Gallicus St. dismisses the past to concentrate on the present as a new beginning (1. 4. 124 f.) 'nemo modum transmissi computet aeui: / hic uitae natalis erit'. To equate the *beneficia* of the present with a second birth is also a topos of political rhetoric, as in Cicero's assessment of his speech which he delivered to the senate on 5 December 63 (*Flacc.* 102) 'o Nonae illae Decembres, quae me consule fuistis! quem ego diem uere natalem huius urbis aut certe salutarem appellare possum': compare *Cat.* 3. 2 and Cicero's notorious line from the poem *De Consulatu Suo* (fr. 17 Morel) 'o fortunatam natam me consule Romam'.

14–15. The poem develops as an εὐχαριστικὸς ὕμνος: the anaphora of *te* with noun phrases in apposition recalls the language of hymns. The hymn is appropriate to the symposiastic context: cf. Virg. *A.* 6. 657 'uescentes laetumque choro paeana canentes', and Norden's note: 'δείπνου mit folgender σπονδή [cf. *immortale merum*] und dem diese begleitenden παιάν'.

14. tene ego: juxtaposition of emperor and poet emphasizes the egalitarianism and informality which St. attributes to Domitian. Cf. *S.* 1. 6. 43–50, describing a banquet to celebrate the Kalends of December, where St. marvels at Domitian's accessibility to the common people; Martial remarks on a banquet at which Domitian dined with all levels of society (8. 50. 7 f.) 'uescitur omnis eques tecum populusque patresque, / et capit ambrosias cum duce Roma dapes'; Suet. *Dom.* 4. 5 describes a public feast in which Domitian participated. The theme of equality is amplified in *cerno iacens* (16) with the paradox that St. is observing the emperor from a recumbent position instead of standing up in his presence.

regnator terrarum: St. presses to its logical conclusion the illusion of a banquet in heaven: his host would have been Jupiter, king of heaven; hence his real host, Domitian, is king on earth. Cf. 4. 3. 128 f. (Domitian as Jupiter's vicegerent) 'hunc iubet beatis / pro se Iuppiter imperare terris'.

14–15. orbisque subacti / magne parens imputes to Domitian both military conquests and power over nature. Power to arrest natural forces is an attribute of heroes and demigods which St. ascribes to Domitian at 4. 3. 135 (cf. 4. 3. 24–6).

16. datur ... datur: for the word-order see 4. 1. 40–1 n. The second *datur*, as well as underlining St.'s incredulity by means of anaphora, introduces a Virgilian reminiscence appropriate to the heroic tone, recalling Anchises' incredulous welcome to Aeneas in the Underworld (*A.* 6. 688) 'datur ora tueri, / nate, tua et notas audire et reddere uoces?'

17. uina inter: anastrophe is frequently attested in poetry when a preposition governs a pair of nouns. A parallel example in St. occurs at *Theb.* 2. 59 'arua super populosque meat'. See N–W ii. 945.

assurgere: the compound form is the *uox propria* when the action is a gesture of respect: see *TLL* ii. 938. 3–38. St. expresses another paradox to illustrate Domitian's *comitas*: the etiquette which he prescribes at the banquet requires St. to flout the convention of rising in the presence of the emperor. See on l. 6.

fas est: court-etiquette is described in religious language. This accords with the atmosphere of the εὐχαριστικὸς ὕμνος and, no doubt, with the attitude of an emperor who claimed for himself divine honours (Suet. *Dom.* 13. 2). This sentence could theoretically be punctuated as a statement or a question. However, after the rhetorical question *tene ego ... cerno iacens* a prosaic answer would be banal, whereas another question sustains the hyperbolic tone.

18. The *ecphrasis* of the Domus Domitiana (18–31) concentrates on the scale and luxury of the building and its decoration, in particular the variety of marble: cf. *S.* 1. 2. 148 ff. (the home of Stella and Violentilla), 5. 36 ff. (the baths of Claudius Etruscus), 2. 2. 85 ff. (the villa of Pollius Felix). In contrast to this selectivity, however, at *S.* 1. 3 he offers a comprehensive description of Manilius Vopiscus' villa: cf. Pliny's detailed accounts of his villas (*Epist.* 2. 17, 5. 6). At *S.* 4. 2, where the environment is only a backdrop for Domitian himself, St. dwells on stunning features to demonstrate that the emperor overshadows even these.

The purpose of an *ecphrasis* of a man-made object is to emphasize the wealth and imagination of its founder: cf. Theoc. 15. 83 (Praxinoa admiring the tapestries in Ptolemy's palace) σοφόν τι χρῆμ' ἄνθρωπος. The *ecphrasis* also flatters the founder by implying that the poet, privileged to have witnessed the monument, describes it for the benefit of those who have not had this privilege: cf. Theoc. 15. 25 (Gorgo's maxim at the sight of the Adonis display) ὧν ἴδες, ὧν εἴπαις κεν ἰδοῖσα τὺ τῶι μὴ ἰδόντι. The grandeur also throws into relief the informality and accessibility of the emperor (cf. l. 17).

St.'s *ecphrasis* displays elegant handling of literary topoi and influences. Line 18 is a reminiscence of Virg. *A.* 7. 170 'tectum augustum, ingens, centum sublime columnis', preserving its predominantly epic features: the spondaic solemnity, the religious flavour of *augustum* (cf. Fordyce on Virg. *A.* 7. 153), and the grandeur of *ingens*, enhanced by its position (Fordyce, *A.* 7. 29). He outdoes the dimensions of Virgil's palace with the paradoxical litotes *non centum insigne columnis*.

Domitian's architect Rabirius designed the Flavian Palace, which was built over the remains of Nero's Domus Aurea in the depression between the Cermalus and the Palatium. It was probably completed in AD 92 and used for state functions: see Mart. 7. 56, 8. 36, *S.* 1. 1. 34. This is the palace described in *S.* 4. 2: see Platner–Ashby, 158–66. South of it on the Palatium Rabirius designed the Domus Augustana, which was probably where Domitian actually lived: see H. Finsen, *Domus Flavia sur le Palatin; Aula Regia — Basilica*, Analecta Romana Instituti Danici II, Supplementum (Copenhagen, 1962) and *La Résidence de Domitien sur le Palatin*, Analecta Romana Instituti Danici V, Supplementum (Copenhagen, 1969).

19. quantae: equivalent to *quot*; also at 4. 3. 49, and Prop. 1. 5. 10, Hor. *O.* 1. 15. 10. Similar uses of *tanti* and *magni* demonstrate a general poetic tendency to prefer the quantitative adjective instead of the numerical one: see Prop. 4. 11. 12, Man. 5. 170, Luc. 9. 34, Val. Fl. 5. 273, with L–H–S 207 and 758, where the phenomenon is regarded as part of a natural reaction against short, weak-sounding words.

Atlante remisso: there is a touch of humour in this phrase, as though Atlas were relaxing on a day's leave; *remitto* carries overtones of informality: cf. Cic. *Cael.* 13 'cum tristibus seuere, cum remissis iucunde ... uiuere'; *S.* 4. 6. 1–4 'forte remittentem curas ... rapuit me cena benigni / Vindicis'; 5. 3. 248 f. 'ubi dulce remitti, / gratia quae dictis?' See *OLD* s.v. *remitto* 9.

20. sustentare: the intensive form of the verb stresses the number of columns required to support a ceiling equivalent to the vault of heaven. The image of the ceiling like the sky is sustained at l. 30. The comparison suggests that the roof was a dome: cf. Platner–Ashby, 170 (a domed room in Nero's Domus Aurea).

20–1. uicina Tonantis / regia: the personification (*stupet*) implies that St. is thinking of a splendidly decorated temple of Jupiter which nevertheless pales into insignificance beside the Flavian palace. The hyperbole is greatest if he is referring to the temple of Jupiter Optimus Maximus Capitolinus. This is the temple which Claudian calls *tecta Tonantis* (*VI cons. Hon.* 44): see L. Jeep, *RhM* 27 (1872), 269–77. It was restored by Domitian (Suet. *Dom.* 5) and was notorious for its cost (12,000 talents: Plut. *Publ.* 15). Hence *uicina* refers to the geographical proximity of the Capitoline and Palatine hills. St. calls the temple *Tonantis regia* to recall that Jupiter is *rex deorum*; his temple, personified, is in awe of Domitian's palace, which implies that Domitian has the status of *rex* on earth.

21. pari . . . sede: the gods are glad that Domitian is accommodated in a palace comparable to the temple of Jupiter Optimus Maximus on the Capitoline. Vollmer understands *numina* as the deities to whom temples nearby were dedicated, but the compliment surely depends upon unanimity in heaven, i.e. *numina* refers to the gods in general.

22. nec . . . caelum: a variation of the theme *serus in caelum redeas* (Hor. *O.* 1. 2. 45): cf. *S.* 1. 1. 106 'nec te caeli iuuet aula'.

   escendere: the accusative of the goal (*magnum . . . caelum*) with *excedere* (M) is very awkward, hence Lundström's suggestion *ne in* for *nec*. But *excedere* is in any case a colourless word; in the context of apotheosis the notion of elevation to heavenly rank is appropriately conveyed by *escendere* (Gronovius). A direct object after *escendere* is attested (especially with modes of transport, e.g. Sen. *Dial.* 7. 23. 4 'escendere . . . vehiculum'). A parallel for St.'s context occurs at Tac. *Ann.* 13. 5. 3 'escendere suggestum imperatoris': just as it is natural to mount a platform, so Domitian on his (presumed) apotheosis may be said to 'mount heaven'.

23. effusaeque impetus aulae: this phrase is a recollection of Lucr. 5. 200, where *impetus* with spatial reference is used in the context of the sky ('quantum caeli tegit impetus ingens'); *impes* is likewise used of spatial extent in Lucr. 4. 416 f. 'despectum praebet sub terras impete tanto / a terris quantum caeli patet altus hiatus' and at 5. 913 f. 'hominem tanto membrorum esse impete natum / trans maria alta pedum nisus ut ponere posset'.

24. campi: Vollmer punctuates with a comma after *liberior* and takes *multum* ἀπὸ κοινοῦ with *campi* and *aetheros*. But *liberior* needs a comparison to give it point: hence Domitius's *campo*. But in an urban context this smacks of the Campus Martius, which would be too limiting for St.'s hyperbole. If, however, with *campi* one supplies *impetu* from *impetus* (23) (see Håkanson, 114), the sense is that Domitian's palatial structure is more spacious than a stretch of open ground. *spatii* (Markland) seems colourless beside *campi*, and a noun alluding to the ground points a contrast with *aetheros* (25).

   operti: the dome of Domitian's palace is so vast that it appears to cover a large part of the sky. Just as the ground area is more spacious than a plain, so the roof-space appears to enclose part of the upper atmosphere, which is precisely the element of the universe which cannot be contained. The sky is naturally assumed to be open: hence *aperti* (ς) is lame. The paradox of a covered sky (*operti aetheros*) is appropriately hyperbolic. The implication that the emperor has put a vault over part of heaven accords with St.'s flattery that Domitian can exercise power over nature: see on ll. 14–15.

25. tantum domino minor: cf. Martial's description of the palace (8. 36. 1) 'par domus est caelo, sed minor est domino'. The charisma and supernatural status which St. accords to Domitian subtly blurs the distinction between man and god. In the following clauses (*ille . . . grauat*) St. amplifies the assertion *domino minor*, and so there should be a colon after *minor*.

penatis: with *implet*, *penatis* is to be understood in its transferred sense as metonymy for 'household': cf. 5. 2. 170 f. 'fama uelocior intrat / nuntius atque tuos implet, Crispine, penatis?', Luc. 5. 536 f. 'ne cessa praebere deo tua fata uolenti / angustos opibus subitis inplere penates'. Domitian's presence and forceful personality dominate the surroundings. St. picks up this theme at l. 40. Pliny makes a prosaic statement of a similar idea at *Pan.* 15. 4 'tectum magnus hospes impleueris'; the hyperbole in St., however, is much more extreme because *penatis* represents a palace, not merely the ordinary dimensions of a *tectum*.

26. grauat: after *implet*, *iuuat* (M) is weak. Furthermore *penatis*, after meaning 'household' with *implet*, would have to be taken with *iuuat* as 'household gods'; this is somewhat strained, and confusing. *grauat* (Schwartz) continues the physical metaphor in *implet*: if Domitian's palace is full of his personality it must be weighed down by it. H. Wagenvoort, *Roman Dynamism* (Oxford, 1947), 114 ff., demonstrates that the quality of *grauitas* was derived from the notion that gods or influential persons were physically heavy: cf. Aeneas in Charon's boat on the Styx (Virg. *A.* 6. 414 f.). St. twice explicitly attributes this feature to Domitian: cf. *S.* 1. 1. 18–20 'exhaustis Martem non altius armis / Bistonius portat sonipes magnoque superbit / pondere', 56 f. 'insessaque pondere tanto / subter anhelat humus'; cf. also *Theb.* 7. 750 f. (of Apollo) 'ingentique uiro magnoque grauatus / temo deo'.

aemulus: it was fashionable to combine different variegated marbles: cf. *S.* 1. 2. 148–57 (the description of Violentilla's house at Rome), 1. 5. 36–43 (Claudius Etruscus' bath), 2. 2. 85–94 (Pollius Felix' villa), Mart. 6. 42. 11–13, Lucian, *Hipp.* 5. *aemulus* refers to the contrasting colours in the decoration (*nitet*, *glaucae*), not, as Vollmer believes, to different uses for the different types: a special use is only specified for marble from Luna (29). Martial conceives of different colours competing with each other (6. 42. 12) 'certant uario decore saxa'. St. sustains the metaphor of competition with *certantia . . . saxa*. This is a modification of the topos of ὑπεροχή ('preeminence'), which is a feature of Hellenistic panegyric: see Curtius, 162 n. 63. Here it is not the encomiast's subject who proves his superiority; instead, inanimate objects (types of marble) are personified competing with each other to win his favour (by proving which is most decorative).

27. mons Libys Iliacusque: for the varieties of marble listed by St. see R. Gnoli, *Marmora Romana* (Rome, 1971), 18 f. *mons Libys* is Numidian marble from Simitthus in north-west Tunisia. *Iliacus* is Synnadian marble quarried at Docimio. *Syene* refers to Aswan in southern Egypt, famed not for marble but for its rose-coloured granite: see Plin. *NH* 36. 63 'circa Syenen uero Thebaidis syenitis quem antea pyrrhopoecilon uocabant', *RE* ivA. 1020 (Kees).

simul atra Syene: some editors have tried connectives to fill the lacuna between *nitet* and *multa* in M, and to remove the asyndeton. *hic* (Baehrens), to balance *illic* (26), requires *nitet* to be lengthened under the ictus, which is an unsatisfactory remedy. But the damage surely extends to *multa*, since it is not quantity but qualities (*nitet, glaucae*) which are being stressed. The corruption probably does not conceal a verb, since *nitet* can be understood with all the subjects listed in the sentence: for a singular verb with a list of subjects attached see Bentley on Hor. *O.* 1. 24. 8. Various epithets have been tried: *Nilaea* (Slater) would create a stylistic imbalance, since Syene would be the only name in the list with an additional geographical epithet; *cumulata* (Phillimore) matches the vast scale of the decoration; *coniuncta* (J. Delz, *Mus. Hel.* 30 [1973], 126) suggests a mosaic arrangement of different-coloured marble, i.e. *opus sectile*; preferable, however, to a generally applicable notion would be *maculata* (suggested to me by Professor Nisbet), alluding to the mottled appearance of *syenites* implied by Pliny's *pyrrhopoecilon* (see previous n.). But ⟨*si*⟩*mul at*⟨*ra*⟩, communicated to me by Professor W. S. Watt (see *WJA* NS 14 [1988], forthcoming), is most appropriate, since it removes the asyndeton and conveys another characteristic ascribed to *Syenites*, its dark appearance (attributed to weathering by Kees, *RE* ivA. 1020. 30 ff.): cf. Diod. 1. 47. 3 λίθου μέλανος τοῦ Συηνίτου, Strabo 17. 1. 33. That this dark stone is the same as the red *Syenites* is proved by the lower courses of the third pyramid at Giza, which are made of red granite called λίθου Αἰθιοπικοῦ at Hdt. 2. 134. 1 and μέλανος λίθου τῶι Θηβαικῶι παραπλησίου at Diod. 1. 64. 7. *ater*, 'murky', forms a characteristically Statian contrast with *nitet*.

28. Chios: marble from Chios was multicoloured: cf. Plin. *NH* 36. 46 'uersicolores istas maculas Chiorum lapicidinae ostenderunt'. Theophr. *Lap.* 7 describes a dark stone in Egypt as translucent like Chian stone, μέλας αὐτόθι διαφανὴς ὅμοιος τῶι Χίωι, hence Coley and Richards ad loc. surmise that Chian marble was probably dark with lighter streaks. At . 1. 3. 36 an unnamed translucent marble with streaks decorates the villa of Manilius Vopiscus: 'picturata lucentia marmora uena'.

glaucae ... Doridi saxa: blue Carystian marble: cf. 1. 2. 149, 2. 2. 93. Doris was daughter of Oceanus and Thetis; the personification of the sea fulfils the human metaphor in *certantia*. The Greek dative *Doridi̇̄* was corrupted to *Doride* (M). Greek datives in Latin texts are prone to corruption; a similar situation obtains at Sil. 9. 478 'aegidi (*Bentley*: aegide *codd.*: aegida *ed. Rom. 1*) praecellant quantum horrida fulmina nosces'; for the dative with *praecello* cf. Sil. 15. 72–4. For the Greek dative in *ī* N–W i. 457 cite two other instances in St. (*Theb.* 3. 521, *Ach.* 1. 285) and two in Catullus (64. 247, 66. 70).

29. Luna: cf. 4. 4. 23 'metallifera Luna'. Carraran marble was quarried at Luna in Etruria and exported as far afield as Gaul and Africa: see Gnoli (op. cit. on l. 27), 229. Strabo (5. 2. 5) records that most of the buildings at Rome and elsewhere in Italy were adorned with it. In the Augustan era it was bluish, but by the time of the elder Pliny the quarries at Luna yielded a radiant white variety (Plin. *NH* 36. 135). Mozley explains St.'s line: Carraran marble, being white, was considered inferior to multicoloured varieties, and so it was only supplied to form the base for columns of more exotic hues. On the quarrying of marble see J. B. Ward-Perkins, *Proc. Brit. Acad.* 57 (1971), 137–58.

31. aurati ... laquearia caeli: the roof of Domitian's palace, designed by the architect Rabirius, is compared with the sky by Mart. 7. 56. 1 f. 'astra polumque pia cepisti mente, Rabiri, / Parrhasiam mira qui struis arte domum'. For ceilings gilded like the star-studded heavens cf. also Man. 1. 532 'haec igitur texunt aequali sidera tractu / ignibus in uarias caelum laqueantia formas', *S.* 4. 3. 19 n. For elaborate gold and ivory inlaid ceilings as a sign of wealth cf. Hor. *O.* 2. 18. 1 f. 'non ebur neque aureum / mea renidet in domo lacunar'. The private houses of the wealthy could boast gilded beams; St. regards these as an item sufficiently luxurious to be mentioned in the description of Manilius Vopiscus' villa (1. 3. 35).

32. Romuleos proceres: this periphrasis for the senate recalls the authority vested in it by Romulus. For the elevated tone of *proceres* see Bömer on Ov. *Met.* 3. 530: the *Metamorphoses* and *Fasti* contain sixteen examples against a single instance in the rest of Ovid's work.

32–3. trabeata ... agmina: periphrasis for the *equites*. The *trabea* was the cloak which they wore on formal occasions including the *transuectio equitum*: see Dion. Hal. 6. 13, Val. Max. 2. 2. 9. It is mentioned as characteristic of them in a periphrasis at 5. 2. 17 f. 'non sanguine cretus / turmali trabeaque recens et paupere clauo': cf. Mart. 5. 41. 5. *agmina* may recall the military origins of qualification for the equestrian class.

34. Ceres Bacchusque: the image of Ceres and Bacchus serving at Domitian's banquet is rooted in the traditional presentation of corn and wine as the gods' first gift to mankind, elaborated in the references to Triptolemus and Lyaeus (Bacchus), 35–7. The image recalls Hephaistos bustling round at Zeus' banquet serving the other gods (*Il.* 1. 597–600). Here it is not fellow-gods but mortals who are receiving divine table-service. The concept of divinities giving Domitian specialist service also occurs at 4. 1. 22 (Minerva weaving Domitian's consular toga).

35. sufficere: a key motif of the poem is whether the standards which Domitian deserves can be attained; the scale of effort required is stressed, by the repetition: cf. *sufficiam* (8). The enjambment and the prominent position of *sufficere* emphasize the toil. The divine context and the verbal arrangement are a reminiscence of Virg. *A.* 9. 802–4 'nec contra uiris audet Saturnia Iuno / sufficere; aeriam caelo nam Iuppiter Irim / demisit'. Both passages share the enjambment; the position of *sufficere* is the same, followed by a sense-pause and elision with an adjective denoting motion through the upper atmosphere and describing a heroic or divine figure; the rhythm of l. 35 is identical with *A.* 9. 803.

aetherii ... (36) Triptolemi: Demeter (Ceres) delegated to Triptolemus the dissemination of corn. This legend, although probably older than the *HHDem.*, is excluded from it, and is first attested in the third quarter of the sixth century on two black-figure vases which depict Triptolemus on a wheeled apparatus, holding ears of corn (J. D. Beazley, *Attic Black-figure Vase-painters* [Oxford, 1956], 308, 309). Later his vehicle acquires wings and is drawn by snakes, the familiars of Demeter: see Richardson on

HHDem. 153, *RE* viiA. 213–30 (Schwenn). Triptolemus appears in full regalia and states his mission at Ov. *Met.* 5. 642–56.

felix ... orbita: *orbita* describes the path of Triptolemus' vehicle through the air: cf. *orbita* of heavenly bodies (*OLD* s.v. *orbita* 2). The root of *felix* denotes fecundity. One would expect a furrow, ploughed and sown, to be called *felix*. Here St. transfers the concept to the invisible rut which Triptolemus' wheel makes in the air; he can call it *felix* not because the air itself is fertile but because Triptolemus in mid-flight scatters the seed upon the earth below.

36. uuifero: *uitifero* (M) cannot qualify *palmite*, whether *palmite* is understood in its primary meaning of 'vine-shoot' or as metonymy for the whole vine. *uitiferus* ('vine-bearing') would describe one of the support trees, not the vine itself or any part of it. The hillsides were bare (*nudos*) before Bacchus planted vines to shade them. Shade is provided by branches, leaves, and bunches of grapes. So *uuifero* is an appropriate epithet for *palmite* in this context. Furthermore, the implications of *uuifero* are in antithesis to *sobria*: the landscape was teetotal before Bacchus introduced the intoxicating properties of the grape. For the personification cf. 4. 3. 12 'sobriasque terras'.

37. Lyaeus: this epithet for Dionysus, derived from λύω, denotes the relaxing of inhibitions. For the topos of the therapeutic qualities of wine cf. Hor. *O.* 2. 11. 17 f. 'dissipat Euhius / curas edaces', and see G. Giangrande, *L'Épigramme grecque*, Entretiens Fondation Hardt XIV (Geneva, 1968), 171 f. This title for Bacchus points the contrast with *sobria*: cf. Horace's word-play at *Epod.* 9. 37 f. 'curam metumque Caesaris rerum iuuat / dulci Lyaeo soluere'.

38–9. St. claims that the twenty-line *ecphrasis* illustrates what did not engage his attention: his eyes were for Domitian alone.

Indisque innixa columnis / robora Maurorum: periphrasis for the fashionable and luxurious *mensae citreae*. At 3. 3. 94 similar periphrases denote the materials of citrus-wood and ivory, 'Massylaque robora et Indi / dentis honos'. *CIL* vi. 9258 attests a common guild of citrus-workers and ivory-workers, *citrarii et eborarii*. The table-tops were of citrus wood (*robora Maurorum*), indigenous to Mauretania and prized by collectors: cf. Plin. *NH* 13. 91 'Atlans mons peculiari proditur silua ... confines ei Mauri, quibus plurima arbor citri et mensarum insania'. The citrus tree sends up new growth when it is cut down, and so the stump grows wider; it also produces burr-wood on its trunk and on its branches which is very decorative when sawn: see R. Meiggs, *Trees and Timber in the Ancient Mediterranean World* (Oxford, 1982), 290. The size of the wooden slabs was a status-symbol, and so they were sometimes joined together to form one enormous surface (Plin. *NH* 13. 97). King Ptolemy of Mauretania was reputed to have commissioned a table of two semicircular surfaces joined together; the finished product was 137 cm in diameter and 7.6 cm thick (Plin. *NH* 13. 93): see Blümner, 124.

St.'s description is hyperbolic: for *robur* in the sense of 'timber' see *OLD* s.v. *robur* 3a; *columna* meaning 'table-leg' is unparalleled, but ivory legs were a fashionable embellishment for tables of citrus, which was a dark wood. Seneca had five hundred of these tables (Dio 61. 10. 3). See D–S ii. 446 n. 73 (Alfred Jacob). The elder Pliny claims that in his day Indian elephants were the major source of ivory, the African supply having been severely depleted through human rapacity (*NH* 8. 7). This may be true: literary references to Indian ivory increase at the end of the first century AD, and African elephants were by now hunted as far afield as Cape Prasum (Ptol. 1. 9. 3), probably to be identified with Cabo Delgado in northern Mozambique: see J. O. Thomson, *History of Ancient Geography* (Cambridge, 1948), 275, E. H. Warmington, *The Commerce between the Roman Empire and India* (London, 1974), 164.

The extravagance of purchasing these tables appalled Cato (Fest. 282 Lindsay). Trends in furniture-design provoked Pliny to treat the theme of greed. The taste for adornment adulterated the plain materials used in the olden days: the combination of a citrus-wood slab with ivory legs would presumably be categorized as greedy and luxurious ostentation, just the same as the ivory relief or veneer criticized at *NH* 16. 232, or the imitation wood manufactured out of tortoiseshell (*NH* 16. 233 'sic lectis pretia quaeruntur ... sic citrum pretiosius fieri').

ex ordine: this phrase recalls the context of domestic duty: cf. Virg. *G.* 4. 376 f. 'manibus liquidos dant ordine fontes / germanae, tonsisque ferunt mantelia uillis', *A.* 1. 703 f. 'quinquaginta intus famulae, quibus ordine longam / cura penum struere', *CLE* 1988. 13 'positis ex ordine rebus'. Silius in his description of Hannibal's feast at Capua (11. 275 f.) echoes Virgil: 'posuisse dapes his addita cura, / his adolere focos, his ordine pocula ferre'. Austin, *A.* 1. 703, captures its essence: 'each of the *famulae* had her proper duty'. In combination with *turmae*, *ex ordine* smacks of regimented drill and crack service.

40. cupido: St. is *cupidus* (ἐπίθυμος), governed by Domitian's magnetism. At 2. 2. 9 ff. Pollius and Polla exercise a similar attraction: '[me] placidi facundia Polli / detulit et nitidae iuuenilis gratia Pollae, / flectere iam cupidum gressus'; at 4. 2. 40 St.'s ἐπιθυμία is more urgent: in the context of the banquet and luxurious surroundings it is a paradox flattering to Domitian that St.'s supreme desire is to keep his gaze fixed on the emperor alone.

41. tranquillum uultus et maiestate serena: Domitian is a model of repose and dignity. The tranquil expression and intense gaze foreshadow the 'Gallienic' style in portraiture of the 250s: see R. MacMullen, *Roman Government's Response to Crisis* (Yale, 1976), 18 f. Cf. also the 'impassivity and stateliness' ascribed to Constantius on his entry into Rome in 357 (Amm. 16. 10. 9 ff.): see M. P. Charlesworth, *JRS* 37 (1947), 36. Charlesworth (34) quotes Xen. *Cyrop.* 8. 1. 42 describing the impassive deportment of Cyrus and suggests (37) that Constantius' pose is part of the imperial image which Diocletian allegedly borrowed from the Persian kings. St.'s description suggests that Domitian already cultivated such deportment; Suetonius' remarks about previous emperors provide further evidence that an ideal of tranquillity in the emperor's bearing was now fashionable: he says that Tiberius was tense and fidgety (*Tib.* 68. 3); he shows Claudius undermining his *auctoritas dignitasque formae* by unseemly behaviour due to his disability and by exhibiting his emotions (*Claud.* 30) 'remisse quid uel serio agentem multa dehonestabant: risus indecens, ira turpior'. (Claudius may have suffered from multiple sclerosis: see A. Esser, *Cäsar und die julisch-claudischen Kaiser im biologisch-ärztlichen Blickfeld*, *Janus*, Suppl. 1, [Leiden, 1958], 167.)

maiestas is an aspect of the relationship between *maiores* and *minores*: gods and men, Rome and other peoples: see R. A. Bauman, *The Crimen Maiestatis in the Roman Republic and Augustan Principate* (Johannesburg, 1967, repr. 1970), 1 ff. Hence it is vested in magistrates as representatives of the *populus Romanus*. Analogous *maiestas* is thus integral to the status of the emperor *vis-à-vis* his subjects, embodying his *dignitas* and *auctoritas*: see *TLL* viii. 156. 1 ff. Domitian's appearance was a source of pride to him (Suet. *Dom.* 18). St. does not describe his features, but alludes to his unmistakable aura (*dissimulatus honos*). His diction comes from the vocabulary of weather: *tranquillum, serena, mulcentem, radios, nitebat*.

42. mulcentem radios: for *mulcere* governing natural forces cf. Sil. 12. 4 'blandis . . . salubre uer zephyris tepido mulcebat rura sereno', *TLL* viii. 1562. 42 ff. St. refreshes the use of this verb by applying it not to the familiar context of storms but with reference to light. Martial also remarks on the serenity of the emperor in a paradoxical phrase which equates him with Jupiter (7. 99. 1 'placidum Tonantem'). The weather-vocabulary contributes to the impression of divinity associated with Domitian: cf. Enn. *Ann.* 446–7 Skutsch 'Iuppiter hic risit tempestatesque serenae / riserunt omnes risu Iouis omnipotentis', Virg. *A.* 1. 254 f. (Jupiter) 'subridens hominum sator atque deorum / uultu, quo caelum tempestatesque serenat'.

The interchangeability of epithets for man and nature reflects the ancient association of the ruler with the heavenly bodies which govern natural phenomena: see O. Weinreich, *NJb* 1926, 647; for the concept of the emperor as νέος Ἥλιος see A. D. Nock, *JHS* 48 (1928), 34 (= *Essays on Religion and the Ancient World*, sel. and ed. Z. Stewart [Oxford, 1972], i. 148). Hence *mulcentem radios* alludes to the association of the ruler with the sun, and *TLL* viii. 1563. 26 is inaccurate in glossing *radios [oculorum]*; Domitian's whole face is aglow (*ore nitebat*): cf. the vision in Rev. 1: 16 ἡ ὄψις αὐτοῦ ὡς ὁ ἥλιος φαίνει ἐν τῆι δυνάμει αὐτοῦ. St. is indeed capable of comparing Domitian's glance to beams of light, but then he makes the comparison explicit (1. 1. 103 f.) 'tua sidereas imitantia flammas / lumina'.

The adoption of sun-imagery continues a feature of earlier imperial propaganda. Gaius is said to have dressed up as Apollo, complete with radiate crown (Philo, *Leg.* 13. 95). Nero was identified with Apollo from early in his reign: see Sen. *Apocol.* 4. 1. 22 f. (with Eden's note), Calp. Sic. 4. 159, *Ecl. Eins.* 1. 37, 2. 38, Luc. 1. 48; his looks were said to recall both Apollo and Mars (Calp. Sic. 7. 83 f.). The image of irradiation was familiar from the crown of rays worn by emperors in coin-portraits, dating from the radiate bust of Augustus minted by Tiberius (Mattingly, *BMC* i. 141). Nero was the first emperor to mint coinage depicting a radiate portrait of himself (Mattingly, *BMC* i. 266 ff.). See further Weinstock, 381–4.

42–3. summittentemque modeste / fortunae uexilla suae: a *uexillum* was a military standard consisting of a cloth banner which was suspended from a transverse bar attached to a vertical pole. (For a description of the only surviving example, preserved in the Pushkin State Museum of Fine Arts in Moscow, see M. Rostovtzeff, *JRS* 32 [1942], 92.) Hence St.'s expression must be a metaphor: Domitian surely did not surround himself with standards and standard-bearers at a banquet. St. is claiming that, despite Domitian's self-effacing gestures (e.g. *mulcentem radios*), his preeminence is unmistakable (*tamen ore nitebat / dissimulatus honos*). The phrase *summittere uexilla* appears to be a calque on *summittere fasces*, the term for dipping the insignia of office as a mark of respect either towards the *populus Romanus* (see Ogilvie on Liv. 2. 7. 8) or from a lesser magistrate to his superior (cf. Plin. *NH* 7. 112). Out of courtesy to his guests Domitian discards the formality which normally characterizes his position. St.'s metaphor is somewhat analogous to the biblical 'hide one's light under a bushel'. The military associations of *uexilla* suit an emperor who prized a military reputation, and they look forward to the impression which St. says that Domitian makes upon foreign foes. Domitian's *modestia* is alleged by Suetonius to have been hypocritical (*Dom.* 2. 2) 'simulauit et ipse mire modestiam'. *modeste* recalls the Epicurean equilibrium maintained by Pollius Felix and mirrored (so St. says) in his surroundings: 2. 2. 28 f. 'nulloque tumultu / stagna modesta iacent dominique imitantia mores'. For Domitian's *pudor* see on 4. 1. 10.

43. ore nitebat: Domitian's high colour (Suet. *Dom.* 18. 1) was variously interpreted: a blush of modesty (Tac. *Hist.* 4. 40. 1); anger (Philostr. *VA* 7. 28); a mask of impudence (Plin. *Pan.* 48. 4, Tac. *Agr.* 45. 2), which is the opposite of St.'s view that, although Domitian tried to hide his distinction, he emitted an aura which gave him away. A divine, tranquil glow is ascribed to Domitian by Martial (5. 6. 9 f.) 'nosti tempora tu Iouis sereni, / cum fulget placido suoque uultu.'

45. ignotae conspectum agnoscere gentes: paradoxically, even tribes at the back of beyond could not fail to recognize Domitian, such was the aura which emanated from him despite his efforts to reduce it; St. exploits the common root of *ignotae* and *agnoscere*. The concept that Domitian was unable to conceal his superiority is reflected in artistic representations where his figure is larger and more prominent than any other, e.g. the Cancellaria relief: see R. Brilliant, *Gesture and Rank in Roman Art; the Use of Gestures to Denote Status in Roman Sculpture and Coinage* (New Haven, Conn., 1963), 101.

46. Rhodopes: south-west of the Haemus range, separating Thrace and Macedonia. According to a Homeric tradition, Thrace was the home of Ares: cf. *Il.* 18. 301, *Od.* 8. 361; see *RE* ii. 642 f. (Sauer). The *exemplum* of Mars exhausted after his exploits in Thrace also illustrates the equestrian statue of Domitian (1. 1. 18 f.). Rhodope was traditionally associated with extreme cold (cf. Virg. *G.* 3: 349–56, Ov. *Her.* 2. 113 'Rhodope glacialis'), remoteness (Virg. *G.* 3. 462), and generally inhospitable terrain (Virg. *E.* 8. 43–5); the reputation of the locale accentuates the relaxation which Mars has won.

47. Gradiuus: *Grādiuus* cannot come from *grădior*, as alleged by Paul. ex Fest. 86. 15 'a gradiendo in bello ultro citroque'. But Grădiuus, where attested, may have arisen from the false etymology (Ov. *Met.* 6. 427, Val. Fl. 5. 650, Sil. 15. 15, 337). The epithet is derived from Grādīuos, the name of an Illyrian deity who became associated with Mars: see E. Norden, *Aus altrömischen Priesterbüchern* (Lund, 1939), 137 n. 1. St. perhaps felt that, in view of the popular etymology, *Gradiuus* was an appropriate epithet in the context of Mars' travels; its juxtaposition with *dimissis equis* makes a neat play upon the (supposedly) pedestrian connotations of the title.

47–8. lubrica ... membra: Pollux' limbs were *lubrica* because all athletes, including boxers, smeared their bodies with oil: see *RE* xvii. 2463 (Pease).

48. Therapnaea ... gymnade: Therapne in the Eurotas valley was particularly associated with the Dioscuri, from where they were said to keep guard over Sparta (Pind. *Nem.* 10. 55): see on 4. 8. 53. So St. (5. 3. 139 f.) naturally depicts Castor and Pollux, victorious after their horse-racing and boxing-match respectively, relaxing in the precincts of their sacred site. St. is not referring to Pollux' fight against King Amycus of the Bebryces (as supposed by Vollmer), which took place on the shores of the Black Sea.

49. Euhan: St., who imagines that the Indians became adherents of the cult of Bacchus when he visited them, portrays them participating in the traditional Bacchic rites and shouting the Bacchic cry (*ululantibus*). Hence he uses the cult-title Euhan for Bacchus here in order to evoke its associations with εὐοῖ: see *RE* vi. 992 (Graf). On the stimulating effect of the bisyllabic chant see J. N. Bremmer, *ZPE* 55 (1984), 279 f. *ululare* is the *uox propria* for ecstatic cries in ritual worship: see Pease on Virg. *A.* 4. 168, *OLD* s.v. *ululo* 2c. For the onomatopoeic effect cf. 1. 3. 85 f. 'cedant uitreae iuga perfida Circes / Dulichiis ululata lupis'.

50. grauis: Vollmer understands 'serious', but this does not fit a hero after successful completion of his labours. *grauis* here functions as a general heroic epithet conveying superhuman proportions of might and physique; Hercules is weighty in bulk and also in authority: cf. Virg. *A.* 5. 437 'stat grauis Entellus nisuque immotus', Sil. 10. 404 'grauis ... Scaeuola bello'; see *TLL* vi. 2. 2278. 40 ff.

horrida iussa: Markland, feeling that *horrida iussa* needed specification, proposed *nouercae* for *reuersus*, alluding to the machinations of Hera whereby Hercules had to perform labours for King Eurystheus of Argos. But the implication in *iussa* is that they refer to the instructions of the person who uttered them, i.e. Eurystheus. They are *horrida* not because of Eurystheus' attitude but because they involve Hercules in danger. *reuersus* gives exactly the right nuance of returning to base, and thus to safety and relaxation.

51. leoni: the name of the animal is commonly used by metonymy for its skin. Examples are collected by Langen on Val. Fl. 6. 704. *leo* denotes the skin of the Nemean lion also at Val. Fl. 8. 126, Mart. 9. 43. 1.

52. parua loquor: St. reiterates the topos of being unable to do justice to a mighty theme: cf. 7 f. He exaggerates the point by referring to his previous examples, two gods and two heroes, as *parua* by comparison with

Domitian; the only suitable illustration left to him is a comparison with Jupiter: cf. Menander Rhetor's prescription for a βασιλικὸς λόγος (*Rhet. Gr.* iii. 368. 23–369. 2 Sp.) ὥσπερ δὲ πελάγους ἀπείρου τοῖς ὀφθαλμοῖς μέτρον οὐκ ἔστι λαβεῖν, οὕτω καὶ βασιλέως εὐφημίαν λόγωι περιλαβεῖν οὐ ῥάιδιον.

†**uultus:** the repetition of *uultus* in the identical position two lines further on arouses suspicion. At l. 54 the thought is entirely appropriate: Jupiter's face glows when he relaxes over a drink of nectar, the heavenly equivalent of wine: cf. Ov. *Met.* 3. 318, 4. 765, Mart. 9. 34. 3, St. *Ach.* 1. 53; Phillimore's *uittas* is not only unnecessary but plainly absurd since the 'middle' use of *diffusus* without reference to the subject's physique would be very strained, and, besides, the notion of Jupiter's wreath stained with spilt nectar is hardly consonant with divine dignity, even in a context illustrating *comitas*. One solution would be to change this second *uultus* to *uultum*, suggested to me by Professor Goodyear, in order to reduce the repetition. But the trouble probably lies with the first *uultus*: after 46–51 a word is required which refers to posture or to appearance in general. The plural *uisus* (Markland) has the wrong reference ('gaze'). *gestus* would be inappropriate, conveying gestures rather than posture. *cultus*, 'elegance', suggested to me by Professor Nisbet, suits the transition in thought from Hercules and his lionskin back to Domitian: it would refer to his appearance overall, not just his clothes, and would thus be appropriate of Domitian's general aspect (*talem*, 44) which generated the comparisons in ll. 46–51. And yet *cultus* refers primarily to external features and would not properly convey Domitian's spontaneous, innate radiance which St. claims is his most striking feature (41–4: cf. 54). Hence no conclusive alternative for *uultus* is apparent.

53–4. mensas ... Aethiopum: a visit by Zeus to the Ethiopians is a conventional feature of epic from Homer onwards: cf. *Il.* 1. 423, *Od.* 1. 22 ff.

55. secreta ... carmina: the Muses and Apollo are the traditional performers at heavenly concerts: Hom. *Il.* 1. 603 f., *HHAp.* 182 ff.; the Gigantomachy is one of their themes: *Theb.* 6. 355 ff., Val. Fl. 5. 692 f. The *carmina* are *secreta* because the Muses are not delivering them to mankind in general, as they usually do, but performing them in private to Jupiter and his hosts the Ethiopians; *secura* (Schwartz) is no more significant.

56. Pallenaeos ... triumphos: Pallene was another name for the Phlegraean fields comprising the southernmost peninsula of the Chalcidice, the site of the Gigantomachy: Hdt. 7. 123. 1–2, Diod. 5. 71, Luc. 7. 150. Mart. 8. 49(50) makes an explicit comparison between Jupiter celebrating after the Gigantomachy and Domitian presiding at a *cena recta*. The theme of the Gigantomachy is attested in both art and literature as an allegorical rendering of historical military campaigns: e.g. the Gigantomachies on the metopes of the Parthenon represented the rout of the Persians, and the Gigantomachy on the Great Altar of Zeus at Pergamum has recently been dated to the last years of the reign of King Eumenes II, celebrating his victory over the Galatians in Asia Minor: see P. J. Callaghan, *BICS* 28 (1981), 115–21; generally, N–H on Hor. *O.* 2. 12. 7.

57–9. St. prays for Domitian's longevity by addressing him directly and expressing the prayer in the form of a wish.

57. **animas ... exaudire:** the metonymy in *animas* ('soul' for 'person') emphasizes the sacral context. *exaudire* is the *uox propria* for granting a suppliant's request: see *TLL* v. 2. 1191. 79 ff.

58. **patriae ... senectae:** Vespasian died aged sixty-nine (Suet. *Vesp.* 24). Hence *bis terque* is a hyperbolic expression of the conventional wish for longevity: cf. on 4. 1. 46 f., 3. 162 f. The present passage is the only example in St. where the desire for longevity is expressed as a prayer. It is prescribed by Menander for the conclusion of a βασιλικὸς λόγος (*Rhet. Gr.* iii. 377. 28–30 Sp.) ἐπὶ τούτοις εὐχὴν ἐρεῖς αἰτῶν παρὰ θεοῦ εἰς μήκιστον χρόνον προελθεῖν τὴν βασιλείαν.

bis terque: this phrase is used loosely to convey indefinite repetition: cf. Ov. *Met.* 4. 516–19 (of the demented Athamas whirling his son round like a stone in a sling) 'parua Learchum / bracchia tendentem rapit et bis terque per auras / more rotat fundae rigidoque infantia saxo / discutit ora ferox'; see *OLD* s.v. *ter* 1b.

59. **rata numina miseris astris:** four Flavians were deified: cf. 1. 1. 96 f. 'ibit in amplexus natus fraterque paterque / et soror: una locum ceruix dabit omnibus astris'. Vespasian was deified by Titus; Titus by Domitian (Suet. *Dom.* 2. 3); Domitilla by Titus or Domitian (cf. Mattingly, *RIC* ii. 312, no. 68, Scott, 48); Domitian's son, born in 73 (Suet. *Dom.* 3), died in childhood and was presumably deified by Domitian even if he died before Domitian's accession: see Scott, 74, with his argument about Domitilla's 'delayed' deification. By prolepsis, *rata* expresses the status which would be accorded to the *numina* by their apotheosis; in deifying individuals, Domitian fulfils their latent divinity: cf. Sen. *Oed.* 572 '"audior" uates ait, "rata uerba fudi..."', and see *OLD* s.v. *ratus* 2b.

60. **templaque des habitesque domos:** the *serus in caelum redeas* theme. St. prays for Domitian to construct more temples for the gods but not to join them yet in their divine abode, i.e. *templa ... des* refers to Domitian's entire programme for building temples, not merely those projects honouring the deified Flavians, and *domos* means human dwellings in general, not specifically (and unimaginatively) the palace. To interpret *domos* as divine dwellings (cf. Barth's *habiles* for *habites*, which, however, contributes nothing noteworthy to the abode of the gods) destroys the climax of flattery: after referring to the Flavian apotheoses and the temple-building programme, St.'s utmost wish for Domitian is that he should remain alive on earth. The chiasmus *templaque des habitesque domos* delays *domos* so as to point the paradox.

61. **nouo Ianum lictore salutes:** the use of *lictor* in the collective singular, *pars pro toto*, is attested at Cic. *Q. fr.* 1. 1. 13, Liv. 28. 27. 15, 33. 1. 6, Sil. 8. 672, 10. 392. For the personification of the new year as the god Janus, and the notion that a new consul in his inaugural ceremony will greet the god, see the speech with which Janus welcomes Domitian upon the assumption of his seventeenth consulship (4. 1. 17–43).

62. **coronatis ... lustris:** *lustrum* was originally the term for a purificatory ceremony, and it became associated particularly with the censors' rites held every five years after the census. Thence it came to denote the censor's term of office and then any period of five years. Perhaps under the

influence of inclusive reckoning, the period became reduced to four years (*TLL* vii. 2. 1884. 30 ff.), and so *lustrum* can describe an Olympiad: cf. *S*. 2. 6. 71–2 'nectere temptabat iuuenum pulcherrimus ille / cum tribus Eleis unam trieterida lustris'. It commonly became used of games which occurred at four-yearly intervals: cf. *S*. 2. 2. 6 (of the Augustalia) 'post patrii . . . quinquennia lustri', *CIL* ix. 2860 (of the Capitoline Games, on the occasion in AD 106 when L. Valerius Pudens, aged thirteen, won a prize) 'certamine sacro Ioui Capitolini lustro sexto claritate ingenii coronatus est'. First prize was an oak-wreath (*S*. 5. 3. 231). When he founded the games, Domitian demonstrated his antiquarian interests by trying to associate the new games with the old Roman *lustrum*: cf. Censor. 18. 13–15 'idem tempus anni magni Romanis fuit, quod lustrum adpellabant . . . rursus tamen annus idem magnus per Capitolinos agonas coeptus est diligentius seruari, quorum agonum primus a Domitiano institutus fuit'. Hence St. may have felt *lustrum* to be the particularly appropriate term here. On the Capitoline Games see Friedländer, ii. 120 f., iv. 264–7.

64. sacra: see on 4 *Pr.* 6.

longo post tempore: what period does St. mean? Interpretations which involve the Capitoline defeat are unconvincing: Härtel, 11, dates it to 94 and interprets *longo post tempore* as hyperbole; Legras, 344, also dates it to 94 and suggests that the disillusioned poet was about to retire when the invitation cheered him up and prompted him to publish Book 4; G. Giri, *RFIC* 35 (1907), 449, dates it to 90 and assumes that St.'s defeat offended Domitian (how?) and resulted in four years of imperial disfavour. But St. is most naturally referring simply to the gap of time since the Alban Games; having referred to future celebrations of the Capitoline Games, he is reminded of his own success at the Alban Games and chooses it to illustrate a happy occasion in the past parallel to that of the dinner.

65. lux evokes the image of joyful day dissipating the miseries of darkness and night: cf. the parodos of the *Antigone* (100 ff.).

Troianae . . . Albae: to help bridge the gap between the landing of the Trojans in Italy and the founding of the city of Rome, tradition has it that Ascanius founded Alba Longa after ruling for thirty years at Lavinium: cf. Virg. *A.* 1. 269 ff., and parallel passages quoted by N. M. Horsfall, *CQ* NS 24 (1974), 111 ff. St. never mentions the town by name without referring explicitly to its Trojan associations: *S*. 3. 1. 61, 4. 5. 2, 5. 2. 168, 3. 38, 227.

66–7. Germanas acies . . . Daca . . . proelia: St.'s theme in his prize-winning entry at the Alban Games was Domitian's action against the Chatti in January 89 for supporting L. Antonius Saturninus in his revolt against Domitian (Suet. *Dom.* 6. 2) and his second campaign against the Dacians in 89 (Suet. *Dom.* 6. 1, Dio. 67. 7). Whether St. merely made reference to the earlier campaigns, against the Chatti in 83 (Suet. *Dom.* 6. 1) and against the Dacians in 86 (Dio 67. 6), or whether he gave them equal prominence alongside the later campaigns we do not know. For the dating of this contest to AD 90 see General Introduction.

COMMENTARY

3

INTRODUCTION

THIS poem celebrates the completion of the Via Domitiana in 95 (Dio 67. 14. 1).[1] It was built along the marshy coastal plain between Sinuessa (6 km north of modern Mondragone) and Puteoli, to shorten the journey between Rome and Naples by eliminating the detour inland to Capua along the Via Appia (Fig. 2). For the ancient itineraries see *CIL* x, p. 58 n. VI. Economic benefits were probably the main aim: the construction of this road has been linked with warehouses for spices (*horrea piperataria*) which Domitian built at Rome in 92.[2] Domitian created an extraordinary post for the official in charge of the construction of this road, a senator (name unknown) who was later *praefectus aerarii Saturni* and consul (*CIL* v. 7812, cf. *Riv. stor. Lig.* 4 [1938], 168 + *AE* 1964, 239) '[. . . curatori uiae n]/ouae faciend(ae) u[sque] / Puteolos, praef(ecto) a[er(arii)] / Saturni, c[o(n)s(uli)] / Soci(i) (uicesimae) libert[at(is)] / [p]atron[o]': see A. Degrassi, *Mem. Acc. Linc.*[8] 11. 3 (1963), 139–69.

Road repairs were undertaken throughout the Empire during Domitian's reign (see Garzetti, 278), but the Via Domitiana was the major new construction project. The propaganda value must have been considerable; Roman leaders had long exploited engineering projects to impress local populations. Caesar bridged the Rhine because a risky boat-crossing 'neque suae neque populi Romani dignitatis esse statuebat' (*BG* 4. 17. 1). A road across the Apennines was one of Caesar's projected enterprises, an extension of his scheme to beautify Rome (Suet. *Jul.* 44. 3) 'uiam munire a mari Supero per Appennini dorsum ad Tiberim usque'. Several ambitious imperial constructions in Campania aroused great admiration: cf. Virg. *G.* 2. 161–4 on Agrippa's *portus Iulius*; Strabo 5. 4. 5–7 on the three tunnels near Naples designed by the Augustan architect Cocceius (from the acropolis at Cumae to the harbour, from under the crater-rim to the shore of L. Avernus, and from Puteoli to Naples under Posilippo), which Frederiksen, 334, points out were negligibly shorter than the overland routes and above all advertised the *magnitudo animi* of their creator; *Anth. Pal.* 7. 379, 9. 708 on the harbour-mole at Puteoli (and also Strabo, cit. above). Campania had seen grandiose but abortive building-projects under Nero: the Stagnum Neronis from Misenum to L. Avernus (never completed) and Nero's projected canal from L. Avernus to Ostia to avoid the dangerous coastline and drain the marshes (Plin. *NH* 14. 61, Tac. *Ann.* 15. 42); St. derides these efforts (see on ll. 7-8), but the Via Domitiana was designed to fulfil the same goals: transport, drainage, and propaganda. Trajan too was admired for his programme of improvements to the road network in Italy: cf. Galen x. 632–3 Kühn, Dio 68. 7. 1. For the view among his subjects that the emperor was directly responsible for these benefits see V. Nutton, 'The Beneficial Ideology', in

---

[1] See General Introduction, n. 18.
[2] See E. H. Warmington, *The Commerce between the Roman Empire and India*[2] (London, 1974), 89.

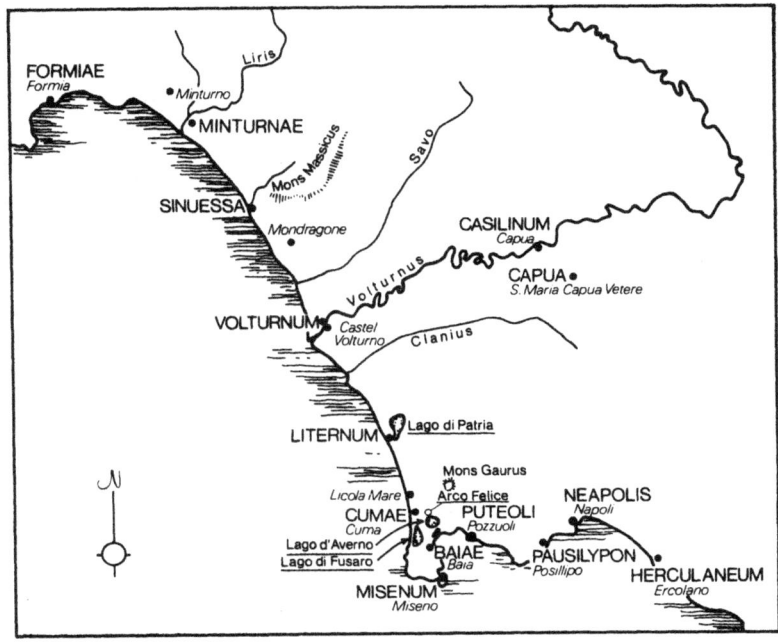

Fig. 2. Map of Northern Campania. Drawing: S. L. Abraham

P. D. A. Garnsey and C. R. Whittaker (eds.), *Imperialism in the Ancient World* (Cambridge, 1978), 209–21.

Terrain, landmarks, and construction could be subjects for encomium. Menander provides general instructions on praising a country (*Rhet. Gr.* iii. 344. 15 ff. Sp.) and a city (iii. 346. 26 ff.), and brief notes on harbours (iii. 351. 20 ff.), bays (iii. 352. 6 ff) and citadels (iii. 352. 10 ff.); praise of cities he expands under the headings of origin (iii. 353. 4 ff.) and accomplishments (iii. 359. 16 ff.) None of his instructions is directly relevant to St.'s poem, and Menander does not deal with roads, but his precedents suggest that in antiquity there was nothing odd about composing encomia for inanimate entities and constructions of this sort.

Building projects also display man's dominion over Nature; for St. they represent the advance of civilization upon a disordered wilderness: cf. the construction of Pollius Felix' villa on the hitherto inaccessible promontory at Surrentum (2. 2. 30–3, 52 f.) 'inde per obliquas erepit porticus arces, / urbis opus, longoque domat saxa aspera dorso. / qua prius obscuro permixti puluere soles / et feritas inamoena uiae, nunc ire uoluptas ... his fauit natura locis, hic uicta colenti / cessit et ignotos docilis mansueuit in usus'. St. attributes to Hercules himself the labour involved in building his shrine at Pollius Felix' villa (3. 1. 19–22) 'deus attulit arces / erexitque suas, atque obluctantia saxa / summouit nitens et magno pectore montem / reppulit': see the discussion by D. Goguey, *Lat.* 41 (1982), 602–13. It is the civilizing aspect which St. above all admires rather than artificiality for its own sake.³

The new road is presented as a miracle wrought by Domitian, and thus, although it is not a panegyric in the formal sense, it recalls the theme of benefaction as a vehicle for praise of the subject in the biographical tradition: cf. Plutarch's praise of the roads built by C. Gracchus, expressing the topoi of utility, beauty, straight routes, paved surfaces, secure foundations, and bridges (Plut. *C. Gracch.* 7. 1) ἐσπούδασε δὲ μάλιστα περὶ τὴν ὁδοποιίαν, τῆς τε χρείας ἅμα καὶ τοῦ πρὸς χάριν καὶ κάλλος ἐπιμεληθείς. εὐθεῖαι γὰρ ἤγοντο διὰ τῶν χωρίων ἀτρεμεῖς· καὶ τὸ μὲν ἐστόρνυτο πέτραι ξεστῆι, τὸ δ' ἄμμου χώμασι νακτῆς ἐπυκνοῦτο. πιμπλαμένων δὲ τῶν κοίλων καὶ ζευγνυμένων γεφύραις ὅσα χείμαρροι διέκοπτον ἢ φάραγγες, ὕψος τε τῶν ἑκατέρωθεν ἴσον καὶ παράλληλον λαμβανόντων, ὁμαλὴν καὶ καλὴν ὄψιν εἶχε δι' ὅλου τὸ ἔργον.

The propaganda value of a road lies chiefly in the feat involved and in the advantages it brings, rather than in the visual impact of the structure itself (especially a cross-country road, remote from large audiences); a roadway looks relatively less impressive than a monument like a building or an arch, hence the symbolism (of a reclining woman holding a wheel and a branch) in coins advertising the Via Traiana. Urban monuments associated with a road promote the achievement of the whole undertaking: Trajan's column commanded a wider audience for Trajan's road along the Danube than the Tabula Traiana on the road itself. Hence poetry is the ideal medium for commemorating a construction with relatively low visual appeal; St. interprets the road as testimony to the *providentia* and *potestas* of the emperor.

The route itself provides a framework for the poem:⁴ ll. 1–66 describe the general terrain and the construction; 67–94 highlight the bridge over the Volturnus, not by straightforward description but by the dramatic technique of attributing to the river-god a eulogy of Domitian as an engineer; 97–113 focus on the triumphal arch where the Via Domitiana branches off the Appia; 114 ff., complementary to the speech delivered by the Volturnus, is a eulogy spoken by the Sibyl of Cumae at the southernmost point of the route. (On St.'s use of divine and mythological spokesmen to express extravagant compliments to his addressees see the introduction to 4. 1.) Cancik, *LK* 34, shows that the two speeches are a development from the introductory catalogue of Domitian's domestic achievements ('Herrscherlob [politisch]'), culminating in the Sibyl's picture of the emperor's cosmic influence. For the combination of *ecphrasis* and encomium that determines the structure of the poem see Cancik, *LK* 108–15, and especially his schematized synopsis (p. 111).

Public ceremonies and celebrations would mark the occasion on which a

³ On the theme of 'marvels of civilization' in the *Siluae* see Pavlovskis.

⁴ An analysis of the poem's structure by Newmyer, 105, confuses content and treatment (e.g. 49–55 are classified as 'personal details of the workers', 61–6 as 'hyperbole'), and in identifying and labelling major subdivisions (e.g. 40–66: 'the road'; 69–96: 'the builder') he mistakenly tries to determine the emphasis of the poem by a simple line-count: e.g. 'Statius accords slightly more space to the Emperor, indicating by structural means that Domitian is the focus of attention.'

POEM THREE 105

building was opened or an engineering project first became operative. Claudius staged a naval battle on the Fucine Lake before opening the tunnel which he had built to drain it into the R. Liris: see Tac. *Ann.* 12. 56. 1 'quo magnificentia operis a pluribus uiseretur, lacu in ipso nauale proelium adornatur', Suet. *Claud.* 21. 6.[5] Such celebrations might be rewarded in verse: cf. Martial's *Liber Spectaculorum* upon the completion of the Flavian Amphitheatre in AD 80. It is tempting to think that St.'s poem was intended as part of such a celebration.

This is the longest hendecasyllabic poem in the *Siluae*: 1. 6 (102 lines) celebrates the festivities sanctioned by Domitian for the Kalends of December; 2. 7 is the *genethliacon* for Lucan requested by his widow (135 lines); 4. 9 is the mock-reproof to Plotius Grypus (55 lines), on which see ad loc. 1. 6 foreshadows St.'s treatment of the imperial theme here; the encomiastic element is present in 2. 7. While 4. 3 is a tribute to Domitian's engineering achievement, 163 hendecasyllables are a *tour de force* to match the subject-matter, and the swift metre is appropriate to the theme. Catullus' successors, especially Martial and St., standardized the spondaic form for the first two syllables of the line, and St.'s hendecasyllabic line generally exhibits word-division after the fifth or sixth syllable: see D. S. Raven, *Latin Metre: An Introduction* (London, 1965), 139 f.

1. **Quis:** cf. the series of questions at 1. 1. 1–7 positing various identities for the sculptor of Domitian's equestrian statue. A question followed by the refutation of possible answers is a technique of priamel to delay and heighten the main theme, which is presented as the true answer: cf. Hor. *O.* 1. 31. 1 ff. The questions at *S.* 1. 1. 1 ff. all imply a divine provenance for the statue, whereas the rejected answers at 4. 3. 4–8 record historical events in Campania and therefore build up an atmosphere of credibility while implying that the present enterprise eclipses the abortive undertakings of the past.

   duri silicis grauisque ferri: St. is referring to the clanging of the workmen's tools against the paving materials. *silex*, flint, is commonly used in construction, especially in paving roads: cf. Liv. 10. 47. 4, *CIL passim*, e.g. x. 5204 'uiam silice sternendam ... curauerunt'.

2. **immanis:** commonly used of very loud noises, especially if harsh and unpleasant: see *OLD* s.v. *immanis* 3c.

   aequori locates the noise on the coastal side of the Via Appia.

3. **saxosae:** not 'stony' (Mozley), since the Via Appia was paved; it was the oldest Roman highway ('regina uiarum', 2. 2. 12), begun by Appius Claudius in 312 BC (Liv. 9. 29, Front. *Aq.* 1. 5, Diod. 20. 36), and the first paving on it outside Rome began in 295 BC (Liv. 10. 47. 4). *saxosus* is here used for *saxeus*, which is the regular adjective for stone constructions: cf. Lucr. 1. 316 'strata ... uiarum saxea', Luc. 4. 15 'saxeus ... pons'.

4. **Libycae ... cateruae:** Hannibal's troops. *Libycus* is used in poetry for

---

[5] After these impressive celebrations the opening ceremony was an anticlimax as the tunnel was not deep enough; but then it was enlarged too much, so that when the ceremony was repeated it provoked a flood and an imperial row (Tac. *Ann.* 12. 57).

'Carthaginian': cf. Ov. *Pont.* 4. 16. 23 'qui ... acies Libycas Romanaque proelia dixit', *OLD* s.v. *Libycus* 2.

5. **peierante bello:** alluding to the 'foedifragi Poeni' (so Politian) and thus establishing the identity of the 'dux aduena' as Hannibal. For the transferred epithet cf. 4. 6. 77–8 'periuroque ense superbus / Hannibal'; Carthaginian untrustworthiness was a byword: see Otto, *Sprichwörter*, no. 1490.

6. **inquietus** implies the tumult and chaos of invasion: cf. Suet. *Tib.* 9. 1 'Comatam Galliam ... barbarorum incursionibus et principum discordia inquietam'.

7–8. For his abortive attempt in 64 to build a canal between Lake Avernus and Ostia Nero was branded as 'incredibilium cupitor' (Tac. *Ann.* 15. 42), 'non in alia re damnosior quam in aedificando' (Suet. *Nero* 31. 1). But Nero can be seen to have made a realistic attempt to overcome the coastal hazards in transporting supplies between Puteoli and Rome; and major engineering projects usually provoked hostility: see Miriam Griffin, *Nero: the End of a Dynasty* (London, 1984), 107 f. Nero's neglect of useful public works was a topos of Flavian propaganda: literary and epigraphic evidence is collected by M. P. Charlesworth, *JRS* 27 (1937), 55 f.

7. **frangit uada:** a canal would cut through the coastal marshes between Avernus and Ostia. For *frangere* = 'cleave' cf. *Ach.* 1. 372 f. 'uolucres ... mollia frangunt / nubila'.

9. **qui:** anaphora of the relative pronoun is characteristic of the high style of sacral language. As the relative clause in hymns denotes the sphere of influence of the deity, so here the implication, complimentary to Domitian, is that his identity is recognizable from the relative clauses describing his feats.

   limina bellicosa Iani: the temple of Janus Quadrifrons: see on 4. 1. 12. *bellicosa*, conjuring up the traditional association of Janus with war, is paradoxically juxtaposed with *legibus et foro*: Domitian's policy is that war is a tool of justice and peace.

10. **coronat:** a poetic synonym for *cingit* (*TLL* iv. 992. 42 ff.), referring to the Forum Transitorium, built by Domitian, which contained the temple of Janus Quadrifrons. *foro*, not *legibus*, is the literal instrument of *coronat*, but by a sort of hendiadys St. alludes to the law-making process in the forum which is exemplified in the next two relative clauses.

11. **qui:** *quis* (M) would limit *legibus* too severely: St. would not suggest that Domitian passed only two worthwhile laws; *qui* sustains the anaphora.

   castae Cereri: the paradox of a mortal doing a deity a favour is complimentary to Domitian: cf. l. 16, and Minerva serving Domitian at 4. 1. 22. *castae* and *sobrias* both convey an air of moral propriety. *TLL* iii. 569. 67 classifies this example of *casta* as a general epithet, i.e. *decens*, *uerecundus*, but its usage here may be more subtle: H. Le Bonniec, *Le Culte de Cérès à Rome* (Paris, 1958), 411 f., interprets *casta* as a reference to sexual taboos connected with the cult of Ceres. His deduction is based on: Tertullian's testimony that chastity was required of priestesses of Ceres in Africa c.200; the obligations of chastity laid upon priestesses of Demeter; Juvenal's claim (6. 50) that most women, being adulterous, would defile the cult of Ceres (although Courtney ad loc. denies a specific allusion to the *castus Cereris*).

11–12. diu ... terras: Campania's fertility led to a proverbial ἀγών: cf. Plin. *NH* 3. 60 'ut ueteres dixere, summum Liberi patris cum Cerere certamen'. By Domitian's vine-edict of 91–2 (Eusebius–Jerome, *Chron.*, p. 191 Helm) or 90 (*Chron. Pasch.*, p. 466 Dindorf) no more vines were to be planted in Italy and half those in the provinces were to be removed (Suet. *Dom.* 7. 2, 14. 2, Philostr. *VS* 520, *VA* 6. 42). Domitian later rescinded this edict (Philostr. *VS* 520). The old view was that Domitian wanted to curb overproduction of wine. But there must have been a demand for it, otherwise farmers would not have neglected other crops in favour of vines: see B. Levick, *Lat.* 41 (1982), 67. Contrast S. Reinach, *Rev. arch.* 1901 (2), 350 f., Millar, 392. Hence Suetonius' explanation coheres with St.'s: the edict was intended to boost the corn-supply, and perhaps also to protect Italian viticulture from external competition: see on 4. 4. 82. R. Duncan-Jones, *The Economy of the Roman Empire* (Cambridge, 1974), 35 n. 4, interprets the edict as moral legislation akin to a licensing law: cf. Philostr. *VS* 520 ἐδόκει τῶι βασιλεῖ μὴ εἶναι τῆι Ἀσίαι ἀμπέλους, ἐπειδὴ ἐν οἴνωι στασιάζειν ἔδοξαν; but Levick, art. cit. 69, observes that a corn-shortage, perhaps caused by an increase in viticulture, could cause riots.

13–15. qui ... formae: Domitian's law against castration in 82: Suet. *Dom.* 7. 1, Mart. 2. 60, 6. 2, 9. 7. 9, *S.* 3. 4. 65 ff., Amm. 18. 4. 5, Philostr. *VA* 6. 42, Dio 67. 2. 3. Philostratus mentions the vine-edict and the castration-edict together so as to record a witticism of Apollonius, λέληθε δὲ ὁ θαυμασιώτατος τῶν μὲν ἀνθρώπων φειδόμενος, τὴν δὲ γῆν εὐνουχίζων. Domitian's edict prohibited *castratio* and θλῖψις. The objection to castration was that it was unnatural: cf. Sen. *Contr.* 10. 4. 17 'principes ... uiri contra naturam diuitias suas exercent: castratorum greges habent', Sen. *Epist.* 122. 7 'non uiuunt contra naturam qui exspectant ut pueritia splendeat tempore alieno?', Quint. 5. 12. 18 f. 'alia quae natura proprie maribus dedit parum existimant decora ... sed mihi naturam intuenti nemo non uir spadone formosior erit'. Domitian's own favourite, Flauius Earinus, was a eunuch, castrated in boyhood (3. 4. 68), before Domitian's edict (73) but painlessly because Asclepius performed the operation: 'haud ullo concussum vulnere corpus' (70). St. equates Domitian's edict with divine prohibition: 'nunc frangere sexum / atque hominem mutare nefas' (3. 4. 74 f.). Likewise the converse is true: Domitian's authority makes unorthodox behaviour *fas*. Cf. 4. 2. 17 n.

13. fortem sexum: as opposed to the 'weak' sex (*mollis*). Hence *mollis* also describes *cinaedi*: Phaedr. 4. 15(16). 1 'tribadas et mollis mares', Mart. 3. 73. 4 (both *cinaedi* and eunuchs). St. hyperbolically postulates universal emasculation were it not for Domitian's intervention.

14. censor: Domitian assumed *censoria potestas* on his return from the Rhine in 84, and became *censor perpetuus* in 85, the first Roman emperor to consolidate his autocratic position by adopting this office. He was keen to present himself as guardian of Roman morals: cf. Suet. *Dom.* 8. 3 'suscepta correctione morum'; St.'s vocabulary here has moral overtones: see on 11 above.

adultos: castration was usually performed before puberty: see M. K. Hopkins, *PCPhS* NS 9 (1963), 79 and n. 1. But Juvenal's claim that eunuchs could sometimes satisfy women's lusts (6. 366 ff.) testifies to post-adolescent castrations: see Courtney's note ad loc. Domitian's prohibition certainly covered *pueri*: cf. Mart. 2. 60. 1 f. 'uxorem armati futuis, puer Hylle, tribuni, / supplicium tantum dum puerile times', 9. 7. 9 f. (Domitian's measure against child prostitution) 'dilexere prius pueri iuuenesque senesque, / at nunc infantes te quoque, Caesar, amant', Amm. 18. 4. 5 'ne ... castraret quisquam puerum'. Domitian's edict presumably forbade castration at any age, and St. covers the general edict in l. 13 and the specific application to post-adolescents in ll. 14 f.

15. pulchrae ... formae: apparently referring to the male physique as a whole: cf. *Priap.* 39. 5 f. 'me pulchra fateor carere forma, / uerum mentula luculenta nostra est'. St. uses the same phrase of women who have good breeding or looks but few morals (5. 1. 51–3) 'laudantur proauis aut pulchrae munere formae, / quae morum caruere bonis, falsaeque (*Heinsius*: falsoque *M*) potentes / laudis egent uerae'.

16. reddit Capitolio Tonantem: from Domitian's legislation St. turns to his public works. The temple of Jupiter Capitolinus, burnt down in 80 (*CIL* vi. 2059), was rebuilt by Domitian in 82: Suet. *Dom.* 5. 1, *S.* 1. 6. 100, Mattingly, *BMC* ii. 351 and pl. 68. 3. Markland notes that St. flatters Domitian the more by reversing the normal order of dedicating a temple to a god: cf. 3. 1. 96–102, where Hercules asks Pollius for a shrine.

17. Pacem propria domo reponit: the Templum Pacis was begun by Vespasian in 71 after the capture of Jerusalem and dedicated in 75 (Suet. *Vesp.* 9. 1, Jos. *BJ* 7. 158), but St. seems to ascribe its completion to Domitian (cf. 4. 1. 13). St.'s claim may be based upon the extensive alterations to the Templum Pacis which were necessitated by the construction of the Forum Transitorium along its north-west side: see J. C. Anderson, *AJA* 86 (1982), 101–10, and *The Historical Topography of the Imperial Fora*, Coll. Lat. (Brussels, 1984), 112, 126–9. Anderson believes that St. confuses Domitian's alterations with the original construction, but the facts must have been well known and it seems more likely that a second dedication (i.e. after the Domitianic alterations) is to be inferred from *reponit*. The notion that the goddess had to vacate her temple while it was being renovated and then Domitian moved her back in again matches the conceit in *reddit Capitolio Tonantem* (see previous n.). A fundamental meaning of *reponere* = 'restore objects to their former position': cf. Val. Max. 5. 1. 6 '[Metellus] litteras misit ut ornamenta templorum suorum a Poenis rapta per legatos recuperarent inque pristinis sedibus reponenda curarent', Tac. *Hist.* 3. 14 'repositis Vitellii imaginibus'. See plan of the imperial fora (Fig. 1) for the asymmetrical development of the south-west façade of the Templum Pacis. The interpretation of alterations in this manner as fundamental construction may lie behind Suetonius' accusation that Domitian took the credit for his predecessors' achievements (*Dom.* 5) 'omnia sub titulo tantum suo ac sine ulla pristini auctoris memoria'.

19. sancit limina Flauuiumque caelum: in the hendecasyllabic metre St. commonly links two related ideas in sentence-units of two or three lines: cf.

11-12, 13-15, 16-17. Hence the two halves of l. 19 should express complementary ideas to form a cohesive whole with l. 18. The legal term *sancit*, with its religious overtones, matches the context of legislation (11-15) and state cult (16-17). The subject is clearly the Flavian cult: *genti patriae*, 18. After ll. 16-17 describing the temples of Jupiter and Pax, the Templum Gentis Flauiae would be a natural topic. But *caluum* (M) is out of the question, since this epithet is excluded from the higher genres: see T. P. Wiseman, *Cinna the Poet* (Leicester, 1974), 148-9. In any case, Domitian was highly sensitive about baldness (Suet. *Dom*. 18. 2), and *Flauium ... caluum* (referring to Vespasian, who was bald) would be no way to denote a late emperor and a god. *lumina* (M) would have to mean *astra* or *sidera* but, although *lumen* is attested of a deified *princeps* (Val. Fl. 1. 16), that is not a precedent for interpreting *lumina* as future generations of deified Flavians.

culmina (Baehrens) ... *cliuum* (Slater) would refer to the Templum Gentis Flauiae. For *culmina* of temples cf. Virg. *A*. 4. 186, 671, Liv. 27. 4. 11, 42. 3. 7. The site of the Templum Gentis Flauiae has been identified as the Quirinal, south of the Alta Semita, probably on the street which is now the Via delle Quattro Fontane; hence *Flauium cliuum* could refer to the Quirinal and would flatter Domitian by implying that the whole Quirinal was known by the temple which he had dedicated there. But the Quirinal was not the only hill with strong Flavian associations, and a phrase describing the temple itself would be more natural: *limina* (ς) is a common metonym for *templum* (*TLL* vii. 2. 1405. 44 ff.) and easily corrupted to *lumina*; but *caluum* as a corruption of *templum* (Otto) or *fanum* (Stange) would be surprising, and neither creates a suitable climax.

caelum (Turnebus), supported by Markland, is a metonym for 'ceiling' at Man. 5. 288 f. 'sculpentem faciet sanctis laquearia templis / condentemque novum caelum per tecta Tonantis', Vitr. 7. 3. 3 'camaris dispositis et intextis imum caelum earum trullissetur'. At 4. 2. 31 St. compares the gilded ceiling of the Domus Domitiana to the sky, 'aurati putes laquearia caeli', which implies that the ornamentation resembled glittering stars: cf. Mart. 7. 56. 1 f. 'astra polumque pia cepisti mente, Rabiri, / Parrhasiam mira qui struis arte domum'. Evidence for ceilings in antiquity decorated like the sky is collected by Karl Lehmann, *Art Bull*. 27 (1945), 1-27. The Templum Gentis Flauiae was probably not domed; domed constructions at this period were almost exclusively tombs, villas, palaces and thermae (including Hadrian's Pantheon, which was part of the Thermae of Agrippa): see Lehmann, 26. However, ceiling canopies decorated like the sky are attested in Nero's Domus Aurea (Lehmann, 12). Gods were depicted amongst the stars: cf. the floor-mosaic from the Villa Rufinella at Tusculum, mid first century AD, showing stars on a blue background with Minerva in the central sphere (Lehmann, 5 f.). Nero's awning in the amphitheatre, 'vela colore caeli stellata' (Plin. *NH* 19. 24), depicted Nero himself in a chariot surrounded by stars (Dio 63. 2). The correspondence between the deified Flavians and stellar decoration on the ceiling of their temple would be a sophisticated conceit. 'Flauium caelum' is a suitable *double entendre*: it actually describes the ceiling of the temple, decorated like heaven; it implies in flattering hyperbole that heaven is guaranteed to be the eternal domain of the Flavian dynasty.

20. segnis populi uias grauatus: Domitian concerning himself with the lot of the people manifests *prouidentia*. For *segnis* of travel cf. Liv. 30. 10. 9 'die segni nauigatione absumpto.'

21. campos ... detinentis: paradox: the level plains, usually facilitating travel, here delay it because of the boggy conditions.

23. grauis: water-logged; hence not *leuis*, as one would expect of sand (nor *cauas*, as Phillimore, app. crit.), but resembling a heavy soil: cf. Cato, *Agr.* 131 'uti [loca] quaeque grauissima et aquosissima erunt'. *grauis* is commonly used in classifying soils, e.g. Plin. *NH* 18. 175 'altum et graue solum'; cf. Cat. 17. 25 'in graui ... caeno'. If *grauis* were proleptic (Bitchofsky), this would cohere awkwardly with the preceding attributive adjectives: cf. 'segnis ... uias', 'campos ... detinentis', 'longos ... ambitus'.

24–6. Three famous areas in the vicinity of the terminus of the Via Domitiana at Puteoli (Dio 67. 14. 1).

24. Euboicae domum Sibyllae: *Euboicae* is a transferred epithet, properly applying not to the Sibyl but to the early Greek colonists on the Bay of Naples: cf. Virgil's reference to Cumae (*A.* 6. 2) 'Euboicis Cumarum ... oris' and to the Sibyl's cave (*A.* 6. 42) 'excisum Euboicae latus ingens rupis in antrum'. For a description of the 'antro' discovered by Maiuri in 1932 which is believed to be the Sibyl's cave, see C. Hardie's note, with diagrams, in *Aeneid* 6, ed. R. G. Austin (Oxford, 1977), 49–58.

25. Gauranos ... sinus: for Mons Gaurus (Monte Barbaro), north-west of Puteoli, see Frederiksen, 37. *sinus* must refer to the lakes at its foot, the Avernus, Lucrinus, and Acherusius: cf. Juv. 8. 85 (oysters from the Lucrine) 'ostrea Gaurana'.

25–6. aestuantis ... Baias: famous for its thermal springs: cf. 3. 5. 96 'uaporiferas ... Baias', Plin. *NH* 31. 4–5. The heating-systems of the baths harnessed this natural phenomenon: see D'Arms, 139–40, with bibliography at n. 112. When Domitian was holding tribunician power for the fifteenth time, i.e. between 13 September 95 and 12 September 96, the citizens of Puteoli formally thanked him for having moved their town towards Rome (*AE* 1973, 137 = 1941, 73). The end of the inscription reads 'colonia Flauia Aug(usta) Puteolana [...] indulgentia maximi diuinique principis urbi eius admota'. Thus St. reflects official propaganda (*admouere*); but underneath lies a reminiscence of the poetic adynaton which conceives of geographical features far apart as contiguous: cf. Hor. *Epod.* 16. 27 ff. 'quando / Padus Matina lauerit cacumina / in mare seu celsus procurrerit Appenninus', Sen. *HF* 374 ff. 'pax ante fida niuibus et flammis erit / et Scylla Siculum iunget Ausonio latus, / priusque multo uicibus alternis fugax / Euripus unda stabit Euboica piger', Sil. 5. 253 f. 'Thrasymennus in altos / ascendet citius colles'.

27–35: having made a vivid start with the road-building, St. now reverts to a chronological approach, beginning with the former hazards and drawbacks of travel along the coastal route.

27. axe ... uno: what vehicle does St. envisage? Vollmer understands the four-wheeled *raeda*, with the back wheels stuck in the mud and only the front wheels moving; but surely the vehicle then would not move at all. For *uno* Heinsius proposed *udo*, which would somewhat pre-empt *mala nauigationis* (31). But *axe* . . . *uno* must refer to the quickest available means of transport, so as to emphasize what a hindrance the terrain was; hence St. must mean the two-wheeled *cisium*: see Blümner, 460. Thus *axe* . . . *uno* must have concessive force and be taken closely with *piger*: even though the traveller was in a swift two-wheeler his progress was laboriously slow.

28. cruce pendula: Housman, in his annotated copy of Vollmer, takes this phrase metaphorically, 'a rack on wheels'. But *pendula* suggests an actual structure precariously poised. *pendere* and its derivatives can denote perching as well as hanging: cf. Ov. *Pont.* 1. 8. 51 'pendentis . . . rupe capellas', Colum. 10. 229 'putator pendulus arbustis'. A *cisium* could be drawn by a single animal or a pair: see D–S i. 1201 (G. Lafaye). The mention of a single draught-animal at l. 34 does not refer to the vehicle on which the *piger uiator* is travelling. Instead of shafts, a *cisium* drawn by two animals could have a single pole with an animal yoked to it on each side. A cruciform shape would thus be made where the pole bifurcated the axle, affording support to a rudimentary seat. In a vehicle with two axles the chassis is relatively stable, but on a bad road a single-axled vehicle tilts at a precipitous angle that makes it a risky perch.

29. sorbebatque rotas: *sorbere*, properly the action of consuming liquids or inhaling, is used of whirlpools, marshes, quagmires, and the like into which persons or objects disappear: cf. Virg. *A.* 3. 422 'Charybdis . . . sorbet in abruptum fluctus', *Theb.* 8. 141 'currus humus impia sorbet', *OLD* s.v. *sorbeo* 3b. The word implies voracity and greed: cf. Plaut. *Bac.* 372 'istas . . . sorores, quae hominum sorbent sanguinem'.

maligna tellus: *malignus* is the *mot juste* for unproductive soil (cf. Virg. *G.* 2. 179 'difficiles . . . terrae collesque maligni', Plin. *Epist.* 2. 17. 15 'terra . . . malignior ceteris [arboribus]'), but here we have, rather, a personification of the ground as deliberately obstructive: cf. *Theb.* 1. 373 'saxa malignis . . . submersa uadis', *TLL* viii. 134. 38 ff.

31. mala nauigationis: the lurching vehicle makes the traveller sea-sick: see M. Lavarenne, *Lat.* 15 (1956), 372 f.; paradoxical beside *in mediis campis*. Cf. Sen. *Epist.* 57. 1 (*en route* overland from Baiae to Naples) 'tantum luti tota uia fuit ut possem uideri nihilominus nauigasse'.

33. tenaces: *tacentes* (M) is nonsense because it is not the silent tracks themselves but the reason for their silence which slows down the journey. *tenaces* suits marshy ground (29–31). Håkanson, 115, quotes Tac. *Ann.* 1. 63 'loca limosa tenacia graui caeno'.

34–5. sub alta . . . statera: literally a type of balance: see on 4. 9. 46. Here it must refer to the animal's harness which is abnormally heavy ('pondus nimium querens') because it is dragging a scarcely mobile vehicle. *alta* suits a high collar, the common harness for equines when they were used as draught-animals: see White, *Technology*, 138 and pl. 139.

35. languida: the horse is exhausted (and therefore slow): cf. Hor. *Epod.* 2. 63–4 'uidere fessos uomerem inuersum boues / collo trahentis languido'.

36. solidum: i.e. *integrum*, denoting an unbroken period of time: cf. Hor. *O.*

COMMENTARY

1. 1. 20 'nec partem solido demere de die / spernit', Sen. *Epist.* 83. 3 'hodiernus dies solidus est, nemo ex illo quicquam mihi eripuit'. St. is referring to the most marshy stretch of the route south of the R. Volturnus and north of the Acropolis of Cumae, to which modern drainage schemes have given the name Bonifica di Licola. With St.'s boast compare the claim (112) that the whole distance (141 Roman miles) can be covered between sunrise and sunset. The feat of completing long journeys made the computation of distances a subject of great interest and the empire's road-network cause for great gratitude: cf. *Anth. Pal.* 14. 121 (*arithmeticon* by Metrodorus on the distance between Gades and Rome).

38–9. For the rhetorical feature of sudden apostrophe after narrative see S. F. Bonner, *Roman Declamation in the Late Republic and Early Empire* (Liverpool, 1949, repr. 1969), 69. Here the apostrophe marks off the description of the bad old road (27–37) from the detailed account of Domitian's project (40 ff.) Apostrophe can express an exaggeration (travellers by land covering the distance more quickly than birds or ships): see J. Martin, *Antike Rhetorik* (Munich, 1974), 284. *Pars pro toto* (*pennae, carinae*) matches the epigrammatic flourish.

40–8. The processes of Roman road-building have been a source of modern controversy (for which see on l. 44): documentary evidence is virtually limited to this passage of poetry, and archaeology has revealed multiple methods of road-construction. P.-M. Duval, *BSAF* 1959, 180, observes that the demands of the terrain and the availability of local materials largely determined the constituents of the road-bed. The excavation of 350 m of the Via Domitiana near Casino Reale at Licola is documented by Maiuri (1928), 181–5, and corroborates St.'s details. The Via Domitiana was continued to Naples when in 102 Trajan completed Nerva's project of resurfacing the Augustan road between Puteoli and Naples (*CIL* x. 6926–8, *RE* Suppl. xiii. 1515–16 [Radke]; the name Via Antiniana attributed to this road in modern references is, to my knowledge, unattested in antiquity). The famous tunnel, the Crypta Neapolitana, which caused tall people to stoop (Petr. fr. 16) and choked Seneca with dust (*Epist.* 57), was built by Augustus' engineer L. Cocceius Auctus (Strabo 5. 4. 5); hence the photograph of the tunnel at White, *Technology*, fig. 101, which is misleadingly ascribed to the Via Domitiana, is not of a Flavian construction.

40. incohare sulcos: a ditch was dug down the central line of the future road-bed, and boundary-ditches (*fossés-limites*) have been discovered approximately 20 m on each side of some major roads, (*loci*) *non aedificandi*: see J. Martens and R. Brulet, *Dossiers de l'archéologie* 67 (Oct. 1982), 32–3. For the *fossés-limites* see also Chevallier, 96 = Eng. tr. 88. Maiuri (1928), 183, records the finished width of the Via Domitiana as 4.4–4.5 m, i.e. fifteen Roman feet (excluding the pavements, which have not survived). Excavated sections of *uiae publicae* vary in width from 3.87 m on the Via Appia to 8.1 m on the Via Flaminia (including pavements): see *RE* Suppl. xiii. 1438 (Radke).

41. rescindere limites: J. André, *REL* 28 (1950), 109–11, demonstrates that *limes* is fundamentally a road and secondly a boundary. He connects *limes* etymologically with *limus*, 'at an angle', i.e. *limes*=a side-road branching off a *uia publica/uicinalis/priuata*: cf. *CIL* ii. 5439 'quicumque limites quaeque uiae quaeque itinera per eos agros sunt', Liv. 22. 12. 2 'transuersis limitibus in uiam Latinam est egressus'. Hence *rescindere limites* = 'cut back the existing track', i.e. widen it and clear away vegetation and topsoil, which was usually done to a width of 16–20 m: see Mertens and Brulet, art. cit. (previous n.). A track did already exist: cf. 27 ff.

41–2. alto / egestu = 'penitus cauare terras', thorough excavation for the road-bed. For this type of poetic repetition, dwelling on a picture, see Henry on Virg. *A*. 4. 584–7. For the diction cf. Curt. 5. 1. 29 (excavations for the bridge over the Euphrates at Babylon) 'quo [limo] penitus ad fundamenta iacienda egesto'.

42. terras: 'soil', often plural: cf. Acc. *trag*. 495 'ut rorulentas terras ferro . . . proscindant', Virg. *G*. 2. 37 'neu segnes iaceant terrae', l. 79 below, *OLD* s.v. *terra* 4a.

43. haustas ... fossas: created by the excavation: cf. Petr. *Sat*. 120 l. 91 'montibus haustis antra gemunt'. The *fossae* are not parallel ditches (for which see *sulci*, 40) but the road-bed itself. Duval, *BSAF* 1959, 179, explains the plural as referring to the construction of the road in sections to accommodate gradual shifts in the angle of direction.

aliter: the excavated earth is replaced by material to facilitate good drainage (see next n.), i.e. *gremium parare dorso*; for the repetition of the same technical idea in successive phrases see on 41–2.

44. summo ... dorso: the cambered surface; *dorsum* denotes a humped protrusion: cf. Virgil's description of a rocky island outcrop whose surface protrudes from the waves (*A*. 1. 109 f.) 'saxa uocant Itali mediis quae in fluctibus Aras, / dorsum immane mari summo', Suet. *Jul*. 44. 3 'Appennini dorsum'.

gremium can describe a topographical depression or hollow, conveying the notion that the earth cradles what is upon it: cf. Apul. *Apol*. 88 'sub ulmo marita cubet, in ipso gremio terrae matris', *TLL* vi. 2. 2324. 11 ff. The use of *gremium* here matches the anatomical flavour of *dorsum*. Since the work of N. Bergier, *Histoire des grands chemins de l'Empire romain* (edn.[1] Paris, 1622; edn.[2] Brussels, 1728; edn.[3] Brussels, 1736), St.'s *gremium* has been erroneously assumed to be a composite reference to the three layers of foundation specified at Vitr. *Arch*. 7. 1: *statumen*, flat stones cemented with mortar or lime; *ruderatio*, pebbles or chips; *nucleus*, gravel or sand. But Vitruvius is describing floors and mosaic pavements; likewise Pliny at *NH* 36. 184–7. Further, the number, depth, and components of the layers constituting road-beds vary extensively in sections excavated throughout the Roman world: see White, *Technology*, 94 f. Chevallier, 94 f. = Eng. tr. 87, summarizes the general components of a Roman road-bed as rubble (sometimes with piles driven in beneath), sand (sometimes interspersed in pockets within the gravel layer), and a cambered surface (not necessarily paved). For a stylized cross-section see Fig. 3; also Chevallier, fig. 13a (the road from Rheims to Trier excavated at Florenville in 1955), White, *Technology*, fig. 94 (a section through the Via Appia excavated in 1813).

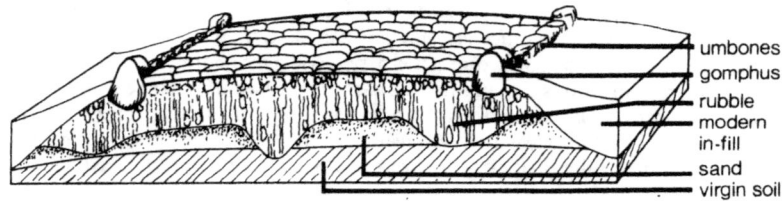

Fig. 3. Roman highway: stylized cross-section. Drawing: S. L. Abraham

45. ne nutent sola: *nutare* is used of earth-tremors and unstable soil: cf. Val. Fl. 6. 169 'tremibundaque pulsu / nutat humus'; St. is thinking of soil-erosion caused by inadequate drainage. With Ovidian *reduplicatio* he repeats this idea in the next one and a half lines; 'nutent . . . maligna' seems a deliberate echo of 28–9, which describe the malevolent landscape hindering the traveller's progress.

46. pressis . . . saxis: *saxum* is both rock in its natural state and dressed stone: for the latter cf. Liv. 36. 22. 11 'tecta . . . caementa et saxa uariae magnitudinis praebebant'. The Via Domitiana was paved: see Pls. 1–2. *pressis* refers to the weight of traffic which necessitates a firm foundation if the road-surface is not to collapse.

cubile: cf. English 'bed', i.e. 'foundation', commonly so used in Latin, as in the elder Pliny's story of the unwieldy lintel in the temple of Diana at Ephesus, whose architect contemplated suicide when the stone appeared not to fit (*NH* 36. 96) 'ea maxima moles fuit nec sedit in cubili, anxio artifice mortis destinatione suprema', *TLL* iv. 1272. 72 ff.

47. umbonibus . . . coactis: *umbo* is used primarily of a protrusion, as the boss of a shield, and is applied to a large stone slab marking boundaries: cf. *Theb.* 6. 352 'hinc saxeus umbo arbiter agricolis'. Hence the *umbones* here must be of comparable size, rammed in ('coactis') on both sides of the road ('hinc et hinc'); presumably the border of stone blocks set vertically to shore up the edges: see Pl. 1. The *margines* (or *crepidines*, pavements) on the outside of the *umbones coacti*, if they existed along the Via Domitiana, must have been raised banks of earth of which no traces remain: see Maiuri (1928), 183; but Duval, *BSAF* 1959, points out that simple buttresses, not necessarily *margines*, could have supported the *umbones*.

48. crebris . . . gomphis: *gomphus* (γόμφος) = *clauus*. The spelling is debatable: *gonfis* (M) reflects the common confusion whereby φ, correctly *ph*, is rendered *f*; our choice between *m* and *n* must be arbitrary, since inscriptions attest γόνφος as well as γόμφος: see A. Souter, *CR* 44 (1930), 116 f. These *gomphi* are boulders set into the kerb along both sides of the road at intervals of 3–9 metres: see Pl. 2. For a sketch of the *gomphi* excavated near Casino Reale at Licola see Maiuri (1928), 183, fig. 2: the oblong section occupies a depth of 0.6–0.7 m below ground, while a triangular portion protrudes 0.5–0.55 m above ground. Maiuri ascribes the term *gomphi* to a decoration in relief in the shape of a nail (*clauus*) at the base of the triangular portion. The *gomphi* I saw on the slopes of Monte

1. The *Via Domitiana* on the slope beneath the Arco Felice. Arrows l. to r. indicate *umbo* and *gomphus* respectively. *Photograph: K. M. Coleman*

2. The *Via Domitiana* on the slope beneath the Arco Felice: close-up of *gomphus* (lower arrow indicates *umbo*). *Photograph: K. M. Coleman*

Grillo bear no trace of any decoration, but may give the impression of reinforcing the *umbones* like stakes in a fence, which may account for their name. They probably, however, have no buttressing function: the chief roads engineer in the Cape Town City Council has described to me local roads constructed of 'stone sets' on the analogy of Roman construction which have not required any such buttressing or pegging. *gomphi* are common also in North Africa and Gaul, and are generally believed to mark the edges of the road where it might become hidden under sand or heavy snow. The sandy stretches along the Via Domitiana, and also the danger of flooding, might necessitate this precaution; but since the *gomphi* continue up the slope of Monte Grillo and under the Arco Felice (on which see l. 98 n.), where neither danger exists, they are presumably continued for consistency of ornament. They have also been explained as mounting-posts or seats, but every 3 m seems too close for that.

iter = *agger*, the more usual word for a roadway, as at 4. 4. 3 'mollis solidus premit agger harenas'. The variant *iter* fits this position in the hendecasyllable line.

49–60. Having described the construction itself, St. now depicts Domitian's road-gangs as miracle-workers. In the Republic soldiers normally built roads, but under Domitian there were no legions stationed permanently in Italy; local labour must therefore have been used for the Via Domitiana, one of the few new roads to be built in Italy under the Empire. Local labour was already conscripted in the Republic to assist in road-works: cf. the gangs recruited for road-repairs in Gaul when Fonteius was praetor (Cic. *Font.* 17). Prisoners might do forced labour: 6,000 Jews worked on Vespasian's canal at Corinth (Jos. *BJ* 3. 10. 10). For St.'s portrayal of the various gangs at work, and the declamatory use of pronouns, cf. 3. 1. 118 ff. (the construction of Pollius Felix' temple of Hercules) 'his caedere siluas / et leuare trabes, illis immergere curae / fundamenta solo' etc.

49. quantae ... manus = *quot manus*: see on 4. 2. 19.

50. hi caedunt nemus exuuntque montis: collecting timber for the construction: see next n.; *caedunt nemus* may perhaps also imply clearing the route: cf. 126 f. 'qui foedum nemus et putris arenas / celsis pontibus et uia leuabit'. The Silua Gallinaria, north of Puteoli, was a pine-forest ('Gallinaria pinus', Juv. 3. 307) known since the Middle Ages as 'Pineta'. Perhaps we are meant to recall Virgil's description of the tree-felling for Misenus' pyre so near by (*A.* 6. 175 ff.). *exuunt* belongs to the metaphor whereby the landscape is 'clothed' with vegetation: cf. Cic. *ND* 2. 98 'riparum uestitus uiridissimos', Liv. 32. 13. 3 '[montes] uestiti frequentibus siluis sunt', Colum. 10. 69–70 'curui uomere dentis / iam uiridis lacerate comas, iam scindite amictus'.

51. hi ferro scolopas trabesque leuant: *scopulos* (M) is intrusive in a couplet dealing with timber (51–2), and while *leuare* is a natural verb to describe planing a piece of wood it is not attested elsewhere of dressing stone: cf., however, Virg. *A.* 5. 305 (of metal) 'Cnosia bina dabo leuato lucida ferro / spicula'. Dressed timber was needed for the superstructure of bridges (see on 69–70) and for causeways, both necessary along the Via Domitiana's soggy route: cf. Labienus' futile attempt to cross a swamp

FIG. 4. Roman causeway: stylized cross-section. Drawing: S. L. Abraham

adjacent to the R. Seine (Caes. *BG* 7. 58. 1) 'Labienus primo uineas agere, cratibus atque aggere paludem explere atque iter munire conabatur'. The causeway excavated beneath the Via Mansuerisca at Hautes Fagnes in Belgium incorporated a timber framework staked to the ground and supporting joists spanned by tree-trunks like railway sleepers, with flagstones on top supporting a cambered surface: for a diagram see Fig. 4; also Chevallier, fig. 14 (=White, *Technology*, fig. 95). Hence *leuant* needs two objects, both referring to timber. A variety of wood, such as *corylos* (hazel), is too specific; a general word is needed to balance *trabes*. Professor Nisbet suggests to me a transliterated form of σκόλοπας (='stakes'), unattested anywhere else in Latin, but plausible in a passage employing the language of technology (cf. *gomphis*, 48), and susceptible of corruption.

ferrum, used loosely of any metal tool, must here mean a type of file: cf. Columella's description of removing a side-shoot from a vine and smoothing over the scar (4. 24. 4) 'si suboles radicibus adhaeret, diligenter explantanda ferroque alleuanda est'.

52. **saxa ligant opusque texunt:** 'theme and variation', substantially the same idea, but repeated from another aspect to attract the reader's attention: cf. on 41–2, and see Henry on Virg. *A.* 1. 546–51. St.'s specification of mortar (53) is supported by Maiuri's findings, since a shaft sunk in the excavated portion of the Via Domitiana revealed a solid layer of *opus caementicium* 0.50 m below the surface: see Maiuri (1928), 184. *opus caementicium* was not cement in the modern sense, but rubble over which liquid cement was poured which created a strong binding: see (e.g.) White, *Technology*, 204 f., and next n. The layer of *opus caementicium* under the surface of the Via Domitiana is unusual, necessitated presumably by the marshy route: see Duval, *BSAF* 1959, 184.

53. **cocto puluere sordidoque tofo:** limestone was reduced to powder by combustion in chalk-ovens: see J.-P. Adam, *La Construction romaine* (Paris, 1984), 69–76. This chalk was then mixed with powdered tufa and water to form a solid mortar. There was a characteristic Campanian tufa which was dark (*sordido*): cf. Vitr. 2. 7. 1 'in Campania rubrum et nigrum tofum': hence there is no need of Heinsius' *torridoque*. Pozzuolana (*puluis Puteolanus*) created mortar which was both watertight and fireproof; on its excellence

see Vitr. 2. 6. 1. The proportions used were one part chalk to two parts pozzuolana, with 15–20 per cent water: see Adam, 77 f. Ernout–Meillet argue that *tofus*, spelt thus at Virg. *G*. 2. 214, is a Campanian word; for the retention of intervocalic *f* they cite *sulfur*, also Campanian.

54. siccant bibulas manu lacunas: once the road has been built, the surrounding land is drained by two methods: water which has collected in hollows is scooped out manually, and streams are diverted (55). *manu*, 'artificially', is very common in the context of constructing features which also occur naturally, e.g. dams or ponds: cf. *Ach*. 1. 108 (Chiron's cave) 'pars exhausta manu, partem sua ruperat aetas', and see *TLL* viii. 356. 29 ff.; so here it is applied to a different process, drainage. For *bibulus* ('thirsty') in the transferred sense of 'full of water' cf. Ov. *Met*. 14. 368 'bibulas ... nubes'; it makes a nice contrast with *siccare* (commonly = 'drain').

55. longe fluuios agunt minores: St. is presumably referring to the diversion of streams into major watercourses to reduce the number of fords and bridges that would be required.

56–8. The historical example of Xerxes' canal through Mt. Athos and his bridge over the Hellespont (Hdt. 7. 21, 33) constitute a pair of well-known rhetorical and declamatory topoi, usually expressing the paradox of trampling on the sea and sailing through the earth; St. avoids this glib antithesis. For the *loci classici* see Isocr. *Pan*. 89, Cic. *Fin*. 2. 112, and for further parallels see Mayor on Juv. 10. 173–84. The rhetorical topos usually treats Xerxes as an example of ὕβρις or transgressing nature: cf. Arnob. *Adu*. *Nat*. 1. 5 'ut ille immanis Xerxes mare terris immitteret et gressibus maria transiret'. But St. alludes to his acts as miracles of human endeavour, with no moral judgement implied. By Juvenal's time scepticism of both feats was expressed (10. 173–6) 'creditur olim / uelificatus Athos et quidquid Graecia mendax / audet in historia; constratum classibus isdem / suppositumque rotis solidum mare credimus'. It is not clear whether St. was sceptical or not; he is concerned to present the topoi as adynata so as to glorify the achievement of Domitian's road.

56. hae ... dextrae: by metonymy for physical labour: the plural of *manus* is similarly used: cf. Sall. *Cat*. 37. 7 'in agris manuum mercede inopiam tolerauerat'.

57. maestum pelagus: sad because its eponymous heroine Helle drowned there: cf. Pind. fr. 189 (ed. Snell–Maehler, 1975), Aesch. *Pers*. 70, Roscher i. 2028 (Höfer/K. Seeliger). *gemens* is appropriate in the context of sounding waves: *TLL* vi. 1762. 64 ff.

58. intercludere ponte non natanti: Domitian's men would be able to construct a conventional bridge as a permanent fixture; Xerxes' bridge was a 'float' (σχεδίη): Hdt. 7. 33, cf. 4. 88 and 97 describing Darius' bridge across the Bosphorus.

59–60. paruus ... Inous ... Isthmos: the feasibility of channelling through the Isthmus of Corinth is included in a list of engineering projects which Quintilian cites as *quaestiones* raised in *suasoriae* (3. 8. 16) 'coniectura est: an Isthmos intercidi, an siccari palus Pomptina, an portus fieri Ostiae possit'. Nero is reputed to have designed a canal across the Isthmus, inspired by the examples of Darius and Xerxes ([Lucian], *Nero* 2). St. claims that Domitian was capable of succeeding where his predecessors had failed (a standard procedure in the λόγος βασιλικός: see *Rhet. Gr.* iii. 376. 31 ff. Sp.). There was a cult of Ino at Lechaeum, on the Isthmus of Corinth, where she was reputed to have met her death: see *RE* xii. 2293 (Eitrem). R. Ellis, *JPh* 13 (1885), 91, objected to the combination of two epithets with one substantive (*paruus . . . Inous . . . Isthmos*), but in reply H. Macnaghten, *JPh* 19 (1891), 135, takes *paruus* closely with *his*: 'an easy task for these'. In this emphatic position, however, *paruus* is rather clumsy. Further, the next phrase attests serious corruption: M's *deuiae* or *cleuiae* was interpreted by Vossius as *cliuiae*, a species of bird with an ominous call: cf. Plin. *NH* 10. 37 'cliuiam quoque auem ab antiquis nominatam animaduerto ignorari, quidam clamatoriam dicunt, Labeo prohibitoriam'. But this reference would seem oddly specific in the context, not to say arcane. An attractive solution for both difficulties, *laurus nisi Deliae* (Constantius Fanensis), is impossible since Delos was no longer an important cult-centre in the first century AD: see *RE* iv. 2500 (v. Schoeffer). *di uiam* (Barth) accords with the notion that divine disapproval hindered projects to channel through the Isthmus of Corinth, unsuccessfully attempted by Demetrius, Julius Caesar, Caligula, and Nero: cf. Plin. *NH* 4. 10 'nefasto, ut omnium exitu patuit, incepto'. *di uia* (Macnaghten) would imply that a route already existed; *di uiam*, conveying an absolute prohibition, is preferable, but since the difficulty with *paruus* persists, I conclude that no satisfactory conclusion has yet been reached.

61–6. After the detailed description in ll. 40–60, this concluding section summarizes the busy atmosphere and relates the enterprise to its geographical setting: the stage is now set for the encomiastic speeches of Volturnus and the Sibyl.

61. feruent litora mobilesque siluae: an echo of the Virgilian phrase 'feruere litora' (*A.* 4. 409, 567). Mozley translates *mobiles siluae* as 'waving woods', but the notion of a breeze is quite extraneous; Heinsius understands hewn timber, 'quia loco mouentur incisae' (cf. 50), which sustains the impression of miracle-working, perhaps with a hint of Domitian as a second Orpheus: cf. Hor. *O.* 1. 12. 7 f. 'uocalem temere insecutae / Orphea siluae'.

62. it ... medias ... per urbes: the tone of these six lines recalls the bustle of the Trojans preparing to leave Carthage (*A.* 4. 397–411): cf. here l. 404 'it ... per herbas'. The settlements 'in the middle', i.e. between the terminal points of the Via Domitiana, were scarcely *urbes*; even Cumae had already declined in the late Republic (see on 65); the sleepy backwaters of Campania are woken by Domitian, who flings open a route to action and prosperity.

64. Gauro: Mons Gaurus, the southern landmark alongside the Via Domitiana: see on 25.

Massicus uuifer: Monte Massico, south-east of Sinuessa; the centre of the vine-growing district in the *ager Falernus*. From its slopes Fabius Maximus is reputed to have watched the farms of Roman settlers being razed by Hannibal all the way to Sinuessa (Polyb. 3. 92). This mountain represents the northern landmark beside the Via Domitiana. St. imagines the echo of the workmen's din being tossed between this peak and Mons Gaurus.

65. quieta Cyme: colonists from Κύμη in Euboea are believed to have founded the Campanian settlement c.740 BC: see L. H. Sackett et al., ABSA 63 (1966), 33, Frederiksen, 59–62. For the Greek spelling cf. Liv. 37. 11. 15, Sil. 8. 531, 11. 288, 12. 60, 13. 492, S. 5. 3. 168, CIL x. 1624 (from Puteoli), TLL Onomasticon ii. 743. 23–8; but contrast Cumas at l. 115 below, representing the usual spelling. Cumae's role as the port of Capua was eclipsed by Puteoli by the end of the Republic as Cumae's harbour became too shallow and restricted for the volume of trade, hence *quieta*: see Frederiksen, 324 f.

66. Literna palus: a colony was founded at Liternum in 194 BC: Liv. 32. 29. 3, 34. 45. 1. The area (modern Lago di Patria) was notoriously swampy: Liv. 22. 16. 4 'Literni harenas stagnaque', Sil. 8. 530 f. 'stagnisque palustre / Liternum', Maiuri, *Passeggiate campane*, 89 ff., Frederiksen, 21.

pigerque Sauo: the Savo (modern Savone) flowed into the sea seven Roman miles south of Sinuessa (*Tab. Peut.*) and five Roman miles north of the Volturnus; it is 50 km long, rising on the slopes of Monte Roccamonfina. The *pons Campanus*, where it was bridged by the Via Appia, was the site of Horace's picnic with Maecenas and Virgil (Hor. *Sat.* 1. 5. 45). Its course is swift as far as Ponte dei Cervi (Frederiksen, 18); thereafter the marshes would have slowed its flow in Roman times, hence *piger*: for the *pigritia* of silted rivers see Aus. *Mos.* 46. The silence and lassitude of the *palus Literna* and the Savo offset the enthusiastic eulogy to be delivered by Volturnus (72–94).

67–96. The R. Volturnus, the third largest in the Apennines (*RE* ixA 1. 861 [Radke]) and the largest in southern Italy, was the major obstacle for the Via Domitiana to cross, and hence an appropriate mouthpiece for an extended eulogy of Domitian. For the convention of a mouthpiece see 4. 1 intro. Cancik, *LK* 109, notes that this excursus enables St. to provide details of features on the route which were not germane to the general building-process. The Volturnus praises Domitian for the practical benefits of his engineering, without pre-empting the prophetic eulogy delivered by the Sibyl of Cumae (124–63). St.'s river-god is somewhat unconventional (see on 67); he would steal a march on the Sibyl if he were to exercise the prophetic powers usually attributed to river-gods: cf. Plin. *Epist.* 8. 8 (the Clitumnus) 'numen ... fatidicum', Eden on Virg. *A.* 8. 62 ff.

67. flauum caput: *flauus* is the *uox propria* of sand (André, *Couleur*, 129), and the constant epithet of the Tiber: Hor. *O.* 1. 2. 13, 8. 8, 2. 3. 18, Virg. *A.* 7. 31, Ov. *F.* 6. 228, *Met.* 14. 448. Hence it is appropriate for the silt-bearing waters of the Volturnus: cf. Ov. *Met.* 15. 714 'multamque trahens sub gurgite arenam'. This epithet also contributes to the impression that the river-god is young, endowed with youthful exuberance: see especially 76–82. River-gods are usually old: cf. Virg. *A.* 8. 31–2 'deus ipse ... Tiberinus ... senior'; but artistic depictions are sometimes youthful, e.g. the relief of Cladeos on the east pediment of the temple of Olympian Zeus:

3. Bust of the river-god Volturnus from the ampitheatre at Capua (now S. Maria Capua Vetere). *Photograph: Fotografia Foglia, Naples*

4. The Volturno near its mouth at Castel Volturno. *Photograph: K. M. Coleman*

see B. Ashmole, *Architect and Sculptor in Classical Greece* (London, 1972), pl. 33–5. For a youthful-looking bust of the river-god Volturnus from an arch of the amphitheatre at Capua see Pl. 3, and contrast the relief of the Danube on Trajan's column (on which see following n.).

68. mollibus ... uluis: river-gods are commonly described with aquatic plants covering their hair: cf. Virg. *A.* 8. 34 (the Tiber) 'crinis umbrosa tegebat harundo', 10. 205 f. 'uelatus harundine glauca / Mincius'. The images of river-gods representing captured territory were carried in processions, and these were portrayed with weed and reeds on their heads: cf. Ov. *Ars* 1. 223 'Euphrates, praecinctus harundine frontem', *Tr.* 4. 2. 41 'uiridi male tectus ab ulua ... Rhenus', *Pont.* 3. 4. 107 f. 'squalidus inmissos fracta sub harundine crines / Rhenus ... portet'. On Trajan's column the god of the Danube is depicted underwater up to his chest, with weed trailing from his head: see P. M. Monti, *La Colonna Traiana* (Rome, 1980), 23; on his arch at Beneventum the river-gods Euphrates and Tigris are similarly depicted: see P. Hamberg, *Studies in Roman Imperial Art* (Uppsala, 1945), 74, C. Pietrangeli, *L'Arc de Trajan à Benevento* (Paris, 1943), pl. xix.

69–70. maximoque ... arcu: Maiuri (1928), 185, reports that a brick pillar which supported the span of the bridge is preserved in the fabric of the medieval castle at Castel Volturno; a number of piers on the opposite bank indicate that a viaduct crossed the lagoon which flowed between the river-bed and a previous watercourse. Even allowing for considerable change in the river-mouth and estuary, the modern bridge carrying the Via Domitiana across the Volturno suggests that the ancient structure must have been an impressive construction with several arches: see Pl. 4.

Piers for a bridge were not necessarily equidistant, probably because the engineers aimed for the easiest footholds on the river-bed (White, *Technology*, 98). But by *maximo ... arcu* St. probably does not envisage one of the supporting arches ('a very large/the largest arch') but the span of the entire bridge (which itself formed an arch, supported by subsidiary arches beneath). In a poem about Domitian's engineering triumph, it is appropriate for the river-god to lean against the bridge rather than a mossy bank (interpreted by Pavlovskis, 20, as contributing to the theme of 'marvels of civilization').

71. raucis ... faucibus: the passage of the *uox* is through the *fauces*: cf. Virg. *A.* 2. 774 'uox faucibus haesit', Quint. 11. 3. 20 'fauces tumentes strangulant uocem'; *fauces* is also used of a river-mouth: *TLL* vi. 1. 397. 69 ff.; St. sustains simultaneously the impression of the actual river and its personification as a god. A transferred epithet denoting sound is common with *os*: cf. Ov. *Am.* 3. 6. 52 (the Anio) 'rauca ora', *Met.* 5. 599 ff. (the Alpheus), *F.* 5. 637 (the Tiber).

talia ... redundat: rarely attested transitive use, derived from its meaning of 'overflow': *OLD* s.v. *redundo* 2; the notion of excess implicit in *redundare* contributes to the picture of the river's youthful exuberance.

72–84. Volturnus' first sentence begins by addressing Domitian in prayer-language (72–5). He then adduces his own changed behaviour as an example of the emperor's miraculous powers (76–80), and thanks him for his intervention (81-4). At l. 76 *et* (M) has been interpreted as anacoluthon, but this figure is odd so near the beginning of the sentence; *en* (Turnebus) conveys the shift of focus from Domitian's powers to their effect on the Volturnus.

72. bone conditor: for *bonus* as part of the vocabulary associated with state leaders see *TLL* ii. 2085. 71 ff. *conditor* denotes someone who arranges or puts together something; hence, while it is often applied to the initiator of a project, the notion of 'founder' is too narrow a definition. Conditor was the god of the storehouse. Weinstock, 183 f., conjectures that Caesar may have experimented with this word as his title before settling for *parens patriae*; *conditor* designated the divinities and heroes who were regarded as original Roman stock, and it became the *uox propria* of Romulus as founder of Rome (Liv. *Pr.* 7). For the founder as subject for praise see Quint. 3. 7. 26 'laudantur autem urbes similiter atque homines. nam pro parente est conditor, et multum auctoritatis adfert uetustas'. Tiberius is recorded as *conditor* of the twelve Asian *ciuitates* devastated by earthquake in AD 17 (*CIL* iii. 7096) 'conditor uno tem[pore XII ciuitatium t]errae motu ue[xatarum]'. The emperor Maximinus is *conditor* of a road repaired at Aquileia in Cisalpine Gaul (*CIL* v. 7989). Domitian was called κτίστης at Priene (Head, 229). For κτίστης of emperors see *RE* xi. 2086 (Prehn). Domitian's measures to prevent the Volturnus flooding bring order out of chaos, hence Volturnus' stress on first beginnings ('amnis esse coepi', 80). *conditor* is an appropriate appellation for Domitian, implying that he has exerted a civilizing influence over hitherto untamed nature and is thus worthy of the dignified title associated with divinities and heroes.

73. uallibus auiis refusum: the river spread into what could otherwise be called *ualles*: cf. Ov. *Met.* 2. 254 ff. 'Nilus in extremum fugit perterritus orbem / occuluitque caput, quod adhuc latet: ostia septem / puluerulenta uacant, septem sine flumine ualles'. Hence dry watercourses which could be used as tracks became impassable when the Volturnus flooded: cf. *Theb.* 1. 358-60 (R. Eridanus) 'puluerulenta prius calcataque flumina nullae / aggeribus tenuere morae, stagnoque refusa est / funditus et ueteri spumauit Lerna ueneno'.

74. ripas habitare nescientem: the Volturnus flooded involuntarily: cf. Hor. *Ars* 390 'nescit uox missa reuerti'. Beyond its banks it was trespassing: cf. Plin. *NH* 5. 57 (the Nile after its seasonal floods) 'reuocatur intra ripas', Ulp. *Dig.* 43. 12. 1. 5 'ripa ... ita recte definietur id, quod flumen continet'. St.'s choice of vocabulary expresses the rationalizing of the Volturnus' course in terms of the emperor's role in keeping nomadic tribes to a fixed abode (see on 4. 7. 50-1): cf. *uictor* (84).

76. ille ego: formula to introduce a reduction in status: see R. G. Austin, *CQ* NS 18 (1968), 110, and cf. the speech of the river-god Ismenus, polluted by the blood of his grandson Crenaeus (*Theb.* 9. 434-7) 'ille ego clamatus sacris ululatibus amnis, / qui molles thyrsos Baccheaque cornua puro / fonte lauare feror, stipatus caedibus artas / in freta quaero uias'. Volturnus uses this formula to express gratitude instead of shame; this paradox contributes to the impression that Domitian's influence over nature works miracles.

COMMENTARY

turbidus minaxque: *turbidus* describes muddied waters (e.g. Virg. *A.* 6. 296 'turbidus hic caeno ... gurges aestuat'), and conveys turbulence and turmoil; for *minax* of disturbed water cf. Quint. *Decl.* 388. 13, p. 436 Winterbottom (a storm at sea) 'exaestuantis fluctus minax facies'. Volturnus, disciplined by Domitian, sees the folly of his former ways.

77. uix passus dubias prius carinas: the R. Volturnus was navigable at least as far as Capua: cf. Liv. 26. 7. 9 (Hannibal prepares to transport his troops across the river) 'nauis in flumine Volturno conprehensas subigi ad ... castellum iussit'. In 212 BC there were officials at Puteoli and at the mouth of the Volturnus in charge of importing grain for the Roman army at Casilinum (Liv. 25. 22. 7); as there was no road from the mouth of the Volturnus inland, the corn must have been shipped upstream: see M. W. Frederiksen, *Puteoli* 4–5 (1980–1), 10.

78. peruiusque calcor: paradoxical with regard to a river. *peruius* contrasts with *uallibus auiis* (73). *calcor* carries overtones of humiliation and defeat: see *TLL* iii. 136. 75 ff. The same conceit of the river trodden underfoot occurs at *Theb.* 1. 358–60 (cit. on l. 73).

79. rapere et rotare: for the imagery cf. Sen. *Nat.* 3. 27. 7 'deuolutus torrens altissimis montibus rapit siluas male haerentes et saxa resolutis remissa compagibus rotat'.

81. gratis ago: the prayer-formula (*TLL* vi. 2. 2204. 6 ff.) and the anaphora of *te* (82) sustain the impression of a hymn (see on 72–84). Human skill in subordinating the natural force of rivers is a topos: cf. Virg. *A.* 8. 726–8, Hor. *O.* 2. 9. 21 f. Nature is usually depicted resenting human interference: the sea was resentful when Agrippa, by building a canal from Lake Lucrinus, opened Lake Avernus to ships (Virg. *G.* 2. 162) 'indignatum magnis stridoribus aequor': cf. Virg. *A.* 8. 728 'pontem indignatus Araxes'. St. habitually attributes to nature the opposite attitude: delight and gratitude at the amenities of civilization, e.g. Manilius Vopiscus' mosaic flooring (1. 3. 55 f.) 'uarias ... picta per artes / gaudet humus'. Volturnus' gratitude is particularly flattering to Domitian, but is paralleled by the behaviour of other natural features, e.g. 1. 4. 79 'patiens Latii iam pontis Araxes' (cf. *A.* 8. 728 cit. above). Through the Volturnus' volte-face St. can implicitly impute miraculous powers to Domitian without transgressing the bounds of credibility; no repetition here of the fantastic legend which recorded the Volturnus in 524 BC flowing backwards (a standard adynaton: cf. Eur. *Med.* 410, Hor. *O.* 1. 29. 10) as a portent that the people of Cumae would repulse their Etruscan aggressors (Dion. Hal. *Ant. Rom.* 7. 3. 3–4. 3).

seruitus implicitly accords with Domitian's self-styled title *dominus et deus*. Volturnus is now at Domitian's service, subject to his power as *arbiter* (see on 83–4). His enslavement is not degrading but a benefit (*tanti est*). The river is attracted by the magnetic force which Domitian's *numen* exerts over the natural world, so that subservience to the emperor is the dominant impulse: cf. Juv. 4. 68 (the fish) 'ipse capi uoluit'. This theme is common in Martial, especially in the *Liber Spectaculorum*: see Sauter, 166–70, Scott, 119–24, O. Weinreich, *Studien zu Martial* (Stuttgart, 1928), 74–155, G. Highet, *Juvenal the Satirist* (Oxford, 1954), 256.

82. cessi: the river no longer floods. As with the initial description of the Volturnus (67–71) St. uses a word applicable both to the river's godhead and to the water itself, i.e. *cedere* = 'yield', 'recede': cf. Sen. *HF* 684 'qualis incertis uagus Maeander undis ludit et cedit sibi'.

83–4. maximus ... ripae: Volturnus gives thanks because a record of Domitian's achievement is preserved for posterity, i.e. in an inscription on the bridge (*legere*). *arbiter* is extended from the judicial sphere to denote absolute authority: cf. Ov. *Tr.* 5. 2. 47 (Augustus) 'arbiter imperii', [Sen.] *Oct.* 488 (Nero) 'generis humani arbiter', Tac. *Ann.* 2. 73. 4 (Germanicus) 'quod si solus arbiter rerum ... fuisset', *CIL* iii. 1090 'Ioui ... rerum rectori fatorumque arbitro'. *uictor perpetuus* conveys Domitian's absolute and permanent control over the river's resources, and sustains the notion of the river's *seruitus* (81): cf. Tac. *Ann.* 14. 13 (of Nero, AD 59) 'hinc superbus ac publici seruitii uictor Capitolium adiit' (derogatory in the context).

85. limite ... beato: places which bring happiness to their inhabitants can be called *beatus*: see *TLL* ii. 1915. 34 ff. The paradox of nature subservient to man means that even a restricting *limes* appears *beatus* to the grateful river.

86–7. malumque ... pudorem: Domitian had the Volturnus dredged to deepen the river-bed by removing deposits of silt. Augustus similarly cleared the channels that carried off flood-waters from the Nile (Suet. *Aug.* 18) 'fossas omnis, in quas Nilus exaestuat, oblimatas longa uetustate militari opere detersit'. Cf. Liv. 39. 44. 5 (clearing drains) 'detergendasque, qua opus esset, cloacas ... locauerunt'. Domitian was concerned to prevent the harbour at the river-mouth from silting up. Modern filtration tests have calculated that the Volturnus carries and deposits 0.5 m^3 of soil annually (regarded by Frederiksen, ch. 1 n. 126, as a conservative estimate), with far-reaching effects: carried by southward-flowing currents, silt from the Volturnus has entirely covered the ancient harbour at Cumae (Frederiksen, 70). For methods of soil-conservation in antiquity (i.e. dredging, and the construction of dams and moles) see White, *Technology*, 103, 109–10.

88–9. ne me puluereum grauemque caeno / Tyrrheni sinus adluat profundi: *grauem caelo* (M) would have to mean 'polluting the atmosphere', which would only apply to stagnant water. *grauem caeno*, extending the idea in *puluereum*, is typical of St.'s duplications in expression: see on 41–2, 45, 52. *obluat* (M) is not attested with certainty anywhere else: see *TLL* ix. 118. 4 ff. *obruat* (ς), approved by Håkanson, 116 f., is explained by Vollmer to mean that the water of the Volturnus used to be so dirty that it sank to the bottom at the river-mouth even though salt-water is usually heavier than fresh water. This, however, is a very technical explanation which St. does not make explicit to his readers: for a description of the normal situation cf. Ov. *Pont.* 4. 10. 59 ff. (the mouth of the Danube) 'copia tot laticum, quas auget, adulterat undas / nec patitur uires aequor habere suas ... innatat unda freto dulcis leuiorque marina est, / quae proprium mixto de sale pondus habet'. *abluat* (Baehrens), 'wash out', is inappropriate of the Mediterranean, where tidal activity is almost negligible.

adluat, 'lap against', describes the motion of the sea at the quayside: cf. Cic. *Ver.* 5. 96 'urbe portus ipse cingitur ... ut non adluantur mari moenia extrema, sed ipse influat in urbis sinum portus'. It conveys the curling of tiny waves around a person's feet at the water's edge: cf. Cat. 65. 6 'pallidulum manans alluit unda pedem'. The notion that the sea should lap against another body of water is something of a paradox, afforded by the semi-personifiction of Volturnus, who regards it as a disgrace (*pudorem*, 87) if the sea should have to lap against the muddy water which lies where, in human terms, his dirty feet would be.

90–1. Cinyphios ... agros: the Volturnus no longer silts up like the R. Bagradas, which rises south of Hippo Regius and flows into the Mediterranean between Utica and Carthage: cf. Luc. 4. 587–8 'se / Bagrada lentus agit siccae sulcator harenae', Sil. 6. 140–1 'turbidus arentis lento pede sulcat harenas / Bagrada'. In its sluggish flow there is no noisy current churning against the banks, hence *tacente ripa*. *agros* requires an adjective which can be applied to the whole area through which the Bagradas flows. The R. Cinyps flows between the Syrtes; for *Cinyphius* = *Libycus* cf. Ov. *Met.* 15. 755 'Cinyphiumque Iubam'. The Bagradas can be appropriately called *Poenus* because it was the major river near Carthage. *Cinyphios ... Poenus Bagrada ... agros* constitutes common word-order in St., e.g. 4. 6. 58, 8. 31, hence the distance between *Cinyphios* and *agros* is not a difficulty. The transposition of the epithets meets Vollmer's objection that the adjective derived from the name of a river which was not particularly famous (*Cinyphius*) does not help to clarify the position of another river. For *serpere* of a winding river cf. Ov. *Tr.* 3. 10. 30 (Danube) 'tectis in mare serpit aquis', Luc. 1. 215 (Rubicon) 'per ... imas serpit ualles'.

92–3. nitente cursu / tranquillum mare: because it is no longer subject to flooding, the Volturnus flows smoothly and its surface is shining instead of ruffled.

94. prouocare Lirim: the Liris, flowing into the sea north of Sinuessa at Minturnae, was the largest river in the vicinity of the Volturnus. In its upper reaches (modern Liri) it is swift, in its lower reaches (modern Garigliano) calm. Its tranquillity was a byword in antiquity: cf. Hor. *O.* 1. 31. 8 'rura quae Liris quieta / mordet aqua taciturnus amnis', Sil. 4. 438 ff. 'Liris ... qui fronte quieta / dissimulat cursum ac, nullo mutabilis imbri, / perstringit tacitas gemmanti gurgite ripas', 8. 399 f. 'Fibreno miscentem flumina Lirim / sulpureum tacitisque uadis ad litora lapsum'. For the topos of 'pre-eminence' see on 4. 2. 26. Cf. St.'s apostrophe to the region where Lucan was born (2. 7. 26 f. 'Tritonide fertilis Athenas / unctis, Baetica, prouocas trapetis') and his injunction to Virgil's birthplace not to challenge Lucan's river (2. 7. 35 'Baetim, Mantua, prouocare noli'). Volturnus' competitive spirit matches his exuberance and the loyalty of the convert.

95–6. pariterque se leuarat ... plaga marmorata: while the river-god was speaking, the construction was completed. Volturnus' speech is inserted between the description of the building-process (40–66) and a review of the completed route (97–113). Vollmer's assumption that the river-god's presence had accelerated the construction is not based on an explicit statement in the text, and thus 1. 1. 61 f. is not comparable ('iuuat ipsa labores / forma dei praesens'). What is the *plaga marmorata*? Kähler, *RE* viiA. 472 ff. s.v. 'Triumphbogen', interprets it as a triumphal arch, but the marbled arch rising like a rainbow (98–9) marks where the Via Domitiana branches off the Appia (see next n.). *huius* (97) refers to the road, whose gateway is an arch at the junction with the Appia; since *huius* refers back to *plaga*, *plaga* should be the road. *plaga* can refer to a strip or stretch of territory: cf. Curt. 6. 2. 13 'qui in Europa sunt, a laeuo Thraciae latere ad Borysthenem atque inde ad Tanaim recta plaga attinent'. *marmorata* is not literally true, since the road was not paved with marble; hence Frère supposes that *dorso* is 'autre chose que celui de la chaussée v. 44'; the secondary meaning of *marmoratus*, 'coated with cement of powdered marble', although attested for the pavements of a road at Gortyna in Crete in the second century AD (*CIL* iii. 14120 'marginibus utrinque constructis lapide silici marmorato'), would not describe the surface of the Via Domitiana, which is cemented 'cocto puluere sordidoque tofo' (53). But *marmorata*, 'marbled', is suitable hyperbole for 'paved'. Vollmer, however, takes *plaga* as 'net', i.e. the bridge, faced with marble, has been thrown like a net over the river's back. A bridge with ornamental trelliswork might look like a net, but the superstructure of bridges with this decoration was usually wooden, not marble, and *se leuarat* does not cohere with the image of a net. But the road itself can be said to 'rise' because its cambered surface (*ingenti* ... *dorso*) is banked up above the level of the sands and marshes along the coastal plain: see on 51.

97–8. ianua prosperumque limen / arcus: at the junction of the Appia and Domitiana at Sinuessa (102). *ianua* can be used broadly of the approach to a place: cf. Ov. *Tr.* 1. 10. 32 (of the Bosphorus) 'hic locus est gemini ianua uasta maris', *TLL* vii. 1. 137. 7 ff. *limen* is used similarly of the edge of a place: see *TLL* vii. 2. 1406. 38 ff. (where, however, St.'s phrase is taken to refer to an archway at the bridge); cf. Mart. 3. 5. 5 (of the covered way between the Via Flaminia and the Tiber) 'protinus hunc primae quaeres in limine Tectae'. Crossing the *limen* of a building can have religious significance (*TLL* vii. 2. 1404. 38 ff., K. Meister, *SHAW* 15 [1924–5], 3. Abh.), hence this arch over the Via Domitiana is said to be *prosperum* ... *limen*.

98. belligeris ducis tropaeis: cf. Martial's description of a triumphal arch of Domitian at Rome (8. 65. 9–11) 'hic gemini currus numerant elephanta frequentem, / sufficit immensis aureus ipse iugis. / haec est digna tuis, Germanice, porta triumphis'; he is said to have erected several: cf. Suet. *Dom.* 13. 2 'Ianos arcusque cum quadrigis et insignibus triumphorum per regionis urbis ... exstruxit'. The triumphal insignia on the arch at Sinuessa presumably celebrated Domitian's triumphs over the Chatti and the Daci (Suet. *Dom.* 6). A similar triumphal arch at the bifurcation of two roads was erected by Trajan in 114 at Beneventum where the Via Traiana branches off the Via Appia towards Brundisium (the Porta Aurea at modern Benevento). The reliefs depict aspects of Trajan's domestic policy and military conquests, and the triumphal frieze extends round all four sides above the architrave: see P. Hamberg, *Studies in Roman Imperial Art*

(Uppsala, 1945), 63, C. Pietrangeli, *L'Arc de Trajan à Benevento* (Paris, 1943) (plates), F. J. Hassel, *Der Trajansbogen in Benevent: Ein Bauwerk des römischen Senates* (Mainz, 1966) with the review-article by F. A. Lepper, *JRS* 59 (1969), 250–61. There were probably at least three arches on the Via Domitiana: this one, the Arco Felice between Cumae and Puteoli, and possibly a third at Puteoli itself: it was customary to erect arches at either end of an imperial progress: see *RE* viiA. 472 ff. (Kähler). Two fragments of relief in quite different styles were found with the inscription at Puteoli cited on ll. 25–6 (*AE* 1973, 137 = 1941, 73). The piece (now in the Philadelphia Museum) which displays the inscription has a Trajanic relief on the reverse: see K. D. Matthews, Jr., *Expedition* 8. 2 (1966), 35. The other fragment, now in Berlin, resembles the style of the Cancellaria Reliefs and is thus believed to be Domitianic, hence Kähler's suggestion that a half-finished arch at the terminus of the Via Domitiana was reused by Trajan for the Via Antiniana (see 40–8 n.) which continued the route down to Naples: see H. Kähler, in *Studies Presented to D. M. Robinson* (St Louis, 1951), i. 430 ff. The only extant arch over the Via Domitiana is the Arco Felice outside Cuma on the road to Pozzuoli, where the road passes through a deep cutting in Monte Grillo. In antiquity it formed a short viaduct connecting the land on each side of the cutting. It is a brick structure, 5.8 m wide and 19.5 m high, with niches for statuettes but no trace of triumphal reliefs: see A. Maiuri, *The Phlegraean Fields*³, tr. V. Priestley (Rome, 1958), 105 and fig. 59, and an excellent photograph in J.-P. Adam, *La Construction romaine* (Paris, 1984). It was suggested by Beloch, 164, that the arch might have originally been an Augustan construction contemporary with Agrippa's project of linking Lake Avernus with the sea (see introduction); but the arch complements the grand highway which it spans, and it is nowadays assumed to be Domitianic: cf. Frederiksen, 28 n. 95.

99. totis Ligurum nitens metallis: marble from Luna, in Liguria; for its dazzling white colour see on 4. 2. 29. *totis* is hyperbole: it took all the mines of Luna to supply the best marble for the arch at Sinuessa.

100. quo ... Iris: *imbri* (M) is otiose in the context of a rainbow. *iri* (ς) involves an inversion, i.e. 'quantus [arcus] nubila qui coronat iri' = 'quanta iris nubila quae coronat arcu'. Heinsius' conjecture avoids this inversion: cf. Man. 1. 713 'suos arcus per nubila circinat Iris'.

101. flectit iter citus: in antithesis to *piger ... uiator* (27–8), proposed by A. Cartault, *JS* NS 2 (1904), 527, and fully discussed by Håkanson, 117 f. *excitus* (M), denoting unease, is inappropriate; with a personal subject for *flectere* the reflexive form is used and never the passive; the corruption could have arisen from haplography.

104. iugalis: the easier the track, the more eager the beasts are to hurry. For *iugales* of a team of draught-animals cf. Virg. *A*. 7. 280 'currum geminosque iugalis', *Theb*. 3. 268 'spumantem proni mandunt adamanta iugales'.

105–6. The comparison is between the weary oarsmen, now fanned by a rising breeze, and the draught-animals, previously exhausted by the difficult route but now picking up speed on the new road. For the apostrophe cf. 39.

107–13. The order in M presents two difficulties: first, St., invoking travellers from the east, apparently recommends a devious route to Rome (107–10); secondly, he then reverses direction, describing the journey south from Rome to Naples (112–13). But St. directs easterners to take an 'easy route', *prono limite*: for this sense of *pronus* cf. Curt. 6. 3. 16 'non mare ... nos moratur, non Ciliciae fauces ... includunt. plana omnia et prona sunt', *OLD* s.v. *pronus* 7. St. thus cannot mean travellers landing at Brundisium, since they would travel straight along the Via Appia through Capua to Rome, and the Via Domitiana would involve them in a detour. The only easterners who would travel to Rome *prono limite* along the Via Domitiana would land at Puteoli (the chief port for eastern cargoes), but *sub axe primo* ('in the east': see Vollmer on 1. 4. 73) naturally suggests the route from Brundisium. To invoke easterners in the middle of a description of the journey south along the Via Domitiana (101 ff.) is odd in itself, but sailing forges a thematic link: Romans on the Lucrine provide a spur for easterners making the voyage round Italy's toe. The southbound journey is summarized in ll. 112–13, and the conclusion to be drawn from this example is expressed in l. 111 'nil obstat cupidis, nihil moratur'. Having demonstrated how much time the new route saves for southbound travellers, St. can now recommend it for the northbound (*ergo*), tactfully casting his advice as an injunction to the eastern nations to do obeisance to the imperial cult at Rome, and concluding the section with an allusion to Domitianic triumphs in the east: see on 4. 1. 40–1. He simultaneously implies that the new road makes it worthwhile for travellers from the east to sail round the toe of Italy and dock at Puteoli, since the onward journey to Rome overland will only take a day. In fact the economic benefits were probably an important incentive for Domitian to build this road; E. H. Warmington, *The Commerce between the Roman Empire and India*[2] (London, 1974), 89, links its construction with warehouses for spices (*horrea piperataria*) which Domitian built at Rome in 92 (see Platner–Ashby, 262 f.).

112–13. Along the Via Domitiana it was 141 Roman miles from Rome to Puteoli. Only a traveller on horseback could have covered this journey in one day, and he would have had to travel at the speed of a messenger conveying an emergency message (Friedländer, i. 281): cf. the news of the Roman defeat at Aquileia, conveyed to Rome in four days (*HA Max.* 25. 2), i.e. at the speed of 130–40 Roman miles per day. See the evidence for travelling speeds compiled by Chevallier, 220–5 = Eng. tr. 191–5.

114–18. The entry of the Sibyl is introduced by a series of questions which convey an atmosphere of mounting suspense: cf. the questions with which Lucan prefaces Appius' visit to the Pythia (6. 86 ff.).

114. fine ... imo: the last stage on the journey southwards from Rome is represented by Cumae, three Roman miles from Puteoli (*Tab. Peut.*). The route along the Via Domitiana, beginning at Sinuessa (101), ends on the Bay of Naples; *uno* (M) would be imprecise.

115. monstrat ueteres Apollo Cumas: *Apollo* by metonymy for his temple, which dominated the original city: cf. Virg. *A*. 6. 9 f. 'arces quibus altus Apollo/ praesidet'. Cumae was traditionally the oldest Greek colony in Italy: cf. Strabo 5. 4. 4 ταύταις δ' ἐφεξῆς ἐστι Κύμη, Χαλκιδέων καὶ

Κυμαίων παλαιότατον κτίσμα, and see on l. 65. The original Greek settlement was built on the lower hill to the south on the acropolis, where there is a temple assumed to be Apollo's on the basis of an unpublished inscription found by Maiuri in 1912 and now lost. This temple is near the underground complex now identified as the Sibyl's cave: see Hardie's note at Virg. *A.* 6. 9 (ed. Austin) and fig. 2. The temple of Zeus was on a higher elevation than the temple of Apollo (Austin, fig. 3) and might be seen to dominate the landscape from the north, but once a traveller had reached the forum the temple of Apollo would be the nearer and more prominent landmark. The Via Domitiana enters the forum from the north; two roads run out on the south side: the Via Baiana due south and the continuation of the Via Domitiana south-east to Puteoli. Hence St. visualizes the Sibyl appearing from her cave near the temple of Apollo, visible to the traveller at the point where the roads out of the forum fork (*fine . . . imo*).

116. albam crinibus infulisque: the Sibyl's hair is white because she is an old woman, granted by Apollo as many years of life (but not of youth) as grains in a fistful of sand: cf. Ov. *Met.* 14. 129 ff. *albus* and its cognates, frequently combined with *canus*, commonly designate what is white with age: cf. Ov. *Met.* 3. 516 'ille [senex] mouens albentia tempora canis', *Her.* 13. 159 'quod ut uideam canis albere capillis', *OLD* s.v. *albus* 5, André, *Couleur*, 67. The Sibyl's head-covering is white because she is priestess to Apollo: cf. Luc. 5. 143 f. (the Pythia) 'crines . . . candida . . . conplectitur infula'. White, symbolic of chastity and purity, was associated with cults: cf. Cic. *Leg.* 2. 45 'color autem albus praecipue decorus deo est, cum in cetero tum maxime in textili', André, *Couleur*, 260 f.

117. uisu fallimur: it is common in the context of epiphanies to doubt the evidence of the senses: cf. Virg. *E.* 8. 108 'credimus? an qui amant ipsi sibi somnia fingunt?', Hor. *O.* 3. 4. 5 'an me ludit amabilis / insania?'

118. Chalcidicas . . . laurus: bay was traditionally associated with the cult of Apollo at Delphi, possessing properties which roused the Pythia to prophecy. The plant, and Apolline cult, had no special connection with Chalcis, but the cave at Cumae did, traditionally settled by colonists from Euboea (see on l. 65).

120. uates sanctior: St., in the capacity of *uates* as a professional poet, must defer to the authority of the Sibyl as mouthpiece of Apollo: cf. Virg. *A.* 6. 65 f. 'sanctissima uates, / praescia uenturi'. The Virgilian associations govern the use of *uates* here, the sole instance in the *Siluae*. For the Augustans' expropriation of this term see J. K. Newman, *The Concept of Vates in Augustan Poetry* (Brussels, 1967).

121-2. The Sibyl is in a prophetic frenzy (ἔνθεος) induced by Apollo: cf. Virg. *A.* 6. 78 (the Sibyl) 'bacchatur uates', 4. 300 f. (metaphorically, of Dido) 'totamque incensa per urbem / bacchatur', Luc. 5. 169 f. (the Pythia) 'bacchatur demens aliena per antrum / colla ferens', Sen. *Ag.* 724 (Cassandra) 'cui bacchor furens?' The Sibyl, possessed by Apollo, actually spoke his words: see E. R. Dodds, *The Greeks and the Irrational* (Berkeley, 1951), 70; hence St.'s choice of the Sibyl of Cumae as his mouthpiece implies an even more august prophet, Apollo himself. The dramatic element of resistance (cf. Virgil's Sibyl, *A.* 6. 77-9) is totally absent.

121. colla rotat: a sign of demonic possession: cf. Quint. 11. 3. 71 'adeo iactare id [caput] et comas excutientem rotare fanaticum est'; more histrionically Lucan's Pythia (5. 170 ff.) 'uittas ... Phoebeaque serta ... ancipiti ceruice rotat', and Valerius Flaccus' Mopsus (1. 208 f.) 'uittamque comamque per auras / surgentem laurusque rotat'.

121–2. nouis ... spatiis: 'uiae spatium' (Ov. *Met.* 8. 794) = 'the length of the road', but 'noua spatia' would be an odd phrase for a newly built road and must mean here territory new to the Sibyl: now that the Via Domitiana has been completed she ventures on to the road for the first time and testifies to the divinity of its founder.

122. uiam ... replet: when used of people occupying a space, *replere* occurs with a plural or a collective singular as subject: cf. *Theb.* 12. 472 'omnis ... aetas tecta uiasque replent'. Applied to one person it achieves a vivid picture of uncontrolled frenzy: the Sibyl in her ravings monopolizes the entire width of the road.

123. profatur: the *uox propria* of making a divine revelation: cf. Lucr. 1. 739 'Pythia quae tripodi a Phoebi lauroque profatur', Petr. *Sat.* 89 l. 4 'Delio profante'.

124. ueniet: prophetic diction: cf. Aesch. *Ag.* 1280 ἥξει γὰρ ἡμῶν ἄλλος αὖ τιμάορος. St.'s anaphora is typical of prophetic language: see R. G. Austin, *CQ* 21 (1927), 103.

manete: in the context of a prophecy this sounds like a formula, exhorting the faithful to suffer patiently until the god brings relief and rewards.

126. foedum nemus et putris arenas: the *nemus* is not the Sibyl's lair (so Stange) but the Silua Gallinaria (50 n.), combined with *putris arenas* (swamps, 66 n.) to represent the difficult terrain along the route. By chiastic arrangement the *nemus* is traversed by *uia* and the *arenas* by *pontibus* (127).

128–38. The prophecy (124–7) is fulfilled by the revelation, a combination of sacral language and ἐγκώμιον βασιλέως. Cf. Anchises' speech revealing Augustus to Aeneas in the underworld (*A.* 6. 791–805), with Norden's analysis at *RhM* 54 (1899), 466–82 (= *Kl. Schr.*, 422 ff.).

128. hic est deus: for the formula οὗτός ἐστιν (with anaphora) in revelatory language see Norden, *Agnostos Theos*, 188, and cf. *A.* 6. 791 'hic uir, hic est'.

128–9. hunc iubet ... / pro se Iuppiter imperare terris: for the widespread Hellenistic and Roman belief that rulers were sanctioned by Jupiter cf. the famous maxims of Callim. *H.* 1. 79 ἐκ δὲ Διὸς βασιλῆες, Hor. *O.* 3. 1. 6 'reges in ipsos imperium est Iouis', and see N–H on Hor. *O.* 1. 12. 50. Domitian surpasses all the leaders in whom Jupiter has vested authority since the Roman race was founded (130–3).

130. subit habenas: for the metaphor of the reins of power cf. Cic. *De Or.* 1. 226 'cui [senatui] populus ipse moderandi et regendi sui potestatem quasi quasdam habenas tradidisset', *S.* 1. 4. 92 f. (Gallicus appointed *praefectus urbi* by Domitian) 'tanti lectus rectoris habenas ... subisti', 5. 1. 37 f. (Domitian) 'deus qui flectit habenas / orbis', *TLL* vi. 3. 2394. 4 ff.

131–3. praescios Auerni ... lucos: Virgilian adjective: cf. *A.* 6. 66 (the Sibyl) 'praescia uenturi'. The *luci* of Avernus are also Virgilian: cf. *A.* 6. 118.

134–6. Superiority over nature (135) is a fit comment on the emperor's hypothetical role as charioteer of the sun (136), but not as peacemaker and warrior (134). But if l. 135 were transposed after l. 136, the progression *bonus ... melior* and *timendus ... potentior* would be lost. Hence I have retained the order of the lines as in M, but instead of punctuating (as conventionally) with a full stop after l. 135, I have put one after 134. This concept lies behind Menander's recommendations for concluding a λόγος βασιλικός (*Rhet. Gr.* iii. 377. 22 ff. Sp.): praise of the emperor, and prayers for his safety, because under his influence good rains produce abundant harvests.

134. paci bonus: explained by *timendus armis*. For the dative after *bonus* cf. Cic. *De Or.* 3. 139 'Critias ... Alcibiades ciuitatibus ... suis non boni', *TLL* ii. 2087. 28 ff., 2097. 71 ff.

136. si flammigeros teneret axis: cf. Luc. 1. 48 'flammigeros Phoebi ... currus', Val. Fl. 5. 581 'flammigeri proles ... Solis'. The sun was recognized as the major climatic factor: cf. Cic. *Rep.* 6. 17 'Sol ... dux et princeps et moderator luminum reliquorum, mens mundi et temperatio', Plin. *NH* 2. 13 'hunc [solem] esse totius mundi animum ac planius mentem, hunc principale naturae regimen ac numen credere decet'. If Domitian were to regulate the behaviour of the sun, he would improve the world climate (triple adynaton, 137–8).

137–8. Triple *exemplum* of climatic adynata to illustrate Domitian's potential influence over nature. The first two elements are alleged to duplicate the same idea, hence Postgate's conjecture of an unattested intransitive *umbraret* to refer to Libya's treeless desert. But Professor Badian has pointed out to me that the first two elements are not tautologous: while India's rivers were catalogued by early authorities, she was simultaneously noted for drought: cf. Plin. *NH* 19. 19 (a type of linen) 'nascitur in desertis adustisque sole Indiae, ubi non cadunt imbres'. Libya, on the other hand, had very few watercourses. Hence St. predicts that rain would fall in India and that Libya would be awash (with rivers). The third element continues the train of thought by predicting a thaw in Thrace: the Great Balkan range was itself snow-capped and commanded plains where the snow did not melt: cf. Theoc. 7. 76 χιὼν ὅς τις κατετάκετο μακρὸν ὑφ' Αἵμον.

139. dux hominum et parens deorum: adapted from Ennius' formula for Jupiter, *diuum pater atque hominum rex*: cf. *Ann.* 203 Skutsch. In the narrow sense *parens deorum* refers to the deification of Domitian's relatives (4. 2. 59 n.), but this expression is also part of the panegyric tradition associating Roman rulers with the kingdom of heaven: cf. Virg. *A.* 9. 642 (to Ascanius) 'dis genite et geniture deos', Sen. *Dial.* 6. 15. 1 '[Caesares] dis geniti deosque genituri', *S.* 1. 1. 74 f. (Lacus Curtius to Domitian) 'salue, magnorum proles genitorque deorum, / auditura longe numen mihi'.

140. cognitum: *conditum* (M) with an abstract subject (*numen*) is very difficult in the sense of *conditum pectore* (so Vollmer). Conceivably *conditum* ('sung of') could refer to the prophecy of ll. 124–7, but in that case St.'s language would have to make it clear that this is the sense required, as at Ov. *Pont.* 4. 10. 75 'conditur a te / uir tanto, quanto debuit ore cani', *TLL* iv. 153. 74 ff. *cognitum* (ς) matches *prouisum* much more closely, referring to the Sibyl's prophetic powers, parallel to the Christian concept of recognizing Christ the man as God incarnate: cf. Tert. *Adv. Prax.* 13. 7 'at ubi uenit Christus et cognitus est a nobis', *TLL* iii. 1503. 60 ff.

141–3. putribus euoluta chartis ... mea dicta: having predicted Domitian's salvation of Campania (124–7, 140), the Sibyl delivers in person her prophecy of his future achievements (147 ff.) instead of entrusting it to the Sibylline books. These books, allegedly brought to Rome under Tarquinius Superbus (Dion. Hal. 4. 62. 1–6, Plin. *NH* 13. 88, Gell. 1. 19. 1), were destroyed by fire in 83 BC and replaced by a new collection. St. envisages the Sibyl's oracular sayings being 'unfolded', both literally and metaphorically, on papyrus rolls; for the metaphor cf. Cic. *Att.* 9. 10. 7 'hanc deliberationem euoluis accuratius in litteris'. The papyrus would be rotting (*putribus*) because of its great age.

142. sollemni prece Quindecim Virorum: the oracular collection on the Capitoline was in the care of a college of priests who, probably under Sulla, came to number fifteen: see G. B. Pighi, *De Ludis Saecularibus* (Milan, 1941), 231 ff., M.-W. Hoffmann Lewis, *The Official Priests of Rome under the Julio-Claudians*, American Academy in Rome, Papers and Monographs 16 (1955), 86 ff. For *sollemnis* of a ritual utterance cf. Sen. *Dial.* 6. 13. 1 'sollemnia pontificii carminis uerba'.

143–4. canentem / ipsam: cf. Aeneas' request to the Sibyl (Virg. *A.* 6. 74–6) 'foliis tantum ne carmina manda, / ne turbata uolent rapidis ludibria uentis; / ipsa canas oro'.

145. quam seriem imminentis aeui: *series* is almost invariably felt as a collective noun and therefore governs a plural genitive, but the sense of a temporal continuum may just admit a singular (*aeui*): cf. Ov. *Tr.* 4. 10. 53 f. 'successor fuit hic [Tibullus] tibi, Galle, Propertius illi, / quartus ab his serie temporis ipse fui'. Even so, *series temporis* ('sequence of time') is a natural expression, but *series aeui* is not (although perhaps helped by the notion of generations: cf. 148 'natis ... abnepotibus'). Hence *aeui* needs to be qualified by a word that will ease the phrase. To make sense at all, *merentis* (M) would need to be given passive force ('longevity which has been deservedly won'); even were this attested, *merentis* would be a pale compliment and it jars suspiciously after *mereris* (144). *uirentis* (Heinsius) and *uigentis* (Saenger) would somewhat pre-empt the prophecy of eternal youth (149), and neither contributes any temporal significance to smooth the expression *seriem aeui*. But *imminentis* (Polster) creates a striking phrase (lit. 'sequence of impending age'), suggesting that Domitian is hovering on the brink of immortality; it also conveys a mild paradox: *imminet* frequently alludes to the proximity of ill fortune or death (*TLL* vii. 1. 459. 71 ff.), which is what the Fates usually contrive for man, but here, instead of impending death, they are responsible for protracted life. *seriem*, derived from *sero* ('bind together'), precisely matches the sense of *pronectant* ('weave on').

147. magnus ... ordo saeculorum: cf. Virg. *E.* 4. 4 f. 'ultima Cumaei uenit iam carminis aetas; / magnus ab integro saeculorum nascitur ordo'. Virgil's phrase, of cosmic relevance, becomes hyperbolic flattery of the emperor.

148. longior: 'longer-lived'; bolder than the instances cited at *TLL* vii. 2.

1640. 58 ff., where an ablative defines the sphere of reference: Ps. Rufinus Jos. *BJ* 4. 6 p. 748 'aeuo pontificum longissimus' (= γεραίτατος), Cypr. Gall. 201 'quinque fuit tantum . . . longior annis'. Also comparable is the use of *longum (cog)nomen* to describe an enduring reputation: cf. Ov. *Am.* 3. 9. 31 'sic Nemesis longum, sic Delia nomen habebunt', *TLL* vii. 2. 1637. 76 ff.

150–2. Three proverbial *exempla* for great age. Nestor and Tithonus are cited together at Prop. 2. 25. 10, Sen. *Apocol.* 4. 17, *S.* 2. 2. 108. Nestor grew old naturally (*annos . . . placidos*); his example is also cited at 1. 3. 110 (of Manilius Vopiscus) 'finem Nestoreae precor egrediare senectae', 3. 4. 103 f. (of Domitian) 'eat oro per annos / Iliacos Pyliosque simul': see Otto, *Sprichwörter*, no. 1223, *RE* xvii. 119 ff. (Schmidt). Tithonus was granted immortality but not eternal youth: see Otto, *Sprichwörter*, no. 1789, *RE* viA. 1518 f. (Wüst). For the Sibyl see 116 n. and Otto, *Sprichwörter*, no. 1639.

153. niualis Arctos: the constellation Arctos (= Septemtriones) was the Bear, and by metonymy designated the north and hence northern regions and peoples: see *TLL* ii. 471. 64 ff. St. refers to Domitian's campaigns in northern Europe, i.e. against the Chatti, Daci, and Sarmatae.

154. magnos Oriens dabit triumphos: traditionally the east had to be conquered: cf. Virg. *A.* 6. 794 f. 'super et Garamantas et Indos / proferet imperium', *S.* 4. 1. 40–3.

155–7. This passage, based on Virg. *A.* 6. 795–805, is explained by Housman, *CR* 20 (1906), 44–5 (= *Cl. Pap.* ii. 650–2). Exploits in the north and east recall the travels of Hercules and Bacchus. Domitian's journey *ultra sidera flammeumque solem* recalls *A.* 6. 795 f. 'iacet extra sidera tellus, / extra anni solisque uias', i.e. 'south of the zodiac and the ecliptic' (Housman). Although Mt. Atlas and the source of the Nile (157) do not lie south of the zodiac, they were believed to do so: cf. Virg. *A.* 6. 796–800. Hence St. echoes Virgil's diction in formulating his prophecy that the emperor will travel beyond the borders of the known world.

155. Euhan: cult-title for Bacchus, attested with certainty in Latin before St. only at Lucr. 5. 741, Ov. *Met.* 4. 15: see Bömer ad loc., Roscher i. 1393 (Steuding). St. found it a useful spondee, the nominative and vocative forms of *Bacchus* and *Liber* being trochaic by nature: *Euhan* occurs eight times in the *Siluae* (*Bacchus/e* four times), five times in the *Thebaid* (*Bacchus/e* eight times, *Liber* five times). As a cult-title it was perhaps fostered in areas of strong Greek influence: cf. *CIL* x. 1948 = *ILS* 5265 (from Puteoli) 'hic Phoebus fuit, hic superbus Euhan'.

159. scandes . . . abnuesque currus: by a bold compression *currus* is the object of both *scandes* and *abnues*: Domitian will mount his chariot on campaign but refuse it in a triumph (like his self-effacing gesture after the Sarmatian campaign: see on 4. 1. 39).

160–1. renatae . . . aulae: for the restoration of the Temple of Jupiter on the Capitoline see on l. 16. *aula* for 'temple' occurs only in St. and Martial: cf. *S.* 3. 1. 10, Mart. 7. 60. 1. The Capitol, and ritual associated with it, is commonly used as an image of permanence: cf. Hor. *O.* 3. 30. 7 ff. 'usque ego postera / crescam laude recens, dum Capitolium / scandet cum tacita uirgine pontifex', Virg. *A.* 9. 446 ff. 'si quid mea carmina possunt, / nulla dies umquam memori uos eximet aeuo, / dum domus Aeneae Capitoli immobile saxum / accolet imperiumque pater Romanus habebit', *S.* 1. 6. 98 ff. 'quos ibit procul hic dies per annos ... dum stabit tua Roma dumque terris, / quod reddis, Capitolium manebit'.

163. senescet: the first two *donec* clauses describe symbols which are capable of enduring (the Vestals' fire and the temple of Jupiter), while the third postulates an adynaton, i.e. *donec* (160) = 'as long as', *donec* (163) = 'until'. Although the subjunctive after *donec* meaning 'until' is attested in early Latin and in Tacitus (L–H–S 629), the indicative is normal and should probably be restored here.

4

INTRODUCTION

THIS poem is a verse-epistle addressed to Vitorius Marcellus, the dedicatee of Book 4 (4 *Pr.* 1–2). His family home is at Teate (4. 4. 85) but he is a practising orator in Rome (37–45) and he has embarked on the senatorial *cursus* (59–60: see below). He is described as a *iuuenis* (45). St. sends his letter to the right bank of the Tiber (6–7), which was a wealthy residential area: see L. Homo, *Rome impériale et l'urbanisme dans l'antiquité* (Paris, 1951), 530, and P. Grimal, *Les Jardins romains*[2] (Paris, 1969), 110.

In 96 Quintilian dedicated to Marcellus the *Institutio Oratoria*, which was written to instruct Marcellus' young son Geta (*Inst. Or.* 1 *Pr.* 6). Hanslik, *RE* Suppl. ix. 1744 s.v. Vitorius 2, infers from Marcellus' capacities as *actor causarum* (37–8) that he may have been a pupil of Quintilian. Odd, then, that the younger Pliny, who was virtually a contemporary of Marcellus and was himself taught by Quintilian (Plin. *Epist.* 6. 6. 3), does not mention him; but see on 4 *Pr.* 24 ff.

Marcellus is perhaps also to be identified with literature in another way: the critic Valerius Probus wrote a letter to a Marcellus about the accentuation of Punic names (Gell. 4. 7). White (1973*a*), 281 n. 13, points out that the pronunciation of Punic (more accurately the scansion of Punic names in Early Latin) is a very abstruse topic to interest our Marcellus. But there is just a chance that his associations with Punic society through his *condiscipulus* Septimius Seuerus (4 *Pr.* 10–11) may have caused him to investigate such matters.

St. gives only two details of Marcellus' political career to date: he had held a magistracy and was designated *curator* of the Via Latina (59–60) '[Domitianus] tuos alio subtexit munere fascis / et spatia obliquae mandat renouare Latinae'. White (1973*a*), 280, supposes that l. 60 refers to Marcellus' post in 95, whereas *mandat* implies that the post is designated for the following year. There is also no need for him to suggest that a year elapsed between Marcellus' praetorship and curatorship. Hence Marcellus is praetor in 95 and designated *curator Viae Latinae* for 96. But it has been doubted whether a praetorian curatorship for individual roads was established before Hadrian's reign: the only curatorship attested before then is that of Q. Decius Saturninus, *curator uiarum Labicanae et Latinae* under Tiberius (*CIL* x. 5393 =

ILS 6286). O. Hirschfeld, *Die kaiserlichen Verwaltungsbeamten bis auf Diocletian*² (Berlin, 1905), 207, thus interprets Saturninus' post as temporary, and he concludes that Marcellus' curatorship was honorary. But St. clearly refers to the *cura Viae Latinae* as the post to which Marcellus has been designated in the normal way. Further, it can be shown from Marcellus' subsequent career that he required a praetorian assignment in 96. Marcellus was suffect consul Sept.–Dec. 105 with C. Caecilius Strabo (*Fast. Ost.* 105). Since the *fasti* do not record a Vitorius as consul in the previous generation, it seems that Marcellus was the first consul in his family. The minimum age for a praetor was thirty, but a year or two older was normal: see Syme, *Tacitus*, ii. 652 f. For nobles and patricians thirty-two was the minimum age for becoming consul. Descendants of imperial consuls, and *uiri militares*, might obtain some years' remission from the standard age of forty-two: see Syme, *Tacitus*, ii. 653–6. If Marcellus was forty-two in 105 he would be thirty-two when he held his praetorship in 95, thus conforming to the usual pattern.

Hence the hint that St. gives at ll. 74–7 is fulfilled: he urges Marcellus' son to complete the senatorial *cursus* (*cunctas . . . curulis*) more quickly than Marcellus has done (*iuuenemque puer deprende parentem*); thus he predicts that Marcellus will gain the consulship and that as a result his son will advance rapidly along the *cursus honorum*.

Was Marcellus equestrian or from a non-consular senatorial family? His wife's background may be a clue. In 95 Marcellus' son Geta was still *paruus* (71) but just old enough (*iam nunc*) to listen to his grandfather's military reminiscences (72–3 n.).[1] The young Geta was *stemmate materno felix* (75). In treating the topos of inherited qualities, St. customarily combines a reference to a child's father and his maternal grandfather: cf. 4. 7. 43 ff., 8. 57 f. So Marcellus married into a family which attests the *cognomen* Geta and a distinguished military record.

A Cn. Hosidius Geta was *legatus Augusti* in Mauretania in AD 42 (Dio 60. 9. 1): see *RE* viii. 2490 s.v. Hosidius 6 (Groag). Either he or a brother Gaius won the *ornamenta triumphalia* in Britain in 43 under Plautius (Dio 60. 20. 4): see *PIR*² H 217, *RE* viii. 2490 s.v. Hosidius 5. Cn. Hosidius Geta was suffect consul with L. Vagellius in September 43 or 45 (*CIL* x. 1401 = *ILS* 6043). Hence Marcellus must have married into this family. If he was equestrian, the Hosidia who married him would have married beneath her station. It seems safe to assume that while a Hosidia might marry into a senatorial family which had not yet produced a consul, she would not marry an equestrian.

Groag (*RE* viii. 2491) postulates that Marcellus' wife could have been either Hosidius Geta's daughter or his granddaughter. But the daughter of a man who was suffect consul in the mid forties would almost certainly be too old to be mother of a small boy in 95, and, further, since Marcellus was now aged about thirty-two and it was almost unheard-of for a man to marry an older woman, Marcellus' wife was probably not more than thirty now, at

[1] Vollmer mistakenly identifies *auus* (73) with M. Vettius Marcellus, property-owner at Teate (Plin. *NH* 2. 199, 17. 245: see on l. 85), who was procurator under Nero (*CIL* ix. 3019 = *ILS* 1377); but this man cannot have been related to Marcellus as his *nomen* is different.

most; if her first child was under ten she was probably in her twenties. If she was Hosidius Geta's daughter and he was suffect consul in his thirties (or, more likely, his forties), then he would have been at least in his mid fifties when she was born. Hence the *auus* must be the famous Hosidius Geta and Marcellus' wife is his granddaughter. (For *auus* meaning 'great-grandfather' see 72–3 n.)

What of the child of this marriage? At the most he could have been nine years old when Quintilian wrote the preface to his sixth book (6 *Pr.* 10), i.e. in the latter half of the period 90–6.[2] Thus he cannot have been born earlier than 87. The dates fit, because his father was probably thirty-two years old in 95, and it was common for a first child to be born to a man in his mid twenties. A C. Vitorius Hosidius Geta was co-opted by the Fratres Aruales in 118 (*CIL* vi. 2078); he was *promagister* in 119, *magister* for 120 (*CIL* vi. 2079, 2080). Vespasian had been the first emperor to encourage the admission to the Fratres Aruales of senators in their early thirties: see Syme, *Arval Brethren*, 15. New admittances might soon be nominated as *magister* (Syme, *Arval Brethren*, 18). Membership of the Fratres Aruales suits the son of a man who was himself from a non-consular senatorial family, and conspicuously loyal to the emperor (see Syme, *Arval Brethren*, 77).

The Arval Brotherhood could lead to distinction (Syme, *Arval Brethren*, 35–42). A certain M. Hosidius M. f. Geta was numbered among seven signatories to a *senatus consultum* of AD 139 in response to a request from the citizens of Cyzicus for a youth club (*CIL* iii. 7060 = *ILS* 7190 = *FIRA*[2] i, no. 48). Since his name precedes that of M. Annius Libo, consul of 128 (*CIL* vi. 10048 = *ILS* 5287), M. Hosidius Geta was himself consular: see H.-G. Pflaum, *Historia-Augusta-Colloquium Bonn 1963* (Bonn, 1964), 113. His tribe was Arnensis, in which Histonium was enrolled, the home territory of Vitorius Marcellus' *adfines*: see, e.g., *CIL* ix. 2844, 2852. He was M(arci) f(ilius); the *praenomen* of Vitorius Marcellus was M(arcus) (*Fast. Ost.* 105).

But can the Arualis and the consular be reconciled? Pflaum, art. cit. 114, suggests that his full name was M. Vitorius C. Hosidius Geta and that by 128 he customarily abbreviated his signature to M. Hosidius Geta. A parallel can be drawn from the nomenclature of C. Ummidius Quadratus, suffect consul in 118 (*PIR* V 603): he was clearly polyonymous but preferred the *nomen* of his maternal grandmother, Ummidia Quadratilla (*PIR* V 606), who came from a distinguished family: her father was C. Ummidius Durmius Quadratus, who was governor of Syria when he died in AD 60 (*PIR* V 600). As an Arualis our man could have been known as C. Vitorius Hosidius Geta by simple substitution of one *praenomen* to the exclusion of the other. Pflaum meanwhile admits that the consular could have been a direct descendant of the distinguished Hosidii Getae by the male line; but it is persuasive that a consular father should produce a consular son, and that co-option to the Fratres Aruales should mark out the young man as a loyal recipient of imperial favour, destined for high position *felix uirtute paterna*.

The general cast of this epistle is Horatian, and it ranges over common

---

[2] For the dating of the *Inst. Or.* see *RE* vi. 1956 f. s.v. Fabius 137 (Schwabe), M. L. Clarke, *G&R*[2] 14 (1967), 33 ff.

138   COMMENTARY

epistolary themes such as the weather, summer holidays, friendship, and the contrast between the circumstances of the writer and his addressee. The Horatian reminiscences, in context and vocabulary but above all in atmosphere and ideas, are conditioned by the fundamental difference in the attitudes of the two poets to their addressees; and perhaps St. is too self-consciously aware of his dignity as an epic poet to be able to write hexameters in the informal tone of Horace's *Epistles*. For an analysis of the contrast with Horace, see Hardie, 164–70.

EPISTVLA AD VITORIVM MARCELLVM: see General Introduction. St. refers to this poem as *epistulam meam* at 4 *Pr.* 8–9. He also uses *epistula* of Horace's *Epistles* (*S.* 1. 3. 104 'seu tua non alia splendescat epistula cura') and clearly intended 4. 4 to convey a Horatian tone.

1–11. A prologue in which St. issues instructions to his verse-letter. Instructions are issued to the *papyrus* at Cat. 35. 2, *carta* at Cat. 36. 1, *liber* at Hor. *Epist.* 1. 20. 1 ff., Ov. *Tr.* 1. 1. 1 ff., Mart. 1. 70. 1; the verse-letter receives instructions for reaching its destination at Ov. *Tr.* 3. 7. 1–2 'uade salutatum ... Perillam, / littera,' *Pont.* 4. 5. 1 ff. 'ite, leues elegi ... protinus inde domus uobis Pompeia petatur'. The personification of the letter eliminates the *persona* of a courier (employed, for example, at Hor. *Epist.* 1. 13).

1. Imitated in a letter from Charlemagne's court to Paulus Diaconus ('curre per Ausoniae non segnis epistola campos'): see Vollmer, 34 and n. 2.

   Euboicos ... campos: the first colonists on the Bay of Naples were from Chalcis in Euboea: cf. ll. 78–9, Vell. Pat. 1. 4. 1 'Chalcidenses ... Cumas in Italia condiderunt', *S.* 4. 3. 24 'Euboicae domum Sibyllae'.

2. uias: from Naples St. is sending his verse-letter to Marcellus in Rome. The route is along the Via Domitiana until it meets the Via Appia at Sinuessa, and thence along the Appia to Rome. Vollmer, taking *crescit* to refer to the bifurcation at Sinuessa, which is at the wrong end of the Via Domitiana, proposed *uia*, 'starting along this road by which the venerable Appia bulges sideways'. Håkanson objects that corruption of *uia* in the ablative phrase *hac ... uia qua* is unlikely, and, if it happened, *uiam* would be more likely than *uias*: he understands 'starting your journey (*uias*) by the route by which (*qua*)', but in such a context *qua* could only mean 'where'. Håkanson thinks that St. was influenced by Mart. 1. 70. 9 'flecte uias hac qua madidi sunt tecta Lyaei', but then it is strange that he should have given *qua* a different meaning. Satisfactory sense is yielded if *crescit* refers to the entire extension of the Via Appia along the Via Domitiana. St. compliments Domitian not by ascribing the construction to *dominus et deus noster* but by presenting the Via Domitiana as an offshoot of the most ancient Roman road (cf. 4. 3. 3 n.).

3. mollis solidus premit agger harenas: paradox: the sturdy foundations of the road rest on an insubstantial bed of sand. *agger*, with or without the defining genitive *uiae*, is the *uox propria* for the foundations and causeway of a road, e.g. Virg. *A.* 5. 273 'uiae deprensus in aggere serpens', *S.* 2. 1. 176 'agmina Flaminio quae limite Moluius agger / transuehit': see *TLL* i. 1309. 17 ff.

5. dextras ... oras: for the desirable residential area on the right bank of the Tiber see intro. above. *ora* is a poetic word for a river-bank (*TLL* ix. 867. 27 ff.), enhanced here by the poetic plural for singular.

flaui ... Thybridis: see on 4. 3. 67.

6. Lydia ... (7) ripa: the right bank of the Tiber is the border between Latium and Etruria: cf. Hor. *O*. 1. 2. 14 'litore Etrusco'. Rival theories claimed that the Etruscans were immigrants from Lydia (Hdt. 1. 94) or an indigenous people (Dion. Hal. 1. 30).

penitus ... coercet: *coercere* is commonly applied to restrictive topographical features, especially river-banks: cf. Liv. 27. 47. 11 'altioribus coercentibus amnem ripis', Ov. *F*. 6. 413 'aquas sua ripa coercet', *S*. 3. 2. 109 'cur uada desidant et ripa coerceat undas [Nili]', *TLL* iii. 1433. 51 ff. Perhaps *penitus* conveys the notion that the banks press upon the water and make the lake deep, which would contrast with the effect created on the surface by the fringe of gardens. For *praetexitur* cf. Virg. *E*. 7. 12 'praetexit harundine ripas Mincius'.

Stagnum Nauale: the Stagnum Nauale built by Augustus in 2 BC was on the right bank of the Tiber (*RG* 23, Suet. *Aug*. 43) and still in use in Titus' day at least (Suet. *Tit*. 7. 3). But Domitian built one too: Suet. *Dom*. 4. 2 'edidit naualis pugnas paene iustarum classium, effosso et circumstructo iuxta Tiberim lacu, atque inter maximos imbres perspectauit', Dio 67. 8. Stone from it was later used to repair the Circus Maximus: Suet. *Dom*. 5 'excitauit ... naumachiam, e cuius postea lapide maximus circus deustis utrinque lateribus exstructus est'. This operation does not necessarily imply total demolition of Domitian's Stagnum, and, in any case, it was presumably performed under a later emperor. Hence Domitian's Stagnum can be assumed to have existed when St. wrote this poem. Traditionally it has been located in the Vatican Valley, although a rival location on the left bank of the Tiber in the Campus Martius in Regio IX was suggested by G. Lugli, *Monumenti antichi di Roma e suburbio* iii (Rome, 1938), 226; Domitian built assiduously in this area: see D. M. Robathan, *TAPhA* 73 (1942), 134–8. Because St. is describing the actual location of Marcellus' home, it is irrelevant to assume that he would sooner refer to a building of Domitian than of Augustus. Hence Augustus' Stagnum on the right bank seems the correct identification.

7. suburbanis ... hortis: *horti suburbani* furnish a suitably Horatian context: cf. Hor. *Epist*. 1. 7. 75–6 'iubetur / rura suburbana indictis comes ire Latinis'. For the private parks along the right bank at this period see P. Grimal, *Les Jardins romains*² (Paris, 1969), 162.

8. egregium formaque animisque: Marcellus combines physical and moral excellence, prescribed in that order by Menander in his rules for encomium (*Rhet. Gr*. iii. 420. 12 ff. Sp.). A. Desmouliez, *REL* 33 (1955), 59, examines the ancient concept that physique demonstrated personality: Marcellus epitomizes *sanitas* and καλοκἀγαθία. This combination is attested in the second-century-BC *elogium* added to the epitaph of L. Cornelius Scipio Barbatus, consul 298 (*CIL* i. 2. 7) 'fortis uir sapiensque, quoius forma uirtutei parisuma fuit'. St. praises his stepdaughter in the same terms (3. 5. 63) 'formaeque bonis animique'. The diction recalls Virgil's description of young Marcellus (*A*. 6. 861) 'egregium forma iuuenem'. The double *-que* (*formaque animisque*) particularly expresses oppositions (H. Christensen, *Archiv für lateinische Lexicographie* 15 [1908], 165–211), as here the parallelism of external and internal features: cf. Ov. *Met.* 7. 347, *Pont.* 2. 7. 71, *Theb.* 3. 254.

9. praesignem: *praesignis* exactly conveys physical eminence. For the original locative sense of pre-adjectival *prae* see E. D. Francis, *YCS* 23 (1973), 25; apposite also in our context are the passages Francis quotes: Plaut. *Trin.* 1115 'hic homost omnium hominum praecipuos', and the metaphor at Plaut. *MG* 1042 'hominem tam pulchrum et praeclarum uirtute et forma'. The topos that heroes are distinctive for their height dates from Homer: cf. *Od.* 6. 229 ff. where Athene makes Odysseus handsome and increases his height so as to attract Nausicaa. Distinctive height becomes a topos of panegyric: cf. Plin. *Pan.* 61. 2 f. (Trajan stands out above his consular colleague).

10. primam ... salutem: St. instructs the letter to address Marcellus by the usual salutatory formula (i.e. *Statius Marcello salutem*) and then to deliver St.'s message (i.e. l. 12 to the end of the poem). *primam* (M) or *primum* (ς)? *primum* would suit the contextual reminiscence of Hor. *Epist.* 1. 8. 15 f. (to his Muse) 'si dicet "recte", primum gaudere, subinde / praeceptum auriculis hoc instillare memento'. But *primam ... salutem* refers to the salutatory formula; for *salus* as 'greeting' cf. 4. 9. 49 'inflatam tibi dixero salutem'. The 'initial greeting' thus represents the beginning of the letter, to be followed *mox* by the rest (*inclusa ... uerba*).

11. haec reddere uerba memento: Ovid likewise instructs his letter to Sextus Pompeius to quote his message verbatim (*Pont.* 4. 5. 30) 'talia uos illi reddere uerba uolo'. *memento* is standard in injunctions giving *mandata*: cf. Hor. *Epist.* 1. 8. 15 f. (cit. in previous n.), Ov. *Tr.* 1. 1. 49 'denique securus famae, liber, ire memento'.

12. Weather (then as now) was an epistolary theme: cf. Hor. *Epist.* 1. 15. 1. ff. St. uses *iam*, particularly in connection with the cycle of the seasons, to evoke a Horatian atmosphere: see on 4. 5. 5. The spring rains in the Mediterranean were equated with the period when the sun had entered the 'watery' sign of Pisces: cf. Virg. *G.* 4. 234 'sidus Piscis aquosi'. Ovid describes the spring equinox as the progression from *Piscis aquosus* to Aries (*Met.* 10. 165). *fuga* describes the passage of time: cf. Colum. 11. 1. 29 'praelabentis ... temporis fuga quam sit inreparabilis, quis dubitet?', Hor. *O.* 3. 30. 5 'innumerabilis annorum series et fuga temporum'.

13. lassat: *laxat* (M) is inconsistent with *fuga ueris*: the thaw occurs at the onset of spring, not at the end. Conceivably, *laxat* could describe cracks appearing in the parched soil. But Professor Nisbet suggests to me *lassat*, 'wearies': now that summer has begun and the daylight lasts much longer, the heat wearies the earth and its population, and the sky, hitherto *uolucrem*, seems lethargic and revolves more slowly. Summer fatigue and the refreshing effects of relaxation are themes in this poem: cf. 32–3 'et nostra fatiscit / laxaturque chelys', 37–8 'te quoque flammabit tacite repetita parumper / desidia'.

Icariis ... latratibus: the dog-star, α Canis Majoris or Sirius, rises at the hottest time of the year, i.e. between mid-July and mid-August: see *RE* iii. 1480 f. (Haebler). It was thus frequently used by metonymy for summer: cf. Virg. *G.* 2. 353 'hiulca siti findit Canis aestifer arua'. The epithet *Icarius* alludes to the legendary bitch Maera which led Erigone, daughter of her master Icarus (or Icarius), to her father's grave. All three were catasterized: Erigone as Virgo; Icarus as Bootes or Arcturus; Maera as Sirius or Procyon. See *RE* vi. 451 (Escher). Thus St. associates the legend with the season when the dog-star rises, and he describes its influence in terms of the barking by which a real dog expresses itself: cf. 1. 3. 5 'nec calido latrauit Sirius astro'.

caelum ... urit: having referred to the revolution of the sky (*uolucrem ... polum*) St. now describes the effect of summer heat on the atmosphere. Normally the dog-star is said to burn up what is on the earth: cf. Virg. *A.* 3. 141 'tum sterilis exurere Sirius agros'. Here it is said to scorch the sky.

14. densae rarescunt moenia Romae: Rome is *densa* because she is heavily populated: cf. (if the text is sound) Cat. 68. 60 'medium densi ... populi'. As people migrate to the hills for the summer the population thins out: cf. *Theb.* 4. 284 'rarescunt alta colonis Maenala'. The juxtaposition *densae rarescunt* creates a neat antithesis.

15. Summer holidays are an epistolary theme, e.g. Hor. *Epist.* 1. 7. 1–9, 16. 15 ff. This subject naturally combines two topoi: the temperate climate outside the city (e.g. Hor. *Epist.* 1. 10. 14–17) and the summer recess (e.g. Mart. 10. 62). For the combination, cf. Seneca's aphorism on country villas (*Ben.* 4. 12. 3) 'salubritatis causa et aestiui secessus'. St. composes a list of resorts outside Rome so as to persuade Marcellus to join the annual migration. Martial composes an almost identical list of summer resorts spurned by a certain Apollinaris in favour of Formiae: 10. 30. 5–7 'non ille sanctae dulce Tibur uxoris, / nec Tusculanos Algidosue secessus, / Praeneste nec sic Antiumque miratur'.

Praeneste sacrum: Praeneste (modern Palestrina) was a fashionable hill resort (cf. Hor. *O.* 3. 4. 23) and the site of the cult of Fortuna Primigenia: see G. Wissowa, *RKR*[2] 259, H. Kähler, *Annal. Univ. Savar.* 7 (1958), 189–246, repr. in F. Coarelli (ed.), *Studi su Praeneste* (Perugia, 1978), 221–72. The famous *sortes Praenestinae* were consulted in her temple; Domitian came every year (Suet. *Dom.* 15. 2).

nemus ... Dianae: the celebrated grove of Diana, three miles outside Aricia, bordered on a lake known as Lacus Nemorensis (or, more popularly, Speculum Dianae: Serv. *ad Aen.* 7. 516), nowadays Lago di Nemi. Aricia was commonly associated with the grove: cf. Ov. *F.* 6. 59 (= Luc. 6. 74) 'nemoralis Aricia', *S.* 3. 1. 56 'Aricinum Triuiae nemus'. For the cult of Diana here, presided over by the homicide *rex sacrorum*, see J. H. W. G. Liebeschütz in *Mysteries of Diana*, Castle Museum Nottingham (Nottingham, 1983), 15 f., A. G. MacCormick, ibid., 19 f. *glaciale*, which properly denotes icy conditions, is used here hyperbolically to evoke the coolness of the grove: cf. 1. 3. 1 'Tibur glaciale'.

16. Algidus ... horrens: Mt. Algidus in Latium was part of the volcanic group of Alban hills adjacent to Tusculum. It was *niualis* (Hor. *O.* 3. 23. 9) and heavily wooded (Hor. *O.* 4. 4. 57 f., Liv. 3. 15. 7), hence *horrens*, which conveys its bristling woods and also its coolness ('shivering' with cold: *algidus* = 'cold', cf. Hor. *O.* 1. 21. 6 'gelido ... Algido'); St. stresses coolness in his list: cf. *glaciale, umbra, frigora*. Mt. Algidus is frequently mentioned as a summer retreat: cf. Sil. 12. 536 f: 'nec amoena retentant / Algida', Mart. 10. 30. 6.

Tuscula ... umbra: Tusculum, 23 km south-east of Rome in the Alban hills, was well wooded. Its site has been identified on the slope of a hill called Il Tuscolo, near Frascati. It was a favourite resort of the wealthy: literary sources mention thirty-eight Romans with villas there: see *RE* viiA. 1487 ff. (McCracken).

17. Tiburis ... lucos Anienaque frigora captant: there were waterfalls on the R. Anio at Tibur, and so they are frequently mentioned together: cf. Hor. *O.* 1. 7. 13 'et praeceps Anio ac Tiburni lucus', Prop. 3. 16. 2–4. The combination of shade and water creates an ideal summer retreat; thus St. on the villa of his friend Manilius Vopiscus (1. 3. 5 ff.), esp. 16–19 'non largius usquam / indulsit natura sibi nemora alta citatis / incubuere uadis; fallax responsat imago / frondibus, et longas eadem fugit umbra per undas'. *lucos* implies sacred groves, and hence a cult of the eponymous hero Tiburnus: cf. 1. 3. 74 'illa recubat Tiburnus in umbra', N–H on Hor. *O.* 1. 7. 13. Shade, water, and rural seclusion provoke a reminiscence from bucolic: cf. Virg. *E.* 1. 52 'frigus captabis opacum', 2. 8 'pecudes umbras et frigora captant'.

18. quae iam plaga mitior: *quaenam plaga* (M) seems too emphatic: see F. Hand, *Tursellinus seu de particulis Latinis commentarii*[4] (Leipzig, 1845), iv. 18, K–S ii. 116 f. *quae iam* (A. Otto, *RhM* 42 [1887], 538) conveys St.'s assumption that Marcellus, in accordance with urbane conduct, has already left Rome, and it matches the repetition of *iam* to point the cycle of the seasons at 12, 14, 23: see on l. 12, and Håkanson, 119–20. *mitis* is frequently applied to a favourable environment: cf. Hor. *O.* 1. 18. 2 'circa mite solum Tiburis', *S.* 1. 3. 15 (also of Tibur) 'ingenium quam mite solo', 3. 5. 79 (Naples) 'mite solum'. To replace the *clamosa urbs* St. hopes that Marcellus will find a more harmonious landscape. Rome is *clamosa* like any rowdy city: cf. Mart. 12. 18. 1 f. 'tu forsitan inquietus erras / clamosa, Iuuenalis, in Subura'; *clamosa* may derive further point from the specific context of Marcellus' forensic career: cf. 41–2 'nec ... queruli ... rogant exire clientes', Sen. *HF* 172 'clamosi rabiosa fori iurgia'.

19. quo ... aere: not merely equivalent to *qua ... regione*; *aere* suggests a breath of fresh air to counter the stifling heat.

20–4. The traditional punctuation *quid? tuus ... amor (dubium ... bonis) Latiis ... domos?* was corrected by Housman, *CR* 20 (1906), 45 (= *Cl. Pap.* ii. 652), who noticed the affinities between this passage and Hor. *Epist.* 1. 3. 9–14 and punctuated accordingly: *quid ... bonis? Latiis ... domos?*. The mutual friend is an epistolary feature: cf. Titius (Hor. *Epist.* 1. 3. 9) and Celsus (Hor. *Epist.* 1. 3. 15). The informal nature of the *Siluae* accommodates in non-epistolary poems this 'mutual friend' feature: cf. 2. 1. 191 ff. (Melior's friend Blaesus), 4. 6. 94 (Vindex' deceased friend Vestinus; the atmosphere of this poem is deliberately Horatian: see 4. 6. 1 n.), 5. 2. 152 (Crispinus' friend Optatus). *amicitia* is the general theme of this poem: cf. 97–100 (St.'s request for advice), 102–5 (concluding *exempla*). Hence the 'mutual friend' feature sustains the main theme.

20–1. tua cura ... / nec non noster amor: reference to the absent friend,

Gallus, is made in language reminiscent of the allusions to the poet Gallus at Virg. *E.* 10. 22 'tua cura, Lycoris', 73 'Gallo, cuius amor tantum mihi crescit in horas'.

23. metalliferae ... Lunae: for the marble-quarries at Luna see on 4. 2. 29. The equable climate made the Ligurian coast an ideal place too for spending a warm winter: cf. Pers. 6. 9.

26. sonus ... mihi circumit auris: St. hints that he is intimate with Marcellus by asserting that if Marcellus is with their mutual friend they are bound to mention St. to each other; he knows this because his ears are ringing. Proverbially the ears of a third party buzz (in English idiom they burn) when he is discussed in his absence: cf. Plin. *NH* 28. 24 'quin et absentes tinnitu aurium praesentire sermones de se receptum est', *Anth. Lat.* 450 Shackleton Bailey (=*PLM* iv. 62 Baehrens) '*De tinnitu auris*'. Despite Vollmer, this motif is not the same as the buzzing in the ears which is one of the physical manifestations of erotic suffering: cf. Sappho fr. 31 L-P ἐπιρρόμβεισι δ' ἄκουαι, Cat. 51. 10 f., *Anth. Pal.* 5. 212.

circumit: would St. have written *circumit* (so M at 3. 5. 59, 4. 8. 11) or *circuit* (so M at 5. 2. 12)? The MSS of the epics are inconsistent; grammarians supply conflicting evidence: Prisc. *GL* ii. 45. 13 Keil states that the *m* was not elided in pronunciation; the writer of the *Orthographia Bernensis* 2 (*GL Suppl.* 296. 5 Keil) claims that it was; Papirianus *ap.* Cassiodorus (*GL* vii. 164. 7–10 Keil) claims that *m* was both written and pronounced before *i* or *u*. But the issue may be decided by the near-contemporary evidence of the Trajanic inscription *CIL* vi. 1548. 3 EXERCITVS SVOS CIRCVMIT. In the noun, less open to the influence of *circumeo*, the form *circuitus* is normal but note CIRCVMITVM at *CIL* vi. 25527. 6 (AD 94).

28. torua Cleonaei iuba sideris: St. again, as at l. 13, designates summer by an astronomical and mythological periphrasis. The *sidus Cleonaeum* (also at Mart. 4. 60. 2) is the constellation Leo, said to be the lion that Hercules killed in the grove of Nemea in the Peloponnese, between Phlius and the city of Cleonae: cf. Pind. *Nem.* 4. 27 ἀγὼν Κλεωναῖος (=the Nemean Games), and see *RE* xvi. 2316 (Meyer). *Cleonaeus* was a common epithet at this period in connection with the story of the Nemean lion: cf. 5. 2. 49, Theb. 1. 487, Luc. 4. 612, Val. Fl. 1. 34, Sil. 3. 33, Sen. *HF* 798, Mart. 5. 71. 3. *torua* may be a reminiscence of the periphrasis for Leo at Cic. *Arat.* 321 'fulgens cedit uis torua Leonis'. The constellation was commonly designated, *pars pro toto*, by its jaws or its mane: cf. German. *Arat.* 149 'horrentis ... iubas et fuluum cerne Leonem', 604 'cum prima iuba radiarit flamma Leonis', Sen. *HF* 948 'rutila iubam / ceruice iactans', [Sen.] *HO* 70 'iactans feruidam collo iubam', Mart. 9. 90. 12 'feruens iuba saeuiet Leonis', Firm. 6. 31. 88 'iuba Leonis', *RE* xii. 1977 (Gundel).

29. assiduo temet furare labori: St. echoes Sleep's words to Palinurus at *A.* 5. 845 'pone caput fessosque oculos furare labori'. In both contexts the implication is that, although the call of duty is ostensibly paramount (for Palinurus to steer the ship, and for Marcellus to plead in court), nevertheless the addressee deserves to take unofficial leave, i.e. *furare* conveys stealth.

COMMENTARY

30. sontis ... pharetras: the epithet *sontis*, transferred from the Parthian archer to his quiver, implies that the Parthians are 'guilty' because they are enemies of Rome; it also suggests their treacherous tactics in shooting over their shoulders when they appear to be in retreat.

arcum ... retendit: the image of the loosened bowstring is common in advice to relax: cf. Hdt. 2. 173. 3, Hor. *O.* 2. 10. 19 with N–H's n.

31–2. Eleos auriga laboribus actis / Alpheo permulcet equos: *Eleis ... laboribus actos / ... equos* (M) would mean that the horses are driven (by the charioteer) in the laborious contest at Olympia. But this interpretation strains the syntax, since with *actos* it is natural to understand *laboribus* as instrumental. Markland emends to *Eleos ... actis*: the horses are said to be 'Olympic' (via the transferred epithet *Eleus*, derived from the territory of Elis surrounding Olympia): cf. Virg. *G.* 1. 59 'Eliadum palmas Epiros equarum'.

32. fatiscit: St.'s own poetry provides the third paradigm for relaxation. After the strenuous activity of the Parthian archer and the Olympic competitor, St. presents his own example in a self-deprecating fashion: *fatiscit* implies a certain decadent submission to *inertia*. There is parallel progression homewards in the train of thought: geographical (Parthia, Greece, Italy) and occupational (warfare, physical [and poetic] contests, poetic composition).

33. laxatur ... chelys: St. uses the metaphor of slackening the strings of his lyre to illustrate his periods of respite from poetic composition. In order to function as an *exemplum* encouraging Marcellus to take a holiday from his forensic work, and in order to match the image of the Parthian and the Olympic team desisting from their activities, *laxatur ... chelys* must imply that St. temporarily ceases to write any poetry at all, rather than that he suspends epic so as to relax with lesser genres.

33–4. uires ... uirtus: the Roman ideal of productive *quies et otium* is expressed via the chiastic arrangement *uires ... uirtus*. Inflections of *uis* and *uirtus* form a common alliterative pair: for examples see E. Wölfflin, *Ausgewählte Schriften* (Leipzig, 1933), 280. *otium* conveys more than merely 'activating qualities of rest' (so J. F. Lockwood in *Ut Pictura Poesis: Studia Enk* [Leiden, 1955], 108); it was proverbially a source of literary inspiration: cf. Cic. *Orat.* 108 'nemo enim orator tam multa ne in Graeco quidem otio scripsit'. The slight oxymoron in *instigat ... quies* conveys the paradox that inactivity can be productive.

35. cantata Briseide: *otium* is also necessary to renew physical activity: as illustration St. cites the *exemplum* of Achilles, who spent his *otium* in poetic composition and was thus stimulated to fight Hector and avenge the death of Patroclus. No source before St. attests that Achilles sang about Briseis, but this detail is in keeping with the Roman tendency to romanticize their relationsip in contrast to Homer's unemotional treatment: see N–H on Hor. *O.* 2. 4. 3. The absent object of desire is a theme for song and lament: cf. Hor. *Sat.* 1. 5. 15–17 'absentem ... cantat amicam / ... nauta atque uiator / certatim'.

37. flammabit: the passive connotations of *desidia* contrast with the vivid action implied by *flammare* to convey the paradox that apparent inertia is a stimulus to action, as in *instigat ... quies* (33–4). The metaphor of the flame of love is extended to other capacities: cf. Cic. *Brut.* 93 'omnis illa uis et quasi flamma oratoris extinguitur'.

tacite: in contrast to the musical accompaniment of Achilles' relaxation (cf. *plectris*), in Marcellus' case silence symbolizes rest.

38. solitos: *solidos* (M) is defended by Vollmer as proleptic, but *solitos* (ς) must be right: the paradox that leisure stimulates renewed activity is expressed by the juxtaposition of *solitos nouus* and of *desidia . . . actus*.

exsultabis: the energetic physical activity implied in the root *salire* matches *actus* (from *agere*).

39. Latiae non miscent iurgia leges: *iurgium*, from *iurgare*, originally a 'terme de la langue familière' (Ernout–Meillet), comes to be used as the technical term for a dispute which is heard before a judge: see *TLL* vii. 2. 667. 3 ff. St. similarly contrasts *quies* with *iurgia* in the list of attractions at Naples (3. 5. 87). Lines 39–42 imply that no litigation was brought before the courts in July. Plin. *Epist.* 8. 21. 2 says that little business was done 'Iulio mense, quo maxime lites interquiescunt'; Sherwin-White ad loc. infers that there were more *dies festi* in July than in any other month, but Pliny may rather mean that business generally slackened off in July, not that there was a legal prohibition on litigation. At any rate St. implies a recess lasting for days on end, not isolated days without business, since he expects Marcellus to spend a continuous period out of Rome. No prosecution was allowed to be initiated after 1 September: see C. G. Bruns, *Fontes Iuris Romani Antiqui*, ed. O. Gradenwitz (Tübingen, 1909), 9; hence the July recess was probably informal rather than stipulated by law. Tacitus implies that this recess may have varied somewhat from year to year (*Ann.* 2. 35. 1) 'res eo anno prolatas haud referrem'.

40. piger annus: when *annus* = 'season' it is usually combined with an adjective which limits it, as here *piger*: see *TLL* ii. 120. 3 ff. Summer is *piger* because of the enervating heat: cf. Hor. *O.* 1. 22. 17–18 'pigris ubi nulla campis / arbor aestiua recreatur aura'.

messes . . . reuersae: *ab urbe condita* construction. *messes* marks the time of year: see *OLD* s.v. *messis* 1b. The compression points the antithesis in juxtaposition with *dimisere*: as harvest-time returns to rural Italy, the courts at Rome correspondingly become empty. This technique is used for paradoxical effect, as at Hor. *O.* 2. 4. 10–12 'ademptus Hector / tradidit . . . Pergama'. During the empire the marked taste for epigrammatic point makes this construction a common vehicle for cryptic expression, e.g. Juv. 6. 8 (parodying Catullus) 'turbauit nitidos extinctus passer ocellos'.

42. uestibulo: if the front door did not open directly on to the street, the space in front of it formed a *uestibulum*: cf. Var. *LL* 7. 81 'qui exit in uestibulum, quod est ante domum', Vitr. 6. 7. 5 'item πρόθυρα Graece dicuntur, quae sunt ante ianuas uestibula', Gell. 16. 5. 3 'C. Aelius Gallus . . . uestibulum esse dicit . . . locum ante ianuam domus uacuum, per quem a uia aditus accessusque ad aedis est, cum dextra sinistraque ianuam tectaque sunt uiae iuncta atque ipsa ianua procul a uia est area uacanti intersita', Mayor on Juv. 1. 132, *OLD* s.v. *uestibulum* 1a, A. G. McKay, *Houses, Villas and Palaces in the Roman World* (London, 1975), 32. This was where a patron's clients congregated: cf. Cic. *Caecin.* 35 'non modo limine tectoque aedium

146   COMMENTARY

tuarum, sed primo aditu uestibuloque prohibuerint', Sen. *Cons. ad Marc.* 10. 1 'ampla atria et exclusorum clientium turba referta uestibula'. The prepositional prefix in *exire* makes it easier to omit the preposition with *uestibulo*.

queruli: the *uox propria* of plaintiffs because they keep asking their advocate to present their complaint in court. If Marcellus' clients let him alone in his summer retreat, that may not have guaranteed him peace; even in his Tuscan villa Pliny did not escape importunate requests, this time from tenants: cf. *Epist.* 9. 15. 1 'tam multis undique rusticorum libellis et tam querulis inquietor', 7. 30. 3 'querelae rusticorum'. The similar *agrestes querelae* at *Epist.* 9. 36. 6 may refer to the morning *salutatio* (see Sherwin-White ad loc.), which is the occasion that St. is describing. Cf. Maternus' defence of the poet's seclusion, contrasted with the demands made on the orator's time (Tac. *Dial.* 12. 1) 'nemora uero et luci et secretum ipsum, quod Aper increpabat, tantam mihi adferunt uoluptatem, ut inter praecipuos carminum fructus numerem, quod non in strepitu nec sedente ante ostium litigatore nec inter sordes ac lacrimas reorum componuntur, sed secedit animus in loca pura atque innocentia fruiturque sedibus sacris'. With *rogant*, understand *te* from *tibi*.

43. centeni moderatrix iudicis hasta: the centumviral court dealt with suits for the recovery of property. The *hasta* of the *iudex* was planted in the Basilica Iulia in front of the jurors' tribunal (Gaius 4. 16), and the court was administered by the *praetor hastarius*/*ad hastam*. *hasta* was used as metonymy for each section of the centumviral tribunal (Quint. 2. 5. 1) or even for the whole tribunal (Suet. *Aug.* 36). St. personifies the *hasta* to represent the jury-panel before whom Marcellus demonstrates his rhetorical fluency. For the functions of the court see Plin. *Epist.* 5. 9 with Sherwin-White's discussion, and *RE* iii. 1935 ff. (Kubitschek).

45. iuuenis facundia praeterit annos: *iuuenis* is acc. pl. (= *iuuenalis*): for the adjectival use cf. Ov. *Met.* 7. 295 'iuuenis ... annos', *Ciris* 45 'iuuenes exegimus annos', Pers. 6. 5 'iuuenes ... iocos', *S.* 3. 1 92–3 'iuuenem ... Parthenopen', *TLL* vii. 2. 737. 8 ff. *facundia* denotes talent in writing, e.g. 3 *Pr.* 5 (Pollius Felix' literary pursuits), or in speaking, as here of Marcellus' forensic skill: cf. 4. 5. 3–4 (addressing Marcellus' *condiscipulus* Septimius Seuerus) 'fortem atque facundum Seuerum / ... saluto'.

46. felix curarum: on the face of it, oxymoron. *felix qui* is a formula of μακαρισμός equivalent to ὄλβιος (μάκαρ, μακάριος) ὅστις. Traditionally the advocate has numerous *curae* which a poet has not: cf. Tac. *Dial.* 11. 3, 12. 1 (quoted on l. 42). But, paradoxically, Marcellus is *felix curarum* because his life of action contrasts favourably (so St. claims) with a poet's *otium*.

46–7. non ... / serta nec imbelles ... laurus: St. makes the traditional comparison between oratory, *artes maximae*, and poetry, *artes mediocres*: cf. Cic. *De Or.* 1. 6–12, 212 f., *Brut.* 3, 70, *Fin.* 5. 7, *Cat. Mai.* 50; although orators might write poetry too, it was a pastime and not a full-time occupation: cf. 4. 5. 60, Plin. *Epist.* 5. 3. 5 f. St. uses this comparison to belittle himself and thus, by contrast, exalt his addressee: cf. Virg. *G.* 4. 559 ff., Prop. 3. 9. The *imbelles ... laurus* of St.'s poetic garland recall Horace's *apologia* to Maecenas (*Epod.* 1. 15 f.) 'roges, tuum labore quid iuuem meo, / imbellis ac firmus parum?'

48–9. magnos accinctus in usus / ... animus: cf. Val. Fl. 4. 593 'animos accinge futuris'; *accingere* is common in metaphors for mental preparedness: see *TLL* i. 303. 9 ff.

50. uentosa ... gaudia famae: St. compares the court-cases in which Marcellus participates with the caprices of popular taste in poetry which St. himself has to face. The shifting direction of winds is an old metaphor for the mutability of fortune, and it comes to illustrate in particular the ephemeral nature of glory: cf. Pind. *Nem.* 6. 29 οὖρον ἐπέων / εὐκλεᾶ, and see J. Péron, *Les Images maritimes de Pindare* (Paris, 1974), 189 ff. This image has a particularly Horatian ring: cf. *O.* 3. 2. 19 f. '[Virtus] nec sumit aut ponit securis / arbitrio popularis aurae', *Epist.* 2. 1. 177 f. (of drama) 'quem tulit ad scaenam uentoso Gloria curra / exanimat lentus spectator, sedulus inflat'.

51–2. geniale ... litus: for St. the Bay of Naples is *geniale* because he has cultured friends to visit there and peace and quiet for composing poetry. The Bay of Naples was renowned as a cultural retreat where the intellectual pursuits of *otium* were being cultivated as early as the second century BC: see D'Arms, 13 ff. Virgil settled there to study philosophy (*Catal.* 5), and Silius retired to Campania and wrote the *Punica* (Plin. *Epist.* 3. 7. 6). For the tradition of pursuing *otium* at Naples cf. Hor. *Epod.* 5. 43 'otiosa ... Neapolis', Virg. *G.* 4. 563 f. 'illo Vergilium me tempore dulcis alebat / Parthenope studiis florentem ignobilis oti', Ov. *Met.* 15. 711 f. 'in otia natam / Parthenopen', Sil. 12. 31 f. 'nunc molles urbi ritus atque hospita Musis / otia'.

52–3. se condidit hospita ... / Parthenope: the foundation-legend of Naples recorded that a Siren called Parthenope was washed ashore in the Bay of Naples and founded the city: see R. M. Peterson, *The Cults of Campania* (Rome, 1919), 174 ff. Parthenope was originally *hospita* in the sense of being a stranger on Italian shores: see *OLD* s.v. *hospita*^{2} 3.

53. tenuis ... chordas: St. is being self-deprecating about his poetry in contrast to Marcellus' forensic career. His reference to Virgil as *magister* (55) implies that he is talking mainly about his career as an epic poet. The strings of his lyre are literally *tenus*, which properly describes slender filament and the like: cf. Cic. *Ver.* 5. 27 'reticulum ... ad naris sibi admouebat tenuissimo lino', Virg. *E.* 1. 2 'siluestrem tenui Musam meditaris auena'; this slender quality also reflects the λεπτότης of the stuff of which his poetry is made: cf. Hor. *Epist.* 2. 1. 225 'tenui deducta poemata filo', Pfeiffer on Callim. *Aet.* 1 fr. 1. 24.

ignauo pollice: with *ignauo*, *pollice* here is literally 'thumb', not 'plectrum' as at 5. 5. 31 f. 'nec eburno pollice chordas / pulso'. *ignauia, segnitia, quies*, equivalent to ληθαργία, are regarded as the antithesis of *uirtus* and constructive activity: cf. Naeu. *com.* 92 'ad uirtutem ut redeatis, abeatis ab ignauia', Sall. *BJ* 1. 4 'sin captus prauis cupidinibus ad inertiam et uoluptates corporis pessum datus est, perniciosa lubidine pauliper usus, ubi per socordiam uires tempus ingenium diffluxere, naturae infirmitas accusatur: suam quisque culpam auctores ad negotia transferunt', *S.* 1. 4. 56 f. (of the illness which attacked Rutilius Gallicus, *praefectus urbi*) 'hinc fessos penitus subrepsit in artus / insidiosa quies et pigra obliuio uitae'. It is noteworthy that Virgil at *G.* 4. 563–4 (cit. on ll. 51–2) asserts that his *otium* has been productive for him (*florentem*) but at the same time he acknowledges the tradition that leisured pursuits are *ignobilis*.

54. Maronei ... templi: Silius rescued Virgil's tomb from neglect. If this undertaking merited a four-line epigram (Mart. 11. 50[49]: for a discussion of this corrupt text, see N. M. Kay's commentary), there may have been more involved than simply preventing a modest grave from becoming overgrown. Silius used to make visits to it as though to a shrine: cf. Mart. 11. 48. 1 'Silius haec magni celebrat monimenta Maronis', Plin. *Epist.* 3. 7. 8 'monimentum eius adire ut templum solebat'. For the recurrence of the word *templum* in this context cf. Virg. *A.* 4. 457 f. (Sychaeus' sepulchral monument) 'fuit in tectis de marmore templum / coniugis antiqui', Sil. 1. 84 ff. (Dido's tomb) 'urbe fuit media sacrum genetricis Elissae / manibus ... templum'. Donatus (*Vit. Verg.* 5. 5. 36) records that the tomb ('tumulus') was on the Via Puteolana two miles outside Naples ('intra lapidem secundum') and that Virgil himself composed an elegiac couplet for it: 'Mantua me genuit, Calabri rapuere, tenet nunc / Parthenope; cecini pascua, rura, duces.' Since the mid fourteenth century it has been identified with a tomb of the *columbarium* type at Piedigrotta, beside the entrance to Cocceius' tunnel through Posillipo, although it is slightly further than two Roman miles from Naples and without any trace of Virgil's elegiac epitaph: see J. B. Trapp, *JWarbCourtInst* 47 (1984), 1–34.

57. (detque precor) ... pergent: Markland punctuated thus and emended *pergant* (M) to *pergent*, so that there is only one parenthetic wish, *detque precor*, which modifies the condition that Marcellus be granted a long life; the rider that Domitian must continue to favour Marcellus is then expressed as the second half of the condition. Vollmer retains *pergant* and defends the traditional punctuation, which makes the parenthesis extend from *detque* to *Latinae* (60), on the grounds that it would be tactless for St. to express the bestowal of the emperor's favour as a conditional clause, and to be diplomatic he would have to express it as a wish. But Vollmer fails to see that Domitian's power is portrayed as flatteringly absolute if his favour is cited as a precondition for the advancement of Marcellus' career (which also undoubtedly happened to be true). Hence St. is predicting the likely pattern of Marcellus' career, given that fate grants him sufficient time and the emperor's favour furthers his appointments. *pergere* is commonly used absolutely (*OLD* s.v. *pergo* 1).

58. posthabito ... Tonante: in the context of his devotion to Virgil (54–5), St. appropriately echoes *A.* 1. 15 f. '[Italiam] quam Iuno fertur terris magis omnibus unam / posthabita coluisse Samo'. Marcellus' devotion to Domitian surpasses his worship of Jupiter; St. outdoes Ovid, who equates Messalinus' veneration of Augustus with his attitude towards Jupiter (*Pont.* 2. 2. 41–2) 'uerbaque nostra fauens Romana ad numina perfer / non tibi Tarpeio culta Tonante minus'.

59. tuos ... fascis: the adjective is emphatic: 'to which you are entitled'; but the nuance lacks a succinct translation.

subtexit: a metaphor from weaving whereby another fabric is woven into a material: cf. *S.* 1. 2. 98–9 (Apollo as patron of elegy as well as of epic) 'incedere uates / maluit et nostra laurum subtexere myrto'. Hence in our context Marcellus' designated curatorship of the Via Latina is said to be woven into his praetorship.

60. obliquae ... Latinae: the Via Latina followed a hilly route, hence *obliquae* (M) is usually taken (e.g. by Vollmer, and by Radke at *RE* Suppl. xiii. 1493) to refer to its precipitous gradients, i.e. *obliquae* = 'at an angle' as opposed to 'flat': cf. Juv. 5. 55 'cliuosae ... Latinae', Paul. Nol. *Carm.* 14. 72 'montosae ... Latinae'. But it is impossible for *obliquus* describing a road to refer to elevation rather than to lateral position. The sun can be said to be *obliquus* because in winter it describes an arc in the sky whereby its position can be measured in relation to its position vertically overhead in midsummer: cf. Sen. *NQ* 1. 8. 7 'cum breuiores dies sunt ... [sol] obliquus est'. But a road is not usually described in terms of elevation. Hence it must be *obliqua* in terms of St.'s geographical point of view. He may be referring to the diagonal direction of the Via Latina across Latium, so that it is roughly *obliqua* in relation to the Via Appia (along which St.'s letter has travelled); while the Via Appia is the main highway running south from Rome, the Via Latina runs south-east to Capua and so the Via Latina could be said to slant away from the Appia. This interpretation seems preferable to *antiquae* (Domitius) which, although creating a neat antithesis with *renouare*, is in itself unremarkable.

62. nigrae ... Thules: the Rhine and Thule form a pair of *exempla* illustrating Roman influence in the north and west. The reference to the Rhine recalls the exploration and subjugation in the British Isles in the early part of Domitian's reign. The Thule sighted by Agricola was possibly one of the Shetlands: cf. Tac. *Agr.* 10. 4 with Ogilvie-Richmond's note. Thule is *nigra* because of the long winter nights (*Pan. Mess.* 15. 3, Plin. *NH* 2. 186 f.) and the drizzle: according to Strabo (4. 5. 5) grain could not be stored out of doors διὰ τὸ ἀνήλιον καὶ τοὺς ὄμβρους. Cf. Albinovanus Pedo's lines on Germanicus' expedition in the North Sea (*ap.* Sen. *Suas.* 1. 15 = *FPL* 115. 12–13, 16–17 Morel = *FPR* 147 f. Büchner) 'aliquis prora caecum sublimis ab alta / aera pugnaci luctatus rumpere uisu ... fugit ipse dies orbemque relictum / ultima perpetuis claudit natura tenebris'.

63. datur: *datus* (M) is altered to *datur* (A). It might seem superfluous, since *ibis* can happily govern *seruare* as well as *frenare*, and the notion of a commission, which is implied in *datur*, is already supplied by the context. Hence Domitius proposed *latus*. But *Histrum* is not an adjective, and in any case phrases of the type *Hesperium latus* (Virg. *A.* 3. 418) are formed with an adjective from the name of a region, not a river: see *TLL* vii. 2. 1029. 1 ff. In support of *datur*, its tense should be noted: Marcellus' future commission is already so intended by the emperor.

63–4. metuenda ... Portae / limina Caspiacae: the Κάσπιαι Πύλαι formed a narrow pass in the Parachoatras range (the Elburz mountains) south of the Caspian Sea between Media and Parthia: cf. Plin. *NH* 5. 99 'etiam ubi dehiscit seque populis aperit portarum tamen nomine unitatem sibi uindicans quae aliubi Armeniae aliubi Caspiae aliubi Ciliciae uocantur'. The exact location is disputed: see J. F. Standish, *G&R*[2] 17 (1970),

17–24. *Caspiacae* here is the only attested instance of the alternative form for *Caspius*: see *TLL Onomasticon* ii 230. *limina* is a mild pun on the name *Portae*. The Caspian Gates are *metuenda* because they represent the distant unknown and the traditional eastern enemy. F. Grosso, *Epigraphica* 16 (1954), 118, cites an inscription from Böyük Dash in Azerbaijan (*AE* 1951, 263) attesting that Domitian posted Legio XII Fulminata to the area which could be designated *Portae limina Caspiacae*. He suggests (*Epigraphica* 17 [1955], 51) that St. is predicting for Marcellus the post of legate in charge of this legion. But it would be inappropriate for St. to appear to suggest any particular appointments; he simply cites four regions where Domitian is known to have concentrated military activity.

66. tarde (M) is intolerable: it would not be complimentary for St. to imply that Marcellus was lumbering and inefficient at putting on his armour. Nor does St. say that Marcellus' breastplate was tight; hence Vollmer is mistaken in referring to *Theb.* 1. 489–90 'Tydea per latos umeros ambire laborant / exuuiae'. The theme of this passage (65–71) is that Marcellus has the physique to be a successful soldier: cf. Prop. 4. 3. 23 'dic mihi num teneros urit lorica lacertos', Hor. *O*. 1. 8. 10–11 'neque iam liuida gestat armis / bracchia'. Two approaches have been tried: an adjective appropriate to heroic physique or an adverb (sometimes entailing transposition after *subeant*) conveying soldierly efficiency. Palaeographic arguments cannot be adduced, because *tarde* is an obvious supplement for a scribe who, once the original adjective or adverb dropped out, found the verse a foot short and looked to *grauem* for the immediate context. Hence certainty as to what St. wrote is unlikely to be reached.

67–8. seu campo pedes ire pares ... seu frena sonantia flectes: St. echoes the description of his addressee's namesake, the younger Marcellus, at Virg. *A*. 6. 880 f. 'seu cum pedes iret in hostem / seu spumantis equi foderet calcaribus armos'. For these alternatives in an encomiastic context Norden cites Pind. *Pyth.* 2. 64 f. ὅθεν φαμὶ καὶ σὲ τὰν ἀπείρονα δόξαν εὑρεῖν, / τὰ μὲν ἐν ἱπποσόαισιν ἄνδρεσσι μαρνάμενον, τὰ δ' ἐν πεζομάχαισι. The allusion to Marcellus' height (*est agmina supra* / *nutaturus apex*) recalls the encomiastic topos at l. 9. The detail of reining in a spirited horse recalls the image in the same context of attack at Ov. *Am.* 1. 2. 15 f. 'asper equus duris contunditur ora lupatis: / frena minus sentit, quisquis ad arma facit'. The subjunctive *pares* makes the likelihood that Marcellus would serve as an infantryman more remote, whereas the hypothesis of his cavalry service is expressed in the indicative (*seruiet*), the normal mood for the protasis in conditions of this type referring to the future.

69. facta aliena canendo: a gerund in the ablative case governing a direct object is a construction attested in early Latin prose, adopted by the Augustan poets for metrical convenience and commonly found in later Latin: see L–H–S 373.

70. uergimus: for *uergimur* (M). When *uergo* is used in the passive, an agent apart from the subject is implied, e.g. *Theb.* 6. 211 'spumantes ... mero paterae uerguntur'. The intransitive use of *uergo* is very common, and there seems no reason why St. should make it passive to convey a middle sense: cf. Sen. *Dial.* 6. 21. 7 'ut non putemus ad mortem nisi senes inclinatosque iam uergere', *Theb.* 1. 391 'rex . . . medio de limite uitae in senium uergens inclinatur'. The sinking and declining motion conveyed by *uergo* evokes the debilitating onset of old age: St. was probably now in his mid forties (see General Introduction), an age at which he was not yet a *senex* but could conceivably be said to be tending towards it. The contrast between himself as man of letters and Marcellus as man of action is thus reinforced by the contrast between his age and Marcellus' youth (45, 74). As here, so also at 3. 5. 13 he portrays himself on the brink of old age so as to make a rhetorical point to his addressee (in this case, his wife) 'auguror . . . patria senium componere terra?'

71. ipse canenda geres: St. pursues the contrast between poet and man of action to express the topos that it is more worthwhile to perform exploits which will become the stuff of poetry than to be a poet: cf. Ov. *Pont.* 4. 8. 71 'sed dare materiam nobis quam carmina maius'.

71–2. paruo . . . exempla parabis / magna Getae: for Marcellus' marriage and his son's future career see intro. above. It was a fundamental ancient belief that it was the duty of the father to furnish his offspring with a model to emulate, and the duty of the child to follow the example of his forebears. Cf. Soph. *Ajax* 548 ff. ἀλλ' αὐτίκ' ὠμοῖς αὐτὸν ἐν νόμοις πατρὸς / δεῖ πωλοδαμνεῖν κἀξομοιοῦσθαι φύσιν. / ὦ παῖ, γένοιο πατρὸς εὐτυχέστερος, / τὰ δ' ἄλλ' ὁμοῖος· καὶ γένοι' ἂν οὐ κακός; Sophocles' passage was the model for Virg. *A.* 12. 435 ff. (the advice of Aeneas to Ascanius) 'disce, puer, uirtutem ex me uerumque laborem, / fortunam ex aliis . . . / tu facito, mox cum matura adoleuerit aetas, / sis memor et te animo repetentem exempla tuorum / et pater Aeneas et auunculus excitet Hector'.

72–3. dignos . . . triumphos: having exhorted Marcellus to provide an example of vigorous public life for his son, St. turns his attention to the boy's *auus*, who is said both to demand that the young Geta should perform worthy achievements and to provide (the opportunity) for him to know about his heritage of triumphs. The issues are as follows: (i) who is the *auus* (for the meaningless *auos* of M)? (ii) is it the old man himself or his memory which is to spur on the young Geta? (iii) is *praestat* with the infinitive acceptable syntax? (iv) is *domi* genitive or locative?

(i) It is argued in the introduction that either Cn. Hosidius Geta, *leg. Aug.* in Mauretania in 43, or else his brother is the grandfather of Marcellus' wife, since either of these men would be too old to be the father of a woman who married Marcellus. It is argued by White (1973*a*), 280 n. 7, that although *aui* (plural) can mean 'ancestors', the singular *auus* ought to refer to a grandfather and not to a member of an earlier generation. But St. himself calls Pollius Felix the *auus* of the great-grandchildren whom St. predicts for him (3. 1. 175 ff.) 'concedamque diu iuuenis spectare nepotes, / donec et hic sponsae maturus et illa marito, / rursus et ex illis suboles noua grexque proteruus / nunc umeris inreptet aui nunc agmine blando / certatim placidae concurrat ad oscula Pollae'; in conjunction with his wife Polla, the *auus* must be Pollius himself and not his son. Hence the *auus* at 4. 4. 73 is the young Geta's great-grandfather.

(ii) Håkanson, 120, claims that the picture of an *auus* who harangued the child in person would be too unattractive for St. to include in a poem to Marcellus, and so he assumes that it is the thought of his ancestor, not his actual presence, which spurs on the child. But we surely have here a *domesticus auctor* whose reminiscences evoke for his great-grandson a parade of valorous forebears.

(iii) For *prestatque* (M), Peyrared suggested *perstatque*, so as to match the exacting tone of *poscit* and to avoid the difficulty of following *praestat* with an infinitive. But a convincing parallel is cited by Håkanson: Sil. 8. 294–6 'numerare parentem / Assaracum retro praestabat Amulius auctor / Assaracusque Iouem'.

(iv) *domi* is a form of the genitive in early Latin, but it comes to be associated exclusively with the locative case: see N–W i. 773 ff. The locative *domi* creates here a neat antithesis in thought between the triumphs of military campaigns and the armchair reminiscences of a former warrior; Hosidius Geta inspires his great-grandson with the story of the exploits which won him the *ornamenta triumphalia* in 43 (see intro.). Hence *dignos ... actus* (72) means exploits worthy of his lineage, i.e. appropriate for the descendant of a household which has been decorated with the *ornamenta triumphalia*.

74. surge, agedum ... deprende: *agedum* is an exclamatory exhortation used in conjunction with another imperative: see *TLL* i. 1405. 67 ff. The image is taken from the chase: cf. Sen. *HF* 224 'fera ... deprensa cursu est'. Geta is to reach the consulship (*cunctas ... curulis*, 77) at a younger age than his father, i.e. St. is doubly flattering to Marcellus by predicting a consulship both for him and for his son.

75. stemmate materno felix, uirtute paterna: for young Geta's maternal ancestry see the introduction to this poem. The notion of *imago parentis* is as old as Hesiod (*Op*. 235) τίκτουσιν δὲ γυναῖκες ἐοικότα τέκνα γονεῦσιν. The topos of physical likeness, which was originally esteemed as proof of paternity, is expanded to include inherited traits of character: cf. Ter. *Hau.* 1018 ff. '... sed, quo mage credendum siet, / id quod consimilest moribus / conuinces facile ex te natum', Ov. *Tr.* 4. 5. 31 f. 'sic iuuenis similisque tibi sit natus, et illum / moribus agnoscat quilibet esse tuum', *Pont.* 2. 8. 31 f. (a plea to Augustus) 'perque tibi similem uirtutis imagine natum, / moribus adgnosci qui tuus esse potest'. St. customarily uses this topos to flatter those of his addressees who are fathers of young children: cf. *S.* 4. 7. 43 f. (of Vibius Maximus' son) 'crescat in mores patrios auumque / prouocet actis', 8. 57 f. (of Julius Menecrates' children) 'his placidos genitor mores largumque nitorem / monstret auus, pulchrae studium uirtutis uterque'. Menander includes this theme in his prescription for epithalamium (*Rhet. Gr.* iii. 404. 27 Sp.) ὀλίγωι ὕστερον διαδέξεται λοχεία Ἄρτεμις καὶ μαιεύσεται, καὶ τέξετε παῖδας ὑμῖν τε ὁμοίους καὶ ἐν ἀρετῆι λαμπρούς.

76. blanda sinu Tyrio ... Gloria: *blanda* conveys the allure of fame: cf. Sil. 6. 614 'blando popularis gloria fuco'. Gloria personified is appropriately robed in purple, the status symbol of antiquity. Tyrian purple, *dibapha*, superior in quality to the Italian, Sicilian, and Greek dyes, is reputed to have been introduced at Rome by P. Lentulus Spinther in 63 BC; it became much sought after: see M. Reinhold, *History of Purple as a Status Symbol in Antiquity* (Brussels, 1970), 43 ff. André, *Couleur*, 103, distinguishes between

Tyrius as a technical term and the poetic use whereby *Tyrius* and *Sidonius*, originally denoting the provenance of the dye, came to be used for purple in general and are applied particularly to clothing.

Gloria's posture is reminiscent of the matriarchal Polla with her lapful of grandchildren (4. 8. 13 f.) 'genitos ... attollit ... benigno / Polla sinu'.

78. sonabam: epistolary imperfect. Most modern editors punctuate so that the letter finishes here, but Frère is right in understanding that it continues to the end of the poem, because the valediction (101 ff.) is clearly addressed to Marcellus and not to the letter. St. here shifts the focus of attention from Marcellus to himself, via a brief excursus (78–86) contrasting their respective locations. The poet's location is a device for ending an epistolary poem with the sentiment 'if only you were here': cf. Hor. *Epist.* 1. 10. 49 f. St. inverts this motif: he writes from the area devastated by Vesuvius, and he hopes that Marcellus' own estate will never be similarly afflicted (85–6).

The last third of St.'s poem is strongly reminiscent of the *Georgics*: *haec ... sonabam* corresponds to *G.* 4. 559 '*haec ... canebam*'; both St. and Virgil allude to the military exploits of the emperor: l. 96, *G.* 4. 560–2; both write from Naples under the guidance of a deity with specifically Neapolitan associations: l. 95 (Apollo), *G.* 4. 564 (Parthenope); both refer to their previously published work: ll. 88 ff. (the *Thebaid*), *G.* 4. 565 f. (the *Eclogues*). The Virgilian reminiscences suggest that St. is trying to present himself as a second Virgil: he portrays himself as Virgil's disciple (54 f.), and at the climax of the poem (97–8) he asks Marcellus whether he judges St. competent to write an imperial epic.

78–9. Chalcidicis ... litoribus: see on l. 1 above.

79. fractas ... Vesuius egerit iras: when referring to Campania St. frequently mentions the eruption of Vesuvius in AD 79: cf. 3. 5. 72 ff., 104, 4. 8. 5. St. compares Vesuvius with Etna (80), which, although active, only seldom erupts violently; he is saying that the main eruption is over, and Vesuvius is now merely showing vestigial signs of volcanic activity. Natural forces are frequently personified as subject to anger (and madness: see note on 86, *insania*): cf. Ov. *Met.* 14. 471 'iram caelique marisque perpetimur', Luc. 10. 316 'uiolenti gurgitis iras', *Theb.* 12. 728 'uentorum ... ira minor', Sil. 12. 610 'grandinis iras'. St. interprets Vesuvius' minor rumblings as evidence that its 'anger', manifest in the violent eruption of 79, is now dissipated: see further on 4. 8. 5. For the expression *iram frangere* cf. *Theb.* 8. 534 f. (of the Lucanian boar) 'in latus iras / frangit'.

How is this minor volcanic activity being manifested? *erigit*, for nonsensical *eriget* (M), would be appropriate of a full-scale eruption: cf. Virg. *A.* 3. 576 (of Aetna) 'uiscera montis erigit eructatis'. It also conveys the rousing of emotions: cf. Sil. 4. 278 'horrisonis ululantibus erigit iras'. But *iras fractas* shows that the main emotion has been spent, although flames are still churning out; *uoluo* is the *uox propria* for causing smoke and flames to billow: cf. Lucr. 6. 691 'crassa uoluit caligine fumum', [Tib.] 3. 4. 86 'flammam uoluens ore Chimaera fero', *OLD* s.v. *uoluo* 7. *egerit* (Avantius), 'discharges', is less spectacular and more appropriate of minor volcanic activity: cf. Luc. 6. 294 f. 'cum tota cauernas egerit et torrens in campos defluit Aetna'.

COMMENTARY

80. aemula: Campania's volcano can rival the most famous of antiquity, Mt. Etna. St. commonly conceives of inanimate nature vying with like resources: cf. 4. 2. 26–7 'aemulus illic / mons Libys Iliacusque nitet'.

Trinacriis ... flammis: Sicily was $T\rho\iota\nu\alpha\kappa\rho\iota\alpha$ because of its triangular shape; the adjective from this name was commonly transferred to features of its landscape, including Etna itself: cf. Cat. 68. 53 'Trinacria rupes', Virg. *A.* 3. 554 'Trinacria cernitur Aetna', and see R. Mayer, *G&R*² 33 (1986), 52.

81. mira fides: antithesis: cf. 1. 3. 20–2 (even the R. Anio seems to reflect Vopiscus' lifestyle) 'ipse Anien (miranda fides) infraque superque / saxeus hic tumidam rabiem spumosaque ponit / murmura'. St. presents the rehabilitation of the devastated landscape round Vesuvius as a metamorphosis; the concept of surpassing credibility occurs naturally in such contexts, e.g. Ov. *Met.* 4. 394 'resque fide maior: coepere uirescere telae'.

credet ... propago: the incredulity of posterity was a topos: cf. Hor. *O.* 2. 19. 1–3 'Bacchum ... / uidi docentem—credite posteri—/ Nymphas', with the parallels adduced by N–H.

82. segetes ... uirebunt: an expression of patriotic faith (Bonjour, 359). Lava deposits around Vesuvius made the soil very fertile (Virg. *G.* 2. 224, Colum. 10. 132 f.), comparable to that at Catana at the base of Mt. Etna (Strabo 5. 4. 8). Titus appointed two consular *curatores* to organize a programme for disaster relief and (urban) restoration (Suet. *Tit.* 8. 4, Dio 66. 24. 3, *CIL* x. 1481). But arable land takes several years to recover from a volcanic eruption, especially if (as in this case, Plin. *Epist.* 6. 16. 16) the volcanic deposits include pumice. The agricultural economy in Campania, already suffering from foreign competition and the expansion of the ports at Ostia and Aquileia, did not recover: see S. Janulardo in *Atti del Congresso Internazionale di Studi Flaviani* (Rieti, 1983), 325–30.

83–4. tanto ... mari: as a result of the eruption the familiar landscape disappeared completely: *rura abiisse*. Hence *toto ... mari* (M) does not refer to a tidal wave. Nor was the coastline permanently altered as a result of the eruption. It was the deposit of lava over the surrounding territory which transformed the landscape. Hence if *mari* is right it must be a metaphor for the lava-stream. But this is unparalleled, hence the conjectures: *toto ... graui* (Saenger) is weak, since *grauis* is too mild to convey the overwhelming force of a volcanic deposit; *fato ... pari* (Slater), although appropriate to the scope of the disaster, pre-empts *fata* at l. 85. But although *mare* itself is not used elsewhere of a lava-stream, the metaphor of waves of lava is attested: e.g. *Aetna* 493 'ingeminant fluctus et stantibus increpat undis'. Tension between fire and flood is a feature in descriptions of volcanoes: cf. Lucr. 6. 669 'ignis abundare Aetnaeus', Virg. *G.* 1. 472 'undantem ruptis fornacibus Aetnan', Sen. *NQ* 2. 30. 1, Sil. 14. 58 ff. So it is quite probable that St. extended the metaphor. But *toto* is odd, since what is required is not a notion of entirety but an exclamation at the extent of the lava-flow. The enormous and relentless flood of lava is what does the damage, i.e. *tanto ... mari* (Marastoni). Such exclamatory demonstratives, although trite, are a feature of St.'s thought, e.g. 4. 6. 35–6 (the beauty of the small statuette) 'tantus honos operi finisque inclusa per artos / maiestas!'

Marastoni points out that conjectures which explicitly connect *mari* with the lava-flow are unnecessary (*tosto* Vollmer, *cocto* Krohn) since the glowing lava has already been mentioned at l. 80 'aemula Trinacriis uoluens incendia flammis'.

84–5. necdum ... apex: cf. Val. Fl. 4. 508 'Veseui letalis apex'. E. H. Bunbury in *Dict. Geog.*, ii. 1284, deduces that St. is probably referring to issues of smoke and vapour from the crater: cf. the wisps of smoke which continually emanate from Mt. Etna.

85. Teate: the chief *municipium* in the territory of the Marrucini, modern Chieti, on the Adriatic coast. St. hopes that Marcellus' home-territory will not suffer a fate similar to St.'s Campania; this may not be mere courtesy, if Pliny reflects a general notion that the area was subject to earthquakes: he twice records (*NH* 2. 199, 17. 245) that on the estate of a certain Vettius Marcellus, a landowner *in agro Marrucino*, an olive-grove and a field of crops exchanged places across a road. For the ablative in -*e*, the normal form with such names (N–W i. 327–8), cf. *CIL* viii. 2628. 9.

86. insania montis: disruptive natural forces are personified as *insania*: cf. Sen. *Suas.* 1. 4 (a storm at sea) 'tantus uentorum concursus, tanta conuulsi funditus maris insania est', Sen. *NQ* 4. 2. 6 (flooding of the Nile) 'rapidam insaniam Nili'. For *insanus* of Vesuvius itself see on 4. 8. 5.

87–100. St. somewhat abruptly introduces the topic of his own *œuvre*, but the motif is adopted from Horace, who sometimes concludes an epistle by referring to his own circumstances (*Epist.* 1. 4. 15 f., 18. 104 ff.) or the situation in his part of the world (*Epist.* 1. 12. 25 ff.). Are we to assume that he and Marcellus were the barest acquaintances, since St. finds it necessary to inform him that he has finished the *Thebaid* and is engaged on the *Achilleid*? White (1973*a*), 280, points out that Marcellus does not appear to have cultivated a literary circle, and he deduces that both St. and Quintilian cultivated Marcellus for the social influence which he could wield as a result of his marital connections. But St.'s 'progress-report' on his work (87–94) leads up to the question of whether he should compose an imperial epic (95–100): he may be genuinely seeking the advice of Marcellus as a person who could sound out the emperor's reactions to such an undertaking. Hence his references to the *Thebaid* and *Achilleid*, couched in poetic imagery, may be seen as a plausible background to his request. St. customarily casts his friends and associates in the role of literary advisors, e.g. Pollius Felix (3 *Pr.* 4–7), Septimius Seuerus (4. 5. 25–8), Vibius Maximus (4. 7. 21–8); he attributes the impetus for the *Thebaid* to his father (5. 3. 233–4) 'te nostra magistro / Thebais urgebat priscorum exordia uatum', and for support during its composition he pays tribute to his wife (3. 5. 35–6) 'longi ... sola laboris / conscia'.

88. Sidonios ... labores: the royal house of Thebes was founded by Cadmus, son of Agenor, king of Tyre. The metaphor of poem as ship turns on *labor*, the word for both literary composition and the toil involved in a sea-crossing (cf. Cic. *Att.* 16. 3. 4 'nauigationis labor').

91. tura dedit: from the ship-metaphor St. turns to the personification of the *Thebaid* as the agent of a sacrifice of thanksgiving for a task completed.

92. uotifera ... ab arbore: dedicatory offerings were commonly hung upon the walls of temples or upon trees (D–S i. 359 [E. Saglio]): cf. Virg. *E.* 7. 24 (to mark the singer's retirement) 'hic arguta sacra pendebit fistula pinu'. Anaxagoras, the carousing lover now scorned, dedicates to Lais the remains of his wreath τὰ λιποστεφάνων διατίλματα μυρία φύλλων (*Anth. Pal.* 6. 71. 1). In St.'s case the *uittae* are the emblem of his poetic profession, not (as frequently in dedications) the actual tools of his trade. Perhaps he does not dedicate his lyre because he is making a thank-offering for a single task completed in the course of his career; he is not dedicating the means of his livelihood upon his retirement.

93. uacuos crinis: 'unadorned hair', i.e. 'bare-headed': cf. Calp. Sic. 5. 72 'cum uacuas posito uelamine costas denudauit ouis'. *uacuus* also has connotations of being disengaged and at leisure, appropriate of a poet between works: cf. Prop. 1. 9. 27 'ubi non liceat uacuos seducere ocellos', Ov. *Ars* 1. 491 'seu pedibus uacuis illi spatiosa teretur porticus'.

infula: properly speaking, the *infula* was a sacred headband of red and white wool (D–S iii. 515 f. [Gustave Fougères]). The *uittae*, usually also of wool, appear generally to have had longer streamers than the *infula*: sometimes the two were combined, so that an *infula* was knotted on to the *uittae* at regular intervals (D–S v. 956 f. [Henri Graillot]). The two terms were commonly confused, and here they are probably used synonymously for the sake of *uariatio* without conveying any distinction.

94. magnus . . . Achilles: *magnus* is the heroic epithet for Achilles: cf. Virg. *E.* 4. 36. St. commonly personifies the *Achilleid* in referring to it by the name of its hero: cf. 4. 7. 23–4 'meus . . . / haeret Achilles', *Ach.* 1. 19 (to Domitian) 'magnusque tibi praeludit Achilles'.

95. arcitenens . . . pater: Τοξοφόρος is an epic epithet for Apollo. He usually restrains the poet from too bold an undertaking: cf. Callim. *Aet.* fr. 1. 22 Pfeiffer; here, however, St. inverts the conventional motif and depicts Apollo urging him on to a more audacious enterprise. It is flattering to Domitian that the god himself is deemed to consider the emperor's military exploits a more worthy subject for epic (*arma . . . maiora*) than one of the most famous Homeric heroes.

96–7. trahit impetus . . . retrahitque timor: since it would be dangerous to refuse Domitian anything, we should assume that he did not want an imperial epic. Then St.'s conventional *recusatio* will be in accordance with the emperor's wishes. St. tactfully does not appear totally unwilling: eagerness (*impetus*) is inhibited by diffidence (*timor*). Poets (like orators) may express humility when challenged to treat a grand (e.g. imperial) theme: cf. Hor. *O.* 1. 6. 9–11 'dum pudor / imbellisque lyrae Musa potens uetat / laudes egregii Caesaris', with N–H. St. expresses the same reticence at *Theb.* 1. 16 ff., preferring a mythological theme to the achievements of Domitian: 'limes mihi carminis esto / Oedipodae confusa domus, quando Itala nondum / signa nec Arctoos ausim sperare triumphos'.

97–8. stabuntne . . . umeri: for the metaphor, see Otto, *Sprichwörter*, no. 1820. It is used in the context of literary undertakings at Hor. *Ars* 39 'uersate diu, quid ferre recusent, quid ualeant umeri'.

99. dic: the language of a formal request, as when the presiding magistrate calls on a senator to deliver his *sententia*: see *TLL* v. 1. 970. 80 ff. The

POEM FOUR 157

expression is appropriate to Marcellus' authoritative position and to the importance of the issue in which he is invited to arbitrate.

99–100. fluctus ... periclis: the compression, achieved by hyperbaton, is characteristic of St. *an* governs *credenda*; *sueta ... nosse* is a participial phrase in apposition to *ratis*.

100. Ioniis ... periclis: St. returns to the nautical image of ll. 88–9. The Ionian Sea was notorious for storms: cf. Sen. *Ag.* 506, Pers. 6. 29, Gell. 19. 1. 1.

101–2. Iamque ... ueta: the theme 'remember me' is a common concluding formula: cf. Sappho fr. 94 L–P 7 f. χαίροισ' ἔρχεο κἄμεθεν / μέμναισ', Nic. *Ther.* 957–8 καί κεν Ὁμηρείοιο καὶ εἰσέτι Νικάνδροιο / μνῆστιν ἔχοις, *Alex.* 629–30, Ov. *Her.* 11. 125, *Am.* 2. 11. 37, [Tib.] 3. 5. 31, Juv. 3. 318. Here, as at 4. 5. 58, the motif is reminiscent of Horace: cf. *O.* 3. 27. 14 'memor nostri, Galatea, uiuas'.

102–3. St. concludes his epistle with mythological *exempla* of loyal friendships which he exhorts Marcellus to surpass: Theseus and Pirithous (103–4), Achilles and Patroclus (104–5). The allusion to Hercules at 102 (*Tirynthius*) presumably introduces his friendship with Telamon as an *exemplum*: cf. 5. 2. 50 'pugnante Alcide et Telamona timebant', *Theb.* 9. 68 'iam Telamona pium, iam Thesea fama tacebat'. But either *nec* is corrupt or else there is a lacuna, since *nec ... cedet* would give the opposite sense to what is required. Since the *exemplum* of Hercules is appropriate to the context, *Tirynthius* is unlikely to be corrupt. A series of three *exempla* would be powerful after the personal appeal by St. to Marcellus (101–2), whereas a general statement between the appeal and the following *exemplum* would be banal: hence no attempt to remove *Tirynthius* has been convincing, e.g. *te mitius* (Politian), *seruantius* (Saenger), *tibi uinctius* (Otto). Frère and Marastoni take *almae pectus amicitiae* in apposition to *Tirynthius* and indicate an abrupt break after *amicitiae*, i.e. aposiopesis. But violent dislocation would be inappropriate in the climax towards the conclusion, and feigned reluctance does not suit St.'s persuasive tone here. Slater, *JPh* 30 (1907), 152, proposed *parcus* for *pectus*. But *pectus amicitiae* is a natural expression (cf. Mart. 9. 14. 2) and, further, the notion that Hercules was generous in bestowing friendship is far less hyperbolic than St.'s prophecy that their mutual devotion will outdo famous demonstrations of friendship from mythology. It is hard to see how an emendation for *nec enim* would heal this very cryptic statement, and so it seems likely that something has fallen out. *almae pectus amicitiae* must belong together, and so there are three possible places where the lacuna may have occurred: after *nec enim*, or after *Tirynthius*, or after *amicitiae*. To posit a lacuna within the first *exemplum* would make the second disproportionately shorter than the other two. But it seems plausible to suggest that a general remark introducing the *exemplum* of Hercules may have fallen out after *nec enim*.

103–4. gloria fidi / Theseos: cf. the ending of the *Diffugere niues* ode (Hor. *O.* 4. 7. 25–8) 'infernis neque enim tenebris Diana pudicum / liberat Hippolytum, / nec Lethaea ualet Theseus abrumpere caro / uincula Perithoo'. St.'s passage is generally reminiscent of Horace's: cf. the similarity in thought, i.e. that the paradigm of loyal friendship is somehow found wanting; the example of Theseus; the diction *neque / nec enim*.

5

INTRODUCTION

This ode is St.'s only extant example of alcaics (see further on l. 4). Like the sapphic ode (*S.* 4. 7) it has a strong flavour of Horace. Horatian reminiscence was fashionable among contemporary lyric poets: Pliny's friend Passennus Paulus successfully imitated the elegiacs of Propertius and the lyrics of Horace (Plin. *Epist.* 9. 22. 2). St.'s own designation for this poem is *lyricum carmen* (4 *Pr.* 10). His injunction to his addressee, Septimius Seuerus, *barbiton ingemina* (60), suggests that Septimius himself may have written lyric poetry, in which case St. may have considered a poem in alcaics an appropriate tribute to him.

The structure of this poem is almost symmetrical. It has been analysed by D. W. T. C. Vessey, *AC* 39 (1970), 517: the first stanza may be regarded as programmatic, i.e. ll. 1-2 announce the eulogy of Septimius Seuerus which occupies stanzas 8–15; poet and addressee are linked in stanzas 1, 7, and, by implication, 15.

St.'s addressee Septimius was born at Lepcis Magna in Libya (29 f.), and he came to Rome in boyhood (39 f.). He was a *condiscipulus* of Vitorius Marcellus, dedicatee of Bk. 4 (4 *Pr.* 11). He was equestrian, and in 95 St. could describe him as a *iuuenis* (4 *Pr.* 10). He was an orator, but he only undertook briefs for *amici* (50–2). He wrote both prose and poetry (57–60), and he attended the Alban Games when St. won his victory (25–8). His family owned property at Veii (54 f.), and so he conforms to the pattern of landowners with forensic or literary interests who comprise St.'s circle of addressees. His activities are the characteristic sources of livelihood for an immigrant, as defined by R. P. Saller, *CQ* NS 33 (1983), 248: composing verses, pleading in court, and performing *officia clientium*: cf. Mart. 3. 88.

The search for Septimius' identity gives rise to two main questions: was he of Italian or native Libyan stock? and was he an ancestor of the emperor Septimius Seuerus?[1] Septimius' father (if not earlier forebears too) had owned Septimius' *paternae sedes* at Veii (see on 54–6). *CIL* xiv. 3004 from Praeneste records a Septimius Seuerus of the tribe Pupinia, which was almost exclusively attested in Italy (see 55–6 n.). But St.'s insistence that his addressee did not exhibit Punic *sermo*, *habitus*, or *mens* (45–6) implies that his appearance belies his origins, i.e. he had Punic blood; hence his mother was probably Punic.

---

[1] These issues have long been debated. P. Monceaux, *Les Africains: Étude sur la littérature latine d'Afrique* (Paris, 1894), 190, connected St.'s friend with the Seuerus addressed by Mart. 2. 6, 5. 80, 11. 57 and mentioned at 7. 38. 2, but Seuerus is too common a *cognomen* for the identification to be conclusive. In the commentary I draw especially on the contributions by T. D. Barnes, *Hist.* 16 (1967), 87–107, and A. R. Birley, *BJb* 169 (1969), 247–80 (esp. 253 ff.), *Bonner Historia-Augusta-Colloquium 1968/69* (Bonn, 1970), 63 f., *Septimius Severus* (London, 1971). A useful summary of the problem by R. P. Saller, *Personal Patronage under the Early Empire* (Cambridge, 1982), 176–8, stresses the paradigm of a municipal family which owed advancement to the influence of kin at Rome. For expanded treatment of these arguments see K. M. Coleman, *PACA* 17 (1983), 85–99.

Was St.'s addressee an ancestor of the emperor?[2] *IRT* 412, from the forum at Lepcis Magna, records that the emperor's grandfather was L. Septimius Seuerus; he was *sufes* of Lepcis (i.e. he held the highest municipal magistracy), and he had served *in decuriis et inter iudices selectos* at Rome. This last occupation (Plin. *NH* 33. 30, 33), provided a means of acquiring entitlement to equestrian rank: by legislation of AD 23 judges were eligible to acquire the equestrian gold ring; Isobel Henderson, *JRS* 53 (1963), 68 f., argues that judges in all the *decuriae* were called *iudices selecti* and were thus eligible for equestrian rank. Hence an ambitious provincial might do jury service as a step towards acquiring equestrian rank. But St.'s Septimius seems to have been content with rural seclusion and selective briefs. Perhaps he recommended for equestrian status a relative, L. Septimius Seuerus, who did jury service at Rome. As St.'s Septimius himself possessed equestrian rank, such a relative would have to be equestrian by census but not by formal rank, e.g. not a brother[3] but a cousin.

St.'s friend seems to have been childless; St. usually makes a complimentary reference to an addressee's heir. He may have left his property to his relative; a lead pipe (*CIL* xi. 3816) inscribed *P. Septimi Geta* (*sic*) was found 8 km from Veii; since Septimius Geta was the name of the emperor's father (*IRT* 607) and brother (*IRT* 541), this pipe attests that property near Veii was associated with someone bearing a family name of the emperor. For an interpretation of *HA Seu.* 4. 5 ascribing to the emperor ownership of property at Veii see on 54-6 below. Since he was *sufes*, the cousin of St.'s Septimius may have returned to Lepcis to pursue a successful career in municipal life, hence both retaining his property at Veii and establishing a family tradition of civic leadership at Lepcis. He, and not St.'s Septimius, was grandfather to the emperor.

1. Parui: St. begins on an Epicurean note familiar from Horace: cf. Lucr. 5. 1118 f. 'diuitiae grandes homini sunt uiuere parce / aequo animo; neque enim est umquam penuria parui', Cic. *Tusc.* 5. 89 (of Epicurus) 'hic uero ipse quam paruo est contentus', Hor. *O.* 2. 16. 13 'uiuitur paruo bene', *Sat.* 2. 2. 1 'quae uirtus et quanta, boni, sit uiuere paruo'. The intellectual climate of St. and his associates was noticeably Epicurean: see R. G. M. Nisbet on Pollius Felix, *JRS* 68 (1978), 1-11. *contentus paruo* is also the slogan, pragmatic rather than philosophical, of Romans in retirement in the country: cf. Tib. 1. 1. 25 'iam possim contentus uiuere paruo'. The simplicity of rustic life is implicit in this claim: cf. Val. Max. 7. 1. 2 'Arcadum pauperrimus ... paruuli ruris fructibus contentus', and the *rusticus mus* at Hor. *Sat.* 2. 6. 116 f. 'me silua cauusque / tutus ab insidiis tenui solabitur eruo'. Circumstances force this attitude upon Cicero, making do without tenants on his property at Astura (*Att.* 12. 19. 1) 'equidem iam nihil egeo uectigalibus et paruo contentus esse possum'. St. frequently deprecates himself to draw a contrast with his addressee: cf. the

---

[2] For a defence of the view that St.'s friend was the emperor's grandfather see Birley, artt. citt. in n. 1 above and *Septimius Severus*, 304.

[3] As supposed by Barnes, art. cit. (n. 1 above), 88.

persona of 'mere poet' at 4. 4. 51 ff. to emphasize Marcellus' prowess as orator and soldier. Here the poet's humble rustic means contrast with Septimius' forensic activity at Rome (49) and the ample resources (54) which enable him to enjoy *otium* writing in the country.

beatus: εὐδαίμων. This term was popularly interpreted as 'rich' in the material sense (*TLL* ii. 1917. 31 ff.); juxtaposed with *parui* for antithetical effect. St. recalls Hor. *Epod.* 2. 1 ff. on rural self-sufficiency: 'beatus ille, qui procul negotiis, / ut prisca gens mortalium, / paterna rura bubus exercet suis'; see also *Epist.* 1. 10. 14 'nouistine locum potiorem rure beato?' Possibly there is also pointed juxtaposition with *ruris*, since *rus* is associated with a simple, frugal existence rather than the riches usually implied by *beatus*.

ruris: here, as frequently, *rus* denotes a piece of land: *OLD* s.v. *rus* 2.

honoribus: the blessings of being a landowner: cf. Hor. *Sat.* 2. 5. 12 f. 'dulcia poma / et quoscumque feret cultus tibi fundus honores', *TLL* vi. 3. 2923. 49 ff. The undertone of privilege associated with *honos* is off-set by the self-deprecating *parui*.

2. prisca ... Alba: for St.'s estate at Alba Longa see General Introduction. The adjective *prisca* is a subtle choice: (i) the Alban League of archaic communities in Latium (Diod. 7. 5, Dion. Hal. 4. 49. 2, 5. 61, Liv. 1. 52. 2, Plin. *NH* 3. 68–70) may have been known as Prisci Latini: see Fest. 253. 1 f. Lindsay 'Prisci Latini proprie appellati sunt hi, qui, priusquam conderetur Roma, fuerunt'; at the least, the term represents a later memory of Rome's earliest neighbours as a unit: see A. N. Sherwin-White, *The Roman Citizenship*[2] (Oxford, 1973), 10; (ii) in the sense of 'old-fashioned' *priscus* comes to denote what is 'strict' or 'severe', hence *prisca Alba* is an apt site for composing poetry to a Seuerus: cf. Cat. 64. 159 'saeua quod horrebas prisci praecepta parentis', Cic. *Har.* 27 'priscam illam seueritatem', *OLD* s.v. *priscus* 3b.

Teucros ... lares: for the foundation-legend of a Trojan settlement at Alba see on 4. 2. 65.

3. fortem atque facundum: *fortem* alludes to Septimius' talent as forensic orator (49 ff.): see *OLD* s.v. *fortis* 6, *TLL* vi. 1. 1147. 79 ff. *facundum* refers primarily to Septimius' literary talent (57 ff.): cf. 1. 2. 3, 3. 1, 2. 1. 114, 3. 1. 65. This example should be added to Wölfflin's list of alliterative pairs containing *fortis* (*Ausgewählte Schriften*, 260).

4. non solitis fidibus saluto: a variation of the formulaic epistolary address: cf. 4. 4. 10 f. 'cui primam solito uulgi de more salutem / ... haec reddere uerba memento'. The litotes is emphatic and avoids the hiatus which *Seuerum / insolito* would create. St. avoids any metrical feature which is uncommon in Horace's alcaics: hiatus after -m only occurs three times in the *Odes* (1. 34. 14, 2. 5. 9, 13. 11). Horace admits hiatus at the ends of lines, but only rarely after a short syllable: see N–H i, p. xli; in *S.* 4. 5 the five instances of hiatus all occur after a long syllable (18, 38, 45, 50, 55). These are St.'s first published alcaics, but presumably he practised composing alcaics in his youth, probably under his father's tutelage: the elder Papinius' syllabus included metre (5. 3. 151 f. 'qua lege recurrat / Pindaricae uox flexa lyrae') and the study of lyric poets (5. 3. 153–6);

'quosque alios dignata chelys' (156) may include Alcaeus. It is possible that St. chose a lyric metre for this poem because the time of year suggested that he should draw on those literary motifs which were most closely associated with praise of spring, i.e. the odes of Horace, especially 1. 4, 4. 7, 12. But the main reason may be that Septimius too wrote lyric poetry (see on 59–60). The place of the programmatic statement within the poem recalls Hor. *O.* 3. 1. 4 'uirginibus puerisque canto'. Implicit in the first three stanzas is the analogy between St.'s adoption of a new metre and nature's resurrection in the spring.

5. iam: anaphora of *iam* (ἤδη) emphasizes the arrival of spring: *Anth. Pal.* 10. 5 (Thyillos), Cat. 46. 1 ff., Hor. *O.* 1. 4. 5, 4. 12. 1 ff., Sen. *Apocol.* 2. 1.

trux ... hiems: the elements are harsh and savage in winter: cf. Virg. *G.* 1. 370 'Boreae de parte trucis'. *trux* is commonly used of savage animals; there may be a suggestion here that winter is a savage creature which has fled to join the bears of the arctic constellation. After *trux*, *concessit* is disarming.

Parrhasias: the epithets *Parrhasius* and *Parrhasis* from Parrhasia, a district in Arcadia between Mt. Lycaeon and the R. Alpheus, come to mean 'Arcadian': cf. Virg. *A.* 8. 344, 11. 31. Following Ovid (*Her.* 18. 152, *F.* 4. 577, *Tr.* 1. 3. 48), they are applied to the constellation of Ursa Maior to allude to the metamorphosis of Callisto, mother of the eponymous leader of the Arcadians, and her subsequent catasterization: cf. *Theb.* 7. 8, 8. 370, Sen. *Phaed.* 288, Mart. 6. 58. 1.

6. altis obruta solibus: mild antithesis: St. conceives of winter being buried in utter darkness (*obruta*) by the longer daylight hours of spring (*altis ... solibus*): cf. the figurative use of *obruo* ('eclipse'), e.g. Val. Max. 1. 1. 9 'obruitur tot et tam inlustribus consulatibus L. Furius Bibaculus', Tac. *Dial.* 38. 2 'causae centumuirales ... splendore aliorum iudiciorum obruebantur'. The compulsion implied in *obruta* is in contrast to the volition of *concessit*. *altus* can describe the elevated position of a body which is not in itself tall; in this sense it is frequently applied to the elevation of heavenly bodies above the horizon: cf. Sen. *Epist.* 122. 1 (of a lie-abed) 'qui alto sole semisomnus iacet', *TLL* i. 1774. 45 ff. In the context of spring it presumably refers to the higher arc the sun describes in the sky instead of the flattened elliptical arc of the winter months when the sun's path is closer to the horizon. With St.'s expression here cf. *Theb.* 5. 459 f. 'iamque exuta gelu tepuerunt sidera longis / solibus, et uelox in terga reuoluitur annus'.

7–8. pontus ac tellus renident / ad Zephyros Aquilone fracto: M is corrupt: 'iam zephiros aquilone fractos'. Early editors retained *iam* in line 8, but although triple anaphora of *iam* in one stanza is attractive, double anaphora is equally convincing: cf. Hor. *O.* 4. 12. 1–4 'iam ueris comites ... iam nec prata rigent'. The Zephyrs traditionally ushered in milder weather: cf. Hor. *O.* 4. 7. 9 'frigora mitescunt Zephyris'. *iam Zephyris Aquilo refractus* (Markland) is an attractive paradox (the force of the north wind broken by the gentle Zephyrs): for *frangere* of the force of winds being decreased cf. Vitr. 1. 6. 8 'uti [uenti] aduenientes ad angulos insularum frangantur', Plin. *NH* 34. 40 'unde maxime flatum opus erat frangi', *TLL*

vi. 1. 1245. 51–62. Bücheler and Krohn proposed *in Zephyros Aquilone fracto*: but, since the north and west winds blow from different directions, *in Zephyros* attaches very awkwardly to *Aquilone fracto*. The ablative absolute makes sense by itself; *ad* for *iam* (M) attaches *Zephyros* to the preceding line: earth and sea display their gratitude at the onset of the spring breezes. The new leaves and the surface of the sea sparkle in the spring sunshine: cf. Ov. *F.* 5. 207 'uere fruor semper: semper nitidissimus annus'. St. interprets this physical manifestation as an emotional response. For the sea's smile cf. Lucr. 2. 559 'subdola cum ridet placidi pellacia ponti'. *renidere* can be a synonym for *ridere*: cf. Egnatius (Cat. 39. 2) 'renidet usque quaque', *OLD* s.v. *renidere* 3. *ad* with *renidere* is logical by analogy with *ridere ad*. A close connection between the third and fourth lines of the stanza occurs throughout the rest of the poem, as in Horace's alcaics: see N–H i, p. xli.

9. cuncta ... (10) arbos: in the sense of 'every', *cunctus* is a Statian neologism: cf. *Theb.* 5. 202 'cuncto sua regnat Erinys pectore'. The archaic tone of *cuncta* matches the archaic termination -*os*. Although elsewhere St. invariably uses *arbor*, *arbos* gives him his preferred long vowel in the fifth element of the alcaic hendecasyllable (twenty-three instances out of thirty). At *O.* 2. 13. 3 Horace uses the grandiloquent *arbos* for mock-religious solemnity.

uernans frondibus annuis: *ueris* (M) is otiose. J. P. Postgate, *Philol.* 64 (1905), 129, punctuated after *ueris*, but the statement *nunc cuncta ueris* would be very banal. *ueri* (Baehrens) seems unnecessary beside *nunc*. *ruri* (Polster) is very weak. *uernans* (Markland) matches *annuis*: the present participle suits the immediacy of the burgeoning spring.

10. crinitur: for *crinitus* (M). The finite verb *crinire* is first attested at *Theb.* 4. 217 'frondenti crinitur cassis oliua'. *crinis* and *crinitus* are used of foliage by technical authors: *TLL* iv. 1205. 17 ff. The participle *crinitus* describes the tassel on a cob at Plin. *NH* 60. 18 'grana in stipula crinito textu spicantur'. The image of foliage as hair is common with *coma*: *TLL* iii. 1752. 75 ff.; *comans*: *TLL* iii. 1755. 28; *comatus* only at Cat. 4. 11. At *Peru. Ven.* 4 with the advent of spring the woods let down their hair: '[uere] nemus comam resoluit de maritis imbribus'.

12. siluere: *statuere* (M) contradicts *inexpertum ... carmen* and *tacita ... bruma*: winter is quiet in the sense that the birds have been silent; the Aquilo (8) was notorious for its roaring: Mart. 1. 49. 19 'Aquilone rauco', Claud. *Ruf.* 1. 242. If *statuere* means 'decided upon' it conjures up oddly premeditated birdsong. Similarly A. C. Clark's *studuere* (J. P. Postgate, *CR* 20 [1906], 322) is wrong, implying that the birds sang. *tacuere* (Phillimore) gives the right sense, but it is grotesque beside *tacita*. Mild tautology, however, is common enough: cf. 29 f. 'in remotis Syrtibus auia / Lepcis'. Hence *siluere* (S. G. Owen, cit. Phillimore, *OCT* 1905) is not offensive; it explains *tacita ... bruma* and contrasts with *carmen*; the *carmen* is *inexpertum* because the birds may have forgotten how to sing after their long silence: cf. Longus, *Daphnis and Chloe* 3. 12. 1 f. Ἤδη δὲ ἦρος ἀρχομένου καὶ τῆς ... χιόνος λῃομένης ... αἱ δ' [ἀηδόνες] ὑπεφθέγγοντο ἐν ταῖς λόχμαις καὶ τὸν Ἴτυν κατ' ὀλίγον ἠκρίβουν, ὥσπερ ἀναμιμνῃσκόμεναι τῆς ᾠδῆς ἐκ μακρᾶς σιωπῆς.

13. St. moves indoors from the description of nature in spring to the topos of the poet *contentus paruo* in his rustic domesticity. This stanza is modelled loosely upon the second stanza of Horace's Soracte ode (1. 9).
  parca tellus: the output of St.'s estate is modest: cf. Mart. 4. 8. 10 'ingenti . . . tenet pocula parca manu'.
  peruigil et focus: the hearth is *peruigil* in two senses: (i) the images of the *penates*, the tutelary gods of the household, were kept in front of the larder: see D-S iv. 376 (J.-A. Hild); the *focus*, where food was cooked, was regarded as their altar: cf. Porph. Hor. *Epod.* 2. 43 'proprie hoc rusticae uitae est focum amare. sacrum autem dixit, quia ara deorum penatium est focus'; (ii) traditionally the poor man has to bank the fire at night to keep it burning (i.e. *peruigil*) while he is asleep; this symbol for poverty developed from the grimy realities of a one-roomed dwelling: cf. Aesch. *Ag.* 774 Δίκα δὲ λάμπει μὲν ἐν δυσκάπνοις δώμασιν; it was used as an epic simile by Apollonius (3. 291 ff.) and adapted by Virgil (*A.* 8. 410 f.) 'cinerem et sopitos suscitat ignis / noctem addens operi': cf. Ov. *Met.* 8. 641 ff.; this motif became a bucolic topos: cf. Theoc. 11. 51 ὑπὸ σποδῶι ἀκάματον πῦρ, Virg. *E.* 1. 82, 7. 49, Mart. 2. 90. 7. In declamation the sooty roof was a symbol of poverty: [Quint.], *Decl. Mai.* 13. 4 'pauperem focum et fumosa tecta'. Cf. Chaucer's *povre wydwe* (*Nun's Priest's Tale* 12) 'ful sooty was hire bour and eek hir halle'. The *locus classicus* for this topos in Latin poetry is at *Moretum* 8 f. 'paruulus exusto remanebat stipite fomes / et cinis obductae celabat lumine prunae'. This topos was probably based on fact, despite G. Bagnani, *Phoenix* 8 (1954), 25, who objects that in St.'s day the *focus* burnt virtually smokeless charcoal; D. West, *Reading Horace* (Edinburgh, 1967), 5, replies with evidence for a fireplace for log-fires in the villa at Boscoreale and points to Horace's references to logs for fuel (*Epod.* 2. 43, *Sat.* 1. 5. 46, *O.* 1. 9. 5, 3. 17. 14, *Epist.* 1. 14. 42, 2. 2. 169).
  For postponed *et* see Norden, comm. on *Aen.* 6, app. III, 402 ff.: cf. Fordyce on Catullus 23. 7 (*nam*). Common connective particles are postponed for metrical convenience, in imitation of Hellenistic practice.
14. lumine: by metonymy for the source of light: cf. Suet. *Jul.* 37. 2 (describing a torchlight procession) 'ascendit . . . Capitolium ad lumina'. This metonymy juxtaposed with *sordidum* affords St. the oxymoron *lumine sordidum*.
15. solantur: prevention rather than cure: since St.'s circumstances are adequate, he is not at risk of having his aspirations disappointed. By fulfilling a person's natural needs, a modest life in the country meets Epicurus' criteria for the good life: cf. *beatus* (1); these ethical overtones are part of the Horatian reminiscence: see C. W. Macleod, *JRS* 69 (1979), 25 = *Collected Essays* (Oxford, 1983), 289.
  exemptus ... (16) Lyaeus: wine is drawn from the jar to contribute to physical and emotional comfort indoors. This is a Horatian motif derived from Greek lyric: cf. Hor. *O.* 1. 9. 7 f. and Alcaeus 338 L-P. In denoting the product by the deity's name St. exploits a type of personification (cf. 4. 3. 11): *ferbuerat* describes fermentation (*TLL* vi. 1. 593. 31 ff.); but the literal image is of the god Bacchus raging, cooped up in a wine-jar: cf. Ov. *F.* 2.

732 (describing drunkenness) 'feruet multo linguaque corque mero', *TLL* vi. 1. 591. 81 ff.

16. modo: old wine was prestigious; St.'s means and requirements are modest: the wine is young and was presumably made on St.'s estate. The keynote is self-sufficiency.

ferbuerat: through dissimilation, *-u-* in the perfect tenses of *ferueo* is usually replaced by *-b-*: see N–W iii. 388. For the corruption to *fer uerat* (M) by way of *feruuerat* cf. the corruption of *Vibium* at 4 *Pr.* 15.

17. non ... (18) nec ... (19) -que: a combination of negative and positive propositions is a characteristic of ancient discourse. It is frequently associated with protestations against luxury (implicit here): cf. Hor. *O.* 1. 31. 3 ff., 2. 18. 1 ff. (with N–H's note), 3. 16. 33 ff. Horace's illustrations are vivified by local colour (e.g. *opimae Sardiniae* [1. 31. 3 f.], *aestuosae* ... *Calabriae* [1. 31. 5], *Liris* [1. 31. 7], *trabes Hymettiae* [2. 18. 3], *Gallicis* ... *pascuis* [3. 16. 35 f.]), but St.'s country estate at Alba seems remote from the reality of regional specialities in breeds and crops.

balant ... (18) mugit: the onomatopoeic *uoces propriae* for bleating and mooing: cf. Var. *Men.* 3 Bücheler 'mugit bouis, oui' balat'.

lanigeri greges: St. also recalls Hor. *O.* 2. 16. 33 ff. comparing Grosphus' wealth with the poet's own humble means and slender Muse: 'te greges centum Siculaeque circum / mugiunt uaccae, tibi tollit hinnitum / apta quadrigis equa, te bis Afro / murice tinctae / uestiunt lanae: mihi parua rura ...'. Horace's *greges* are apparently cattle (N–H), but St. conflates this reference with the one to sheep, so that Horace's detail *uestiunt lanae* becomes *lanigeri* (cf. Virg. *G.* 3. 287 'lanigeros ... greges'). The contented farmer owns a thousand sheep: cf. Theoc. 11. 34 (the Cyclops), Virg. *E.* 2. 21 (Corydon).

18. uacca ... adultero: St.'s lowing cow (generalizing singular) is perhaps modelled on Horace's whinnying mare (cit. previous n.). The bull is portrayed as her lover (*adulter*); the anthropomorphic term is used for humorous effect: cf. Hor. *O.* 1. 17. 7 (of goats) 'olentis uxores mariti', with N–H's n.

19. siquando: modifies *canenti*. St. contrasts the perpetual absence of flocks and herds, and the resulting silence, with his own voice spasmodically reciting his compositions.

20. mutus: contrasting with *canenti* and paradoxical with *reclamat*: St. exploits the phenomenon of echo. Silent places are commonly thus personified: cf. Sen. *HF* 536 'mutis tacitum litoribus mare', *S.* 2. 1. 67 'muta domus, fateor, desolatique penates'.

21. Alba is both the rustic venue for St.'s compositions and the site of his greatest competitive achievement; as at 4. 7. 21–4 St. returns to the subject of his addressee by recalling a personal triumph in which his friend lent him support.

23. regina bellorum uirago: Minerva, goddess of war and patron of the arts; Domitian celebrated the Alban Games in her honour: Suet. *Dom.* 4. 4. *uirago* is antonomastic for Minerva: cf. Ov. *Met.* 2. 765 'belli metuenda uirago', 6. 130 'flaua uirago', *Theb.* 11. 414 'cruda uirago'.

24. Caesareo ... auro: the prize at the Alban Games was a gold wreath: cf.

4. 2. 67 where Domitian invests St. with *Palladio . . . auro*. This interchangeability emphasizes the special relationship which Domitian claimed to enjoy with Minerva: see on 4. 1. 22.

redimiuit: *peramauit* (M) is unparalleled; it would be coined by analogy with *peramans* (Cic. *Att.* 4. 8a. 3) and *peramanter* (Cic. *Fam.* 9. 20. 3); the idea contained in the instrumental ablative *auro* would be very awkwardly expressed. *reparauit* (Cruceus) could not refer to compensation for the Capitoline defeat (so Phillimore), since the Alban victory probably came first (see General Introduction); but it might be taken as equivalent to ἀμείψατο, 'took in exchange', 'requited', implying that in some sense the winning entry at the Alban Games was dedicated to Minerva and that Domitian's prize was the manifestation of her approval. But a less tortuous explanation is required by *decorauit* (Markland) or, more attractive still, *redimiuit* (Baehrens): for the transference whereby the poems are garlanded instead of the poet cf. Suet. *Claud.* 11. 2 'comoediam . . . coronauit'.

25. dulce periculum: oxymoron echoing Horace's phrase for Bacchic possession (*O.* 3. 25. 18 ff.) 'dulce periculum est, / o Lenaee, sequi deum / cingentem uiridi tempora pampino'. When St. competed in the Alban Games Septimius evidently gave him encouragement and moral support; at competitions in his youth he was encouraged by his father (5. 3. 220 ff.).

27. Castor: Septimius encouraged St. like Castor encouraging Pollux in his boxing-match against King Amycus of the Bebryces, an incident from the Argonautic legend: cf. Ap. Rh. 2. 1–7, 62–4, Theoc. 22. 27–134, Val. Fl. 4. 99–102, 226 ff. Similarly at 5. 3. 220–4 St.'s father witnessing his son's early competitions is likened to a man watching his son at the Olympic Games.

27–8. cunctos . . . strepitus harenae: *strepitus* conveys the whole uproar of the fight, including the thudding of fists (cf. Juv. 14. 19 'qui gaudet acerbo plagarum strepitu') and the yells of onlookers: cf. Hor. *Epist.* 2. 1. 203 'tanto cum strepitu ludi spectantur', Theoc. 22. 91 f. (of Castor's fight with Amycus) Βέβρυκες δ' ἐπαύτεον, οἳ δ' ἑτέρωθεν / ἥρωες κρατερὸν Πολυδεύκεα θαρσύνεσκον.

29. in remotis Syrtibus: Lepcis Magna was situated on the North African coast between the two Syrtes (Plin. *NH* 5. 27): the Gulf of Sidra to the south-east and Gabès to the south-west, 250 miles apart. They are *remotis* not from each other but from Rome: cf. *auia* (mistaken by T. D. Barnes for *auita*, 'ancestral': *Hist.* 16 [1967], 87). St. exaggerates the inaccessibility of Lepcis to imply that it was a very backward place, so that he can then contrast the illustrious Septimius with his lack-lustre origins. In fact Lepcis was up-and-coming: in 110 under Trajan it received colonial status and Roman citizenship for its inhabitants: cf. *CIL* viii. (1. 5), 10, 11, *RE* xii. 2075. 22 (Dessau). Praise of the subject's birthplace was a topos of encomium. But even Menander admits that if the place was insufficiently distinguished it could be omitted: *Rhet. Gr.* iii. 370. 9–11 Sp. St.'s flattery involves turning the topos upside-down: cf. Horace's reference to his own circumstances (*Epist.* 1. 20. 20 ff.) 'me libertino natum patre et in tenui re / maiores pennas nido extendisse loqueris, / ut quantum generi demas uirtutibus addas'.

COMMENTARY

30. Lepcis: originally called Νεάπολις (see Ps.-Scylax 109, 110 Müller, Dionys. Per. 205 Müller), identified as Λέπτις by Strabo (17. 3. 18) and (with the addition of Μεγάλη) by Ptolemy (4. 3. 3). In Latin inscriptions *Lepcis* is almost always attested. Of the three instances of the spelling *Leptis*, two occur on imported marble cut elsewhere (*IRT* 530) and the third dates from the late fourth century (*IRT* 474). *Lepcis Magna* is first found as an official title under Trajan (*IRT* 302, 355); Pliny *NH* 5. 27 (where the spelling *Leptis* may be a scribal error) specifies the epithet Magna to avoid confusion with the Byzacene town Leptis. For a full discussion see *IRT*, pp. 73–6.

30–1. Indicas / messis: Septimius' birth in Lepcis is presented as a miracle comparable to two adynata. This passage is reminiscent of a Horatian adynaton comprising the appearance of exotic crops in poor soil (*Epist.* 1. 14. 21–3) 'fornix tibi et uncta popina / incutiunt urbis desiderium, uideo, et quod / angulus iste feret piper et tus ocius uua'. For adynata in general see E. Dutoit, *Le Thème de l'adynaton dans la poésie antique* (Paris, 1936) and discussions cited by N–H on Hor. *O*. 1. 29. 10. India, abundant in exotica, produced two harvests annually: cf. Diod. 2. 35. 3, Plin. *NH* 6. 58. Both India and Arabia traditionally represent distant places that produce luxury exports (also associated at 4. 1. 41–2).

31–2. odoratis ... Sabaeis: *Sabaeae* concludes the third line of the alcaic stanza at Hor. *O*. 1. 29. 3. St. is probably referring to incense, a major product of Arabia and associated in literature with the Sabaei: cf. 2. 6. 86 'odoriferos exhausit flamma Sabaeos', 4. 8. 1 f. 'templa Sabaeis / nubibus ... imple', and see on 4. 1. 42. St. describes choicest eastern perfumes by the same epithets at 5. 3. 42 f. 'nec ... rara Sabaei / cinnama, odoratas nec Arabs decerpit aristas'.

rara / cinnama: an exotic import at Rome. Pliny claims that quality cinnamon was all the more scarce because only the thinnest twigs produced the choicest spice (*NH* 12. 91). J. I. Miller, *The Spice Trade of the Roman Empire* (Oxford, 1969), 154, explains that Chinese cassia and Malayan cinnamon, being the spices imported to Rome from furthest afield, brought with them an aura of mystery.

33. quis non: a Horatian formula to introduce an adynaton: cf. *O*. 1. 29. 10 f., expressing, as in St., an unfulfilled remote possibility rather than a strict adynaton.

in omni uertice Romuli: periphrasis punning on Septimius' name. Septimius seems so Roman that one would think he had been there as a baby. The reference to Rome as Romulus' hills (actually only the Palatine was included in the traditional settlement: Liv. 1. 5. 1 ff.) subtly compares Septimius to Romulus and Remus, who were abandoned beside the Tiber in infancy and are frequently portrayed crawling on the grass: see D. W. T. C. Vessey, *AC* 39 (1970), 515. St. stakes for Septimius an exaggerated claim to all seven hills.

34. dulcem: an affectionate, almost sentimental epithet for Septimius as a child: 'dear little'.

35. fonte Iuturnae: Iuturna was the name of a deity associated with a spring at Lavinium, which Servius claims provided water so pure that it was used in Roman sacrifices (*A.* 12. 139). But after the reference to the seven hills (33–4) St. must mean the spring of the same name (Lacus Iuturnae) in the forum at Rome near the Temple of Vesta: see Platner–Ashby, 308, 311 ff., *RE* x. 1348 f. (Latte). The deity's festival, the Iuturnalia, was celebrated on 11 January, and a temple was erected to her in the Campus Martius (Ov. *F.* 1. 463). On the characteristic *-urn-* suffix for place- and river-names of Etruscan origin see Latte, *RR* 77. St. here adapts the topos whereby foreigners are depicted drinking from their local rivers. Septimius, paradoxically, is so naturalized that Roman water of great sanctity would be his refreshment. Contrast Mart. 11. 96, in which he accuses a pushy German immigrant of drinking from the Aqua Marcia at Rome as though it were the Rhine. The topos can be traced to Hom. *Il.* 2. 824 f. (the Trojan clan from Zeleia drank the water of the Aesepus): see E. Norden, *Sitzungsberichte der Kgl. Preuß. Akad. d. Wiss.* 1917, 668–79 = *Kleine Schriften zum klassischen Altertum* (Berlin, 1966), 184 ff. and n. 19. St.'s pains to attribute *urbanitas* to Septimius attest a prevalent xenophobia at Rome: cf. the nutritional image at Juv. 3. 84 f. 'usque adeo nihil est quod nostra infantia caelum / hausit Auentini baca nutrita Sabina?'

35–6. relictis / uberibus: one would think that Septimius had abandoned his *alma mater* (Lepcis) for a surrogate (Rome). *pastum* suggests that the *fons Iuturnae* was more nourishing than ordinary water and equivalent to a mother's milk (cf. *uberibus*). Children were believed to imbibe the moral character of a surrogate through her milk: cf. Gell. 12. 1. 20 'in moribus inolescendis magnam fere partem ingenium altricis et natura lactis tenet, quae iam a principio imbuta paterni seminis concretione ex matris etiam corpore et animo recentem indolem configurat', and see H. D. Jocelyn, *PCPhS* 17 (1971), 52. Hence the claim that the subject was suckled by a mysterious wet-nurse is a topos (usually derogatory but here encomiastic) to account for deceptive appearances: cf. Theoc. 3. 15–16 νῦν ἔγνων τὸν Ἔρωτα· βαρὺς θεός· ἦ ῥα λεαίνας / μαζὸν ἐθήλαζεν, δρυμῶι τέ νιν ἔτραφε μάτηρ, Dido's invective against Aeneas (Virg. *A.* 4. 366 f., based on Hom. *Il.* 16. 34 f.) 'duris genuit te cautibus horrens / Caucasus, Hyrcanaeque admorunt ubera tigres', with Gellius' observation (loc. cit.) 'non partionem solam tamquam ille, quem sequebatur, sed alituram quoque feram et saeuam criminatus est'.

37. nec mira uirtus: an echo of Hor. *O.* 3. 5. 29 'nec uera uirtus' at the same position in the alcaic stanza. St. ascribes to Septimius' upbringing the essentially Roman quality of *uirtus* in his nature, and he says that this quality is not surprising since Septimius was brought up in Italy.

37–9. Ausonum / portus ... intras: harbours represent the immigrant's first contact with his new territory and its promise of security and rest: see Bonjour, 488. The epic tone of *Ausonum portus* suggests a parallel between Septimius' voyage and the arrival of Aeneas and his crew to found Rome after their journey from Carthage. He left Africa too young to know his place of birth. *uadosus* was the *uox propria* of the Syrtes (Man. 4. 600, Luc. 5. 484 f.) and of that part of the Mediterranean (Sall. *Jug.* 78. 2, Plin. *NH* 5. 26).

39. adoptatus: the new home is personified as the adoptive parent of the

168   COMMENTARY

immigrant: cf. 35–6 n. Naples adopts as her *alumni* Pollius Felix from Puteoli (2. 2. 97) and St.'s father from Velia (5. 3. 106). Since on adoption a son lost the right of inheritance in his old family, the image implies that he has settled permanently in Italy.

39–40. Tuscis / gurgitibus puer innatasti: St. may be referring literally to Septimius' having swum in the Tiber in his childhood. *Tuscus* commonly occurs in periphrases for the Tiber, e.g. Hor. *O*. 3. 7. 27 f. 'nec quisquam citus aeque / Tusco denatat alueo'. *gurges* and its plural commonly occur by metonymy for 'river': cf. Val. Max. 1. 8 *ext*. 19 (of the Bagradas) 'cruore suo gurgitibus inbutis'. City-dwellers swam in the Tiber: see N–H on Hor. *O*. 1. 8. 8, and *RE* Suppl. v. 847 ff. (Mehl).

41. inter pignora curiae: Septimius was brought up among senators' sons; his *condiscipulus* Vitorius Marcellus (4 *Pr*. 11) was probably one of them. Septimius was equestrian, *inter ornatissimos secundi ordinis* (4 *Pr*. 11), but St. remarks on his aristocratic temperament, *indole patricia* (44): cf. *nobilitate ingenita* (Tac. *Ann*. 1. 29. 1). For the (complimentary) topos 'birds of a feather flock together' cf. the epigram quoted by Pliny (*Epist*. 4. 27. 6) γιγνώσκων ὅτι / τοιοῦτός ἐστιν, οἷσπερ ἥδεται συνών.

42–3. contentus ⟨artae⟩ lumine purpurae / crescis: M attests a lacuna of two syllables between *contentus* and *lumine*. *contentus* implies modest circumstances: hence *artae* (Burman), alluding to the *angustus clauus* of the equestrian tunic which Septimius took in exchange for the stripe of the *toga praetexta* when he came of age (*crescis*). With Septimius' modest aspirations cf. the elder Seneca's son Mela (Sen. *Contr*. 2 *Pr*. 3) 'paterno contentus ordine'. *contentus* might disguise the fact that Septimius was not eligible for senatorial status, but it is more likely that he was *eques equo publico* and that St. is implying that he could have had the *latus clauus*, which would give him the right to stand for office, had he asked for it. It is rash, however, to interpret the effusive superlative of *inter ornatissimos secundi ordinis* as categorical evidence that Septimius was *eques equo publico*; but it remains plausible. Horace calls Maecenas, content with equestrian rank, 'equitum decus' (*O*. 3. 16. 20); contrast his description of the cumulative worries of wealth and political responsibility at *O*. 3. 1. 41 ff. (where *purpura* likewise denotes the office of which it is a symbol) 'quodsi dolentem nec Phrygius lapis / nec purpurarum sidere clarior / delenit usus'. St.'s image perhaps alludes to the traditional equestrian epithet *splendidus* (*OLD* s.v. *splendidus* 4b).

43. immensos labores: antithesis between Septimius' restricted ambition (*contentus*, *artae*) and his unbounded pursuit of duty (*immensos*). The status of the ruling class is earned by the responsibilities of government: cf. Virg. *A*. 1. 33.

45. non ... non ... (46) non: St. continues the theme of how Septimius' appearance belies his origins: three negative statements with triple anaphora of *non* lead to the climactic claim *Italus, Italus*. To us this may sound patronizing or even hypocritical, but the Romans saw nothing to be ashamed of in their chauvinism. To be a compliment, however, it must imply that Septimius had non-Roman parentage: see A. Birley, *Septimius Severus* (London, 1971), 38, R. Syme, *CPh* 74 (1979), 13 (=*Rom. Pap*. iii. 1133). Note that St. does not call Septimius 'Romanus': see 46 n.

sermo Poenus: not 'language': it would be banal to compliment Septimius on not speaking Punic in Rome, pace F. Millar, *JRS* 58 (1968), 130. 'Manner of speaking' is appropriate: cf. Cic. *Q. Fr.* 1. 3. 3. (of Tullia) 'effigiem oris, sermonis, animi mei'. The emperor Septimius Seuerus is supposed to have sounded as though he came from Africa: *HA Seu.* 19. 9 'Afrum quiddam usque ad senectutem sonans'; it is alleged that his sister could scarcely speak Latin (*HA Seu.* 15. 7). By *sermo* St. may perhaps mean idiom as well as intonation and inflection, i.e. a North African Latin comparable to Australian or Canadian or South African English today. With St.'s compliment cf. Messala's criticism of Latro (Sen. *Contr.* 2. 48) 'ingenium illi concessit, sermonem obiecit'. Note, however, that the literary and epigraphic evidence for *Africitas* collected in the last century has since been shown to be second-century mannerism: see P. Monceaux, *Les Africains: Étude sur la littérature Latine d'Afrique* (Paris, 1894), refuted by M. Dorothy Brock, *Studies in Fronto and His Age* (Cambridge, 1911), 161–261; see too W. Kroll, *RhM*^{2} 52 (1897), 569–90.

habitus: not 'clothing', since the three aspects which St. mentions must be innate characteristics if Septimius is to betray his origins involuntarily; not 'personality', which is conveyed in *mens* (46); 'physical features' is appropriate if Septimius had Punic blood in him which did not show, e.g. if only one parent was Punic, whereas, if he was of pure Punic descent, St. would be defying visible evidence.

46. externa ... mens: St. assumes the superiority of Romans over provincials; foreign elements which met with Roman approval were assimilated to the *mens domestica et ciuilis*: cf. Cic. *Balb.* 55 on the adoption of Greek rites in the worship of Ceres. *externus* carries connotations of treachery: cf. Tac. *Hist.* 3. 5 'ne inter discordias externa molirentur', 4. 32 'neue externa arma falsis uelaret'. Vollmer may be right to see an allusion to *Punica fides*; the metropolitan could say such things to the *assimilado* without risk of giving offence.

Italus, Italus: a reminiscence of Hor. *O.* 3. 3. 18 'Ilion, Ilion' at the same place in the stanza. St. compliments Septimius by calling him 'Italus' instead of 'Romanus' because 'Italus' was a more exclusive designation: anyone of non-Italian origin who became a citizen could be called 'Romanus', but only native Italians were 'Italus'. Septimius is so naturalized that he appears 'Italus'.

47. turmis: perhaps the *turmae equorum publicorum*: see on 42–3 and 4. 1. 25, where *turmae* represents the *equester ordo*.

48. alumni: native to Rome or to Africa? Since it would be a gross insult for St. to claim that some Romans were untrustworthy enough to be Africans, he must mean that in Rome there were Africans who did Africa credit.

49. est et: verbal and contextual reminiscence of Hor. *O.* 3. 2. 25 f. 'est et fideli tuta silentio / merces': Horace says that a discreet person reaps the just reward for *fides*; in Septimius' case, being articulate wins him renown.

frementi: *fremere* can describe the noise crowds make: cf. Sen. *Contr.* 9. 1. 4 'uidebatur mihi omnis maiorum meorum circa me turba fremere'; hence it also describes places filled with a hum of sound, usually, but not necessarily, man-made: cf. Virg. *A.* 11. 299 'fremunt ripae crepitantibus undis', *S.* 2. 2. 50 'haec pelagi clamore fremunt ... tecta.'

uox hilaris: contrasting with the indistinguishable hubbub in the background (*frementi . . . foro*). For *hilaris* (M) Markland proposed *habilis* as more appropriate to the dignity of the law-courts. But *hilaris* is supported by Ov. *Pont.* 4. 4. 37 'hos [sc. patres] . . . ubi facundo tua uox hilarauerit ore': cf. Cic. *Brut.* 44 (describing the pleasure of listening to an orator) 'huius [sc. Periclis] suauitate maxime hilaratae Athenae sunt'.

50. uenale: although under Claudius the *lex Cincia* of 204 BC (Tac. *Ann.* 11. 5. 3), revived under Augustus (Dio 54. 18. 2), was finally abolished (Tac. *Ann.* 11. 7. 8, 13. 5. 1–2, 42. 2), the ideal of altruistic advocacy persisted: cf. Quint. 12. 1. 25 'non enim forensem quandam instituimus operam nec mercennariam uocem', 12. 7. 8 'nam quis ignorat quin id longe sit honestissimum ac . . . dignissimum, non uendere operam nec eleuare tanti beneficii auctoritatem, cum pleraque hoc ipso possint uideri uilia quod pretium habent?' (with Austin's n.), and see Mayor on Juv. 7. 124. One's first duty in advocacy was to one's *amici*: cf. Tac. *Dial.* 5. 5 'quid est tutius quam eam exercere artem qua semper armatus praesidium amicis, opem alienis, salutem periclitantibus . . . ferat'.

51. ensis ... uagina quiescit: St. applies to oratory a metaphor borrowed from Horace's simile about his satires (*Sat.* 2. 1. 39 ff.) 'sed hic stilus haud petet ultro / quemquam animantem et me ueluti custodiet ensis / uagina tectus'.

52. ni: *ni* (*ς*) for *ne* (M) is right: Septimius refrains from taking on cases unless his friends ask him, not for fear that he will be asked. The present subjunctive indicates the rarity of the contingency. Septimius' altruistic behaviour is exemplified in his support of St. at the Alban Games (25–8).

53. rura ... et quies: *quies* (ἡσυχία) is a prerequisite for literary composition. Favourable surroundings are in turn a prerequisite for *quies*: cf. 1. 3. 20–3 (of Manilius Vopiscus' villa) 'ipse Anien ... tumidam rabiem spumosaque ponit / murmura, ceu placidi ueritus turbare Vopisci / Pieriosque dies et habentis carmina somnos'.

As sometimes in Horace's odes, the philosophical persuasion of the addressee determines the cast of thought: St. composes contentedly in rustic simplicity and seclusion, just as Septimius refrains from earning a public reputation at the Bar, and frequently retreats to the country to compose prose and verse (57–60). The antithesis between *rus* and *forum* is a topos inherited from declamation: cf. Quint. 2. 4. 24 'rusticans uita an urbana potior?' Contrast Septimius' *condiscipulus*, Vitorius Marcellus, for whom relaxation is not a worthy ideal in itself but a means to acquire the renewed vigour necessary for engaging successfully in public life: cf. 4. 4. 33–4.

54–6. nunc ... nunc ... nunc: triple anaphora signalling three different country retreats where Septimius enjoys *quies*. Hence *in paternis sedibus et solo / Veiente* is hendiadys and, *pace* Frère (on 4 *Pr.*), *frondosa Hernica* and *Curibus uetustis* do not also refer to Septimius' father's lands. *paternis* may mean only that the land had belonged to Septimius' father, not that the Septimii were originally Italians with their ancestral home at Veii. The attractions of specific locations in the Italian countryside is reminiscent of Horace's alcaic ode 3. 4, especially 9 ff., 14 ff., and 22 ff. After its dramatic conquest by Camillus in 396 BC, Veii (modern Isola Farnese) declined in importance; hence here it epitomizes rustic quiet and seclusion: cf. Prop. 4. 10. 27 ff. 'heu Vei ueteres! et uos tum regna fuistis, / et uestro posita est aurea sella foro: / nunc intra muros pastoris bucina lenti / cantat, et in uestris ossibus arua metunt', Flor. 1. 12 'hoc tunc Veii fuere. nunc fuisse quis meminit? quae reliquiae? quod uestigium? laborat annalium fides, ut Veios fuisse credamus'. Septimius' imperial namesake has also been linked with Veii: at *HA Seu.* 4. 5 the meaningless *unum fundum inuenit etiam* was emended by M. Hammond, *HSCPh* 51 (1940), 142, to *unum fundum Veientem*, suggesting that the emperor Septimius Seuerus ultimately inherited the estate at Veii which had belonged to the father of St.'s addressee.

55–6. frondosa supra / Hernica: the Hernici were a tribe in Latium of ancient origins. Their name was derived from the Sabine word for 'rock': cf. Virg. *A.* 7. 683 f. 'gelidumque Anienem et roscida riuii / Hernica saxa colunt', Fest. 89. 24 Lindsay 'Hernici dicti a saxis quae Marsi herna dicunt', G. J. M. Bartelink, *Etymologisering bij Vergilius* (Amsterdam, 1965), 48 f. Their territory comprised the upper valley of the Trerus (modern Sacco) and part of the Apennines, still heavily wooded in the nineteenth century (*frondosa*): see *Dict. Geog.*, i. 1059 ff. (Bunbury). *supra* indicates an elevated position, hence Frère identifies Septimius' retreat as Capitulum Hernicum in the neighbourhood of modern Piglio. The Hernici were conquered by Q. Marcius in 306 (Liv. 9. 42 f.) and do not feature in subsequent history; hence they symbolize seclusion. *CIL* xiv. 3004 is an undatable inscription from Praeneste recording a Septimius Seuerus who was *patronus municipii*. Frère suggests that this Septimius is St.'s addressee and that he was *patronus* of Capitulum Hernicum 'd'où la pierre serait venue à Préneste'. Since Praeneste and Capitulum Hernicum are 20 km apart, this hypothesis seems far-fetched. T. D. Barnes, *Hist.* 16 (1967), 89, points out that the Septimius of the inscription could be the father of St.'s addressee or a descendant, not necessarily St.'s Septimius himself. But the inscription does show that the Septimii Seueri were enrolled in the tribe Pupinia, almost exclusively attested within Italy. Lepcitanes who gained citizenship while Lepcis was a *municipium* were enrolled in the Quirina; those enfranchised after it became a *colonia* were enrolled in the Papiria. Hence this evidence supports the thesis that Septimius Seuerus was of Italian extraction. But A. Birley, *BJb* 169 (1969), 255, arguing that St.'s Septimius may not be related to the Septimius of the Praeneste inscription, suggests that the father of St.'s addressee was a native of Lepcis, who was enfranchised *c.*AD 79 and took the *nomen* of the legate of Legio III Augusta, who, he postulates, may have been the Septimius Flaccus on campaign in the Sahara in the first century AD (Ptol. 1. 8. 4); this citizen, conforming to the pattern at pre-colonial Lepcis, would have been enrolled in the tribe Quirina. This squares with the claim (*HA Seu.* 1. 2) that the emperor's forebears were *equites Romani* before the general grant of citizenship (i.e. before AD 110). But for a different explanation for the equestrian status of the Septimii Seueri, see intro. above.

56. Curibus uetustis: Cures, the site of two modern villages, Correse and Arci (*Dict. Geog.*, i. 719 f. [Bunbury], *RE* iv. 1814 [Hülsen]), was a Sabine stronghold under T. Tatius (Liv. 1. 13, Virg. *A.* 8. 638), hence important in the early history of Rome but insignificant later: cf. Ov. *F.* 2. 135 'paruique Cures', Strabo 5. 3. 1 Κύρης δὲ νῦν μὲν κωμίον ἐστίν. The epithet *uetusti* alludes to its ancient role in Rome's history: *Quirites*, the venerable term for the Roman people, was popularly derived from Cures and was thus believed to record the incorporation of the Sabines into Rome under Romulus: cf. Var. *LL* 6. 68 'Quirites a Curensibus; ab his cum Tatio rege in societatem uenerunt ciuitatis', Liv. 1. 13. 5 'ita geminata urbe ut Sabinis tamen aliquid daretur Quirites a Curibus appellati', Ov. *F.* 2. 476 ff. 'qui tenet hoc nomen [Quirinus], Romulus ante fuit / siue ... seu quia Romanis iunxerat ille Cures', Fest. 304. 3 ff. Lindsay. It is appropriate to the immigrant Septimius' assimilation within Roman society for St. to associate him with a site which reputedly gave the Romans a venerable title (although the etymology is almost certainly false: see R. E. A. Palmer, *The Archaic Community of the Romans* [Cambridge, 1970], 157).

57. pones: *uox propria* for setting down in writing: cf. Cic. *Brut.* 219 'ut ne in scripto quidem meminisset quid paulo ante posuisset', *OLD* s.v. *pono* 18. As at 4. 7. 53–6 the final stanza reveals that the addressee is a writer.

57–8. uocibus et modis / passu solutis: *passim* (ς), defended by Frère as *omni tempore*, would contradict the demands of prose rhythm: cf. Cic. *De Or.* 3. 176 'liberat immutatione ordinis, ut uerba neque alligata sint ... neque ita soluta ut uagentur'. With *passu* (Markland) St. combines the traditional definition of prose as *oratio/uerba soluta modis* (e.g. Cic. *Orat.* 183, Ov. *Tr.* 4. 10. 24) with the concept of prose rhythm free from the strictures of metrical feet: cf. [Tib.] 3. 7. 36 'quique canent uincto pede quique soluto', Pers. 1. 13 'scribimus inclusi, numeros ille, hic pede liber'. *passus* is grandiloquent for *pes*: cf. St.'s description of his father's prose paraphrase of Homer (5. 3. 159–61) 'tu par assuetus Homero / ferre iugum senosque pedes aequare solutis / uersibus et numquam passu breuiore relinqui'.

58–9. memor ... nostri: for this formula to conclude a poem, and the Horatian touch, see on 4. 4. 101–2.

59–60. uerecundo ... sub antro: it was fashionable for literary men to exhibit self-effacing *pudor* or *modestia*: cf. Plin. *Epist.* 7. 25. 1 'o quantum eruditionis aut modestia ipsorum aut quies operit ac subtrahit famae', and Martial describing Nerva's reticence about his literary talent (8. 70. 4) 'cum siccare sacram largo Permessida posse / ore, uerecundam maluit esse sitim'. The *timor* which keeps St. from writing an epic about Domitian is slightly different since it is a legitimate qualm about a specific undertaking (see on 4. 4. 96–7). Caves were associated with poetic composition; St.'s phrase is a reminiscence of Horace's alcaics (2. 1. 39 f.) 'mecum Dionaeo sub antro / quaere modos leuiore plectro'. Characteristically, St. inverts the Horatian context: Horace's injunction for him and his Muse to seek inspiration together is replaced by St.'s wish that his own example will inspire Septimius to composition.

latentem / barbiton: the βάρβιτος was a type of lyre, details unknown: see *RE* iii. 4 f. (von Jan). The word, though rare in Latin, occurs in Horace: *O.* 1. 1. 34, 32. 4, 3. 26. 4. Here it appears to be a metaphor for lyric poetry: cf. the common use of *lyra*, as at Hor. *O.* 4. 3. 23 'Romanae fidicen lyrae', Ov. *Pont.* 4. 16. 28 'Pindaricae fidicen tu quoque, Rufe, lyrae'. Thus Septimius composed lyric as well as writing prose; hence it is appropriate for St. to address him (and proffer his example *memor nostri*) in lyric metre.

60. ingemina: *TLL* vii. 1. 1518. 8 glosses St.'s phrase *sc. una mecum*, but St. appears to envisage a totally independent enterprise for Septimius: St. urges him, writing prose in rural seclusion, to play his lyre again too; the contrast with prose-writing implies lyric composition, not a mere recital. *ingeminare* is used of repeated or resumptive action: cf. Val. Fl. 2. 168 f. (the Lemnians' display of affection for their threatened homes) 'oscula iamque toris atque oscula postibus ipsis / ingeminant'.

6

INTRODUCTION

THIS poem is addressed to Novius Vindex, after a dinner-party at which he displayed a statuette of Hercules he had in his possession. Martial 9. 43 and 44 are on the same theme (see below). Vindex was a poet (4 *Pr.* 14, 6. 30, 99 ff., Mart. 9. 43. 14 'docti Vindicis') and an art connoisseur (22 ff.). He was apparently not a senator, or else had retired from office, since for the seven known senators whom St. addresses in the *Siluae* the senatorial post most recently held is specified, except for Rutilius Gallicus, who was retired. Vindex has been tentatively identified with M. Aufatius P. f. Arn. Vindex Nouius Probus *praef. equitum* of *AE* 1893, 50: see *PIR* N 156, *RE* xvii. 1221 (Stein). His friend Vestinus (94) may be the subject of an epicedion by Martial in approximately 88 (4. 73).[1] White (1975), 287 n. 35, conjectures that Martial may therefore have known Vindex too since 88; this is plausible but not definite. St. calls Vindex *noster* (4 *Pr.* 13), an appellation too vague to prove or disprove a long association.

What was the type and provenance of Vindex' statuette? A colossal statue of Hercules, corresponding in posture and attitude to the description by St. and Martial of the Epitrapezios, was excavated in 1960 at Alba Fucens: see F. de Visscher, *AC* 30 (1961), 67–129. The skyward gaze (Mart. 9. 43. 3) and seated position are the same, but the club and wine-cup are held in opposite hands to the specification at Mart. 9. 43. 4 (de Visscher, 108). Since the colossal version displays considerable detail and refinement, de Visscher, 93, argues that Lysippus, to whom Vindex' miniature is attributed (4. 6. 37, 109, Mart. 9. 43. 6, 44. 6), carved an original colossus of which the Alba Fucens statue is a copy. But it is possible that the original miniature was also by Lysippus, since he is known to have made reduced versions of his own Parthenos and the Tyche of Antioch: see Robertson, 473.

[1] Martial's Vestinus died young (4. 73. 7 f. 'tunc largas partitus opes a luce recessit / seque mori post hoc credidit ille senem'). St.'s claim that Vestinus while still in his youth lived up to his ancestry may imply an early death (4. 6. 93 f. 'scit adhuc florente sub aeuo / par magnis Vestinus auis').

While it is possible that Vindex' statuette was indeed Lysippus' original miniature, a copy, perhaps Hellenistic, seems more likely (although St. implies [22–31] that Vindex collected authentic pieces): the Hellenistic age favoured *objets d'art*, including bronze statuettes, and Lysippean styles;[2] furthermore, whereas until the first century BC 'free' copies, made by hand, exhibited clear deviations from their models, the invention of the pointing process enabled exact copies to be made, by mechanical means, that the untutored eye could not distinguish from the originals: see G. M. A. Richter, *Ancient Italy* (Ann Arbor, Mich., 1955), 35, 105 ff.

Central to any hypothesis about the genesis of Vindex' statuette is the meaning of the term ἐπιτραπέζιος: does it describe a figure depicted 'at table' or a figure intended for display 'on a table'? If the colossal version was known as ἐπιτραπέζιος, this would have to refer to its pose since a colossus could not function as a table ornament. De Visscher, 47 f., interprets Hercules' pose as evidence that he was depicted partaking of the sacrifice which was made to him: cf. τράπεζα, *sacra mensa*. He deduces (94, 99) that the type became popular as a figurine to preside over family meals: cf. 4. 6. 32 'castae genius tutelaque mensae', Mart. 9. 43. 12 'priuatos gaudet nunc habitare lares', *ILS* 3442 (from Tivoli) restored as 'Herculi domestico'. Thus an older meaning, 'Hercules at table', could have been replaced by the notion 'Hercules on a table': see Robertson, 473. But if ἐπιτραπέζιος described a figure at a table it would surely imply the *accubatio* position, whereas both Vindex' statuette and the colossus are not reclining but sitting (on a rock, in the case of Vindex' statuette [58]), which does not belong to the context of a formal banquet and τράπεζα. Hence ἐπιτραπέζιος seems to be an epithet acquired by the miniature, either Lysippus' own or a copy, alluding to its potential as a table decoration.[3] The colossal version was probably not originally known as ἐπιτραπέζιος.

To what genre is 4. 6 to be ascribed? It is the longest hexameter poem in *S.* 4, occupying the central position in the metrical arrangement of poems 3–9 (see General Introduction). It begins in a chatty, discursive style reminiscent of the *Sermones* of Horace, above all 1. 9. Lines 20–31 eulogize Vindex' qualities as an art connoisseur. At l. 32 the subject is revealed to be a statuette

---

[2] See W. Lamb, *Greek, Etruscan and Roman Bronzes* (London, 1929) (= *Ancient Greek and Roman Bronzes* [Chicago, 1969]), 195 f.

[3] Hesychius twice uses ἐπιτραπέζιος of Phoenician deities: cf. Hesych. E 78, p. 239 Latte εὐφραδής· Πάταικος ἐπιτραπέζιος, Γ 60, p. 377 Latte Γιγγρών, οἱ δὲ Γιγῶν· Πάταικος ἐπιτραπέζιος. οἱ δὲ Αἰγύπτιον Ἡρακλέα. Hesychius defines the Πάταικοι (s.v.) as θεοὶ Φοίνικες, οὓς ἱστᾶσι κατὰ τὰς πρύμνας τῶν νεῶν. Ch. Picard, *RA* 1911/1. 261, concludes that Ἐπιτραπέζιος = Πάταικος and that statues of Hercules corresponding to the Tyrian god Melqart were displayed as protective figureheads on ships; hence he deduces that Lysippus sculpted his original statue for Alexander when, forbidden by the Tyrians to sacrifice to Melqart, he had besieged Tyre: cf. Diod. 17. 40. 2, Arr. *Anab*. 15. 7, 16. 7, 8, Curt. 4. 2. But de Visscher, 95 n. 53, observes that the basic function of the Πάταικοι is apotropaic (hence their appearance on ships' prows) and that only two of them, Euphrades and Gingron, are called ἐπιτραπέζιος; he thus concludes that in these two instances the gods' apotropaic function was transferred from sea-voyages to household celebrations. What is clear from Hesychius' definitions is that ἐπιτραπέζιος denotes the role of a divinity rather than the pose in which it was customarily represented.

of Hercules belonging to him. An *ecphrasis* of the statuette (32–58) is followed by discussion of its previous owners (59–88), culminating in a eulogy of Vindex himself (89–109).

Works of art are a common subject for epigrams in the *Greek Anthology*: cf. especially the groups about Myron's statuette of a heifer (9. 713–42, 793–8), Lysippus' statues of Alexander (16. 119–22) and Kairos (16. 275), and see P. Laurens, *REL* 43 (1965), 320. Hence Mart. 9. 43 and 44 belong in this tradition. But in St.'s much longer poem the element of *ecphrasis* is subordinate to the broader theme of complimenting Vindex on his taste, knowledge, wealth, hospitality, and friendships. Nevertheless, characteristics of ecphrastic epigram remain.[4] Likewise in prose Pliny's letter to Annius Seuerus (3. 6), commissioning an inscribed base for the bronze statue of an old man which he had bought for the temple of Jupiter at Comum, combines *ecphrasis* (3. 6. 2 f.) with the broader aim of self-advertisement. Sherwin-White (on *Epist.* 3. 6. 5) observes that the absence of specifications as to the size of base required proves that Pliny revised this letter for publication; it is also possible that the detailed *ecphrasis* may be an expansion of what Pliny originally wrote to Annius Seuerus.

The flood of Greek works of art to Rome with the conquest of Greece, Asia Minor, and southern Italy in the third and second centuries BC is widely recognized in antiquity: cf. Cic. *Ver.* 2. 4. 50–2, Plin. *NH* 33. 148, Liv. 27. 10. 7, G. Becatti, *The Art of Ancient Greece and Rome*, tr. J. Ross (London, 1968), 288. Art-collecting became a pursuit to which the wealthy devoted much *otium* and attention: see Friedländer, ii. 329. It represents the taste for luxury in a Horatian passage contrasting the extremes of excess and deprivation (Hor. *Epist.* 2. 2. 180 ff.) 'gemmas, marmor, ebur, Tyrrhena sigilla, tabellas, / argentum, uestes Gaetulo murice tinctas / sunt qui non habeant, est qui non curat habere'. For a contemporary illustration cf. Plin. *Epist.* 3. 7. 8 (of Silius Italicus' materialism) 'plures isdem in locis uillas possidebat, adamatisque nouis priores neglegebat. multum ubique librorum, multum statuarum, multum imaginum', Sen. *Breu. Vit.* 12. 2, and see O. Vessberg, *Studien zur Kunstgeschichte der römischen Republik* (Stockholm, 1941), 1. Abteilung, J. J. Pollitt, *The Art of Rome ca. 776 BC–AD 337: Sources and Documents* (Englewood Cliffs, NJ, 1966, reissued Cambridge, 1983) and *TAPhA* 108 (1978), 155–74. The pretensions of amateurs who boast of their Corinthian bronzes are parodied at Petr. *Sat.* 50. Bogus collectors are mocked by Martial at 4. 39, 9. 59. 7 ff. A pedigree of distinguished owners enhanced the snob-value of a work of art: cf. Hor. *Sat.* 1. 3. 90, 2. 3. 21, Mart. 8. 6. 1 ff., Juv. 6. 156 f., 12. 44 (with Courtney's note), 47, Sen. *Dial.* 9. 1. 7 'mensa non uarietate macularum conspicua nec per multas dominorum elegantium successiones ciuitati nota', *HA Tyr. Trig.* 30. 19. But the taste and culture of St.'s host are above reproach: he was a connoisseur, dividing his time between poetic composition and art appreciation (30 f.). This devotion to his hobbies earned him the tribute of St.'s poem (4 *Pr.* 14 ff.).

Despite St.'s protestations that Vindex was knowledgeable and discerning,

---

[4] Discussed in the commentary ad locc. See generally P. Friedländer, *Johannes von Gaza und Paulus Silentiarius. Kunstbeschreibungen justinianischer Zeit* (Leipzig, 1912), 62 ff.

most of the opinions which St. expresses about the statuette (and which presumably originate with Vindex himself: see below) are *loci communes* (noted in the commentary ad loc.). These banal observations presumably reflect the general level of art criticism in wealthy Roman circles, despite the impression which Cicero gives in the *Verrines* that cultured people set great store by discussion about works of art: see P. Zanker, *Fondation Hardt* 25 (1979), 287 f. But indisputably this poem, by implication, celebrates Vindex' wealth: he collected old masters (20 ff.). If Lucullus commissioned a statue of Felicitas from the contemporary artist Arcesilaus for one million sesterces (Plin. *NH* 35. 156, adopting Detlefsen's conjecture), we may assume that classical Greek masterpieces would be extremely valuable.[5]

Verbal and thematic similarities between this poem and Mart. 9. 43 suggest a common source, presumably the instructions of Vindex himself: see Hardie, 71. Martial does not mention the dinner-party. The Horatian setting and contrived casualness of *forte* (1) suggest that the occasion is literary rather than authentic, 'a specific (but artificial) "occasion"' (Hardie, 130): see too the discussion of this poem by Vessey, *ANRW* 2794–8. But if St. had never been a guest at his house Vindex would surely have considered impertinent St.'s compliments (12 ff.) about the cultured conversation between them. Hence this *cena* may be a composite occasion to form a context for the commissioned poem. R. B. Steele, *CPh* 25 (1930), 334, sets out the similarities between the diction of St. and Martial, but he mistakenly interprets them as echoes of Martial by St., on the assumption that Martial's poems date from 94 and St.'s from 95; but since topicality was vital, all three poems must have been produced as soon as Vindex put his statuette on display. They should thus be dated to 94.

1–31. This is the only poem in the *Siluae* to begin in narrative form. The tone and setting are Horatian, ll. 1–31 forming a prologue which includes the eulogy of Vindex as an art connoisseur (20–31), 'thirty lines which laboriously strive for the chatty idiom of Horace' (White [1975], 286). The scene is thus set for the *ecphrasis* (32 ff.), whereas Martial's epigrams (9. 43, 44) depend for their brevity and impact on complete exclusion of any 'setting'. It seems unlikely that this prologue was added for publication, since its compliments are clearly meant for Vindex, and without it the poem is less directly encomiastic. It also loosely corresponds to an invitation-poem, combining thanks to Vindex with a notice of the invitation (3), oblique allusion to the type of menu (5 ff.), and summary of the entertainment (12 f.): for these characteristic topics see E. Lowell, *AJPh* 103 (1982), 184–8.

1. Forte: cf. Hor. *Sat.* 1. 9. 1 'Ibam forte uia Sacra'. *forte* marks the beginning of a narrative: cf. Hor. *Epist.* 1. 7. 29, Liv. 42. 49. 1.

1–2. Phoeboque leuatum / pectora: inspiration is interpreted as possession by Apollo: cf. Virg. *A.* 6. 78 (religious inspiration) 'bacchatur uates, magnum si pectore possit / excussisse deum.' St. portrays himself as the professional epic poet, relaxing after hours spent composing, and glad

---

[5] The authenticity of Vindex' latest acquisition is a separate issue, discussed above.

that Vindex' invitation (3) engages him in conversation on literary topics (12 f.), whereas Horace, mulling over some verses (*Sat.* 1. 9. 2 'nescio quid meditans nugarum, totus in illis'), resents being interrupted. St.'s phrasing disguises the fact that, by the operation of *amicitia* fundamental to his livelihood, he was obliged to accept invitations to dinner (see White [1978], 76), and that while he always protests that epic is his *métier* (1 *Pr.* 5 ff; 4 *Pr.* 28, 4. 87 ff., 7. 21–4), his *amici* cultivate him for the type of composition reflected in the *Siluae*: cf. Mart. 9. 97. 9 f. 'rumpitur inuidia quod sum iucundus amicus, / quod conuiua frequens, rumpitur inuidia'.

2. **patulis ... Saeptis:** the Saepta Iulia were in the Campus Martius between the Pantheon and the Temple of Isis: see Nash ii. 291 and pls. 1052–4. Originally voting enclosures, they were used under the early empire for public displays (especially gladiatorial fights) until the Flavian Amphitheatre (Colosseum) was dedicated in AD 80. In that year the Saepta were severely damaged by fire (Dio 66. 24) but immediately rebuilt and thereafter converted into an enormous market: cf. Mart. 9. 59. 1–2 'in Saeptis Mamurra diu multumque uagatus, / hic ubi Roma suas aurea uexat opes', 10. 80. 3–4 '... gemitus imo ducit de pectore quod non / tota miser coemat Saepta feratque domum', 2. 57. 1 f. It was a fashionable place to walk, and hangers-on might pick up dinner-invitations there: cf. Mart. 2. 14. 5 (the notorious Selius) 'si nihil Europe fecit, tunc Saepta petuntur'. See *RE* iA. 1724 ff. (Rosenberg).

3. **iam moriente die:** St. absolves himself from suspicion of waiting for an invitation since *cena* usually began before sunset; Pliny's uncle finished dinner in daylight during summer and within the first hour of darkness during winter (*Epist.* 3. 5. 13), and Martial reserves the ninth and tenth hours for it (4. 8. 6 f.), i.e. between half-past two and five in summer and between half-past one and three in winter: for the modern equivalent of the Roman hours of the day see the table, derived from Marquardt, at Courtney, 59.

3–4. **rapuit me cena benigni / Vindicis:** the echo (of Hor. *Sat.* 2. 8. 1 'ut Nasidieni iuuit te cena beati') is more exalted than the original: cf. Virg. *A.* 6. 460 (Aeneas to Dido) ~ Cat. 66. 39 (the *coma* to Berenice), Hor. *Epist.* 2. 1. 256 (Augustus and Parthia) ~ Cic. fr. 17 Morel (Roma and Cicero's consulship: see Brink's note on Horace's line). For a comparable sequence, setting an important occurrence against a general background depicting people at leisure, cf. Petr. *Sat.* 27. 1 'nos interim uestiti errare coepimus ... immo iocari (otiari *Heinsius*) magis et circulis ludentum (*Heinsius*: ludentem *codd.*) accedere, cum subito uidemus senem caluum'. *benignus* carries a nuance of 'generous' as well as 'kind': cf. Hor. *O.* 1. 9. 5 ff. 'dissolue frigus ligna super foco / large reponens atque benignius / deprome quadrimum Sabina, / o Thaliarche, merum diota'.

5. **inconsumpta:** the spiritual nourishment which St. derived from the meal with Vindex continued to sustain him long after the transient satisfaction of the edible content had disappeared: cf. the aphorism attributed to the Athenian Timotheus the day after a meal with Plato (Cic. *Tusc.* 5. 100) 'uestrae quidem cenae non solum in praesentia, sed etiam postero die iucundae sunt'. The notion that mental discipline (i.e.

philosophy) constitutes true nourishment is Epicurean: cf. Epic. *Epist.* 3, p. 64. 12 ff. Usener. To enjoy gastronomic delights is to indulge in *ludibria uentris*, deceptive pleasures.
6. **epulas diuerso a sole petitas:** cf. Hor. *Sat.* 2. 2. 120 f. 'bene erat non piscibus urbe petitis, / sed pullo atque haedo'. The import of luxury goods from the distant east (*diuerso a sole*), which gained momentum after the defeat of the Achaean League (146 BC), is frequently denounced in moralizing writers, notably the elder Pliny: see Friedländer, ii. 146–64.
7. **uina ... perpetuis aeuo certantia fastis:** the vintage was dated on the amphora with the consuls' names: cf. *CIL* iv. 5520 'C. Pomponio C. Anicio cos. ex fund. Badiano diff. id. Aug. bimum'. Mature wine from an exceptional vintage was highly prized: cf. the reputation of wine laid down in the consulship of Opimius (121 BC): Cic. *Brut.* 287 '[uino] ita uetere ut Opimium aut Anicium consulem quaerat', Vell. 2. 7. 5 'Opimius, a quo consule celeberrimum Opimiani uini nomen', Petr. *Sat.* 34. 6 'Falernum Opimianum annorum centum', Plin. *NH* 14. 55, 94, Mart. 1. 26. 7 'testa sed antiqui felix siccatur Opimi', 3. 82. 24, 9. 87. 1, 10. 49. 2.
8–9. **quid Phasidis ales / distet ab hiberna Rhodopes grue:** to contrast with *medio ... Helicone petitus / sermo* (12 f.). St. parodies the precious and sterile debates in which gourmets engage, 'exacta tenui ratione saporum' (Hor. *Sat.* 2. 4. 36). The relative excellence of products from different localities is debated at Hor. *Sat.* 2. 2. 31 ff. 'unde datum sentis, lupus hic Tiberinus an alto / captus hiet? pontisne inter iactatus an amnis / ostia sub Tusci?', and traditional reputations associating products and places are listed at 2. 4. 32 ff. 'murice Baiano melior Lucrina peloris, / ostrea Circeis, Miseno oriuntur echini, / pectinibus patulis iactat se molle Tarentum': cf. the discerning palate at Juv. 4. 139–43 'nulli maior fuit usus edendi / tempestate mea: Circeis nata forent an / Lucrinum ad saxum Rutupinoue edita fundo / ostrea callebat primo deprendere morsu, / et semel aspecti litus dicebat echini'. *Phasidis ales* is the species of pheasant (*Phasianus colchicus*) associated with the R. Phasis which flows into the Euxine: see D'Arcy Thompson, *Birds*, 298 ff. It was regarded as very exotic: cf. Petr. *Sat.* 93. 2 'ales Phasiacis petita Colchis / atque Afrae uolucres placent palato, / quod non sunt faciles'. The rarity of this bird is weighed against the winter crane to show the sterility of the gourmets' concerns, since cranes were renowned in antiquity for the long migration southwards which made them unobtainable in Europe during winter: see D'Arcy Thompson, *Birds*, 71. Crane were native to Thrace, denoted here by Mt. Rhodope in the Haemus range: cf. Virg. *G.* 1. 120 'Strymoniae ... grues'. Both crane and goose-liver (see next n.) were on Nasidienus' menu (Hor. *Sat.* 2. 8. 87 f.).
9–10. **quis magis anser / exta †ferat†:** gourmets discuss which geese produce the best pâté, i.e. which have the fattest liver. To this end, geese were force-fed on figs: cf. Hor. *Sat.* 2. 8. 88 'pinguibus et ficis pastum iecur anseris albae', and see André, *Alimentation*, 132 f. From the Greek verb for this process, συκόω, was derived συκωτόν for liver (mod. Gr. συκῶτι) and, by a calque, Latin *ficatum*, whence the Romance words for liver (e.g. Fr. *foie*, It. *fegato*). *magis* is the right word in gourmets' discussions: cf. Hor. *Sat.*

2. 2. 29 f. (peacock compared with chicken) 'carne tamen quamuis distat nil hac magis, illam / imparibus formis deceptum te petere! esto', *Epist.* 1. 15. 22 f. 'tractus uter pluris lepores, uter educet apros, / utra magis piscis et echinos aequora celent'. But *magis . . . exta ferat* is not Latin for *maiora exta ferat*. Hence the corruption must lie with *ferat*. Attempts have been made to replace it with an adjective, since *magis* with an adjective is attested as a periphrasis for a comparative: cf. Prop. 1. 10. 27 'humilis magis', Mart. 5. 68. 2 'flaua magis', 7. 2. 2 'fida magis'. But while *ferax* (denoting the capacity for being productive) and *satur* (cf. Pers. 6. 71) are both attractive, they govern the genitive and cannot be construed with *exta* as accusative of respect. The only solution would be to replace *ferat* with a verb meaning 'fatten'.

10. cur Tuscus aper generosior Vmbro: Umbrian boar is an approved gourmet dish at Hor. *Sat.* 2. 4. 40 f. 'Vmber et iligna nutritus glande rotundas / curuat aper lances carnem uitantis inertem'. *generosus* ('choice') belongs to the pretentious vocabulary of the epicure: cf. Hor. *Sat.* 2. 4. 31 'sed non omne mare est generosae fertile testae', *Epist.* 1. 15. 18 'generosum et lene requiro'.

11. lubrica ... conchylia: cf. Hor. *Sat.* 2. 4. 30 'lubrica nascentes inplent conchylia lunae'.

12. nobis uerus amor: the passion which St. and Vindex share for literature is genuine, whereas the debates between gourmets about the relative merits of (e.g.) pheasant and crane are an affectation and a sham: cf. 31 'hic Aoniis amor auocat antris'.

12–13. medio ... Helicone petitus / sermo: *sermo* (= λέσχη) is the *uox propria* for after-dinner conversation: cf. Callim. *Epig.* 2. 3 Pfeiffer ἥλιον ἐν λέσχηι κατεδύσαμεν, Hor. *O.* 3. 21. 9 f. 'Socraticis madet / sermonibus', *Sat.* 2. 6. 71 'sermo oritur, non de uillis domibusue alienis', Plin. *Epist.* 3. 12 'Socraticis tantum sermonibus abundet'. The topic was literature, derived from the heart of the Muses' haunts. Vindex was a poet (30); *hilares . . . ioci* (13), reminiscent of Catullus' evening with Caluus (Cat. 50), may suggest that St. and Vindex spent part of the evening composing spontaneous verse: cf. Cat. 50. 4 ff. 'scribens uersiculos uterque nostrum / ludebat numero modo hoc modo illoc, / reddens mutua per iocum atque uinum'. But we should probably not think of a tête-à-tête. St. cultivates an impression of intimacy and confidentiality with his patrons which excludes mention of other parties, excepting individuals of particular significance to the patron (see on Vestinus, 1. 94). *petitus sermo* contrasts with *epulas . . . petitas* (6): imports to satisfy physical appetites are pretentious extravagance, but for intellectual sustenance the search must be pursued to the very sources of inspiration.

15–16. alter / Castor = the constellation Gemini, i.e. the Dioscuri. With twins, one of the pair is commonly named for both, or the name of one is used in the plural to designate the pair: cf. (for the Dioscuri) Hor. *O.* 3. 29. 64 'geminus ... Pollux', Tac. *Hist.* 2. 24. 2 'locus Castorum uocatur', *Anth. Lat.* 197. 18 Riese 'Castoribus simpli rite dicantur equi'; (for the Haedi) Hor. *O.* 3. 1. 28 'impetus ... orientis Haedi', Prop. 2. 26. 56 'purus et Haedus erit'. This usage in literary Latin, discussed by A. J. Bell, *The Latin*

Dual and Poetic Diction (London–Toronto, 1923), 3 ff., is found also in cult and in place-names, and is shown by Wackernagel, *Kl. Schr.* i. 544–5, to have Indo-European ancestry.

For the development of the tradition associating the Dioscuri with the underworld see Roscher i. 1155–6 (A. Furtwängler): originally they both simply died; then they together spent alternate days on earth and beneath it (cf. Pind. *Nem.* 10. 103 ff. μεταμειβόμενοι δ' ἐναλλὰξ ἁμέραν τὰν μὲν παρὰ πατρὶ φίλωι Δὶ νέμονται τὰν δ' ὑπὸ κεύθεσι γαίας ἐν γυάλοις Θεράπνας); finally, the tradition which St. follows, the twins changed places with each other on alternate days (cf. Virg. *A.* 6. 121 f. 'si fratrem Pollux alterna morte redemit / itque reditque uiam totiens', with Norden's note).

17. iunctaque utinam Tirynthia luna: for the ellipse of *esse* in exclamations see L–H–S 421. The paradigm for the miraculously extended night is the occasion when Heracles was conceived of Zeus and Alcmene in two nights joined as a continuous one (*iuncta luna*): cf. Prop. 2. 22. 25 f., Ov. *Am.* 1. 13. 45 f., Hyg. *Fab.* 29. The other version, which St. follows at *Theb.* 6. 288, 12. 301, is that the night was not double but triple: cf. Apollod. 2. 4. 8, Diod. 4. 9. 2. St. here follows the Argive tradition that Heracles was brought up at Tiryns instead of Thebes: cf. Diod. 4. 10. 2.

18. Erythraeae Thetidis signanda lapillis: cf. Mart. 10. 38. 4 f. 'o nox omnis et hora, quae notata est / caris litoris Indici lapillis'. It was customary to commemorate a happy day with a white mark on the calendar: cf. Cat. 68. 148 'quem lapide illa diem candidiore notat', Hor. *O.* 1. 36. 10 'Cressa ne careat pulchra dies nota', Plin. *Epist.* 6. 11. 3 'o diem (repetam enim) laetum notandumque mihi candidissimo calculo', Otto, *Sprichwörter*, no. 299. This habit was derived from a Thracian custom of putting a white pebble in an urn for each happy day: cf. Plin. *NH* 7. 131.

Pearls were fished in the *rubrum mare*: cf. Tac. *Agr.* 12. 6 f. 'margarita . . . in rubro mari uiua ac spirantia saxis auelli'. In St.'s day *rubrum mare* could mean part or all of the sea between Suez and Sri Lanka: see Goodyear on Tac. *Ann.* 2. 61. 2. St.'s reference may be general: cf. Plin. *NH* 9. 106 'Indicus maxime has mittit oceanus', Amm. 23. 6. 85 'apud Indos et Persas margaritae reperiuntur in testis marinis robustis et candidis'. But he probably means specifically the Persian Gulf, which was famous for its pearls: cf. Plin. *NH* 9. 106 'praecipue autem laudantur circa Arabiam in Persico sinu maris Rubri'. For the distribution of pearl-fisheries in the ancient world see *RE* xiv. 1687–9 (Rommel). *Erythraeis* (M) is untenable (despite Mart. 5. 37. 4 'nec lapillos praeferas Erythraeos') since *Thetidis*, awkward on its own, requires an epithet.

19. genium ... perennem: the night of Vindex's party possessed a quality of divinity derived from the divinely inspired literary conversation; its memory can never be erased. For the quality of inspiration which guarantees immortality cf. Mart. 6. 60. 9 f. 'nescioquid plus est, quod donat saecula chartis: / uicturus genium debet habere liber'.

20. mille ... species aerisque eborisque: *mille* = 'innumerable': cf. Ov. *Rem.* 526 'mille mali species', Pers. 5. 52 'mille hominum species', *TLL* viii. 980. 80 ff. Statuettes and small reliefs were sometimes made of ivory (G. M. A. Richter, *The Sculpture and Sculptors of the Greeks* [Yale, 1929], 107). St.

does not appear to be thinking of ivory in combination with other materials, e.g. chryselephantine or akrolithic statues (Richter, 106).

21. locuturas mentito corpore ceras: for the topos of lifelike art cf. Ov. *Met.* 10. 250 f. (Pygmalion's statue) 'uirginis est uerae facies, quam uiuere credas, / et, si non obstet reuerentia, uelle moueri'. *mentiri* suggests imitation of alien properties: cf. Virg. *E.* 4. 42 'nec uarios discet mentiri lana colores', Quint. 2. 15. 25 'colorem fuco et uerum robur inani sagina mentiantur'. The notion of unintentional deception is common in the context of sculpture: cf. *Anth. Lat.* 748. 3 Riese 'mentitur gemma uolatum [aquilae]', Oros. *Hist.* 2. 19. 15 '[imagines] quae superstitione miserabili uel deum uel hominum mentiuntur', *TLL* viii. 781. 22 ff. The attributive use of the future participle is common in imperial poetry to express a hypothesis: see K–S i. 761, L–H–S 390. Here *locuturas* stands for a relative clause with ellipse of the protasis. For wax statues intended as permanent works of art (as opposed to bronze casting by the *cire perdue* process) cf. Plin. *Epist.* 4. 7. 1 (Regulus' statues of his son in various media including *cera*), 7. 9. 11 (statues of Mars, Minerva, Venus, and Cupid), *RE* Suppl. xiii. 1358 (Büll, Moser). St. does not appear to mean ancestral wax *imagines* such as decorated the *atria* of the noble, but statuary comparable with bronzes and ivories.

22. edidici: Vindex taught St. to recognize a thousand works by different sculptors; *ediscere*, 'to learn (a list) by heart' can be used of visual memorization: cf. Prop. 4. 3. 37 'cogor et e tabula pictos ediscere mundos', *TLL* v. 76. 4 ff.

24. non inscriptis ... signis: statue-bases were inscribed with a dedication and occasionally the name of the sculptor, as Martial claims for Vindex' statuette (9. 44. 5 f.) 'inscripta est basis indicatque nomen. / Lysippum lego, Phidiae putaui' (where 'Lysippum' [*codd.*] has been upheld by Housman, *JPh* 30 [1907], 246–7 [= *Cl. Pap.* ii. 724–5]); for two statue-bases at Corinth dated to *c.*325 BC and inscribed Λύσιππος ἐπόησε see B. Powell, *AJA* 1903, 29–32. For signatures on statuary see G. M. A. Richter, op. cit. (on l. 20), 120, M. Guarducci, *Epigrafia greca* iii (Rome, 1974), 377–561, G. Kaibel, *Epigrammata Graeca ex lapidibus conlecta* (Berlin, 1878; repr. Hildesheim, 1965), index s.v. 'artificis nomen', M. Bua, *Mem. Acc. Linc.*[8] 16 (1971–2), 13. Vindex' statuette was either an original or an accurate copy (see intro.), because from the first century BC signatures appeared on the statues themselves and no longer on the base: see G. M. A. Richter, *JRS* 48 (1958), 13. St. apparently means here that, by dint of studying Vindex' collection under his guidance, he will be able to recognize the work of any of the old masters when he sees one of their statues without an ascription. An unscrupulous owner, of course, could display copies but nevertheless pass them off as originals: cf. Eucrates (Lucian, *Philopseudeis* 18), who claimed to own in his collection works by both Myron and Polycleitus.

25. hic answers the question introduced by *quis* (22). *haec* (M) is superfluous; the objects of *monstrabit* are specified with anaphora of the relative pronoun (*quae ... aera, quae marmora, quod ebur, quod, linea quae*) and a summarizing demonstrative is clumsy and unnecessary. *hic*, emphasizing Vindex as the

COMMENTARY

embodiment of learning and discernment, underlines Vindex' role as teacher (*monstrabit*).

docto ... Myroni: cf. 44–5 'docti / artificis', Mart. 8. 50(51). 1 'quis labor in phiala? docti Myos anne Myronos?' *doctus* can describe a person who excels in a particular skill: cf. Ov. *Met.* 3. 168 (of the deftest nymph attending Diana) 'doctior illis ... Crocale ... capillos colligit in nodum', *TLL* v. 1758. 46 ff. Myron and Polyclitus are invariably included in the canon of Greek sculptors: cf. *Rhet. Her.* 4. 9, Cic. *De Or.* 3. 26, Lucian, *Somn.* 8. Vindex was a connoisseur of the same artists as Pollius Felix: cf. 2. 2. 63–7, identical with our list except for the omission of Praxiteles. Vindex was acquainted with *Myronis aera*, not merely the cow for which he was popularly famous: cf. Plin. *NH* 34. 57 'Myronem ... bucula maxime nobilitauit celebratis uersibus laudata' (i.e. in the Greek epigrams cited in the intro. above), *Aetna* 597 'gloria uiua Myronis', *RE* xvi. 1124 ff. (Lippold), Robertson, 339–44.

25–6. uigilata ... aera: the artist, like the poet, pursues a lonely vigil (φρουρά) into the small hours. This was a traditional manifestation of the πόνος of composition: cf. Callim. *Epig.* 27. 3 f. Pfeiffer χαίρετε λεπταί / ῥήσιες, Ἀρήτου σύμβολον ἀγρυπνίης, Lucr. 1. 142 'noctes uigilare serenas', Hor. *Ars* 268 f. 'uos exemplaria Graeca / nocturna uersate manu, uersate diurna', Juv. 1. 51 'haec ego non credam Venusina digna lucerna', *OLD* s.v. *lucerna* 1b.

26. uiuant ... caelo: cf. 2. 2. 67 'Polycliteo iussum est quod uiuere caelo'. Artistic creation is commonly represented as a birth: cf. *Anth. Pal.* 16. 257. 2 (a statue of Dionysus) γενεὴν εὗρε Μύρων ἑτέρην. The reverse, that the artist cannot truly bring about a rebirth, also becomes a topos: cf. *Anth. Pal.* 16. 352. 1–4 (a statue of Porphyrius the charioteer) πλάστης χαλκὸν ἔτευξεν ὁμοίιον ἡνιοχῆι· / εἴθε δὲ καὶ τέχνης ὄγκον ἀπειργάσατο, / ὄγκον ὁμοῦ καὶ κάλλος· ὅπερ φύσις ὀψὲ τεκοῦσα / ὤμοσεν· Ὠδίνειν δεύτερον οὐ δύναμαι, and for a photograph of this epigram inscribed on the statue-base see A. Cameron, *Porphyrius the Charioteer* (Oxford, 1973), pl. 10b. For Praxiteles, a fourth-century Athenian sculptor, see *RE* xxii. 1788 ff. (Lippold), Robertson, 386–96.

27. ebur Pisaeo pollice rasum: Pheidias, son of Charmides of Athens, was associated above all with Olympia for the celebrated ivory statue of Zeus in his temple there: see *RE* xix. 1919 ff. (Lippold), Robertson, 322 ff. The exact location of Pisa, which was in the vicinity of Olympia, is unknown. It was destroyed in 570 BC, and the plunder financed the building of Zeus' temple (Paus. 5. 10. 2): cf. *S.* 3. 1. 140 'Pisaeus ... Iuppiter'. Pisa becomes synonymous with Olympia in both poetry and prose, Greek and Roman: see *RE* xx. 1754. 58 ff. (Meyer).

28. Polycleteis ... spirare caminis: Polycleitus' statues are so realistic that they seem to come to life when he casts them. For his reputation see *RE* xxi. 1707 ff. (Sieveking), Robertson, 328–40.

29. ueterem ... Apellen: the most famous painter of antiquity, and the only one whom St. mentions: cf. St.'s compliment to Domitian (1. 1. 100) 'Apelleae cuperent te scribere cerae', 2. 2. 64, 5. 1. 5, Quint. 12. 10. 6 'floruit autem circa Philippum et usque ad successores Alexandri pictura praecipue, sed diuersis uirtutibus ... in genio et gratia, quam in se ipse maxime iactat, Apelles est praestantissimus', *RE* i. 2689 ff. (Rossbach), Robertson, 492 ff. *ueterem* does not distinguish Apelles from the preceding examples, but rather summarizes a characteristic common to them all: they lived long ago; for this sense of *uetus* cf. Quint. 1. 4. 3 'ueteres grammatici', *OLD* s.v. *uetus* 5b, and for the comparable use of *senex* see on 4. 9. 20.

longe fateatur: the drawing gives the onlooker evidence from which he deduces that Apelles was the artist; this is a common metaphor: cf. Flor. 4. 12. 62 'ipse hominum color ab alio uenire caelo fatebatur', *TLL* vi. 1. 342. 55 ff.

31. Aoniis ... antris: Vindex' art-collecting is a diversion which seduces him from poetic composition, represented here by the haunts of the Muses. Their home on Mt. Helicon in Boeotia, and thus poetic inspiration itself, are commonly designated in poetry by the adjective *Aonius*, derived from Ἄονες, a Boeotian tribe: see *RE* i. 2657 (Hirschfeld). St. is particularly fond of this periphrasis: e.g. the Muses are 'sorores Aonides' (5. 3. 122), 'Aonias ... diuas' (1. 4. 20).

32. castae ... mensae: Vindex' dinner-table was the setting for pure intellectual enjoyment and not the indulgence of physical cravings: cf. Cic. *Cael.* 9 'nemo hunc M. Caelium in illo aetatis flore uidit nisi ... in M. Crassi castissima domo cum artibus honestissimis erudiretur'.

33. cepit: St. uses the language of love-poetry to describe the effect upon him of the statuette's distinction and majesty: cf. *Anth. Pal.* 12. 99. 1 ἠγρεύθην ὑπ' Ἔρωτος, Prop. 1. 1. 1 'Cynthia primum suis miserum me cepit ocellis', Ov. *Her.* 16. 92 'his [blanditiis] poterant pectora nostra capi', *TLL* iii. 337. 74 ff.

34. satiaui: the result of being enthralled by the statuette is that however much St. feasts his eyes on it his appetite can never be assuaged. The faculty of vision is exercised by St., not the statuette; *satiauit* (M) would leave *uisu* unattached to any agent. For the close connection between *uisu*, modal ablative, and the subject of the clause cf. *Ach.* 1. 126 'tacito lustrat Thetis omnia uisu', Plin. *NH* 7. 16 'qui uisu ... effascinent interemantque quos intueantur'. Cf. the ablative with *lumina satiare* to express the sight which is seen, akin to the ablative here expressing the mode of vision (*S.* 5. 1. 174–5) 'nec sole supremo / lumina sed dulci mauult satiare marito'.

35–6. tantus honos operi finisque inclusa per artos / maiestas: for the paradox that a great personality can be depicted in a small work of art cf. *Anth. Pal.* 9. 776. 4 (Diodorus' epigram on a miniature depicting Queen Arsinoe) εἰμὶ δ' ἀνάσσης / εἰκών, καὶ μεγάλης λείπομαι οὐδ' ὀλίγον, 16. 120. 2 (on Lysippus' statue of Alexander) τίν' ὅδι χαλκὸς ἔχει δύναμιν, Mart. 14. 171 Βρούτου παιδίον *fictile* 'gloria tam parui non est obscura sigilli: / istius pueri Brutus amator erat'. The oxymoron 'great in small' with reference to physical dimensions is a similar topos: cf. 37 f. 'paruusque uideri / sentirique ingens', Mart. 9. 43. 2 'exiguo magnus in aere deus', Sen. *Epist.* 53. 11 'magni artificis est clusisse totum in exiguo'.

36. deus ille, deus: *geminatio* suits religious language, for instance at epiphanies (i.e. Lysippus' statuette of Hercules is the embodiment of a god): cf. Lucr. 5. 8 (of Epicurus) 'deus ille fuit, deus', Virg. *E.* 5. 64 'deus, deus ille'.

36–8. seseque tuendum / indulsit, Lysippe, tibi, paruusque uideri / sentirique ingens: the godhead revealed to the artist is a topos; *tuendum* (Schrader) avoids the clumsy repetition with *uideri* (37) but retains the sense of *uidendum* (M). Cf. *Anth. Pal.* 16. 81 (Philip on the statue of Zeus at Olympia) ἦ θεὸς ἦλθ' ἐπὶ γῆν ἐξ οὐρανοῦ, εἰκόνα δείξων, / Φειδία· ἦ σύ γ' ἔβης τὸν θεὸν ὀψόμενος, 179 (Antipater of Sidon on the Aphrodite Anadyomene by Apelles), 216 (Parmenion on a statue of Hera by Polycleitus), 9. 505 (where the artist achieves the image of Terpsichore even without her appearing to him). Behind this topos lie the imaginative processes of artistic creation which are interpreted as φαντασίαι or εἰδωλοποιίαι (Longinus 15. 1), the artist's 'visions' ('visualizations' is the less emotive translation advocated by Russell ad loc.) whereby he conjures up his subject before his eyes and uses his skill to make his audience see it too: cf. Longinus 15. 1 (of oratory) ἤδη δ' ἐπὶ τούτων κεκράτηκε τοὔνομα [ἡ φαντασία] ὅταν ἃ λέγεις ὑπ' ἐνθουσιασμοῦ καὶ πάθους βλέπειν δοκῇς καὶ ὑπ' ὄψιν τιθῇς τοῖς ἀκούουσιν. Longinus cites the mad scene of Euripides' *Orestes* as an example of a poet's φαντασία (15. 2) ἐνταῦθ' ὁ ποιητὴς αὐτὸς εἶδεν Ἐρινύας· ὃ δ' ἐφαντάσθη, μικροῦ δεῖν θεάσασθαι καὶ τοὺς ἀκούοντας ἠνάγκασεν. The Latin term is *uisiones*: cf. Quint. 6. 2. 29 'quas φαντασίας Graeci uocant (nos sane uisiones appellemus), per quas imagines rerum absentium ita repraesentantur animo ut eas cernere oculis ac praesentes habere uideamur, has quisquis bene ceperit is erit in adfectibus potentissimus'. The term itself probably belongs to the jargon of the rhetorical schools (A. Trendelenburg, *Progr. zum Winckelmannsfeste*, no. 70 [Berlin, 1910], 3), but it applies also to the vivid evocation of an image in the plastic arts: cf. Quint. 12. 10. 6 (of the painter Theon of Samos) 'concipiendis uisionibus quas φαντασίας uocant Theon Samius ... est praestantissimus'. Lysippus, by his φαντασία of Hercules, was able to create for his audience a truly lifelike representation, so that even the statuette's tiny dimensions conveyed to the onlooker's imagination the strength and stature of Hercules. Lysippus was renowned for the realism of his figures: cf. Prop. 3. 9. 9 'gloria Lysippo est animosa effingere saxa', Quint. 12. 10. 9 'ad ueritatem Lysippum ac Praxitelen accessisse optime adfirmant'; allied to this is his reputation for very detailed execution: cf. Plin. *NH* 34. 65 'propriae huius uidentur esse argutiae operum custoditae in minimis quoque rebus'.

40–2. The statuette displays a physique capable of performing the feats attributed to Hercules. St. cites the killing of the Nemean lion and the episode aboard the Argo where Hercules underestimated his own strength and broke his oar in half: cf. Ap. Rhod. 1. 1167 ff., Val. Fl. 3. 476 ff.

42. Argoos: the adjectival form of a proper name to replace a possessive adjective is frequently a mark of high poetic style: see E. Löfstedt, *Syntactica* i² (Lund, 1942), 107 ff. These adjectives are more frequent in Latin poetry than in Greek, although in Mycenaean and Aeolic they were the normal form of patronymic.

43. †ac† spatium: the rest of this line, 'tam magna breui mendacia formae', is a self-contained epigram expressing the antithesis that a tiny work of art can exercise a grand deception over the senses. This is a suitable aphorism after the description of the statuette's magnificent physique fit to undertake the labours of Hercules. *ac* has no proper function. *nec spatium* (Phillimore), if it means anything, is banal. *hoc spatium* (Politian) is harsh in apposition to *mendacia*. *an spatio* (Domitius) destroys the brevity and punch of the epigram. Housman (in his copy of Vollmer) must be right in suspecting that a line has fallen out. *hoc . . . haec* seems to point towards triple anaphora, and another feat to illustrate the realism of the statuette's anatomy would achieve the customary triple *exemplum*. Professor Russell suggests to me the shouldering, perhaps, of Mt. Atlas, e.g. 'hae spatium ⟨immensum caeli terrasque tenebant / ceruices⟩: tam magna' etc.

45–6. curis ... fingere: '*curis* ... is an unhappy word' (E. Courtney, *BICS* 13 [1966], 99), hence manifold attempts to replace it with (i) an adjective of size qualifying *mensae* (which is unnecessary, since the contrast with *ingentis ... colossos* is implicit), (ii) a noun with *fingere* to contrast with *animo uersare*. But *cura* is indeed the *uox propria* of artistic endeavour (= $\pi\acute{o}\nu o s$), and is frequently so used in the *Siluae*: cf. l. 1 above 'forte remittentem curas', 1. 3. 104 'seu tua non alia splendescat epistola cura', 5. 64 'nitenti ingenio curaque puer', 5. 2. 71 'tibi Pieriae tenero sub pectore curae', 3. 34 'tacitisque situm depellere curis', Hor. *Ars* 261 'aut operae celeris nimium curaque carentis', *TLL* iv. 1462. 44 ff.

46. ingentis animo uersare colossos: two interpretations are possible here: either, continuing the notion of *tam magna breui mendacia formae* (43), St. is referring to artistic vision (see on 36–8) whereby in his imagination the artist is able to project enormous stature on to a small work, or else he is complimenting the artist on producing in miniature a work which he is already planning to execute on a grand scale. For the latter interpretation cf. 1. 3. 50 f. 'quicquid et argento primum uel in aere minori / lusit et enormis manus expertura colossos'. This interpretation is supported by the following *exempla* of giants and divinities who could not have rehearsed their work with only a small amount of material (47–9). If this interpretation is right it supports the theory that both the miniature Epitrapezios and the colossus at Alba Fucens may be by Lysippus (see intro.).

47. Idaeis ... Telchines in antris: the Telchines, credited with the first workings in iron and bronze (Strabo 14. 2. 7), represent for St. great experience in metal-working. As the sons of Poseidon (*RE* vA. 210. 33 ff. [Herter]) they were associated with the sea and islands, and Rhodes was said to be their home. St. here identifies them with the Daktyloi, who discovered metallurgy and worked the forges of Zeus in the caverns under Mt. Ida in Crete: see *RE* vA. 224. 14 ff. (Herter), iv. 2018 ff. (Kern).

48. stolidus Brontes: one of the Cyclopes, famous for their strength and their metalwork: cf. Hes. *Theog.* 146 $\mathit{i}\sigma\chi\acute{u}s$ τ' ἠδὲ βίη καὶ μηχαναὶ ἦσαν ἐπ' ἔργοις, *RE* xi. 2328 ff. (Eitrem). For his name see Hes. *Theog.* 140, Apollod. 1. 1. 2, Virg. *A.* 8. 425, Nonn. 14. 52. He represents for St. brute strength in a metalworker: cf. Liv. 28. 21. 10 'maior usu armorum et astu facile stolidas uires minoris superauit'.

48–9. polit ... Lemnius: Lemnos, which has no volcano, was given one in the literary tradition: see W. Burkert, *CQ* ns 20 (1970), 5. It was particularly associated with the legend and cult of Hephaistos (Vulcan): cf. Virg. *A.* 8. 454 'pater ... Lemnius', *RE* viii. 315. 56 ff. (Malten). Hephaistos' role as divine blacksmith goes back to Homer: see *RE* viii. 330. 31 ff. His smithy was located beneath the volcano: cf. Val. Fl. 2. 332 ff. *polit* describes the finishing touches: cf. Virg. *A.* 8. 426 f. 'his informatum manibus iam parte polita / fulmen erat', 435 f. 'aegidaque horriferam, turbatae Palladis arma, / certatim squamis serpentum auroque polibant', Apul. *Met.* 6. 6 'currum ... Vulcanus aurifex subtili fabrica studiose poliuerat'. Vulcan here represents the exquisite workmanship of a god.

49. exigua ... ludere massa: *massa* is raw substance, here molten bronze; a large amount is usually implied: cf. Luc. 6. 403 'calidae ... pondera massae'; occasionally the magnitude is made explicit: cf. Ov. *Met.* 5. 81 'multae ... massae ... cratera'. Hence the specification of a small amount creates an oxymoron which in turn reinforces the adynaton: the legendary prototypes of the skilled metalworker could not practise on a miniature scale and produce the equivalent of the Hercules Epitrapezios. *ludere* suggests that small-scale works are light-hearted, a trial run, and true art can only be produced on a large scale: cf. 1. 3. 51 'in aere minori lusit', Plin. *Epist.* 1. 20. 5; for this notion as a literary metaphor see on 4 *Pr.* 29–30.

50. torua: see on l. 54.

epulis ... remissis: 'relaxed': cf. l. 1 'remittentem curas', 1 *Pr.* 10 'stilo remissiore', Sen. *Dial.* 7. 12. 2 'sapientium remissae uoluptates et modestae ac paene languidae sunt'. St. cites three legends in which Hercules is depicted drinking, to illustrate the pose of the statuette (56 f.).

51. parci domus ... Molorchi: cf. 3. 1. 29 'pauperis arua Molorchi', *Theb.* 4. 159 f. 'quas in proelia uiris / sacra Cleonaei cogunt uineta Molorchi'. Molorchus, the rustic who entertained Hercules before his encounter with the Nemean lion, became the epitome of the χερνήτης. The story can be traced to the *Aetia* of Callimachus (*Aet.* 3 frr. 54–9 Pfeiffer, H. Lloyd-Jones and P. Parsons [eds.], *Supplementum Hellenisticum* [Berlin, 1983], nos. 254–69), where it is conjectured to have been the first story in Book 3: see P. Parsons, *ZPE* 25 (1977), 46 f. Martial cites Molorchus to make a different comparison, flattering to Vindex (9. 43. 13 f.) 'utque fuit quondam placidi conuiua Molorchi, / sic uoluit docti Vindicis esse deus'.

52. Tegeaea sacerdos: cf. 3. 1. 40 ff. 'te Maenalis Auge / confectum thiasis et multo fratre madentem / detinuit'. St. is following the tradition whereby King Aleos of Tegea made his daughter priestess of Athene in order to thwart the Delphic oracle, which prophesied that she would bear a son who would murder his uncle; Hercules raped her when he was drunk, and she bore Telephus: see *RE* ii. 2301. 56 ff. (Wernicke). Mt. Parthenius, east of Tegea, was sacred to Auge (Callim. *H.* 4. 70 f.), and she was depicted in the temple of Athena Alea in Tegea (Paus. 8. 45. 4). For local resonances of the legend see N. M. Horsfall, *JRS* 63 (1973), 72.

54. adhuc torua ... Iunone: after Hercules was cremated on Mt. Oeta, in the mountain-range between Thessaly and Aetolia, he underwent apotheosis and is pictured enjoying the pleasures of heaven, usually with Hebe as his consort: cf. 3. 1. 26 f. 'haustum . . . tibi succincta beati / nectaris excluso melior Phryge porrigit Hebe'. In some versions Juno becomes reconciled to Hercules in heaven, but St. characteristically imagines that at first she maintains her disapproval (*adhuc torua*): cf. her disparaging attitude towards Hercules' former shrine on Pollius' estate (3. 1. 104 f.) 'sed proxima sedem / despicit et tacite ridet mea limina Iuno'. The repetition of *torua* within five lines (cf. 50 'torua effigies') is surprising, but in both instances the word is singularly appropriate. *toruus* is a favourite word with St.: thirty-eight instances in the *Thebaid*, three in the *Achilleid*, twelve in the *Siluae*.

56–7. marcentia ... / pocula: *marcere*˙ and its derivatives frequently describe the enervating effects of wine: cf. *Theb.* 4. 667 '[Bacchus] ore et pectore marcet', Amm. 21. 12. 15 'largiore potu saginisque distenti marcebant milites', 31. 5. 6 'Lupicinus . . . diu discumbens uino marcebat et somno', *S.* 1. 6. 33 'marcida uina largiuntur'. The present participle usually describes what becomes enervated: cf. Colum. 10. 428 'Satyros . . . bracchia iactantes uetulo marcentia uino'; it can also describe what is enervating: cf. Sil. 15. 743 'senex marcentibus annis', Tac. *Germ.* 36. 1 'Cherusci nimiam ac marcentem diu pacem inlacessiti nutrierunt'. The container is frequently a metaphor for the contents: cf. Cat. 27. 2 'inger mi calices amariores', Hor. *Epist.* 1. 5. 19 'fecundi calices quem non fecere disertum?' But here there is an opposition between *tenet*, suggesting an actual cup, and *marcentia*, evoking the metaphor.

57. clauae meminit manus: cf. Mart. 9. 43. 4 'cuius laeua calet robore, dextra mero'. For *memini* with inanimate subject and object cf. *Theb.* 6. 711 'iam . . . procul meminit dextrae seruatque tenorem / discus'. Hercules' hand automatically keeps his club at the ready; without it his identity would be incomplete.

aspera sedis: cf. Mart. 9. 43. 1 'dura sedens porrecto saxa leone / mitigat'. For *e*-stem nouns of the third declension with an alternative nominative ending -*is* see N–W i. 279 ff.

58. et cultum Nemeaeo tegmine saxum: *colere*, implying adornment and embellishment, pays tribute to the status of the lionskin as symbol of Hercules' heroism: the dignity in *cultum* contrasts with the rugged outdoor setting which *saxum* denotes.

59. Digna operi fortuna sacro: the *sententia* introduces a new topic: cf. the location of the equestrian statue of Domitian, introduced by 'par operi sedes' (1. 1. 22).

59–60. Pellaeus ... regnator: Alexander, born at Pella in Macedonia, was chief patron of Lysippus, who is reputed to have been the only artist permitted to cast statues of him in bronze (Plin. *NH* 7. 125). Lysippus' numerous portraits of Alexander included depictions of him as a child (Plin. *NH* 34. 63). St's assertion that the statuette first belonged to Alexander is at least a plausible claim, since Alexander particularly fostered the cult of Heracles: claiming descent from Heracles he used Heraclean iconography on his coinage: see J. Tondriau, *RPh* 23 (1949), 47 f., M. Bieber, *Alexander the Great in Greek and Roman Art* (Chicago, 1964), 48 f. and 61; during his Indian campaigns he constantly drew parallels between himself and Heracles: see P. A. Brunt, *G&R*² 12 (1965), 209 ff.; his son by Barsine he named Heracles: cf. Plut. *Alex.* 21. 4, Brunt, *RFIC* 103 (1975), 22–34.

61. comitem occasu secum portabat et ortu: Pliny (*NH* 34. 48) attests the practice of carrying Corinthian bronzes as talismans (but his assertion that Alexander's tent was supported by statues probably reflects a mistranslation of σκηνή: see Jex-Blake and Sellers ad loc.; it should refer to the canopy over the chariot which carried his corpse: cf. Diod. 18. 26). *occasus . . . et ortus* (believed by Nauke to be accusative of direction) cannot refer to Alexander's travels because he did not go west. But a phrase meaning not 'everywhere' but 'all the time' is equally appropriate. The ellipse of *solis* is attested when the reference is clearly to time of day (or night): cf. Tac. *Hist.* 3. 86 'praecipiti in occasum die'. In Heinsius' conjecture, the ellipse is eased by the conjunction of *occasu* and *ortu*.

62. prensabatque: *praestabat* ('held out', 'offered'), referring back to the banqueting context of l. 60, is very bald and abrupt, and it is nonsense to imply that Alexander offered the statuette to anyone else. *prensabat*, favoured by Housman, suits the image of someone clasping a mascot.

62–3. diademata ... / abstulerat dederatque: the *diadema*, principal emblem of the Persian kings, was part of the hitherto exclusively Persian attire which Alexander adopted when he claimed succession to the thrones of Persia: see Weinstock, 333 and n. 1. 'Giving and taking away' is a manifestation of divine omnipotence: cf. Hor. *Epist.* 1. 18. 111 'sed satis est orare Iouem qui ponit et aufert', N–H on Hor. *O.* 1. 34. 12.

64. ab hoc: the statuette was the source from which Alexander derived encouragement; *ab hoc ... petebat* (before action) is balanced by *huic ... narrabat* (afterwards). *ad hoc* (M), even with Vollmer's interpretation (*ad hoc* [*numen*]), is meaningless.

65. acies ... opimas: St. alludes to Alexander in the role of a victorious Roman general honoured with the *spolia opima*: cf. Hor. *O.* 4. 4. 51 'sectamur ultro quos opimus fallere ... est triumphus', Sil. 9. 430 'opimae caedis honor'.

66. siue catenatos Bromio detraxerat Indos: the myth of Dionysus' conquests in India gained currency after Alexander's campaigns: cf. Diod. 3. 63. 4, Roscher i. 1119, 1145 (E. Thraemer). Perhaps the original kernel of a myth about Dionysus in the east was embellished after Alexander's conquests. The catalogue of the statuette's illustrious owners is designed to flatter Vindex; hence the mortal Alexander is portrayed as superior to the divine Dionysus in that he takes for himself Dionysus' prisoners of war: cf. 4. 3. 16 n. For *detrahere* with a personal object cf. Ov. *Rem.* 545 'qui timet ... nequis sibi detrahat illam'.

67. seu clusam magna Babylona refregerat hasta: Herodotus records that Babylon was originally enclosed by a fabulous wall, fifty cubits broad and two hundred cubits high, but that after the walls were destroyed in the reign of Darius it remained indefensible (Hdt. 1. 178, 3. 150). In 331 it surrendered to Alexander without a siege. *clusam* here reflects the tradition that Babylon was at this time well fortified and would have been difficult to besiege: cf. Curt. 5. 1. 17, Juv. 10. 171. Whatever the historical facts, St.

portrays Alexander's might in the antithesis *clusam . . . refregerat. hasta* represents his military strength: cf. the use of *cuspis* at *Catal.* 3. 6 (also of Alexander) 'cetera namque uiri cuspide conciderant'.

68–9. seu Pelopis terras libertatemque Pelasgam / obruerat bello: in 336–5 Alexander campaigned to establish his hegemony over Greece; this was ratified by the League of Corinth. The movement of the triple *exemplum*, from India through Babylon to Greece (66–9), accommodates a paradoxical climax (69–70).

70. Thebanos . . . excusasse triumphos: of all his successes the only one about which Alexander felt guilty was the destruction of Thebes in 335: cf. Plut. *Alex.* 13. 2 ὕστερον μέντοι πολλάκις αὐτὸν ἡ Θηβαίων ἀνιᾶσαι συμφορὰ λέγεται. St. may be hinting that Alexander was embarrassed at the destruction of Hercules' birthplace; the epithet *Tirynthius* (17, 90) does not mean that in this poem St. was exclusively adopting the legend that Hercules was born at Tiryns. *excusasse*, 'attempted to justify', is the tactic of the unrepentant: cf. Ov. *Her.* 2. 77 (of Theseus' desertion of Ariadne) 'quod solum excusat, solum miraris in illo'.

72. letale merum: when Alexander was dying of fever he drank wine to slake his thirst and became delirious (Plut. *Alex.* 75. 4). St. here reflects the hostile tradition which alleges that the wine was poisoned: cf. Curt. 10. 10. 17, Just. 12. 14. 9. Drinking *merum*, unmixed wine (ἄκρατος), suggests in this context a desperate gesture: for the distinction between *merum* and *uina* in Seneca see Tarrant on Sen. *Ag.* 878 'merumque in auro ueteris Assaraci trahunt'. At [Sen.] *HO* 572 the drunken Hercules is *uictus mero*.

73–4. By ascribing to the statuette two standard portents of disaster St. achieves a climax of πάθος. To the tradition of Alexander's fatal drinking-bout with Medius (Plut. *Alex.* 75. 3, Arr. *Anab.* 7. 25) St. adds the unlikely but affecting detail that he took the statuette with him.

74. aera . . . sudantia: 'sweating', properly the condensation of moisture on metal, stone, or ivory surfaces under certain atmospheric conditions, was interpreted as an omen: cf. Cic. *Diu.* 2. 58 'umor adlapsus extrinsecus, ut in tectoriis uidemus austro, sudorem uidetur imitari'. Hence statues are said either to 'sweat' or to 'weep': cf. Virg. *G.* 1. 480 'maestum inlacrimat templis ebur aeraque sudant', and see Pease on Cic. *Diu.* 1. 98.

supremis . . . mensis: *supremus* here denotes the last of a lifetime: cf. Tac. *Ann.* 1. 13. 2 'supremis sermonibus', *OLD* s.v. *supremus* 4. The irony of a grim omen in the midst of a feast, which should be a cheerful occasion, is reinforced by the pathos of *supremus* with its connotations of death.

75. Nasamoniaco . . . regi: Hannibal is given the status of a barbarian king. The Nasamones were a tribe in Libya who occupied the area south-west of Cyrenaica as far as the Great Syrtis; the adjective *Nasamoniacus* came to denote 'African' in general: cf. *S.* 2. 7. 93 'Nasamonii Tonantis' = - Jupiter Ammon, Sil. 1. 408, 6. 44. In this context the epithet may be emotive, associating Hannibal with the rebellious tribe whom Domitian had crushed in 85 or 86, prompting him to boast (Dio 67. 4. 6) Ναοαμῶνας ἐκώλυσα εἶναι.

77–8. periuro . . . ense superbus / Hannibal: for the notorious *Punica fides* cf. 4. 3. 5 'peierante bello'. The enemy who defies Rome is guilty of arrogance (stressed here by the emphatic word-order and enjambment): cf. Liv. 23. 7. 5 'Pyrrhi superbam dominationem'.

79. dira ... portantem incendia: *dirus* is conventionally applied to Hannibal: cf. Hor. *O.* 3. 6. 36, Juv. 7. 161; Claudius Sanctus, one-eyed like Hannibal, is given the same epithet at Tac. *Hist.* 4. 62. 2 'dux ... effosso oculo dirus ore'. *portantem* implies that the destruction of Rome was Hannibal's aim but not his achievement. The statuette is portrayed as a patriotic Roman Hercules hating Hannibal although it is venerated by him.

80–1. Lenaea ... / dona: offerings of wine; the epithet is derived from Ληνεύς (Ληναῖος), a title of Dionysus: cf. Virg. *G.* 3. 510 'latices Lenaei', *A.* 4. 207 'Lenaeus honos'. Vollmer saw that St. is thinking of the offerings which Hannibal made at Gades in the temple of Hercules (Tyrian Melqart: cf. Arr. *Anab.* 2. 16. 4) out of the plunder from Saguntum: cf. Sil. 3. 14 ff. The reverse chronology (Rome, Gades, Saguntum) would match the order of events which St. quotes from the career of Alexander (see on 68–9). St. treats the statuette as a manifestation of Hercules himself, and ascribes to it opinions and emotions, exploiting the paradox that although the statuette represents a divine hero it is under the control of a mortal villain: cf. the emphasis on the statuette's reluctance (*oderat, maerens*) and Hannibal's impiety (*sacrilega face, immeritae ... Sagunti, polluit*). The identification of the god with his statue is a remnant of the primitive belief that they were the same thing: see Courtney on Juv. 13. 115. This identification could also lead to the reverse of Hannibal's behaviour here, as when the cult-image was punished for a disaster: see Gow on Theoc. 7. 108.

82–3. arces / ipsius: Hannibal razed Saguntum in 219: cf. Polyb. 3. 17. 9, Liv. 21. 15. 3, Flor. 1. 22. 6, [Victor], *Vir. Ill.* 42. 2. Its foundation is repeatedly attributed to Hercules by Silius: cf. 1. 271 ff. 'prima Saguntinas turbarunt classica portas ... haud procul Herculei tollunt se litore muri, ... quis nobile nomen / conditus excelso sacrauit colle Zacynthos', 509 etc. Coins from Saguntum display the head of Hercules, but this image is probably to be identified with Melqart rather than with the Greek Heracles: see G. F. Hill, *Ancient Coins of Hispania Citerior*, American Numismatic Society Notes and Monographs 50 (New York, 1931), 115. Saguntum was originally an Iberian settlement, believed to be Greek by false derivation of its name from Ζάκυνθος: see Hill, 111. For Greek influence in the coastal towns of eastern Spain, exercised from Massilia, see C. H. V. Sutherland, *The Romans in Spain* (London, 1939), 15.

83. immeritae ... Sagunti: the feminine form occurs frequently: cf. Liv. 21. 19. 1 'Sagunto excisa'. The outbreak of the Second Punic War was attributed to Carthaginian treachery and aggression in attacking Saguntum, which was in Roman *fides*: see (e.g.) Polyb. 3. 6–30, Liv. 21. 1–19; St., of course, was untroubled by modern doubts.

84. populis furias immisit honestas: *populis* (pl.) cannot refer solely to the Saguntines, who committed mass suicide rather than submit to Hannibal: cf. Sil. 2. 592 ff., Flor. 1. 22. 6. Hence it must refer also to the Romans, since Saguntum was in their *fides* and their representations to

Carthage on her behalf were repulsed. The avenging spirits are *honestae* for St. because Saguntum and Rome were wronged; the oxymoron *furias . . . honestas* forms the climax to the series of paradoxes which characterize Hannibal's ownership of the statuette. *immisit* is oddly ambiguous (although perhaps only in our impartial age), because grammatically it could mean that the Punic army let loose its honourable frenzy on the Romans and Saguntines.

85–8. The third illustration of the statuette's distinguished ownership is Roman: L. Cornelius Sulla Felix the dictator, fabulously rich from the spoils of the Mithridatic campaigns, and also devoted to Hercules, to whom he consecrated a tithe of his property (Plut. *Sulla* 35. 1). His campaigns in the east reputedly first exposed Roman soldiers to various forms of depravity, including the taste for looting works of art (Sall. *Cat.* 11. 6): cf. Val. Max. 2. 8. 7 'iam L. Sulla . . . ut Graeciae et Asiae multas urbes, ita ciuium Romanorum nullum oppidum uexit'. For his ostentatious triumph in 81 see Plin. *NH* 33. 16. Sulla is specifically known to have plundered the sanctuary of Zeus Eleutherios (Paus. 10. 21. 6) and stolen a Hippocentaur by Zeuxis, which was lost when the ship carrying it was wrecked *en route* to Italy (Lucian, *Zeuxis* 3). St. stresses Sulla's patrician ancestry (*claros . . . penatis*, 87). The assertion that the statuette was *felix* in the pedigree of its owners recalls Sulla's *cognomen*. Although this initial impression of Sulla is favourable, l. 107 conforms to the conventional view: cf. Suet. *Tib.* 59. 2 'felicem sibi non tibi, Romule, Sullam.'

88. felix dominorum stemmate signum: cf. Mart. 8. 6. 1 ff. 'archetypis uetuli nihil est odiosus Aucti . . . argenti furiosa sui cum stemmata narrat / garrulus'. On the snob-appeal of an item associated with a distinguished series of owners see intro.

89–109. The triple *exemplum* (Alexander, Hannibal, and Sulla) leads to a volte-face in the climax: neither court-life nor royal society await the statuette, but the Epicurean tranquillity already adumbrated in St.'s description of Vindex' life-style (12–31).

91. ambit: cf. Virg. *A.* 4. 283 f. 'quo nunc reginam ambire furentem / audeat adfatu?', Hor. *O.* 1. 35. 5 f. 'diua . . . te pauper ambit sollicita prece / ruris colonus'; 'the word suggests the ingratiating blandishments of a canvasser or office-seeker' (N–H), creating here an ironical contrast with *honos*.

91–3. casta ignaraque culpae / mens domini cui prisca fides coeptaeque perenne / foedus amicitiae: Vindex, cultivating 'private' virtues in a secluded lifestyle, contrasts with the ostentatious public figures who are alleged to have owned the statuette before him. St. stressed Alexander's fear of death (72–4), Hannibal's cruelty, arrogance, and untrustworthiness (77) and especially his impiety (82 ff.); Vindex possesses instead a clear conscience (*ignara . . . culpae / mens*), innocence (*casta . . . mens*) and old-fashioned loyalty (*prisca fides*). *foedus amicitiae* expresses the obligations of *amici* topwards each other which form the basis of Roman social relations: cf. Cat. 109. 6, Ov. *Tr.* 3. 6. 1, Sil. 17. 75, Apul. *Met.* 6. 3, and see Housman on Man. 2. 582. The scene which St. describes at the beginning of the poem exemplifies this ethic. As a specific illustration of its lasting nature (*perenne foedus*: cf. Cat. 109. 6 'aeternum ... foedus') St. cites Vindex' devotion to the memory of his deceased friend Vestinus (see next n.).

94. Vestinus: probably to be identified with the man lamented by Martial who was wealthy and died young (Mart. 4. 73. 7 f.). Because of his illustrious ancestry ('par magnis Vestinus auis') he is thought to be the son of M. (Iulius) Vestinus Atticus, *consul ordinarius* of 65 (PIR^2 I 624), and nephew of L. Iulius Vestinus, an *eques* favoured by Claudius (*CIL* xiii. 1. 1668), prefect of Egypt *c*.59 and probably the man to whom Vespasian entrusted the restoration of the Capitol (Tac. *Hist.* 4. 53): see *RE* viiiA. 2. 1788 s.v. Vestinus 1 (Hanslik), Syme, *Arval Brethren*, 22 f. Several times in the *Siluae* St. mentions friends of his addressees (see on 4. 4. 20–4). In this case he gives no hint that Vindex had established any memorial to Vestinus' memory such as the *Blaesianum* which Melior set up for the *collegium scribarum* to keep the anniversary of Blaesus' birthday: cf. *S.* 2. 3. 76 f., Mart. 8. 38. 8 ff. But Vestinus left large legacies (Mart. 4. 73. 7 'largas partitus opes'), and after his death his friends still enjoyed his munificence: cf. Mart. 4. 73. 5 'iam sibi defunctus caris dum uiuit amicis'. St.'s description of Vindex, 'in carae uiuit complexibus umbrae', corresponds to Martial's phrasing about Vestinus at 4. 73. 5 (cit. above). This suggests that Vindex received a legacy from Vestinus; perhaps he spent it on a new statuette for his art collection.

96. laeta quies: the statuette will share Vindex' Epicurean ideal of cultured leisure, sheltered from the strife of public life with which Alexander, Hannibal, and Sulla were engaged; 'nec bella uides pugnasque ferocis' (97) also recalls Hercules' labours (cf. 'fortissime diuum') and contrasts with the intellectual atmosphere of the statuette's new environment. The ideal of *quies* cultivated by St.'s addressees is associated above all with Pollius Felix: cf. 3 *Pr.* 1 f. 'Polli dulcissime et ... quiete dignissime'.

98. amantis tempora laurus: *laurus* was the symbol and attribute of Apollo: see M. B. Ogle, *AJPh* 31 (1910), 304 ff. As Apollo was god of inspiration, so his plant became the symbol of both prophecy and poetry. Hesiod composed holding a bay wand (Paus. 9. 30. 3): cf. Hes. *Theog.* 30. The bay-wreath was worn by poets: cf. Ov. *Ars* 2. 495 f. 'sacris induta capillis / laurus erat: uates ille uidendus adit', Hor. *O.* 3. 30. 15 f. 'mihi Delphica / lauro cinge uolens, Melpomene, comam'. See further Ogle, 306 ff. *carmina* (M) is objectionable because of the repetition in *carmine* (99) and because it is odd to personify bay by making it love an abstraction like poetry instead of some physical entity to which the plant might cling: cf. Virg. *G.* 4. 124 'amantes litora myrtos'. *tempora* (Markland) completes the trio of references to the poet's emblems: cf. 5. 3. 112 'illa tuis totiens praestant se tempora sertis'.

99. sollemni ... carmine: almost exclusive to sacral contexts: see *TLL* iii. 463. 84 ff., 472. 54 f. From the list of Herculean exploits which Vindex is to include in his poem St. seems to envisage a hymn: cf. *Pan. Lat.* 9(4). 10. 2 'ibi adulescentes optimi discant, nobis quasi sollemne carmen praefantibus, maximorum principum facta celebrare ... ubi ante aras quodammodo suas Iouios Herculiosque audiant praedicari Iuppiter pater et Minerua socia et Iuno placata'.

quantus: the triple anaphora conveys the heroic stature of Hercules: cf. Diomedes' description of Aeneas (Virg. *A.* 11. 283 f.) 'experto credite quantus / in clipeum adsurgat, quo turbine torqueat hastam'.

100–5. St. offers a summary of sample contents for Vindex' poem comprising ten paired exploits from the ἔργα, πράξεις, and πάρεργα of the Hercules legend. This list bears some resemblance to the arrangement of the choral ode at Sen. *Ag.* 808–66, where ll. 829 ff. celebrate thirteen exploits of Hercules, grouped roughly according to type, eight of which reappear here. In contrast to this eclectic approach, mythographers attest the emergence (with slight variations in arrangement) of a 'canon' of labours: see the table at *RE* Suppl. iii. 1021 f. (Gruppe).

100. Iliacas Geticasque domos: this first pair alludes to Hercules' adventures in two royal households. At Troy he rescued Hesione from the sea-monster and subsequently killed her father Laomedon for failing to surrender the horses of Zeus which Laomedon had promised him as a reward: cf. Hom. *Il.* 5. 649 ff., Diod. 4. 42, Apollod. 3. 12. 7. For Hesione see Roscher i. 2592 ff. (Drexler). *Geticas ... domos* denotes the palace of Diomedes, king of the Bistones in Thrace; the adjectival form of *Getae*, the name of a tribe on the lower Danube in Thrace, commonly = 'Thracian': cf. *Theb.* 6. 348 'Getici ... Diomedis'. Hercules' capture of the man-eating horses of Diomedes was usually categorized as the ninth labour: see Roscher i. 1022 (L. v. Sybel), *RE* Suppl. iii. 1053 ff. (Gruppe).

100–1. niualem / Stymphalon ... iugis Erymanthon aquosis: the labours of ridding Stymphalus of its anthropophagous birds and Erymanthus of its boar are designated here by the sites themselves. The birds infested a lake in the territory of Stymphalus in north-east Arcadia, dominated by Mt. Cyllene in the north; St. is referring to a spur of this mountain (Στύμφαλος ὄρος, Ptol. 3. 16. 14). Heracles scared the birds with a rattle made by Hephaistos (Diod. 4. 13); according to Apollodorus (2. 5. 6) he subsequently shot them: see *RE* ivA. 434 (Türk), Suppl. iii. 1041 ff. (Gruppe). Mt. Erymanthos in Arcadia has a high level of precipitation because of its jagged ridges and deep gullies: see *RE* vi. 569. 4 ff. (Philippson). St. follows the tradition that this mountain was the site of the boar-hunt: see *RE* vi. 566. 18 ff. (Escher); Heracles delivered the boar alive to Eurystheus.

102–3. pecoris possessor Hiberi ... saeuae Mareoticus arbiter arae: St. cites two exploits situated in the west and involving giants. The monster Geryon lived on the island of Erytheia in Oceanus (Hes. *Theog.* 290, 294, 981 f.). This was traditionally given a Spanish location at Gades (Pherec. *FGrH* 3 F 18 (b): cf. Apollod. 2. 5. 10, Sil. It. 16. 195) or near Tartessos (Stesich. fr. 7 = *PMG* 184 Page), or identified with another island nearby (Hdt. 4. 8 etc). For the autonomasia cf. Ov. *Met.* 9. 184 f. 'pastoris Hiberi / forma triplex'. Hercules' tenth labour was the capture of Geryon's cattle: see Roscher i. 1633–6 (Voigt), *RE* Suppl. iii. 1061 ff. (Gruppe). For representations of the myth on vases see M. Robertson, *CQ* NS 19 (1969), 207–21. The killing of Busiris belongs to the πάρεργα. Busiris was a king in the Nile delta, designated here by allusion to Lake Mareotis near Alexandria, who sacrificed strangers to Zeus and then ate them: cf.

Pherec. fr. 33, *RE* iii. 1074. 53 ff. (Hiller v. Gaertringen). The oxymoron *saeuae . . . arbiter arae* emphasizes the injustice perpetrated in the name of a barbarian Zeus.

104. penetrata tibi spoliataque limina mortis: two exploits in the underworld. In some versions of the Alcestis story Hercules descended to Hades (*penetrata . . . limina*) to rescue her: cf. Lucian, *Dial. mort.* 23, Apollod. 1. 9. 15, Hyg. *Fab.* 51, Roscher i. 234 (Engelmann). Hercules' crowning labour was the capture of Cerberus, hound of Hades, first documented at Hom. *Od.* 11. 623 ff. and illustrated copiously in ancient art: see Roscher i. 234 (Immisch). St.'s allusion to this action as plunder (*spoliata . . . limina*) hints at the image of the swashbuckling folk-hero in the background: cf. 50 ff.

105. flentis Libyae Scythiaeque puellas: two adventures involving the seizure by force of property guarded by groups of women.

The garden of the Hesperides where golden apples grew πέρην κλυτοῦ Ὠκεανοῖο (Hes. *Theog.* 215 f.) became associated with Atlas and was located by one tradition in Africa: cf. Ap. Rhod. 4. 1396 ff., Diod. 4. 26. 2, Iuba, *FGrH* 275 F 6, Apollod. 2. 5. 11; on 'Libya' see 4. 8. 12 n. below. For his eleventh labour Hercules killed the dragon at the entrance to the garden, seized the apples, and delivered them to Eurystheus: see Roscher i. 2594 ff. (Seeliger).

Scythiae puellas are the Amazons: cf. [Sen.] *HO* 1185 'Amazon Scythico sub axe genita'. The Scythians were generally associated with both the northern and southern shores of the Euxine, and the Amazons were frequently denoted by reference to the R. Thermodon, which flows through Pontus into the Euxine east of the River Halys: cf. *S.* 1. 6. 56 'Thermodontiacas . . . turmas', Sen. *Oed.* 481 'Thermodontiacae', Roscher i. 272. 35 ff. (Roscher). The ninth labour of Hercules was to obtain the girdle belonging to the Amazon queen, Hippolyte (or Melanippe): cf. Ap. Rhod. 2. 779, 967, Diod. 2. 46, 4. 16, Apollod. 2. 5. 9, Val. Fl. 5. 132. This theft in itself could explain the Amazons' tears, but St. may be hinting at the version in which Hercules killed their queen: see Roscher i. 269. 6 ff. (Roscher).

106–9. Vindex' verse panegyric could not have been rivalled by any of the statuette's former illustrious owners, nor could a more discerning critic have gazed on Lysippus' work of art: St. draws together Vindex' two enthusiasms (cf. 30 f.). Sulla's voice is *horrida* because he pronounced the proscription lists.

106. Macetum: *metri gratia* for *Macedones* in dactylic poetry, derived from Μακετία, the old name for Macedonia (Hesych. *M* 18 Latte): cf. Man. 4. 762, Luc. 10. 16, Sil. 15. 287, St. *Ach.* 1. 202, and see P. Kohlmann, *Philol.* 34 (1876), 570 f.

108. muneris auctor: the statuette is the work (and hence the gift) of its sculptor: cf. Mart. 9. 43. 6 'nobile Lysippi munus opusque uides', *OLD* s.v. *munus* 7.

7

INTRODUCTION

THIS poem is a sapphic ode addressed to Vibius Maximus (4 *Pr.* 14–15). His *nomen* is attested in the *titulus* as 'Viuium' and at 4 *Pr.* 15 as 'Viuium', 'Niuium', or 'Vinium'. The restoration of 'Vibium' was proposed by H. Nohl, *Hermes* 12 (1877), 517, recognizing that contemporary evidence attests several Vibii Maximi. Nohl's restoration is opposed by F. Delarue, *Sic. Gymn.* 29 (1975), 173–203, who argues for the name Viuius, citing *CIL* iii. 9780 (a Viuius Maximus in Dalmatia). But the evidence of the *titulus* is in any case derived from the *Praefatio* (see General Introduction), and the variant readings at 4 *Pr.* 15 show that confusion existed. Hence the weight of contemporary evidence argues for Nohl's restoration.

There are four main candidates for Vibius' identity: (1) C. Vibius Maximus, prefect of cohors III Alpinorum in Dalmatia mid-94 (*CIL* xvi. 38); (2) P. Vibius Maximus, *eques Epitaurensis*, signatory for a grant of citizenship to a soldier from Dalmatia in Rome in AD 71 (*CIL* xvi. 14 = *ILS* 1991); (3) Vibius Maximus, addressee of Mart. 11. 106; (4) C. Vibius Maximus, prefect of Egypt 103–7 (Plin. *Epist.* 3. 2, *P. Oxy.* iii. 471). St.'s addressee was identified with candidates 3 and 4 by R. Syme, *Hist.* 6 (1957), 480–7 (= *Rom. Pap.* i. 353–60), but now, following White (1973*b*), Syme, *Hist.* 34 (1985), 326–9, identifies him with candidate 2.

Vibius was born in Dalmatia: cf. ll. 13–20, White, 298. Syme, *Hist.* 6, 485 f., mistakenly identifies him with a Maximus from Verona (Mart. 1. 7, Plin. *Epist.* 6. 34). The first legate of Dalmatia, appointed by Augustus in AD 9, was a Vibius Postumus (Vell. Pat. 2. 115. 4 ff.). Vibii were common in Dalmatia throughout the empire: see J. J. Wilkes, *Dalmatia* (London, 1969), 209, 253, 307. If St.'s friend was descended from a native Dalmatian family, his nomenclature would reflect the *nomen* of an emperor or a Roman official in Dalmatia, but the only senatorial family in Dalmatia whose *nomen* is known to have been taken by natives upon enfranchisement is the Calpurnii Pisones: see Wilkes, 293, 331. Hence St.'s friend must have been descended from Italian immigrant settlers. By 94, when this poem was probably written (see General Introduction), he had held the highest of the three *militiae equestres* as *praefectus alae* (46 f.). Hence he cannot be identified with candidate 1, because *praefectus cohortis* would be demotion from *praefectus alae*: see Syme, *Hist.* 6, 481 f.

St.'s reference to gold-mining (14–16), formerly interpreted by Syme, *Hist.* 6, 481, as a hint that Vibius was involved in Dalmatian finances as *procurator*,[1] is now ascribed (by White, 297, and Syme, *Hist.* 34, 327) to the conventional picture of Dalmatia: cf. *S.* 1. 2. 153, 3. 3. 90, Mart. 10. 78. 5. Possibly, however, Vibius' family had inherited mining interests in Dalmatia from the first legate, Vibius Postumus (see above), whom Augustus is said to

---

[1] A common misconception: see (e.g.) H.-G. Pflaum, *Les Carrières procuratoriennes équestres sous le Haut-Empire romain* i (Paris, 1960), no. 65; Sherwin-White, Plin. *Epist.* 3. 2, even alleges that St. 'mentions [Vibius] as in charge of mines'.

have entrusted with the task of taking over and developing the native mineworkings (Flor. 4. 12. 10). But Florus is unreliable as a sole source, especially as he apparently confuses Vibius Postumus with Octavian's legate in Pannonia in 34 BC, whom he names as Vinnius (4. 12. 8).[2]

Was Vibius in Dalmatia on an official appointment? White, 297 ff., believes not, inferring from 4 *Pr.* 17–18 and 4. 7. 29 that Vibius was free to return from Dalmatia whenever he liked, and noting St.'s practice of mentioning his addressees' highest civil and military honours. If Vibius held an official post in Dalmatia, St. would surely have made this explicit. Compare the *propempticon* to Maecius Celer, about to depart for Syria as legionary legate (3. *Pr.* 14, 3. 2. 105, 121): St. dilates on the dangers to be faced abroad (83 ff.); he lists the curiosities Celer should see (106 ff.); postulating the day of Celer's return, he explicitly refers to official recall (127 f.) 'ergo erit illa dies qua te maiora daturus / Caesar ab emerito iubeat decedere bello'. White, 298, suggests that Vibius returned to Dalmatia because he wanted his son to be born there. Seneca's family furnishes a likely parallel: their *nomen* Annaeus being Etruscan or Illyrian (Syme, *Tacitus*, ii. 784 f.), they were originally Italian immigrants to Baetica; three successive generations were born there (Mart. 1. 61. 7 f.). The elder Seneca (*PIR*[2] A 616), born *c.*50 BC (see Miriam Griffin, *JRS* 62 [1972], 5), came to Rome *c.*36 and returned to Corduba *c.*8 BC to marry; three sons were born to him in Spain but he returned to Rome by AD 5 (Sen. *Contr.* 4 *Pr.* 2–4) and had his children brought up there; even his son Mela (*PIR*[2] A 613) returned to Corduba to marry, and had his own son Lucan brought to Rome as a baby (Vacca, *Vit. Luc.*). Hence Vibius probably returned to Dalmatia to marry and beget an heir. St.'s deferential attitude to Vibius as *fidus monitor* for the *Thebaid* (25) and his relief that Vibius has escaped *orbitas* suggest that Vibius was perhaps approaching middle age: see White, 298. Thus his son's grandfather who served under Domitian against the Sarmatae in AD 92–3 (49–51), perhaps as legionary legate or the emperor's *comes* (Syme, *Hist.* 34, 328),[3] must be Vibius' father-in-law, since his own father would probably have been too old.

White, 299 f., identifies St.'s Vibius with candidate 2, signatory to a grant of citizenship in his capacity as *eques Romanus*. This identification suits St.'s picture of Vibius as a leisured and wealthy family man, but it seems incompatible[4] with Syme's conclusion that St.'s friend is candidate 4, the future prefect of Egypt, who suffered *damnatio memoriae*.[5] Since Vibius had apparently been absent from Rome at least since the *Thebaid* was finished (i.e. *c.*92), he would not be available to achieve the prominence in public life which would earn appointment to one of the top equestrian posts nine years later. Perhaps he had taken refuge in Dalmatia to avoid falling foul of Domitian: cf. Tac. *Agr.* 42,

---

[2] Dio 49. 38. 1, 3 names Octavian's legate as Fufius Geminus.

[3] Syme's former suggestion, *Hist.* 6, 486, was consular legate of Pannonia; but at this time Pannonia was probably under L. Neratius Priscus (*ILS* 1033): see W. Eck, *Chiron* 12 (1982), 320, Syme, *Hist.* 34, 328 n. 30.

[4] Sherwin-White, introduction to Plin. *Epist.* 3. 2, identifying St.'s friend with the prefect of Egypt, implies that the *eques Epitaurensis* is a relative.

[5] For the prefect's career see A. Stein, *Die Präfekten von Ägypten in römischer Zeit* (Berne, 1950), 50 ff.

Syme, *Tacitus*, i. 69 n. 6. But a promising careerist was hardly likely to absent himself from Rome unless he had already fallen foul of the emperor, in which case this poem would surely not have appeared in Book 4.

Finally, candidate 3, the addressee of Mart. 11. 106 'Vibi Maxime, si uacas hauere, / hoc tantum lege; namque et occupatus / et non es nimium laboriosus. / transis hos quoque quattuor? sapisti'. Syme originally suggested (*Hist.* 6, 482) that Vibius was *occupatus* because he held an official post but *non nimium laboriosus* because it was the Saturnalian holiday-season; at *Hist.* 34, 329, he upholds his consequent identification of this man with the future prefect of Egypt. But the epigram is sarcastic: Martial's addressee always protests that he is *occupatus*, which is an excuse not to undertake anything (*non nimium laboriosus*). Hence he is unlikely to have spent time assisting an epic poet. Thus St.'s Vibius is probably to be identified with the *eques Epitaurenis*(2) alone.

Vollmer regards this poem as 'der Hauptsache nach ein γενεθλιακόν'. *S.* 2. 7; 4. 7, and 4. 8 have all been ascribed to the genre of *genethliaca* (Newmyer, 24 f.), but 2. 7 is the only one which St. himself so styles (2 *Pr.* 24). The birthday poem in Latin is represented by: Tib. 1. 7, 2. 2, [Tib.] 4. 5, 6, Prop. 3. 10, Hor. *O.* 4. 11, Ov. *Tr.* 3. 13, 5. 5, Pers. 2, Mart. 7. 21–3, 9. 52–3, 10. 24, Paul. Nol. *Carm.* 12–28, Sidon. Apoll. *Carm.* 17, Ennod. *CSEL* vi. 424 ff., *Anth. Lat.* 638 Riese. Common elements are announcement and eulogy of the day, invocation of the subject's *genius*, praise of the subject, prayer for him: for these elements and the poet's freedom in combining or incorporating them see V. Buchheit, *Philologus* 105 (1961), 91. For topoi derived from birthday cult see *RE* vii. 1143 (Schmidt), F. Cairns, *Hermes* 99 (1971), 149–55, van Dam, *Comm.* 451. Rhetorical prescriptions for a *genethliacon* in prose (Ps.-Dion. ii. 266–8 Us.–R., *Rhet. Gr.* iii. 412 f. Sp.) exclude elements from religious cult, presumably because the Greeks had no real counterpart to the *genius*.

St. defines the theme of 4. 7 as a request to Vibius Maximus to return from Dalmatia (4. *Pr.* 17–18). The topic of Vibius' son's birthday arises from this theme half-way through the poem, and its treatment displays two elements from *genethliacon*: eulogy of the day itself (31 f.) and a prayer for the subject (41–56). Van Dam, *Comm.* 451 n. 2, defines this poem as that subsidiary type of *genethliacon* which offers general good wishes, but it is more accurate to say that it is a poem blending request for the addressee's return with elements of *genethliacon* which celebrate the birth of the addressee's son.

This poem is St.'s sole extant example of sapphics: 4. 5 is his only other extant example of lyric metre. For the relative chronology see on l. 6. As in Seneca's sapphics (stanzas at *Med.* 597–606 and continuous repetition of the longer line at *Phaed.* 274–324), St. invariably displays a caesura after the fifth syllable in the longer line, never (as sometimes in Horace) after the sixth. Although the third and fourth lines are closely connected in each stanza, St. never allows a single word to straddle them both, nor does he admit either hiatus or elision at this point: see Raven, *Latin Metre* 143–5.

1–12. *Recusatio* of epic. St. orders his Muse to turn from epic to a lesser genre (1–4), asks Pindar's sanction to compose lyric (5–8), and announces his new subject (9–12): cf. his *apologia* for turning from epic to the theme of

Claudius Etruscus' baths (1. 5. 1 ff.). In the original circumstances of composition, when St. was offering a reason for interrupting his epic composition to write a personal poem, these *recusationes* must have sounded less forced than they do in the middle of a collection of occasional verse. The *recusatio* in Roman literature, strongly influenced by Callimachus' manifesto in the second edition of the *Aetia*, was used both as a vindication of the short poem and as an excuse for declining partisan commissions: see N–H i. 82. *Recusatio* plays for St. yet another role: it is an excuse not to reject but to accept a (carefully concealed) commission, and St. is asking for respite from a genre very familiar to him instead of declining a new one. Another variation is that St. asks for only a temporary reprieve from epic (*paulum*, 6): cf. Ov. *Am*. 3. 1. 67 'exiguum uati concede, Tragoedia, tempus'. The Callimachean *recusatio* and its treatment by the Roman poets are analysed by W. Wimmel, *Kallimachos in Rom* (Wiesbaden, 1960). For a different type of *recusatio*, declining an imperial theme in favour of a conventional mythological epic, see 4. 4. 96–7 n.

1. **lato spatiata campo:** traversing the broad territory of epic is contrasted with keeping to the narrow circle of lyric. The wide scope of epic is usually illustrated by the metaphor of the sea: cf. Callim. *H*. 2. 106 οὐκ ἄγαμαι τὸν ἀοιδὸν ὃς οὐδ' ὅσα πόντος ἀείδει, Prop. 3. 9. 3 f. 'quid me scribendi tam uastum mittis in aequor? / non sunt apta meae grandia uela rati', Hor. *O*. 4. 15. 3 f. 'ne parua Tyrrhenum per aequor / uela darem', Wimmel, *Kallimachos in Rom*, 230. St. here visualizes epic composition not as a sea-voyage but as a gallop round the race-track, contrasted with the tightly controlled dressage of lyric (3–4): cf. Ov. *Am*. 3. 15. 18 'pulsanda est magnis area maior equis'. (Wimmel, 106 n. 3, is wrong to interpret *campo* as the battlefield: this could be neither the battlefield of Thebes, since *iam diu* specifies St.'s current epic composition, nor the battlefield of Troy, since the extant portion of the *Achilleid* takes place before the Trojan War, and St. was still in the early stages of the work: cf. 23–4.) *sociata* (M) with *campo* (dative) is meaningless, and to interpret *campo* as ablative and understand *mihi* is very awkward and artificial. *satiata* (ς) coheres awkwardly with *campo*, which is surely much better suited to a context of physical activity: *spatiata* (ς) suits the dimensions of *lato campo*, and forms a semantic contrast to *in minores / contrahe gyros*. A broad stride is required to keep up with epic: cf. 5. 3. 159 ff. 'tu par assuetus Homero / ferre iugum senosque pedes aequare solutis / uersibus et numquam passu breuiore relinqui'.

2. **Erato:** the assigning of different provinces to the Muses was a gradual development which did not preclude the Roman poets from addressing them on occasion without regard to their particular sphere: see U. von Wilamowitz-Moellendorf, *Die Ilias und Homer*[2] (Berlin, 1920), 474 n. 1, N–H on Hor. *O*. 1. 24. 3, *RE* xvi. 724 ff. (Mayer). But the address to Erato here does seem to have special point. She is primarily associated with love-poetry (by etymology, Ov. *Ars* 2. 16, *F*. 4. 195 f.): see *RE* vi. 354 (Escher). Her summons is clearly appropriate in epithalamium (1. 2. 49). She is twice invoked in epic: at Ap. Rh. 3. 1 f. to tell the story of Jason and Medea in the second half of the work, and hence at Virg. *A*. 7. 37 to

introduce the plot of the second hexad. The proem of the *Achilleid* is addressed to *diua* (*Ach.* 1. 3), perhaps no more specific than the θεά of the *Iliad*. But Erato would be a suitable candidate, since the action of the extant portion of the *Achilleid* is centred upon the love-affair between Achilles and Deidamia. Different Muses can be invoked at different points in a single work: cf. Virg. *A.* 1. 8 (nameless), 7. 37 (Erato), 9. 525 (Calliope). St. now asks Erato to inspire a lyric poem so that he can request Vibius' return to Rome to ensure the rescue of the *Achilleid* from its current difficulties.

3. ingens opus: *ingens* suits the scale and the vocabulary of epic: see K. E. Ingvarsson, *Eranos* 48 (1950), 66–70. Poets writing in 'lesser' genres customarily feel threatened by pressure to undertake a 'greater' genre (epic or tragedy): cf. Ov. *Am.* 3. 1. 69 f. 'teneri properentur Amores, / dum uacat: a tergo grandius urguet opus'.

3–4. in minores / contrahe gyros: the discipline of the training-ring: cf. Cic. *De Or.* 3. 70 'sed si his contenti estis atque eis etiam, quae dici uoluistis a me, ex ingenti quodam oratorem immensoque campo in exiguum sane gyrum compellitis', *Off.* 1. 90 'in gyrum rationis et doctrinae duci oportere', Hor. *O.* 2. 9. 23 f. 'intraque praescriptum Gelonos / exiguis equitare campis', Prop. 3. 3. 21 'cur tua praescriptos euecta est pagina gyros?', Colum. 10. 225 ff. 'ne mea Calliope cura leuiore uagantem / iam reuocat paruoque iubet decurrere gyro / et secum gracili connectere carmina filo'. *contrahe* (cf. *compellitis* at Cic. *De Or.* 3. 70, cit. above) may suggest that a lunge was used. *gyrus* (στροφή) describes the figure known in equitation as 'volte', i.e. parading in circles: cf. Virg. *A.* 11. 695, Ov. *Ars* 3. 384, Tac. *Germ.* 6. 3, P. Vigneron, *Le Cheval dans l'antiquité gréco-romaine* (Nancy, 1968), 95 f.

5–8. For the prayer-formulae (pronoun, appositional phrase, imperative, explanatory clause) see Norden, *Agnostos Theos*, 144 f.

5. regnator lyricae cohortis: the mention of Pindar in a sapphic ode in which the poet renounces the grand style recalls Hor. *O.* 4. 2; for the impression this ode made on St. see *S.* 5. 3. 151–2 (cit. on 4. 5. 4 above), correcting 'numerisque fertur / lege solutis' in vv. 11–12. The grand term *regnator* is appropriate for Pindar because (i) as supreme lyric poet he exercises *regnum* over the rest, (ii) his grandiloquent themes, aristocratic background, and regal patrons argue an affinity with royalty. *cohors*, here suggesting an entourage, is fundamentally a group of people with a common characteristic: cf. Sen. *Epist.* 22. 11 'tota ... cohors Stoicorum', *TLL* iii. 1551. 17 ff., English 'court'. St. uses it twice of the Muses: cf. *S.* 1. 2. 248 f. 'eat enthea uittis / atque hederis redimita cohors', 5. 3. 91 'Pallas doctique cohors Heliconia Phoebi'. The term λυρική ποίησις replaced μελική ποίησις during the first century BC, and *lyricus* became the normal Latin term (despite Gell. 2. 22. 1 'legi solitum erat ... uetus carmen melici poetae'): see R. Pfeiffer, *History of Classical Scholarship* (Oxford, 1968), 182 f.

6. noui ... iura plectri: *iura* implies authority (exercised, here, in lyric composition): cf. Man. 2. 465 'Pisces ... pedum sibi iura reposcunt'. The language here echoes Horace's boast to his Muse that he is innovating in

Latin (*O.* 1. 26. 10 ff.) 'hunc fidibus nouis, / hunc Lesbio sacrare plectro / teque tuasque decet sorores': for the conventional nature of this claim see N–H ad loc. Vollmer thinks that St. is claiming to be the first Roman poet to write a lyric *genethliacon*. But (i) this poem cannot be classified as a *genethliacon* (see intro.), (ii) in the context of his appeal to the Muse to turn from epic to lyric St.'s claim to originality must be purely personal: lyric is a new genre for him. Hence 4. 7 was composed before 4. 5. The alternative explanation, that St. means that the sapphic metre is a novelty, is not the obvious sense yielded by the text. St. does not respect chronology in his arrangement of the poems, and so this lyric is placed beside 4. 8 as they both deal with birthdays: on the arrangement, see General Introduction.

7–8. tuas cantu Latio sacraui ... Thebas: Pindar was born in Thebes (*Isthm.* 1. 1 fr. 198). *Latio* points the contrast of a Greek theme treated in Latin. The hope that St.'s poem immortalized Thebes is also a compliment to Vibius, who gave him advice (25–8).

9. carmen tenuare: cf. Virg. *E.* 6. 5 'deductum dicere carmen', Hor. *Epist.* 2. 1. 224 f. 'cum lamentamur non apparere labores / nostros et tenui deducta poemata filo', Prop. 3. 1. 5 'dicite quo pariter carmen tenuastis in antro'. These expressions are derived from the Callimachean ideal of perfection within narrow dimensions: cf. *Aet.* fr. 1. 24 Pfeiffer Μοῦσαν ... λεπταλέην. In *Maximo ... tenuare* St. characteristically plays on his friend's name: cf. l. 32 n., and see 4. 9 intro. on 'Grypus'.

10–11. ab intonsa capienda myrto / serta: the poet's garland, usually of bay, is a symbol of his powers as *uates* and a legacy from Hesiod: cf. Hes. *Theog.* 30 δάφνης ἐριθηλέος ὄζον, A. Kambylis, *Die Dichterweihe und ihre Symbolik* (Heidelberg, 1965), 173 ff. Myrtle was sacred to Venus (Plin. *NH* 15. 119), and myrtle garlands are usually associated with her: see *RE* xvi. 1182 (Steier). Ovid's Muse in the *Amores* wears a myrtle garland to suit the erotic subject (*Am.* 1. 1. 29 f.). A garland of unaccustomed material is a metaphor for St.'s new genre (see on 6), and the obvious material to choose is myrtle since it is associated with Erato in another context, i.e. as the Muse of love-poetry. The bushy garland of the epic poet is usually contrasted with the garlands denoting other genres, which are stripped of their leaves: cf. Virg. *G.* 3. 21 f. 'ipse caput tonsae foliis ornatus oliuae / dona feram', Prop. 4. 1. 61 'Ennius hirsuta cingat sua dicta corona'. On these analogies *intonsa ... myrto* denotes the wrong garland for this context. But since St.'s theme in the first three stanzas is that lyric is a new departure for him, he is using *intonsus* to denote material from a bush not previously pruned by him rather than 'not stripped of its leaves': see *TLL* vii. 2. 30. 52 ff. Hence St.'s use becomes a most artful deviation from the usage of his predecessors.

11. nunc maior sitit: *sitis* (M) is impossible, since a greater thirst would require not a purer river but a larger one to slake it, and traditionally epic is the large river while the lesser genres are the uncontaminated spring: cf. Callim. *Epig.* 28. 3 f. Pfeiffer οὐδ᾽ ἀπὸ κρήνης / πίνω, H. 2. 110 ff., Prop. 3. 3. 5 f. 'paruaque tam magnis admoram fontibus ora, / unde pater sitiens Ennius ante bibit', Man. 2. 7 ff., Wimmel, *Kallimachos in Rom*, 226 ff. But St. must now turn to an uncontaminated spring because his river of epic inspiration is running dry; hence *sitit* (Saenger) hints at St.'s difficulties with the *Achilleid*, which are illustrated by the circus metaphor in ll. 21–4: cf. Cic. *Q. fr.* 3. 1. 11 'poema ad Caesarem quod institueram incidi ... ipsi fontes iam sitiunt'. While there is no natural opposition between *maior* and *castior*, the underlying topos, associating the pure spring with lesser genres, balances the equation.

12. **castior amnis** is a calque: since καθαρός (*purus*) means both 'physically unsullied' and 'chaste', St. makes *castus* (= 'chaste') a synonym for καθαρός (= 'unsullied').

13. **dulci Latio:** since *dulcis* is an adjective frequently applied to family relationships and hence to native territory, Bonjour, 427 f., assumes that Vibius came from Latium; but St.'s argument (17–20) that he resists the temptations of his native district is meant to encourage Vibius likewise to leave Dalmatia. Hence *dulcis* must simply convey the charms of Latium rather than denote native associations.

14. **Dalmatae montes:** on Vibius' Dalmatian origins see intro. The Flavian poets traditionally associated Dalmatia with gold: cf. *S.* 1. 2. 153 'robora Dalmatico lucent satiata metallo', 3. 3. 90 'Dalmatico quod monte nitet', Mart. 10. 78. 5 ff. 'felix auriferae colone terrae, / rectorem uacuo sinu remittis / optabisque moras, et exeuntem / udo Dalmata gaudio sequeris'. A vein of gold found near the surface in Dalmatia during Nero's reign yielded fifty pounds of gold in one day (Plin. *NH* 33. 67). Mining was especially intense in the Bosnia-Hercegovina basins: cf. E. Pašalić, *Glasnik Zemaljskog Muzeja u Sarajevu* 9 (1954), 75.

14–15. **Dite uiso / pallidus fossor redit:** since mining was associated both with wealth and with activity underground, the Greeks commonly played on the names Pluto and Plutos: cf. Posid. F 240 a E–K = F 48 Jacoby = Athen. 6. 233 E (quoting Demetrius of Phalerum) ἐλπιζούσης τῆς πλεονεξίας ἀνάξειν ἐκ τῶν μηχῶν τῆς γῆς αὐτὸν τὸν Πλούτωνα, F 239 E–K = F 47 Jacoby = Strabo 3. 2. 9 παρ' ἐκείνοις ὡς ἀληθῶς τὸν ὑποχθόνιον τόπον οὐχ ὁ Ἅιδης, ἀλλ' ὁ Πλούτων κατοικεῖ. Hence the Romans connected *Dis* and *diues*: cf. Cic. *ND* 2. 66 'Diti patri ..., qui diues, ut apud Graecos Πλούτων', Quint. 1. 6. 34 'a contrariis aliqua sinemus trahi, ut ... Ditis, quia minime diues'. The miner's lack of suntan is interpreted as pallor at having seen the god of the underworld. *redit* recalls the mythical heroes (Hercules and Aeneas) who visited the underworld during their lifetime on earth. The native mine-workings in Dalmatia which Augustus exploited involved tapping the 'placers', superficial deposits of sand or gravel in stream-beds: cf. Flor. 4. 12. 10 'fodere terras ... aurumque uenis repurgare', J. F. Healy, *Mining and Metallurgy in the Greek and Roman World* (London, 1978), 49. But this passage is evidence that by Domitian's era the Romans in Dalmatia were testing the schist (foliated rock containing layers of mineral deposits): see O. Davies, *Roman Mines in Europe* (Oxford, 1935), 187.

15–16. **eruto ... / concolor auro:** three colours were distinguished for gold in antiquity: red (*rutilus*), tawny yellow (*flauus, fuluus*) and pale yellow (*pallidus*): see André, *Couleur*, 155. Catullus derides Iuuentus' lover as 'inaurata pallidior statua' (81. 4). *pallor* was traditionally a sign of fear (χλωρὸν δέος, Hom. *Il.* 7. 479, 8. 77, *Od.* 11. 45): see *TLL* x. 1. 122. 76 ff., 129. 69 ff., 138. 31 ff., André, *Couleur*, 143. Comparison between the pallor of the mine-worker and the colour of gold is a topos: cf. Luc. 4. 297 f. 'tam longe luce relicta / merserit Asturii scrutator pallidus auri', Sil. 1. 231 ff. 'Astur auarus / uisceribus lacerae telluris mergitur imis / et redit infelix effosso concolor auro'.

17–20. This stanza rests on the assumption that native territory exerts an attraction which is in conflict with the call of duty. This tension is frequently expressed in terms of a citizen's two loyalties: to his home territory and to the *res publica* of Rome: see Bonjour, 96 ff. In the *Siluae* this conflict is a common motif, but it is usually expressed in purely personal terms, regardless of political factors: Vibius should forsake Dalmatia for Rome where St. needs his help, not (ostensibly) to advance his own career in public life. *S.* 3. 5 is predicated entirely upon Claudia's reluctance to forsake her home at Rome in order to accompany her husband as his dutiful wife. St.'s own affection for the Bay of Naples, his birthplace, is a prominent theme in *S.* 3. 5: cf. also 4. 5. 21 f. (Alba) 'terra primis post patriam mihi / dilecta curis'. The superiority of Baiae over Dalmatia as an attractive residence here reinforces the argument: if seductive Baiae cannot keep St., why should Dalmatia (unattractively presented in the previous stanza) keep Vibius?

18–19. portu retinent amoeno / desides Baiae: *amoenae* is a *uox propria* of Baiae: cf. Hor. *Epist.* 1. 1. 83 'nullus in orbe sinus Baiis praelucet amoenis'. Seneca argues that its beauty contributed to its moral decadence: cf. *Epist.* 51. 10 'effeminat animos amoenitas nimia nec dubie aliquid ad corrumpendum uigorem potest regio'. *amoenitas* is a quality which can undermine sober values: cf. Tac. *Ann.* 14. 31. 7 (the colony at Camulodunum) 'nec arduum uidebatur excindere coloniam nullis munimentis saeptam; quod ducibus nostris parum prouisum erat, dum amoenitati prius quam usui consulitur'. Hence the seductive charms of Baiae (*portu . . . amoeno*) cultivate idleness (*desides*): *desidia* denotes sloth, whereas *otium* more commonly (but not invariably) has overtones of productive leisure: see J.-M. André, *L'Otium dans la vie morale et intellectuelle romaine* (Paris, 1966), 93 n. 19.

19–20. liticenue notus / Hectoris armis: an alternative tradition named Misenus as companion of Odysseus and not a trumpeter: cf. Strabo 1. 2. 18. St. follows the Virgilian tradition, which probably derives from Roman antiquarians: cf. *A.* 6. 166 f. 'Hectoris hic magni fuerat comes, Hectora circum / et lituo pugnas insignis obibat et hasta', N. M. Horsfall, *JHS* 99 (1979), 39 f. The promontory south of Cumae which is still known as Punte di Miseno commemorates his death by drowning while he was *en route* to Italy with Aeneas: cf. *S.* 5. 3. 167 f. 'propiore sinu lituo remoque notatus / collis'.

21. Paralysis is a common metaphor for mental inertia, including lack of inspiration: cf. Ov. *Tr.* 5. 12. 21 f. 'adde quod ingenium longa rubigine laesum / torpet et est multo, quam fuit ante, minus'. Even though St. has not succumbed to the temptations of *desides Baiae*, Vibius' absence makes him fall prey to *torpor*. The word-order, *nostris . . . Camenis* encircling *sine te*, illustrates St.'s dependence on Vibius. *sine te*, originally a religious formula (N–H on Hor. *O.* 1. 26. 9), conventionally expresses the poet's need for the stimulus of inspiration or patronage: cf. Virg. *G.* 3. 40 ff. 'interea Dryadum siluas saltusque sequamur / intactos, tua, Maecenas, haud mollia iussa: / te sine nil altum mens incohat', *S.* 5. 3. 237 f. (to his father) 'labat incerto mihi limite currus / te sine'. St. combines his recognition of Vibius' role with the traditional image of the Muses and Apollo as sources of inspiration, implying that if Vibius were there to attract them they would visit St. He pays a similar compliment to Rutilius Gallicus, whose inspiration he requests even before that of the deities whose assistance is vital for composition: cf. 1. 4. 19 ff. 'ast ego nec Phoebum, quamquam mihi surda sine illo / plectra, nec Aonias decima cum Pallade diuas / aut mitem Tegeae Dircesue hortabor alumnum: / ipse ueni uiresque nouas animumque ministra, / qui caneris'.

22–3. Thymbrae / rector: a cult-title of Apollo was derived from his famous temple at Thymbra in the Troad: cf. Eur. *Rh.* 224, 508, Virg. *G.* 4. 323, *A.* 3. 85, Strabo 13. 1. 35. In the context of the *Achilleid*, St.'s reference to this aspect of Apollo's cult may be pointed if he knew of the tradition whereby Achilles murdered Troilus in this temple and was himself murdered there in turn: cf. Philostr. *Her.* 20. 16 f., Hyg. *Fab.* 110, Serv. *Aen.* 3. 321, 6. 57 etc., *RE* viA. 697. 42 ff. (Kruse).

23–4. primis meus ecce metis / haeret Achilles: St. resumes the racing image of the first stanza. The personification of the *Achilleid* (cf. 4. 4. 94) affords the paradox of the πόδας ὠκὺς Ἀχιλλεύς immobilized in a chariot accident. The *metae* are the turning-posts in the circus, usually represented by three obelisks standing on each end of the *spina* which ran down the middle of the race-track; they can be seen clearly in mosaics and frescos, but often all that remains on site is the semi-circular base at the end of the *spina*: see H. A. Harris, *Sport in Greece and Rome* (London, 1972), 191 and fig. 13. *primae metae* might distinguish the first turn of each lap (at the far end of the track) from the turn at the end opposite the *carceres* (see D–S i. 1190 [Bussemaker, E. Saglio]), but St. surely means here that in Vibius' absence the *Achilleid* foundered at the earliest possible moment, i.e. at the first turn of the first lap: cf. Cic. *Cael.* 75 (Caelius' first moral crisis) 'in hoc flexu quasi aetatis . . . fama adulescentis paululum haesit ad metas notitia noua mulieris'.

25. monitore: the word suits a preceptor of the young: cf. Hor. *Ars* 163 '[iuuenis] monitoribus asper', *S.* 5. 3. 146 ff. 'hinc tibi uota patrum credi generosaque pubes / te monitore regi moresque et facta priorum / discere'. The image of the *lima* shows that *monitor* is used here of a critic.

26. It was traditional for Roman poets to allude to the completion of a work in terms of the process involved: cf. Cat. 1. 1 f. 'cui dono lepidum nouum libellum / arida modo pumice expolitum?', Prop. 3. 1. 8 'exactus tenui pumice uersus eat'. The *lima* is a metaphorical extension of this motif: in Cicero and Horace *limatus* conveys an ideal of refined style (Cic. *Brut.* 93 'limatius dicendi . . . genus', Hor. *Sat.* 1. 10. 65 f. 'fuerit limatior idem / quam rudis et Graecis intacti carminis auctor'); *limae labor* (Hor. *Ars* 291) is a traditional metaphor for the Callimachean πόνος of literary revision (cf.

S. 3. 2. 143 'laboratas ... Thebas'). In particular the *lima* represents the process of critical editing and revision, frequently entrusted to an *amicus*: cf. Mart. 5. 80. 12 f. '[libellus] quem censoria cum meo Seuero / docti lima momorderit Secundi', Plin. *Epist.* 1. 2. 5 'quo magis intendam limam tuam, confitebor ... me ... ab editione non abhorrere', 8. 3 'nunc rogo ut ... particulas qua soles lima persequaris', 5. 10. 3 'perfectum opus absolutumque est, nec iam splendescit lima sed atteritur'. St. approaches the metaphor literally (*Thebais cruciata*): the *lima* would hurt.

27. audaci fide: *audacia* (τόλμα) is a literary topos applicable in a variety of contexts: see Brink on Hor. *Ars* 9 f., *TLL* ii. 1243. 8 ff., 1248. 2 ff., 1256. 22 ff. It describes the unconventional element in the *Siluae* which alarmed Pollius Felix (3 *Pr.* 4): see General Introduction, n. 37. Here St.'s imitation of Virgil (cf. 4. 4. 54–5) is itself construed as *audacia*. Since the *Thebaid* was a success (Juv. 7. 82 ff.), *audaci fide*, written in hindsight, carries a hint of pride. Whereas at *Theb.* 12. 816–17 St. was displaying conventional modesty in presenting his new work before the public, here the circumstances are different: if the credit is to be worth sharing with Vibius it must be exalted, and surely at the moment of resting from the genre St. can take legitimate pride in its success. For the motif of referring to the poet's birthplace instead of naming him cf. 4. 2. 9 n.

28. gaudia: the poet's πόνος is also his reward: cf. Virg. *G.* 3. 291 ff. 'sed me Parnasi deserta per ardua dulcis / raptat amor; iuuat ire iugis, qua nulla priorum / Castaliam molli deuertitur orbita cliuo'. Postgate's *grandia* destroys the antithesis.

29. damus ... ueniam: the *persona* of the indignant poet won over by the force of circumstances of his *amicus* recurs at 4. 8. 44.

30. fundasti uacuos penatis: by metonymy *penates* = *domus*: cf. 4. 8. 23 *larem*. Children are the foundations which stabilize the home (by ensuring the continuation of the family line): cf. [Sen.] *Oct.* 532 'digna ... nostram subole fundaro domum', Plin. *Epist.* 4. 21. 3 'unus ex tribus liberis superest, domumque pluribus adminiculis paulo ante fundatam desolatus fulcit ac sustinet', *TLL* vi. 1. 1562. 21 ff.

31. o diem laetum: a formula for expressing pleasure or congratulations: cf. Plin. *Epist.* 6. 11. 1, 3 'o diem laetum! ... o diem (repetam enim) laetum notandumque mihi candidissimo calculo!', *Rhet. Gr.* iii. 412 Sp. (rules for *genethliacon*) μετὰ τὰ προοίμια τὴν ἡμέραν ἐπαινέσεις καθ' ἣν ἐτέχθη ὁ ἐπαινούμενος, Ps.-Dion. ii. 266 Us.-R. ἐπεὶ γὰρ ἀρχὴ τῆς γενέσεως τῆς ἑκάστου ἡ ἡμέρα, ἐφ' ἧς ἐγένετο, ἀναγκαῖόν που ὀλίγα ἄττα καὶ περὶ τῆς ἡμέρας εἰπεῖν οἷον ἐγκωμιάζοντα τὸ προσόν, εἰ ἄρα ἴδιόν τι ἔχει παρὰ τὰς ἄλλας ἡμέρας, ἐπισημαινόμενον. The birth of the child is celebrated almost like the *aduentus* of a general in a triumphal procession (*uenit ecce*): cf. Hor. *O.* 4. 2. 41 ff. 'concines laetosque dies et Vrbis / publicum ludum super impetrato / fortis Augusti reditu forumque / litibus orbum'.

32. Maximus alter: another punning antithesis on the name (see l. 9 n.), a superlative (in the exclusive sense) being incompatible with an alternative.

33–40. St. congratulates Vibius on having escaped *orbitas*. Cf. the delight of an old man whose only daughter presents him with a grandson, thereby saving his *hereditas* from passing to the *gentiles* (Cat. 68. 123 'impia derisi gentilis gaudia tollens'): see A. Watson, *The Law of Succession in the Later Roman Republic* (Oxford, 1971), 180. Childless persons (*orbi*) were at a legal disadvantage: under Augustus' marriage legislation, *lex Iulia de maritandis ordinibus* (18 BC) and *lex Papia Poppaea nuptialis* (AD 9), they were forbidden to inherit more than half a legacy, while the rest (*caducum*) was allotted to another beneficiary, provided he had children, or, failing that, to the state *aerarium* (and, later, the *fiscus*): see A. Berger, *Encyclopedic Dictionary of Roman Law* (Philadelphia, 1953), 377 f., Kaser, i. 724 f., G. Rotondi, *Leges Publicae Populi Romani* (Hildesheim, 1966), 443–5, 457–62. But the literary sources (as here) stress what are usually considered the social disadvantages of *orbitas*, i.e. the unflagging attentions of *captatores*: flattery and gifts anticipated the reward of a handsome legacy. The fullest treatments of this theme occur at Hor. *Sat.* 2. 5 (Teiresias' advice to Ulysses), Plin. *Epist.* 2. 20, 8. 18, Juv. 12. 93–130, and frequently in Martial, e.g. 12. 90: see Friedländer, i. 213–16. Vollmer believes that St.'s stress on this theme reflects his fear of *orbitas* on his own account and also echoes the official programme of encouragement to boost the birth-rate. Both these influences may be contributory factors, but prima facie Vibius' own circumstances and the general climate of opinion despising the practice of legacy-hunting explain the inclusion of this topos. Throughout these two stanzas, verbal oppositions reflect the innate hypocrisy of *captatio*: *fugienda* (33) / *premit* (34), *inimicus heres* (34), *uotis* (34) / *funus* (36).

35–6. optimo poscens (pudet heu) propinquum / funus amico: the gist of M (*optimo ... propinquo ... amici*) is that the heir prays for his benefactor to die, but the passage must be corrupt since both *propinquo* and *amici*, apparently referring to the *orbus*, cannot grammatically designate the same person. The substantive *propinquo* would imply kinship between *orbus* and *heres*, whereas the context requires the *heres* to be simply an *amicus*. The same objection applies to Postgate's extended parenthesis *pudet heu propinqui* ('shame on a relative'). Håkanson (123) demonstrates that *propinquum funus* (5) adds a further scandalous point: the *heres* prays not only for his benefactor's death but that it will occur soon: for the expression cf. *Theb.* 9. 714 f. 'leti ... propinqui / effugium'. There is little to choose between *optimo ... amico* (dative) and *optimi ... amici* (genitive). Håkanson argues for the genitive on the grounds that *optimi* would be easily corrupted to *optimo* before *poscens*. But an indirect object after *poscens* is more subtle, implying greater malice than the possessive case. Some wild solutions provoke comment: the vocative *amici* (Vollmer) or *amice* (R. Argenio, *RSC* 9 [1961], 213–6) would introduce a laboured and belated address, whether to anonymous persons or to Vibius himself; the adverbial *amice* (Frère), a type of adverb very unusual in poetry (Axelson, 62), would in this position trail lamentably.

37. orbitas: the metonymy creates anaphora with l. 33, stressing the unity of the two stanzas.

nullo ... fletu: it was considered unnatural for the deceased not to be mourned: cf. Lucil. 691 Marx 'nullo honore, heredis fletu nullo, nullo funere'. Hence Teiresias advises Ulysses as *captator* to feign tears (Hor. *Sat.*

2. 5. 103 f.) 'si paulum potes, illacrimare: est / gaudia prodentem uultum celare': cf. Pub. *Sent.* H. 19 'heredis fletus sub persona risus est'.

38–40. St. uses vocabulary common to the contexts of inheritance and war (*capta, spoliis, ignem*) to imply that the *captator* pursues the *orbus* like a soldier fighting for booty. For the technical sense of *capere* cf. the legal phrase 'take an inheritance' and see *TLL* iii. 327. 2 ff.

39. imminens: usually it is death which hovers: cf. Cic. *Tusc.* 1. 91 '[mors] cotidie imminet', Tib. 1. 10. 33 f. 'quis furor est atram bellis accersere Mortem? / imminet et tacito clam uenit illa pede'. The notion of menace also suits the heir, whose sole motivation is *auaritia*: cf. Cic. *Ver.* 2. 2. 134 'auaritia semper hiante atque imminente', Hor. *O.* 4. 7. 19–20 'cuncta manus auidas fugient heredis, amico / quae dederis animo'.

40. computat ignem: by common metonymy *ignis* = *rogus*. The *captator* even grudges the cost of the pyre. A true mourner would spare no expense: cf. 3. 3. 33 ff. (to Claudius Etruscus) 'tu largus Eoa / germina, tu messis Cilicumque Arabumque superbas / merge rogis; ferat ignis opes heredis et alto / aggere missuri nitido pia nubila caelo / stipentur cineres', 2. 4. 33 ff. (Melior's parrot) 'at non inglorius umbris / mittitur: Assyrio cineres adolentur amomo / et tenues Arabum respirant gramine plumae / Sicaniisque crocis'. Hence Teiresias' cynical advice to Ulysses (Hor. *Sat.* 2. 5. 104 ff.) 'sepulcrum / permissum arbitrio sine sordibus exstrue; funus / egregie factum laudet uicinia'. It was Roman practice to make provision for one's funeral by appointing someone to make appropriate arrangements and by stipulating the maximum proportion of the estate which was to be spent (*impensae funeris*); any savings accrued to the heirs: cf. Ulp. *Dig.* 11. 7. 12. 3, *CIL* vi. 10229. 114. If no person was appointed by the testator, his heirs were responsible for the funeral: cf. Ulp. *Dig.* 11. 7. 12. 4. Presumably the need to appoint a specific person was more urgent if the heirs were not on the spot: see D–S ii. 1402 (Édouard Cuq).

41–4. Rhetorical theory prescribed that in the case of a child the orator should praise his family, birth, and nature, and then predict future greatness for him (*Rhet. Gr.* iii. 412 Sp.), or pray for his future (Ps.-Dion. ii. 269 Us.–R.). The distinction of Vibius' son's ancestry and hopes for his future are combined in the topos of children emulating their forebears, obviously a handy technique when parent (or grandparent) is the encomiast's patron: cf. 4. 4. 74 ff., 8. 57 ff., 5. 2. 51 ff. (Vettius Bolanus).

41. generosus: probably referring to the child's maternal line; his maternal grandfather was perhaps senatorial: see intro.

42. non multis iter expeditum: a career of outstanding merit.

43–4. auum ... / prouocet actis: the notion of challenging one's predecessors belongs to the topos of *exempla uirtutis*, combining *laudatio temporis acti* with encomium of the coming generation. So Pliny, of Vetricius Spurinna's son Cottius, who died young (*Epist.* 2. 7. 4) 'tanta ei sanctitas grauitas auctoritas etiam, ut posset senes illos prouocare uirtute, quibus nunc honore adaequatus est'.

45–52. For the military posts of Vibius and the child's grandfather (*tu* balanced by *ille*) see intro.

46. Eoum ... Oronten: the Orontes (modern 'Asi), the chief river of Syria, symbolizes the east: cf. Prop. 2. 23. 21 f. 'et quas Euphrates et quas mihi misit Orontes, / me iuuerint', Juv. 3. 62 'iam pridem Syrus in Tiberim defluxit Orontes'. For the accusative termination *-en* for Greek nouns see Housman, *JPh* 31 (1910), 236–66 (= *Cl. Pap.* ii. 817–39).

48. Castore dextro: the extension of *dexter* to mean 'favourable' originates from the belief in a propitious side in augury: see *TLL* v. 1. 924. 12 ff. In Homer Castor was a horseman and Pollux a boxer: cf. Hom. *Il.* 3. 237 (= *Od.* 11. 300), *RE* v. 1093. 29 ff. (Bethe). Castor was adopted as in some sense the patron of the *equites*: cf. the ceremonial parade, *transuectio equitum*, associated with the cult of the Dioscuri and held annually on 15 July to commemorate the battle of Lake Regillus, in which the Dioscuri were believed to have assisted the Romans (Dion. Hal. 6. 13. 1 f.). See further *RE* v. 1105. 22 ff. (Bethe), Latte, *RR* 173–6.

49–50. inuicti rapidum secutus / Caesaris fulmen: *inuictus* was a common epithet of deities (especially Jupiter), adopted for the ruling emperor since Augustan poetry: see Latte, *RR* 352, Sauter, 153–9. St. consistently dwells on the theme of the emperor's invincibility: cf. 4. 1. 39–42, 3. 153–9, 8. 61 f. 'inuicti Caesaris ... / numina'. *inuictus* occurs frequently in Martial, once also in connection with Domitian's campaign against the Sarmatae (7. 6. 7 f.) 'rursus, io, magnos clamat tibi Roma triumphos / inuictusque tua, Caesar, in urbe sonas'; this association suggests that Domitian was particularly ambitious for this campaign to succeed, and correspondingly sensitive about disparaging reactions (see on 4. 1. 39). Jupiter's *fulmen* becomes a symbol for the force and speed of heroes or (as here) emperors: cf. Quint. 8. 6. 71 'Herculis impetum ... fulmini dicit similem', *S.* 2. 7. 67 (of Julius Caesar) 'fulmen ducis inter arma diui', *TLL* vi. 1. 1527. 83 ff. In a more general sense the emperor's acts are likened to the strike of Jupiter's thunderbolt, symbolizing ineluctable omnipotence: cf. Ov. *Tr.* 1. 3. 11 f. 'non aliter stupui, quam qui Iouis ignibus ictus / uiuit et est uitae nescius ipse suae', 3. 5. 7 f., 5. 3. 31 f. For the association of Domitian with Jupiter see on 4. 3. 128–9, Sauter, 54–78 (*fulmen*: 64), Scott, 116.

50–1. refugis amaram / Sarmatis legem dederit: for the Sarmatae, nomadic peoples in the regions north-east of the Caspian Sea, see T. Sulimirski, *The Sarmatians* (London, 1970). *refugis* refers to the scorched-earth policy of the trans-Danubian peoples, well known to the Romans, by which they tried to foil invasion: cf. Hdt. 4. 126 f., Plato, *Lach.* 191 A, Hor. *O.* 1. 35. 9 'profugi Scythae', 4. 14. 42 'profugus Scythes', Ov. *Pont.* 1. 2. 83 ff., Luc. 6. 50. This mobility in itself implies their nomadic way of life, free from the shackles of property: cf. Strabo 7. 3. 4, 17–18, Sen. *Phaed.* 71 'uacuisque uagus Sarmata campis'. Hence the paradoxical *amara lex*: settlement, a blessing of civilization, is a punishment for a nomadic people; the expedition was a punitive exercise to avenge the legion massacred in 84 (Suet. *Dom.* 6). Civilization by (force of arms and) legislation was Rome's mission: cf. Virg. *A.* 6. 851 ff. 'tu regere imperio populos, Romane, memento / ... pacique imponere morem, / parcere subiectis et debellare superbos'. St.'s review of the careers of his father's pupils visualizes these ideals in practice (5. 3. 185 ff.) 'et nunc ex illo forsan grege gentibus alter /

iura dat Eois, alter compescit Hiberas, / alter Achaemenium secludit Zeugmate Persen, / hi ditis Asiae populos, hi Pontica frenant, / hi fora pacificis emendant fascibus, illi / castra pia statione tenent'. See F. Christ, *Die römische Weltherrschaft in der antiken Dichtung* (Tübingen, 1938), 113 f., V. Nutton, 'The Beneficial Ideology', in P. D. A. Garnsey and C. R. Whittaker (eds.), *Imperialism in the Ancient World* (Cambridge, 1978), 209–21.

53–6. As in the lyric counterpart to this poem (4. 5 to Septimius Seuerus), the last stanza links the interests of St. and his *amicus* by revealing that this *amicus* was also a writer.

54–6. omne ... mundi senium remensus / orsa Sallusti breuis et Timaui / reddis alumnum: Vibius wrote a world history. But *omne ... mundi senium remensus* cannot be construed as an echo of Cat. 1. 5 f. (to Nepos) 'ausus es ... / omne aeuum tribus explicare cartis'; hence there is no foundation for Hardie's surmise (173) that Vibius may have been especially fond of Catullus or Verona.

Who was *Timaui alumnum*? The Timauus (modern Timavo) flows into the Adriatic 20 km east of Aquileia (cf. Mart. 4. 25. 6), i.e. over 100 km from Patauium. But in epic Patauium is misleadingly designated by the Timauus (cf. Luc. 7. 193 ff.), following Virg. *A.* 1. 242–8, where Antenor, approaching Italy from the coast of Illyricum, crosses the Timauus to reach Patauium; hence Virgil's topography is correct, although the subsequent location of Padua near the Timauus is not. But clearly *Timaui ... alumnum* means Livy: cf. Quint. 8. 2. 1 'in Tito Liuio ... putat inesse Pollio Asinius quandam Patauinitatem. quare ... et uerba omnia et uox huius alumnum urbis oleant'.

E. Opelt, *RAC* v. 948, regards Vibius and the anonymous epitomator at Mart. 14. 190 as candidates for writing the first known epitome of Livy. But since Vibius wrote a world history, his work was not a mere epitome of Livy, who wrote exclusively Roman history. Nor can *orsa Sallusti breuis ... reddis* refer to a separate treatment of Sallust's content, since his material is in any case covered by Livy. Sallust and Livy were commonly contrasted in antiquity: cf. Quint. 10. 1. 102 (quoting Seruilius Nonianus) 'pares eos magis quam similes'. *breuis* suggests that Vibius' style emulated Sallust's renowned compression: cf. Quint. 4. 2. 45 'illa Sallustiana breuitas', 8. 3. 82 'est uero pulcherrima [breuitas] cum plura paucis complectitur, quale Sallusti est', 10. 1. 102 'immortalem Sallusti uelocitatem'. The educative value of simplified historical writing was recognized in antiquity: cf. Plut. *Cat. Mai.* 20. 5, *Mor.* 14 E. Livy was to be preferred to Sallust as a school text because of his clarity: cf. Quint. 2. 5. 19 'eorum candidissimum quemque et maxime expositum uelim ut Liuium'. Thus Vibius wrote a simplified world history, combining the conciseness of Sallust with the clarity of Livy, so that the young could receive moral instruction from the lessons of the past. From the Augustan period onwards, selectivity of material (*breuitas* in a different sense from the Sallustian criterion discussed above) is an ideal embraced by those writers, especially universal historians, who concentrate on clear exposition of major themes: cf. Vitr. 5 *Pr.* 5 'quo facilius ad sensus legentium peruenire possint, breuibus uoluminibus iudicaui scribere', Vell. Pat. 1. 55. 1 'admonet promissae breuitatis fides quanto omnia transcursu dicenda sint', Flor. *Pr.* 3 'in breui quasi tabella totam eius imaginem amplectar', and see A. J. Woodman, *CQ* NS 25 (1975), 275–88 (but *caue* his implication, 286 f. n. 5, that Vibius was an epitomator). See further K. M. Coleman, *PACA* 16 (1982), 25–7.

8

INTRODUCTION

THIS poem, written from St.'s estate at Alba (cf. 39), commemorates the birth of a third child to Julius Menecrates (PIR^2 I 430), a Neapolitan ('municipem meum', 4 *Pr.* 18) and son-in-law of St.'s important patron, Pollius Felix (*PIR* P 419), to whom Book 3 is dedicated. Since the trio comprises two boys and a girl (25 ff.), and a grandson and granddaughter to Pollius are already mentioned at 3. 1. 176, the baby must be a boy. Pollius was from Puteoli (2. 2. 96); it is suggested by Beloch that his family had been among the original colonists of 194 BC. He owned a lavish estate at Surrentum (the subject of *S.* 2. 2 and 3. 1): see R. G. M. Nisbet, *JRS* 68 (1978), 1–11. In AD 65 a Pollius Felix owned an estate at Pausilypon (modern Posillipo) west of Naples (*ILS* 5798), perhaps the father of St.'s patron (see *PIR* P 419), or else the man himself, since St.'s friend was old enough to have three grandchildren by AD 94 (see D'Arms, 223). The daughter of St.'s wealthy patron married Julius Menecrates, who was equestrian: see 4 *Pr.* 20–1 (discussed in intro. to 4. 9), where Plotius Grypus, contrasted with Menecrates, is *maioris gradus*. Beloch, 375, suggests that St.'s man may be descended from the Menecrates, freedman of Sextus Pompeius, who was sent to devastate Volturnum and other parts of Campania during the second triumvirate (Dio 48. 46), but proof is lacking. Vessey, *Statius and the Thebaid*, 22, suggests that Menecrates may have been a pupil of St.'s father, who taught the *generosa pubes* of Naples (5. 3. 146).

St. describes this poem as an *ecloga* (4 *Pr.* 18) in which he offers congratulations to Menecrates (*gratulor*, 4 *Pr.* 19). It is largely in epistolary form, but heightened with hymnic elements at the beginning and the end (1–14, 45 ff.). St. does not classify it as a *genethliacon*, although the subject requires elements of *genethliacon* to be included: see 4. 7 intro. For a discussion of this poem see D. W. T. C. Vessey, *AC* 43 (1974), 257–66.

1–3. Pande ... Parthenope: the topos that places rejoice at the birth of citizens who do them credit dates back to *HHAp.* 61 (Delos rejoicing as the birthplace of Apollo): cf. Theoc. 17. 64 ff. (Cos rejoicing over the birth of Ptolemy Philadelphus); the birthplaces or homes of distinguished persons are deemed fortunate: cf. *S.* 2. 7. 24 ff. (Baetica, birthplace of Lucan), 3. 4. 12 ff. (Pergamum, birthplace of Flavius Earinus), 5. 3. 104 ff. (Naples, *patria* of St.'s father). The first Cumaean settlement at Naples was called Parthenope after the Siren of that name. Her cult may have antedated the settlement (Frederiksen, 91), and was maintained when the original foundation was replaced by Neapolis (Lutatius Daphnis *ap.* Serv. Dan. on Virg. *G.* 4. 563, Liv. 8. 22. 5, Ps.-Scymnus 251 f., Vell. Pat. 1. 4. 1). In accordance with an oracle, torch-races were established in honour of Parthenope (and Ceres: see on l. 50), reputedly on the occasion of a visit to Naples by the Athenian general Diotimos: cf. Timaeus, *FGrH* 566 F 98, Lycophr. *Alex.* 732–7, Strabo 5. 4. 7. The torch-race was a common act of expiation, apparently inaugurated on this occasion by the Neapolitans with Athenian assistance: see Frederiksen, 105. Parthenope's tomb was venerated at Naples near the coastline (but mistakenly situated on the R. Clauius by Lycophr. *Alex.* 717–21, probably in error for the Sebethus: see R. W. Peterson, *The Cults of Campania* [Rome, 1919], 176, Frederiksen, 105).

1. Pande foris: most temples were kept shut except on special occasions: see Wissowa, *RKR*² 476 f. Cf. Lucan's description of the people of Larisa welcoming the vanquished Pompey as though he were victorious (7. 713 ff.) 'omnibus illa / ciuibus effudit totas per moenia uires / obuia, ceu laeto; promittunt munera flentes: / pandunt templa, domos; socios se cladibus optant'.

uittata ... templa: *uittae sacrae*, woollen fillets, garlanded the doors of temples on festal days (Prop. 4. 9. 27), and were draped round the pillars and hung on pilasters: see D–S v. 954 (Graillot).

1–2. Sabaeis / nubibus: for Arabian incense see on 4. 5. 31–2. Cf. Ov. *Met.* 11. 247 f. '[Peleus] deos ... pecoris fibris et fumo turis adorat'.

2. pecudum fibris spirantibus: entrails of sacrificial victims had to be examined as soon as the animal was slaughtered, i.e. before the organs changed their appearance. The throbbing entrails of the victim were said to be still 'breathing', because in ancient medicine the blood-vessels were believed to be also the channels for the respiratory system; this theory, first expressed by Diogenes of Apollonia, is repeated in the Hippocratic corpus and by Galen: see C. R. S. Harris, *The Heart and the Vascular System in Ancient Greek Medicine* (Oxford, 1973), 26, 41, 320. Cf. Virg. *A.* 4. 64 'spirantia consulit exta', Sen. *Thy.* 755 f. 'erepta uiuis exta pectoribus tremunt / spirantque uenae', *Theb.* 4. 463 ff. 'Manto ... semineces fibras et adhuc spirantia reddit / uiscera'.

5. insani solatur damna Vesaeui: in Stoic terms natural calamities were explained as irrational rage (see on 4. 4. 79) displayed by natural forces which were hampered or restricted: cf. Sen. *NQ* 6. 17. 1 (subterranean air-currents causing earthquakes) '[aer] cum offenditur ac retinetur insanit et moras suas abripit'. The ultimate cause of natural disasters was popularly regarded as Jupiter's displeasure, vented on the surrounding area: cf. 5. 3. 207 f. (the eruption of Vesuvius, AD 79) 'pater exemptum terris ad sidera montem / sustulit et late miseras deiecit in urbes'. The birth of a child to Julius Menecrates is proof that divine favour smiles upon Naples again: see D. W. T. C. Vessey, *AC* 43 (1974), 261. The spelling *Vesaeuus*, attested at Virg. *G.* 2. 224, hints at savagery: see O. Keller, *Lateinische Volksetymologie* (Leipzig, 1891), 351. For references to the 'madness' of volcanoes cf. 'Insani Montes' (a volcanic range in Sardinia), Lucr. 2. 593 'eximiis ... furit ignibus impetus Aetnae', *Aetna* 530 'lapides ... furere accensos', Sen. *HF* 106 'qui caminis ignis Aetnaeis furit'.

POEM EIGHT 211

6. secreta: Naples was a place of seclusion and retirement (ἀναχώρησις): cf. Hor. *Epod.* 5. 43 'otiosa ... Neapolis', *S.* 3. 5. 85 f. 'pax secura locis et desidis otia uitae / et numquam turbata quies somnique peracti', *RE* xvi. 2121. 59 ff. (Philipp).

7. socii portus: the port of Naples at Puteoli was the single most important factor in the prosperity of Campania, being engaged in commerce with the east (see 4. 3. 107–13 n.), with Rome, and with the hinterland: see Frederiksen, ch. 14 (= revised version of *RE* xxiii. 2036 ff.). For factors threatening this prosperity see on 4. 4. 82. Like Naples (6) and Surrentum (9) it was connected with Menecrates' family, being the birthplace of Pollius Felix (2. 2. 96).

7–8. dilecta ... miti / terra Dicarcheo: *Pŭtĕŏli* will not fit into dactylic verse, hence St.'s circumlocution. The original Greek settlement on the site of Puteoli was called Δικαιάρχεια: cf. Plin. *NH* 3. 61 'Puteoli colonia Dicaearchia dicta'. Frederiksen, 87, defends the assertion of Jerome (*Chron.*, ed. Helm p. 104) and Stephanus of Byzantium (s.v. Ποτίολοι) that it was a Samian foundation, despite Hülsen (*RE* v. 546) and Mommsen (*CIL* x, p. 182). For the form Dicarcheus for the eponymous founder's name see 3. 1. 92, 5. 75 (both genitive); it is derived from the adjectival form *Dicarcheus* standard among the Roman poets, the second syllable (*-ae-*) being dropped *metri gratia*: for the range of spellings see *TLL Onomasticon* iii. 139. 53 ff. For an adjective as a by-form of the name cf. the nomenclature of gods, e.g. Βάκχιος for Βάκχος. To the eponymous founder is attributed the affection traditionally felt by divinities towards places specifically under their protection: cf. *S.* 2. 2. 4 f. 'qua Bromio dilectus ager, collisque per altos / uritur et prelis non inuidet uua Falernis', Hor. *O.* 2. 6. 18 'amatus Aulon fertili Baccho' with N–H. *miti* contains a *double entendre*: it describes mild personality (*TLL* viii. 1152. 74 ff.) and also denotes an equable climate: for the topos and also the climatic allusion cf. 3. 5. 102 'caraque non molli iuga Surrentina Lyaeo'.

8–9. plaga cara madenti / Surrentina deo: cf. previous n.. *madere* can denote excessive drinking: see *TLL* viii. 34. 18 ff.; at *S.* 3. 1. 41 Hercules (brother of Dionysus) is *multo fratre madentem*; at Hor. *O.* 2. 19. 18 Bacchus is *uuidus*. For the fertility of the lava soil around Surrentum see Beloch, 261, and for Surrentine wine cf. *S.* 2. 2. 4 f. (cit. previous n.), Blümner, 199.

9. sertis altaria cingat: cf. 1 *uittata ... templa*; garlands were hung on altars on festive occasions including birthdays: cf. Prop. 3. 10. 19 f. 'inde coronatas ubi ture piaueris aras, / luxerit et tota flamma secunda domo', Hor. *O.* 4. 11. 6 ff. 'ara castis / uincta uerbenis auet immolato / spargier agno', D–S i. 351 (Saglio).

10. materni ... litus aui: St. includes Surrentum in the list of festal areas so that he can compliment Pollius Felix, Menecrates' father-in-law. For his villa at Surrentum see *S.* 2. 2, D'Arms, 220 f., P. Mingazzini and F. Pfister, *Forma Italiae, Regio I. Latium et Campania*, ii: *Surrentum* (Florence, 1946), 54 f., 132 f., pls. i, xviii. It is built on the only suitable stretch of coast: cf. 2. 2. 15 f. 'monti ... interuenit unum / litus'; St. implies that the whole shore is known as Pollius' property (*litus aui*).

11. **similis contendit reddere uultus:** a combination of the topos of 'pre-eminence' (see on 4. 2. 26) and the topos of family resemblance: cf. Theoc. 17. 44, 63 f., Virg. *E.* 4. 17, *S.* 1. 2. 271 ff. 'cumque tuos tacito natura recessu / formarit uultus, multum de patre decoris / plus de matre feras', 3. 3. 114 (Claudius Etruscus' wife) 'sibimet similis natorum gratia monstrat', and see on 4. 5. 45.

St. concludes this poem with the hope that the grandchildren will emulate their grandfather's personality; for the belief that character reflects physique, derived from the Homeric ideal of ἀρετή, cf. Hom. *Od.* 2. 270 ff. (Athene's discourse to Telemachus on legitimacy and heredity), and see on 4. 4. 8.

12. **Libyca praesignis auunculus hasta:** *auunculus* is either a maternal uncle or a grandmother's brother (hence not a paternal relative, *patruus*, as supposed by Vollmer and Frère). Since St. is concerned to compliment Pollius' family and he nowhere mentions the children's grandmother (see next n.), *auunculus* is presumably the children's uncle rather than their great-uncle. Vollmer's objection, that no son of Pollius is mentioned at 2. 2 or 3. 1, is an inconclusive *argumentum ex silentio*. This uncle apparently won a military decoration, the *hasta pura* ('praesignis . . . hasta') in an African campaign. *Libya* often denotes North Africa in general (cf. Enn. *Ann.* 302 Skutsch 'Europam Libyamque rapax ubi diuidit unda', *OLD* s.v. *Libya*), hence *Libycus* for 'African': cf. Hor. *O.* 1. 1. 10 (grain from Africa) 'quidquid de Libycis uerritur areis'. But in the absence of any further definition, *Libyca hasta* would be assumed to refer to Domitian's subjugation of the Nasamones in 85 (see on 4. 6. 75). Klass (*RE* xxi. 1422) postulates that the son of St.'s Pollius may be the C. Pollius Felix who set up a gravestone to his wife at Lambaesis in Numidia (*CIL* viii. 3940 = 18440). But the presence of his wife is awkward, since it suggests two unlikely circumstances: either she accompanied her husband on campaign or else they settled there; the identification is unconvincing. Beloch, 269, suggests that the Marcus Pullius recorded on the *fasti* of Puteoli as *duumuir* for the year 104 might be a descendant of Pollius. It could be this son, returned to his home town to occupy high office after an absence in which he gained distinction in imperial service: cf. the hypothesis regarding the grandfather of the emperor Septimius Seuerus, 4. 5 intro.

13–14. **sibi genitos putat attollitque benigno / Polla sinu:** Polla, wife of Pollius (2. 2. 10), treated Pollius' grandchildren as her own: cf. the similar contrast of *auus* with Polla, mentioned by name, at 3. 1. 177 ff. 'suboles noua grexque proteruus / nunc umeris inreptet aui, nunc agmine blando / certatim placidae concurrat ad oscula Pollae'; hence Polla must be Pollius' second wife, and stepmother to Menecrates' wife (Miriam Griffin, cit. R. G. M. Nisbet, *JRS* 68 [1978], 3). *tollere liberum* was the technical term for the father's symbolic act acknowledging the legitimacy of his child: see Kaser, i. 65, 345 f. Scooping children into the lap is a gesture of maternal affection, usually *sinu excipere* (or *suscipere*): cf. 1. 2. 110 (Venus and Violentilla), 2. 7. 38 (Calliope and Lucan), *Peru. Ven.* 78 (Venus and Cupid). Polla's action, combining these two motifs, acknowledges her husband's grandchildren as her own heirs. (For a different view, that Polla contemplated adoption, see D. W. T. C. Vessey, *AC* 43 [1974], 262.) Polla was a wealthy woman: cf. 2. 2. 151 ff., Nisbet, *JRS* 68 (1978), 2; *benigno* conveys material munificence.

14. macte, o iuuenis: after the hymn-like invocation to Parthenope and injunctions to the surrounding district and to Pollius' family to rejoice at the birth, St. addresses Menecrates himself in elevated language. Vocatives normally stand alone in Latin; *o* is a solemn Graecism. In conjunction with *macte* (*TLL* viii. 24. 2 ff.) it conveys religious solemnity and *pietas*: cf. Val. Fl. 6. 547 f. (Jason to Argus) 'macte o nostrum genus et iam certa propago / Aeoliae necopina domus'. The following clause explains how Menecrates qualifies for this religious epithet (cf. 25).

14-15. tanta ... / lumina: *tanta = tot*: see on 4. 2. 19 *quantae. lumen* is an honorific metaphor for a distinguished citizen: cf. Cic. *Sull.* 5 'ornamenta ac lumina rei publicae', *S.* 1. 4. 39 f. 'quae tum patrumque equitumque notaui / lumina et ignarae plebis lugere potentis!', *TLL* vii. 1821. 13 ff.

15-16. dulci strepit ecce tumultu / tot dominis clamata domus: for *clamata* cf. *Theb.* 5. 461 f. 'iam noua progenies partusque in uota soluti, / et non speratis clamatur Lemnos alumnis'. *dulcis tremit tumultus* (M) is objectionable because *tremit* primarily conveys unease or fear, and the vivid phrase *tot dominis clamata domus*, which is naturally the main idea, is uncomfortable in apposition to the abstract *tumultus*. *strepit* is appropriate of the noise in a house full of children, and *dulci ... tumultu* allows *domus* its natural prominence as subject of the sentence. Håkanson, 124, compares *Theb.* 1. 516 f. 'uario strepit icta tumultu / regia'. *strepit* points the oxymoron in *dulci ... tumultu*, conveying adult tolerance of children's noise.

16. procul belongs to an apotropaic formula: cf. Cat. 62. 92 'procul a mea tuos sit furor omnis, era, domo', with Kroll's note.

16-17. atra ... / Inuidia: the traditional colour for jealousy is *liuidus*, hence *liuentia lumina*: see André, *Couleur*, 174 f. *ater* is the adjective associated with death (e.g. Virg. *A.* 6. 429 'atra dies') and hence poison (*A.* 2. 221 'atro ... ueneno'). It describes sources of fear or distress (e.g. Hor. *O.* 3. 14. 13 'atras ... curas') and the emotions themselves (eg. Virg. *A.* 12. 335 'atrae Formidinis'). It is associated with jealousy in metaphors of poison: cf. Hor. *Epod.* 6. 15 'si quis atro dente me petiuerit', Sil. 11. 547 f. 'atro ueneno / Inuidiae nigroque undantia pectora felle', André, *Couleur*, 51 f.

17. alio liuentia lumina flectat: *pectora flectas* at *Theb.* 8. 119 conveys submission, whereas *flectat* here implies evil intent: *lumina* coheres perfectly, and matches the root notion in *Inuidia*. Markland cites, *inter alia*, *S.* 5. 1. 138-41 'quis iussit iniquas / aeternum bellare deas? nullamne notauit / illa domum, toruo quam non haec lumine figat / protinus et saeua proturbet gaudia dextra?' Common dactylic words, especially in the fifth foot of a hexameter, are easily interchangeable in copying: for the reverse corruption, *lumina* for *pectora*, see Man. 1. 416, corrected by Bentley.

18-19. alba / Atropos: for the propitious colour cf. 4. 3. 146 'candidae Sorores'. It is usually by the colour of the threads they spin that the Fates indicate their approval; white, purple, and gold augur well: see *RE* xv. 2482 (Eitrem).

19. lauro: the arrangement of the double *et* ('et alba Atropos et patrius ... Apollo') requires the phrase *senium longaeque decus uirtutis* to be the sole object of *promisit*, and so *laurus* (or *lauros*), adopted by all modern editors, cannot be right. Phillimore (apparatus) suggested *alebat* for *et alba* to remove the awkwardness of the double *et*, but *alba* is appropriate in the context (see previous n.). The wishes for longevity and *uirtus* (18) are conventional, whereas *laurus* would specifically refer to military glory or poetic achievement, neither of which is mentioned in the concluding prayer for blessings on Menecrates' children (55 ff.). Bay, believed to possess prophetic properties, was regarded as the material whereby Apollo made known his wishes: cf. 4. 3. 118 and see on 6. 98. Hence *lauro* expresses the agency whereby Apollo makes his promise: cf. Lucr. 1. 739 (= 5. 112) 'Pythia quae tripodi a Phoebi lauroque profatur', Aristoph. *Plut.* 39 τί δῆτα Φοῖβος ἔλακεν ἐκ τῶν στεμμάτων.

20. Ausoniae pater augustissimus urbis: the language of Augustan propaganda: cf. 4. 2. 18, 5. 37.

21. ius ... tergeminae ... prolis: the *ius trium liberorum* originated with Augustus' legislation to promote the birth-rate: see on 4. 7. 33–40, Kaser, i. 724 f. It was granted sparingly to the ineligible as a favour: cf. Plin. *Epist.* 2. 13. 8 (an emperor judged by Sherwin-White to be Nerva) 'trium liberorum ius ... quamquam parce et cum delectu daret ... indulsit', 10. 95 (Trajan) 'quam parce haec beneficia tribuam'. This grant, which Martial received separately from Titus and Domitian ('Musarum pretium ... mearum', 2. 92. 2), features in the list of successes for which he boasts that he was envied (9. 97. 5–6). We hear mostly of favours to married people who were childless through natural causes, as Pliny at *Epist.* 10. 2 and Voconius Romanus at *Epist.* 2. 13. 8: cf. Mart. 2. 91. 5 f. 'quod fortuna uetat fieri permitte uideri'. Galba granted this privilege only temporarily, 'ad certum praefinitumque tempus' (Suet. *Galba* 14. 3). A condition was attached to the grant which Trajan made to Suetonius (Plin. *Epist.* 10. 95 'ea condicione qua adsueui').

22–3. Lucina pium ... / intrauit repetita larem: by fulfilling the prerequisites for the *ius trium liberorum* Menecrates demonstrates his family's *pietas*. Lucina, goddess of childbirth, attended every woman in confinement; Latte, *RE* xiii. 1648, compares the phenomenon of the male *genius* and the female *Iuno*: cf. Plaut. *Truc.* 476 'ut uenerem Lucinam meam'.

24. donis numquam mutata sacratis: St. prays that in succeeding generations Menecrates' male descendants will each themselves father three children, thus perpetuating the family and sustaining the standard implied in the emperor's grant of the privilege. The privilege (*dona*) is *sacrata* in the first instance because it comes from Domitian (see on 4 *Pr.* 6) and then because Lucina's ministrations turn the fiction into a reality. For *mutare* with the ablative of respect cf. Hor. *Ars* 60 'siluae foliis ... mutantur' and Brink's note. For the encomiastic expectation that the family line will continue cf. 3. 1. 177 ff. (quoted on 13–14 above).

25–6. et proles ... aucta uirili / robore: *et* gives the second reason why St. calls Menecrates *macte* (14). Male stock ensures the continuity of the family name; at Virg. *A.* 6. 784 Rome is blessed with men to be her citizens and warriors, 'felix prole uirum'.

26. sed ... laetanda et uirgo: *et* is emphatic. A daughter born to a *iuuenis* guarantees that he will see grandchildren in his own lifetime. Between twelve and fifteen years is estimated to have been the average age of marriage for Roman girls: see on l. 60 'pube sub ipsa'.

27. aptior: a weakened comparative, since no woman can possess *uirtus*; St. uses the attributive polar comparative to stress the antithesis, in default of a μέν ... δέ construction in Latin: cf. 4. 7. 11–12 above, Gell. 16. 18. 4 'longior mensura uocis ῥυθμός dicitur, altior μέλος.' Since the girl may be expected to bear grandchildren for Menecrates before the boys beget them, *citius* may be a genuine comparative which thus attracts the other epithet into the same degree. Markland, objecting that this line disrupts the sequence of thought, recommended that it be relocated after l. 32 or else deleted. But a neat *sententia*, predicting that Menecrates' children will realize their father's hopes for them, fits well enough here.

28. maternis Helene iam digna palaestris: Helen's mother was Leda, wife of Tyndareos, king of Sparta. Girls as well as boys participated in the activities of the Spartan *palaestra*: cf. Prop. 3. 14. 1 f. 'multa tuae, Sparte, miramur iura palaestrae, / sed mage uirginei tot bona gymnasii', Xen. *Lac.* 1. 4, Eur. *Andr.* 595, Plut. *Lyc.* 14. Even before she could walk (cf. *reptabat*) Helen was beautiful enough to be worthy of the palaestra.

29. Amyclaeos ... fratres: the Dioscuri are first recorded as Helen's brothers at *Il.* 3. 238, although Helen is not included there among Leda's children: see *RE* vii. 2826 ff. (Pfuhl). Amyclae, on the R. Eurotas, is recorded as the home of Pollux at Virg. *G.* 3. 89 'Amyclaei ... Pollucis', and of both the Dioscuri at Ov. *Her.* 8. 71, *Theb.* 7. 413: see *RE* i. 1999 s.v. Amyklaios 2 (Jessen).

31. admouere iubar mediae duo sidera lunae: Menecrates' sons are like two stars flanking the moon. The usual encomiastic topos is that the subject surpasses other people like the moon (or the sun) outshining other heavenly bodies: cf. Sappho 34 L-P ἄστερες μὲν ἀμφὶ κάλαν σελάνναν / ἂψ ἀπυκρύπτοισι φάεννον εἶδος / ὅπποτα πλήθοισα μάλιστα λάμπηι / γᾶν, Hermocles, *Hymn Dem.* 11 f. (= *Coll. Alex.* 174. 11 f. Powell) ὅμοιον ὥσπερ οἱ φίλοι μὲν ἀστέρες, / ἥλιος δ' ἐκεῖνος, *S.* 2. 6. 36 'quantum praecedit clara minores / luna faces', Hor. *O.* 1. 12. 46 ff. 'micat inter omnis / Iulium sidus uelut inter ignis / luna minores' with N–H. But St. wants to imply not that Menecrates' daughter eclipses his sons but that all three are a credit to him, i.e. the moon sheds its soft light while the stars shine brilliantly around it. *iubar*, used originally of the morning star, is first applied to other heavenly bodies by Ovid: see Tarrant on Sen. *Ag.* 463.

32. queror haud facilis ... questus: *queror* frequently governs an internal accusative of the type *uerba queror* (Ov. *Met.* 9. 304) or *iusta queror* (St. *S.* 3. 2. 78): see *OLD* s.v. *queror* 1d. Our example, however, seems to be the only instance where *queror* appears in the *figura etymologica* whereby verb and substantive are derived from the same stem (L–H–S 38 f.). This figure can accommodate an epithet to qualify the cognate noun (as here): cf. Cic. *Agr.* 2. 44 'cur non eosdem cursus cucurrerunt', E. C. Woodcock, *A New Latin Syntax* (London, 1959), 8. The litotes in *haud facilis ... questus* accommodates the collocation of *facilis*, which implies compliance, with *questus*, which implies disagreement: cf. Hor. *O.* 2. 12. 26 'facili saeuitia negat', *TLL* vi. 1. 61. 22 ff.

33. quantum irascuntur amantes: St.'s anger demonstrates his affection for Menecrates: cf. Ter. *Andr.* 555 'amantium irae amoris integratio est', Otto, *Sprichwörter*, no. 76. St.'s show of displeasure at having heard the news of Menecrates' child's birth 'on the grapevine' ('uulgari ... fama') instead of by special messenger ('ingenti non uenit nuntia cursu / littera', 36–7) is both an excuse for his delay in writing the poem and a literary device to make the poet seem independent and forthright, thereby relieving the sustained encomium and simultaneously creating some opposition for the children's charms to conquer: compare the *ira* which St. feigns in his *hendecasyllabi iocosi* to Plotius Grypus (4. 9).

35. uagiret: the *uox propria* of babies' crying: cf. Cic. *Sen.* 83 'ut ex hac aetate repuerascam et in cunis uagiam', Sen. *Dial.* 7. 26. 4 'uos ... uagire uelut infantes miserrimos', *OLD* s.v. *uagio*.

39. Albano ... cadum sordentem ... fumo: wine was matured in a *fumarium*, i.e. an upper room situated above the *focus*: cf. Colum. 1. 6. 20 'apothecae recte superponentur his locis, unde plerumque fumus exoritur, quoniam uina celerius uetustescunt, quae fumi quodam tenore praecoquem maturitatem trahunt', Hor. *Sat.* 2. 4. 72 'rectius Albanam fumo ·duraueris uuam', Mart. 10. 36. 1 ff. 'inproba Massiliae quidquid fumaria cogunt, / accipit aetatem quisquis ab igne cadus, / a te, Munna, uenit', Blümner, 71. Hence a sooty container symbolizes a mature wine: cf. Hor. *O.* 3. 8. 9 ff. 'hic dies anno redeunte festus / corticem adstrictum pice dimouebit / amphorae fumum bibere institutae / consule Tullo', Tib. 2. 1. 27 'fumosos ... Falernos', Ov. *F.* 5. 518 'fumoso condita uina cado', Mart. 12. 82. 11 'fumosae ... lagonae', Juv. 5. 33 ff. 'cras bibet Albanis aliquid de montibus aut de / Setinis, cuius patriam titulumque senectus / deleuit multa ueteris fuligine testae'.

40. creta signare diem: the phrase *cantu signare diem* (M) accords with the precept that the actual day of birth should be praised (see on 4. 7. 31), but there are three difficulties associated with *cantu*: (i) *signare*, implying a means of identification which is visibly perceptible, is uneasy with *cantu*; Goodyear's *insignire* would solve this difficulty, but two others remain: (ii) the sequence is muddled, moving from music (*redimire chelyn*, 38) to wine (39) and back to music; (iii) *cantu* is repetitive before *cano* (41). *creta* (Bentley, n. on Hor. *O.* 1. 36. 10), referring to the custom of using white markers against special days (see on 4. 6. 18), is appropriate in the context and also implies a colour-contrast (typical of St.) with *sordentem ... fumo* (39).

43–4. hilaris circumstat turba tuorum / defensatque patrem: cf. 10 'turba nepotum', 3. 1. 178 'agmine blando'. The military image in *defensat* and *agmine* (44) conveys a sentimental picture of Menecrates' children as his bodyguard.

45. Di patrii: collectively all the gods with Neapolitan connections; then Apollo (47), Ceres (50), and the Dioscuri (52) are specifically mentioned: cf. Virg. *G.* 1. 498 f. 'di patrii Indigetes et Romule Vestaque mater, / quae Tuscum Tiberim et Romana Palatia seruas'. The *Reihengebet* and reiterated vocatives (*tu*, 47; *tuque*, 50; *uos*, 52) resume the hymnic form with which the poem began.

46. Abantia classis: the Abantes were the legendary inhabitants of Euboea, which was called Ἀβαντίς after them: cf. Hom. *Il.* 2. 536, 541 ff., 4. 464, Hes. fr. 296 Merkelbach and West, *RE* i. 13 (Toepffer). For Euboean colonization on the Bay of Naples see on 4. 3. 65.

47. ductor: ἡγήτωρ. *dux* was originally used only for ὁδηγός; the Ennian phrase *ductores Danaum* translates Δαναῶν ἡγήτορες (Hom. *Il.* 11. 816): see M. Leumann, *Kl. Schr.* (Zürich, 1959), 147 n. 1. Hence *ductor* is suitable for Apollo as οἰκιστής. His special connection with seafaring and the role played by the Delphic oracle in the colonizing movement lie behind his role as patron deity of colonization: see *RE* ii. 18 (Wernicke). For Neapolitan coins depicting aspects of the cult of Delphic Apollo see A. Sambon, *Les Monnaies antiques de l'Italie* (Paris, 1903), 246 ff. (Apollo's head), 271 ff. (his tripod).

48. uolucrem: Venus' dove, sent by Apollo to show the way to the first Euboean settlers: cf. 3. 5. 79 f. 'Parthenope cui mite solum trans aequora uectae / ipse Dionaea monstrauit Apollo columba', Vell. Pat. 1. 4. 1 'huius classis cursum esse directum alii columbae antecedentis uolatu ferunt, alii nocturno aeris sono'. The motif of birds guiding mortals to new lands, first attested in Greek sources at Hdt. 2. 55 (the Libyans), is traced by Norden, comm. on *Aen.* 6, pp. 173 f.

49. Eumelus: *Eumeliss* (M) was commonly read as *Eumelis*. A Eumelis is attested as eponymous god of a Neapolitan phratry (*IG* xiv. 715) Εὔμηλον θεὸν πατρῷον φρήτορσιν Εὐμηλειδῶν. He was commonly assumed to be the father of Parthenope, so that the statue was believed to be of Parthenope herself: see R. W. Peterson, *The Cults of Campania* (Rome, 1919), 170 n. 2, 184. But Housman, *CR* 20 (1906), 46 (= *Cl. Pap.* ii. 653), noting that Achelous was father of all the Sirens including Parthenope (Sil. 12. 33 f.), observes that M's reading points to *Eumelus*, 'whoever Eumelus may have been', since *-iss* is a common error in M for *-us*. *felix* thus gains point in conjunction with *Eumelus* (εὔμηλος = 'rich in sheep'). Who, then, was represented on the statue, worshipping Apollo's dove? Frère postulates the phratry-god: see *RE* vi. 1078 (Schiff). But a god ought to be receiving, not bestowing, worship. A hero, or a prominent Neapolitan citizen, seems more likely.

50. Actaea Ceres: the cult of Demeter, first brought to Cumae by the Chalcidians, was particularly associated with Attica because of the Eleusinian Mysteries. Hence St., describing a ritual akin to the Mysteries (see following n.), addresses the Ceres of Neapolitan cult by the epithet *Actaea*. Ceres was worshipped in Naples as Demeter Thesmophoros (*IG* xiv. 702). Torchlight dances occurred at the Attic Thesmophoria: cf. Aristoph. *Thesm.* 101 ff., 280 f., 1150 ff., L. Deubner, *Attische Feste*[2] (Hildesheim, 1966), 53 f. Torch-races were established in honour of Ceres when the Athenian Diotimos visited Naples in the fifth century BC (Timaeus, *FGrH* 566 F 98 = Schol. Lycophr. *Alex.* 732): see 1–3 n. Priestesses of the cult are attested at *IG* xiv. 702, 756a, 760, *CIL* x. 1812, and priestesses for the temple of Ceres at Rome were supplied from Naples and Velia (Cic. *Balb.*

55). The site of Ceres' temple in Naples has been identified by a votive deposit of terracotta figurines of Demeter dating from the fifth century BC, discovered in 1933 on the acropolis of the original Palaeopolis under the site of the Medical Faculty: see M. Napoli, *Napoli greco-romana* (Naples, 1959), 142.

51. uotiuam taciti quassamus lampada mystae: silent torch-carrying was part of the ritual in the mysteries of Demeter (*HHDem.* 59–61), reflecting Demeter's search for Kore as she roamed over the earth carrying lit torches (*HHDem.* 47 f.). Ritual silence was inspired by awe of the deity, and should be distinguished from the silence enjoined on initiates to prevent cult-secrets' being divulged: see Richardson on *HHDem.* 478 f. Ceres had her initiates (μύσται) also in Rome: cf. *CIL* vi. 32433 'Cereris ... mystes'. St. was apparently an initiate in the Neapolitan cult (cf. *quassamus*); Naples was after all his birthplace and his place of retirement.

52. Tyndaridae: the Dioscuri, sons of Tyndareus (see on 28 and 29). A Roman temple erected to them was incorporated into the church of San Paolo Maggiore in the ninth century but was almost totally destroyed in the earthquake of 1688; fragments remain in the façade. An inscription from the temple, copied in the fifteenth century (*IG* xiv. 714), records that the temple was begun by one Ti. Iulius Tarsus (presumably the recipient of a grant from the emperor Tiberius) and completed by a freedman named Pelagon; hence it can be dated to the first century AD. For the temple and inscription see L. Correra in *Atti Acc. Arch. Nap.* 23 (1905), 2. 220–1, A. Campana, *Arch. Cl.* 25–6 (1973–4), 84–102. The dedication of statues to the Dioscuri by two contestants in the Augustalia in AD 171 is attested by *IG* xiv. 748. A coin type depicting a beardless male face with a galloping horseman on the reverse is thought to represent the Dioscuri: see Sambon, op. cit. (on l. 47), 192.

52–3. horrenda Lycurgi / Taygeta: the mountain range of Taygetos, reaching a height of 2,200 m, dominates Sparta. In one tradition it was the birthplace of the Dioscuri (*HH* 17. 3, 33. 4). Lycurgus, the legendary Spartan lawgiver (*RE* xiii. 2442 ff. s.v. Lykurgos 7 [Kahrstedt]), was reputed to have appointed a place at the foot of Mt. Taygetos where weaklings were to be exposed (Plut. *Lyc.* 16. 1–2). Hence Taygetos, heavily wooded, is *horrenda* both for its gloomy appearance (cf. Liv. 9. 36. 1 'silua erat Ciminia ... inuia atque horrenda') and for its reputation. For the neuter plural termination, used here *metri gratia*, cf. Virg. *G.* 2. 488, Val. Fl. 4. 329, Sil. 4. 363.

53. umbrosae ... Therapnae: in Laconia, south-east of Sparta; the site of the most famous cult of the Dioscuri: see *RE* v. 1098 (Bethe), vA. 2359 f. (Bölte). Here and at 5. 3. 140 ('uirides ... Therapnae') it is wooded: cf. Colluthus 224 ναιομένην ὑπὸ δάσκιον οὔρεος ὕλην ... Θεράπνην. But Bölte (*RE* vA. 2353 f.) attributes this tradition to poetic fantasy, since Therapne is waterless and the soil is unsuitable for trees.

54. patriae: after the lengthy specification of the *di patrii* (45–53), St. makes his simple request. *patrii* (M) would be very awkward with *penates*, since an invocation of the tutelary gods of the household would be bathos after the preceding *Reihengebet*, and *hos* would be left without any obvious reference.

patrii as a vocative (= *di patrii*) would be very abrupt and unnatural. For a dative (*patriae*) after *seruare* cf. 3. 4. 101 f. (Earinus' prayer for Domitian) 'dominum . . . orbi seruare uelis'. See further Håkanson, 124 f.

55. fessam aeuo ... urbem: a play on the (later) name for the old settlement, Palaeopolis, contrasted with the new (*uiridique in nomine*, 56), i.e. Neapolis: see on ll. 1-3.

crebris ... laboribus: it is unclear whether St. had any particular vicissitudes in mind. The legend that the Cumaeans destroyed the original settlement out of jealousy for its prosperity (see on 1-3) would not alone account for *crebris*. It is more likely that St. is thinking of natural disasters, i.e. earthquakes and eruptions of Mt. Vesuvius; a serious earthquake is recorded in AD 62: cf. Tac. *Ann*. 15. 2, *CIL* x. 1406. Sen. *NQ* 6. 1. 2 dates this earthquake to 5 February 63, but his consular date is regarded as an interpolation and the date given by Tacitus, generally reliable on chronology, is to be preferred: see M. Hammond, *MAAR* 15 (1938), 29 f. There was evidence of previous volcanic activity: cf. Strabo 5. 4. 8, Vitr. 2. 6. 2, Diod. 4. 21, and see *RE* viiiA. 2436 (Radke). The eruption of AD 79 spread ash over the countryside as far as Misenum, 30 km west of Vesuvius (Plin. *Epist*. 6. 20. 13–16). This fall-out of ash was caused by a *nuée ardente* ('nubes atra et horrenda', Plin. *Epist*. 6. 20. 9) on the second day of the eruption: see H. Sigurdsson, S. Cashdollar, and S. R. J. Sparks, *AJA* 86 (1982), 49. Naples, between Vesuvius and Misenum, must have been affected.

57–8. St. follows his custom of citing father and maternal grandfather as worthy models for the rising generation: cf. 4. 4. 70 ff., 7. 43 ff. *nitor*, 'splendour', carries with it a hint of the wealth which has facilitated Pollius' elegant lifestyle: cf. 3. 3. 147 ff. 'quam diues in usus / natorum totoque uolens excedere censu, / testis adhuc largi nitor inde adsuetus Etrusci, / cui tua non humilis dedit indulgentia mores', 2. 2. 10 (of Pollius' wife) 'nitidae iuuenilis gratia Pollae'. St. is frank about the advantages which wealth can bring: cf. 'uoce opibusque iuuent' (56), 'et opes et origo' (59).

59. et opes et origo: in both categories St. is probably thinking of the girl's maternal grandfather. For a similar use of *origo* at 1. 4. 69, referring to Rutilius Gallicus' grandfather, see R. Syme, *Arctos* 18 (1984), 152 f. St. predicts that Menecrates' daughter will marry a senator; *origo* disguises the fact that the family was equestrian: see intro.

59–60. lampade prima / patricias intrare foris: a metaphor for marriage derived from the procession lit by *faces nuptiales* which led the bride to her new home: cf. 1. 2. 3 ff. 'procul ecce canoro / demigrant Helicone deae quatiuntque nouena / lampade sollemnem thalamis coeuntibus ignem'. St. is not implying that Menecrates' daughter will have more than one marriage, but that her family's wealth and connections will secure for her a marriage with an élite family at the earliest marriageable age (see next n.), whereas others only climb the social ladder in subsequent marriages.

60. pube sub ipsa: a Roman girl was deemed to reach maturity (and hence acquire the capacity to make a will) at twelve (Gaius, *Inst*. 2. 113). The average age of girls in the upper classes at the onset of puberty was thirteen, and the average age at marriage is estimated to have been between twelve and fifteen; marriage and consummation are both attested, although rarely, for girls who had not yet attained puberty: see K. Hopkins, *Population Studies* 18 (1965), 309–27.

61–2. inuicti Caesaris adsint / numina: a grant of the *latus clauus* from the emperor, which qualified a man to stand for senatorial office, was the established procedure for entering the senate from the time of Claudius: see Millar, *Emperor*, 290 ff., quoting this passage (293) as 'a reflection of the normal and gradual process of advancement into the senate'. Pliny asked this favour (probably of Nerva) for his friend Sextus Erucius (*Epist.* 2. 9. 2) 'ego Sexto latum clauum a Caesare nostro, ego quaesturam impetraui'.

62. limen pulsare: nowadays a threshold is notional, but in antiquity it was tangible, a raised block over which one stepped to enter the building, and hence came to be used by metonymy for the door itself: cf. Sil. 6. 73 'limina pulsabat tecti', *OLD* s.v. *limen* 2b. Visitors kicked against it to gain admission: cf. Callim. *H.* 2. 3 καὶ δή που τὰ θύρετρα καλῶι ποδὶ Φοῖβος ἀράσσει; the *uox propria* in Latin is *pulsare*: cf. Hor. *O.* 1. 4. 13 f. 'pallida Mors aequo pulsat pede pauperum tabernas / regumque turris', *S.* 5. 3. 209 ff. (St. following in his father's footsteps) 'me quoque uocalis lucos Boeotaque tempe / pulsantem, cum stirpe tua descendere dixi, / admisere deae'.

9

INTRODUCTION

This poem is addressed to Plotius Grypus on the occasion of the Saturnalia (4 *Pr.* 22): see *PIR* P 384, *RE* xxi. 593 f. s.v. Plotius 5 (Hoffmann). St.'s tone in this poem, combining familiarity and reproof, reflects the egalitarian atmosphere of the Saturnalia, when social inferiors were treated as equal to their superiors: cf. Hor. *Sat.* 2. 7. 4 'age, libertate Decembri ... utere', *Anth. Lat.* 395. 48 Riese 'nunc tibi cum domino ludere, uerna, licet'. Hence St. promises Grypus a *dignius opusculum* one day; meanwhile the convention of gift-giving at the Saturnalia (see on 23–45) provides him with the opportunity for a literary joke, 'hendecasyllabos quos Saturnalibus una risimus' (4 *Pr.* 22). Martial also writes poems dealing with Saturnalian presents: apart from the *Xenia* (Book 13) and *Apophoreta* (Book 14), which are short epigrams designed to accompany various gifts, he frequently satirizes the convention of gift-giving and attitudes towards it: cf. 4. 46, 88, 7. 53, 72.

Hendecasyllables recall Catullus and are evidently considered appropriate for Saturnalian jocularity: cf. *S.* 1. 6, also in hendecasyllables, describing Domitian's public feast for the Saturnalia. The hendecasyllables which Pliny composes in odd moments of *otium* embrace a wide variety of themes, some rather *risqué* (*petulantiora paulo*), and also of moods, including levity and indignation: cf. *Epist.* 4. 14. 3 'iocamur, ludimus, amamus, dolemus, querimur, irascimur, describimus aliquid modo pressius modo elatius, atque ipsa uarietate temptamus efficere, ut alia aliis quaedam fortasse omnibus placeant'. By ending Book 4 with a hendecasyllabic poem Catullan in inspiration, St. is asserting for the book as a whole a spirit of informality in pointed defiance of the critics of the *Siluae* (see on 4 *Pr.* 24 ff.).

The subject as well as the metre recalls Catullus, especially Poem 14 to Calvus, reproving him for a Saturnalian present of a volume of *pessimi poetae*. Specific verbal echoes (noted in the commentary) contribute to a highly 'literary' tone. This points up the exaggerated invective against Grypus' *libellus* which turns the poem into a satire on poor literary taste and the absence of social graces. The theme is predicated upon an elegant calque on Grypus' name. It is derived from γρύψ (= 'griffin'),[1] but the adjective γρυπός = *nasutus* ('hook-nosed'); *nasutus* has a secondary metaphorical meaning, describing a person with discerning taste: cf. Phaedr. 4. 7. 1 'tu qui nasute scripta destringis mea', Mart. 12. 37 'nasutus nimium cupis uideri, / nasutum uolo, nolo polyposum', 13. 2. 1 ff. 'nasutus sis usque licet, sis denique nasus, / quantum noluerat ferre rogatus Atlans ... non potes in nugas dicere plura meas / ipse ego quam dixi', 1. 3. 5 f. 'maiores nusquam rhonchi: iuuenesque senesque / et pueri nasum rhinocerotis habent', K. M. Coleman, *PACA* 14 (1978), 9 f. In all, the teasing note, familiar from Catullus (and also Cicero and Horace), is not meant to be taken seriously; but such geniality may be a subtle form of flattery.

Grypus' identity poses two problems, resulting in opposing views: (i) that he was equestrian, and held the post of *praefectus uehiculorum*: see Eck (1975), id., *Organisation*, 89–99; (ii) that he was senatorial and held an extraordinary appointment: see F. Bérard, *MEFR* 96 (1984), 259–324 (hereafter Bérard).

The text attesting Grypus' rank is 4 *Pr.* 21, where Grypus, compared with Julius Menecrates, is described as *maioris gradus iuueni[s]*. Menecrates, also young (*splendidum iuuenem*, 4 *Pr.* 19), was equestrian: cf. 4. 8. 59–62. The natural interpretation of *maioris gradus* is the obvious distinction between the *ordo equester* and *ordo senatorius*, i.e. *gradus* = *ordo*: cf. *TLL* vi. 2. 2152. 57 ff.[2] The alternative explanation is that Grypus was of higher equestrian status then Menecrates. In that case *splendidum iuuenem* (4 *Pr.* 19) would imply a contrast with the appellations *egregius*, *perfectissimus*, and *eminentissimus* which, by the end of the second century, came to distinguish grades of *equites* according to the seniority of their posts: see Millar, *Emperor*, 289 and n. 70. But *splendidus* is best taken as the regular epithet of an *eques* (*OLD* s.v. *splendidus* 4b) rather than indicating low equestrian rank, since in the prefatory notice to a book it would be rude for St. to imply that one of his equestrian patrons was inferior to another, whereas the distinction between *eques* and senator implies no disgrace to the *eques*. Furthermore, as noted by Bérard, 262, St. predicts that Menecrates' *opes et origo* (4. 8. 59) will secure a senatorial marriage for his daughter, and entry to the senate for his sons, which suggests that Menecrates was of high equestrian status. Hence Grypus was senatorial, and therefore cannot have held the equestrian post of *praefectus uehiculorum*. Eck, however, tries to reconcile Grypus' rank with the post of *praefectus uehiculorum*[3]

---

[1] γρύψ = 'gryps' = 'gryp(h)es' = 'gryp(h)us': see *TLL* vi. 2. 2340. 80 ff.

[2] Despite the classification of our passage at *TLL* vi. 2. 2152. 43, whereby *gradus* is equated with *auctoritas* or *dignitas*; but that would imply a slight to Menecrates.

[3] *praefectus uehiculorum* was equestrian: see Eck, *Organisation*, 90.

by arguing, (1975), 384, that Grypus, having completed the equestrian *tres militiae* and held the post of *praefectus uehiculoruom*, subsequently entered the senate. Since a man was technically a *iuuenis* up to the age of forty (Eck [1975], 384 n. 108), Grypus could be old enough to have qualified for the senate in this way before St. wrote the preface to Book 4.

Grypus' unusual *cognomen* suggests that he is most likely to be the son of Plotius Grypus[4] (*PIR* P 385, *RE* xxi. 593 s.v. Plotius 4 [Hanslik], W. Eck, *Senatoren von Vespasian bis Hadrian* [Munich, 1970], 104), who was suffect consul in 88 (April: *CIL* vi. 2065 b 65; October: *ILS* 5161 k). Eck [1975], 383, suggests that he was the son of Plotius Firmus (*PIR* P 382, *RE* xxi. 592 f. s.v. Plotius 2 [Klass]), who was *praefectus praetorio* under Otho (Tac. *Hist.* 1. 46. 1, 81. 2, 2. 46. 2, 49. 3) and who Eck suggests may have been the consular's brother; but the *cognomen* is more likely to be inherited from a father than bestowed by an uncle. Similarly, if E. Champlin is right in identifying Pegasus the jurist as a Plotius (*ZPE* 32 [1978], 269–78), Grypus was probably the jurist's nephew rather than his son. But even though Grypus was probably the consular's son, alternative possibilities remain for his rank since a senator's son was technically equestrian until he entered the senate, and might even choose to retain equestrian rank permanently: cf. Seneca's brother Mela (*PIR*[2] A 613).

Related to this issue is Grypus' career (15–19). His initial forensic activity (15–16), delivering speeches in the fora and before the centumviral court (see on 4. 4. 43), took place before (*priusquam*, 16) he received an appointment from the emperor (17–19) 'te Germanicus arbitrum sequenti / annonae dedit omniumque late / praefecit stationibus uiarum'. Was this one post or two? The first clause describes supervision of the corn-supply, specifically provisions for a mobile train (*sequenti annonae*). Hence *sequenti* (*OLD* s.v. *sequor* 11) suggests that the first area of control, like the second, was connected with official journeys.

As often, St. paraphrases the technical terms designating stages in his addressee's *curriculum vitae*: cf. 4. 4. 59 f., 7. 47. *annona* designates the army's provisions, and hence the commissariat accompanying the emperor and his military retinue on a journey: cf. Plin. *Pan.* 20. 3 (of Trajan) 'nullis in exigendis uehiculis tumultus, nullum circa hospitia fastidium: annona quae ceteris'. *hospitium*, originally the technical term for hospitality extended towards authorized persons on journeys, comes to mean a stopping-place along the route (= *mansio*, σταθμός): see the discussion by S. Mitchell, *JRS* 66 (1976), 127.[5] Hence *stationibus* is used here, *metri gratia*, for *mansionibus*. Thus

---

[4] The father's *praenomen* is variously attested: L. (*ILS* 5161 k), D. (*Fasti Potentini*: see N. Alfieri, *Ath.* ns 26 [1948], 110–34); D. at *CIL* vi. 2065 b 65 is a supplement. The *Fasti Potentini* make mistakes with *praenomina*: cf. M. Arrius Celsus for (Ti. Iulius Candidus) Marius Celsus, *cos. suff.* 86 (*PIR*[2] I 241); Minicius Faustinus, *cos. suff.* 91 (*PIR*[2] M 609) whose *praenomen*, given as D. on the *Fasti Potentini*, should be Cn., as on the military diploma (*AE* 1961, 319).

[5] In the city a *statio* was where people stopped to relax: cf. Plin. *Epist.* 1. 13. 2 (of people delaying before going in to a recitation) 'plerique in stationibus sedent tempusque audiendi fabulis conterunt', 2. 9. 5 (soliciting support) 'itaque prenso amicos, supplico, ambio, domos stationesque circumeo'.

while Domitian was travelling Grypus arranged the commissariat and accommodation for the imperial train. These arrangements, however, fell under the responsibilities of the *procurator*: cf. Caelius Florus, *procurator*, who made arrangements for Trajan's journey through Lycia (*IGR* iii. 738 = *TAM* 2. 3, no. 908, sect. IVa): see F. Millar, *JRS* 53 (1963), 199.

But was Grypus in charge of journeys in Italy or abroad? The title *Germanicus* to designate the emperor (17) might be considered appropriate to a military context, implying that Grypus was involved with arrangements for Domitian's campaign against the Sarmatae, but metrical considerations seem more compelling. Further, *omnium ... late ... uiarum* is too general to refer to a military campaign in a particular area (Bérard, 280–1 n. 70), and since journeys through provinces were supervised by the individual *procuratores* Grypus' sphere of influence seems to have been Italy.[6]

Eck (1975), 384 f., deduces from *praefecit* (19) that Grypus held a *praefectura*. But *praeficio* is not necessarily a technical term: cf. Cic. *Plan.* 62 'sin ... emimus quem uilicum imponeremus, quem pecori praeficeremus', *OLD* s.v. *praeficio* 1c. Eck asserts, (1975), 384, that Domitian did not create extraordinary posts for senators, and that a young senator lacking in experience would not have been extrusted with important dispositions in a military campaign. But since Grypus' post was apparently confined to Italy, it is possible that he was *praepositus annonae* (Bérard, 300 f.), organizing Domitian's departure from Italy in 92 for the campaign against the Sarmatae.[7] Another possibility remains: not only campaigns but also tours of inspection involved complex administration for feeding and accommodating the entourage of officials, soldiers (the emperor was always accompanied by an *ala*), and household retainers, especially if the emperor had pretentious tastes: cf. Philo, *Leg.* 252–3 (Gaius' projected visit to Alexandria).[8]

The alternatives can be summarized as follows. The duties which St. describes at 4. 9. 17–19 correspond to those of *praefectus uehiculorum*, but to have held that post Grypus must be understood to have entered the senate only afterwards. But if he was a senator we may assume with Bérard an

---

[6] Eck, *Organisation*, 99, deduces that the jurisdiction of the *praefectus uehiculorum* was restricted to Italy in the 1st and 2nd c. AD, but nevertheless conjectures elsewhere, (1975), 384, that Grypus went north.

[7] Since Domitian is reputed to have delegated command in battle to his generals (Dio. 67. 6) it is not certain that he led the Sarmatian campaign himself.

[8] Domitian was a demanding traveller: Pliny, having praised Trajan for his modest travelling requirements (*Pan.* 20. 3, cit. above), contrasts his behaviour with Domitian's demands and extravagance on his return journey from the east in 93 (*Pan.* 20. 4) 'quam dissimilis nuper alterius principis transitus, si tamen transitus ille, non populatio fuit, cum abactus hospitium exereret, omniaque dextera laeuaque perusta et attrita ... persuadendum prouinciis erat illud iter Domitiani fuisse, non principis'. Even Domitian's mode of transport was different (Suet. *Dom.* 19) 'in expeditione et agmine equo rarius, lectica assidue uectus est'. Germanicus provides a precedent for a member of the imperial house choosing a personal aide to make his travelling-arrangements: cf. his 'requisitions edict' entrusting arrangements for his visit to Egypt in AD 19 κατὰ τὴν Βαιβίου τοῦ ἐμοῦ φίλου καὶ γραμματέως προσταγήν (E–J no. 320 = Zucker and Wilamowitz, *SBA* 1911. 796–7), i.e. Baebius (*PIR*² B 9) was an *amicus* (and apparently *ab epistulis*) of Germanicus.

extraordinary appointment, *praepositus annonae*, either during the Sarmatian campaign or for a civilian tour. If Grypus had distinguished himself in the *tres militiae* it is perhaps odd that St., so quick to mention his patrons' honours, does not say so; indeed, he implies that Grypus was engaged in a forensic career when Domitian chose him. On balance, the likelihood that he was the consular's son, and hence eligible by birth for senatorial rank, makes it easier to suppose an extraordinary post. Since he is nowhere mentioned outside this poem and its prefatory notice, we cannot know whether his later career crowned this precocious success.

1. **iocus iste:** the diction immediately establishes the parallel with the relationship between Catullus and Caluus: cf. Cat. 50. 4 ff. 'scribens uersiculos uterque nostrum / ludebat numero modo hoc modo illoc, / reddens mutua per iocum atque uinum', 14. 6 f. 'isti di mala multa dent clienti, / qui tantum tibi misit impiorum'. Hence, although by this time *iste* is often virtually equivalent to *hic*, it here retains its second-person connotations and implies derision.

1–2. **libellum... libello:** cf. Cat. 14. 12 ff. 'di magni, horribilem et sacrum libellum! / quem tu scilicet ad tuum Catullum / misti, continuo ut die periret, / Saturnalibus, optimo dierum'. For the rhetorical figure cf. Quint. 9. 3. 36–7 'interim uariatur casibus haec et generibus retractatio: "magnus est dicendi labor, magna res" ... fit casibus modo hoc schema quod πολύπτωτον uocant'. Where, as here, the repeated word occurs in the same place in successive lines, the tone is often mocking: cf. Mart. 4. 46. 1 f. 'Saturnalia diuitem Sabellum / fecerunt: merito tumet Sabellus'. See L–H–S 707 f., Lausberg, 328, p. 646, E. Breazale, *Stud. Phil. Univ. N. Carolina* 14 (1917), 306 ff. An autograph copy was a suitable present at the Saturnalia or for a birthday: cf. Mart. 5. 18. 4 'praeter libellos uernulas nihil misi', 10. 18(17). 1 ff. 'Saturnalicio Macrum fraudare tributo / frustra, Musa, cupis ... queritur nugas obticuisse meas', *S.* 2. 3. 62 (to Melior) 'haec tibi parua quidem genitali luce paramus'.

3. **urbanum:** an element of sophistication will redeem a tasteless *iocus* and elevate it to wit: see E. S. Ramage, *Urbanitas: Ancient Sophistication and Refinement* (Oklahoma, 1973), 120 f. For the notion that a witty insult manifests *urbanitas* cf. Cic. *Cael.* 6 'maledictio ... nihil habet propositi praeter contumeliam; quae si petulantius iactatur, conuicium, si facetius, urbanitas nominatur'. In St.'s phrase Catullan reminiscence is again paramount, *urbanus* implying an awareness of what is socially appropriate: cf. Cat. 39. 7 f. '[Egnatius] hunc habet morbum, / neque elegantem, ut arbitror, neque urbanum'. In particular St. is alluding to the breach of literary taste perpetrated by Suffenus (Cat. 22. 2, 9 ff.) 'homo est uenustus et dicax et urbanus ... haec cum legas tu, bellus ille et urbanus / Suffenus unus caprimulgus aut fossor / rursus uidetur'.

4. **si post hoc aliquid mihi remittas:** the subjunctive distances the likelihood that Grypus can redeem himself, and contrasts with the fact of his tastelessness expressed by the indicative in the next conditional clause (5). For a subjunctive in the protasis and *possum* in the indicative in the apodosis see L–H–S 327. The echo at the end ('ne ... remittas', 54–5) is

also a Catullan feature: see J. Vahlen, *Opusc. Acad.* (Leipzig, 1908), ii. 215–34; here the echo constitutes the witty denouement: St., having demanded recompense from Grypus, asks him not to make it in hendecasyllables.

5. **Grype:** the reiterated vocative in the same position in the line is a feature of epigram which serves to focus the reader's attention on the addressee: cf. Cat. 25. 1, 4, Mart. 1. 11. 2, 4 (and *passim*) with Citroni's n.

perseueras: punning on the derivation from *seuerus*, to create oxymoron with *ludere*: St. suggests that Grypus is laying on the joke with a heavy hand. For the opposition of *seuerus* to *iocus* cf. Plaut. *Poen.* 1169 f. 'quod ego dixi per iocum, / id euenturum esse et seuerum ac serium'.

6. **licet ... computemus:** St. suggests that they add up what their respective gifts amount to: cf. *CIL* ix. 2689 from Aesernia, recording a dialogue between serving-wench and traveller calculating the account, which begins 'copo: computemus'.

7–10. The motif of listing the external features of the *libelli* is derived from Catullus' assessment of what Suffenus' book looked like (Cat. 22. 6–8), combined with the agonistic element of a comparison between the two.

7. **purpureus:** the trimmings on the outside of a papyrus roll could be stained for smart editions: the *paenula* (διφθέρα, a protective cover); *lora* (thongs for fastening, Cat. 22. 7); *umbilici* (rollers; see on l. 8); *titulus* (σίλλυβος, index). Cf. Mart. 3. 2. 7 ff. 'cedro nunc licet ambules perunctus / et frontis gemino decens honore / pictis luxurieris umbilicis / et te purpura delicata uelet / et cocco rubeat superbus index', 11. 1. 2 '[liber] cultus Sidone non cotidiana', 1. 117. 16, 10. 93. 4., and see Birt, *Buchwesen*, 64 ff., *Abriß*, 329 ff.

nouus ... charta: fresh papyrus was highly esteemed: cf. Cat. 22. 4 ff. 'puto esse ego illi milia aut decem aut plura / perscripta, nec sic ut fit in palimpseston / relata: cartae regiae nouae bibli', 'royal sheets of new papyrus', and see R. G. M. Nisbet, *PCPhS* 24 (1978), 96 f. Papyrus could be reused by washing off the ink with a sponge: see Birt, *Abriß*, 290; even a moistened finger could erase non-metallic ink: see H. Erman in *Mélanges Nicole* (Geneva, 1905), 119 ff. Hence palimpsest (παλίμψηστος) can be either scraped parchment or washed papyrus. When Cicero praises Trebatius' economy in a letter of 53 BC he must be referring to papyrus (*Fam.* 7. 18. 2) 'quod in palimpsesto [scribis], laudo parsimoniam tuam'.

8. **binis decoratus umbilicis:** St.'s book is evidently superior to the normal variety with only one *umbilicus*. Properly the navel or umbilical cord, it is used in a transferred sense of objects resembling the navel, i.e. central protrusions (cf. ὀμφαλός): cf. Cic. *Ver.* 4. 106 (of Henna) 'qui locus, quod in media est insula situs, umbilicus Siciliae nominatur'. When a Roman book was closed, the centre was a hollow portion in the middle, and a protrusion would be formed by the boss on the end of the roller around which the papyrus was wound. When a book was stored in a bookseller's pigeon-hole, or else in a *capsa*, the boss would form a handle for pulling it out of storage; twin bosses (i.e. one at each end) would be unnecessary. But Professor Julian Brown has pointed out to me that a book which was primarily meant for display (the ancient equivalent of the

coffee-table publication) might well boast two bosses; and St.'s book, with its scarlet dust-jacket, appears to have been such an edition: cf. Mart. 3. 2. 9 f. 'pictis luxurieris umbilicis, et te purpura delicata uelet'. More than one *umbilicus* for a volume is also implied at Mart. 1. 66. 11, 4. 89. 2, 5. 6. 15, 8. 61. 4. The phrase *usque ad umbilicum* (or *umbilicos*) means reaching the end of a roll ('right down to the boss[es]'), i.e. it comes also to denote the hollow centre: cf. Mart. 4. 89. 1 f. 'ohe, iam satis est, ohe, libelle, / iam peruenimus usque ad umbilicos'. Birt, *Abriß*, 329, takes *umbilicus* as the rod which formed the roller, but it would surely be nonsense to speak of two rollers for a single scroll. Frère, ad loc., envisages a hollow cylinder which was slipped inside the scroll to protect it from dust and to be used as a roller; being hollow it could accommodate another one. But a dust-jacket inside seems superfluous, and *decoratus* implies visible embellishment, not merely a useful gadget. Lucian speaks of gilded ὀμφαλοί, which surely must have been visible to be worth gilding; they too occur in conjunction with a brightly coloured dust-jacket (διφθέρα): cf. Lucian, *Merc. Cond.* 41 χρυσοῖ μὲν οἱ ὀμφαλοί, πορφυρᾶ δὲ ἔκτοσθεν ἡ διφθέρα; cf. also, of a single ὀμφαλός, Lucian, ibid. and *Ind.* 7.

9. praeter me: the elliptical use of the pronoun instead of noun and possessive adjective sounds colloquial; it probably develops by analogy with *sine* (= 'without [the help of]'): cf. Prop. 3. 23. 5 'illae iam sine me norant placare puellas', *OLD* s.v. *sine* 4. St.'s *libellus* required his personal contribution in composing the poems, as well as the cost of the raw materials. What sort of book was this de luxe *libellus*? Everywhere else in the *Siluae*, *libellus* describes individual poems (1 *Pr.* 3, 17, 28, 2 *Pr.* 16, 3 *Pr.* 3, 12, 24), and a whole book is always *liber* (2 *Pr.* 4, 22, 3 *Pr.* 8, 4 *Pr.* 1, 3, 9, 33). But a single poem would not constitute a suitable gift at the Saturnalia, when whole books were recommended (cf. Mart. 14. 183–96), and it is clear that even Grypus' paltry gift was a collection of writings (see on 20). It is also clear from Martial 5. 6 that a selection from a *liber* could be issued in a smart edition: see White (1974), 45. The term *libellus* in Martial can be a synonym for *liber*, but always with deprecatory or apologetic overtones: cf. 5. 2. 5 f., where the first four books (*libellos*) are contrasted with the fifth (*liber*), and see E. T. Sage, *TAPhA* 50 (1919), 168. St.'s use of *libellus* here is modelled on Catullus, especially 14. 12 'horribilem et sacrum libellum', where a book of some size is indicated by its contents ('tot ... poetis', 5). A de luxe edition of Martial's Book 1 costs five denarii, i.e. twenty sesterces (1. 117. 17). A copy of Book 13 (*Xenia*), which is half as long, costs four sesterces, but at two sesterces it would still make a profit (13. 3. 2 ff.). Since St. is citing a cost-price with no profit-margin (hence the force of *praeter me*), if we envisage a *libellus* the length of Martial's *Xenia* ten asses (= 2.5 sesterces) suggests very costly materials. De luxe materials would merit professional copying; either St. had a trained slave whose duties included copying, or else he borrowed the services of someone else's slave, just as on occasion copying was done for Cicero by Atticus' slaves: see R. Sommer, *Hermes* 61 (1926), 389–422, summarized by E. J. Kenney, *CHCL* ii. 20. If St. did not have his own copyist, any cost involved in copying must be included in *decussis*. At any rate (despite

Vollmer) *praeter me* seems unlikely to mean that St. copied his poetry himself.

decussis: from Plautus onwards (*con*)*sto* is found with the ablative to express price (L–H–S 129). The anomalous ending here is the indeclinable form, regular in the singular when there is no adjective to impose declension (as at Pers. 5. 191 'et centum Graecos curto centusse licetur'): cf. Lucil. 1153 Marx, Var. *LL* 9. 81, *Men.* 404 Bücheler (= Gell. 15. 19. 2), and see *TLL* v. 1. 248. 35 ff.

10. tu rosum tineis situque putrem: *tu* is emphatic, contrasting with *noster* (*libellus*), 7; it is separated from the verb (*donas*) by twelve lines of hyperbole categorizing the shortcomings of Grypus' gift. A book long unused must have been outdated and unpopular. The book-worm, ἐχθίστη Μούσαις σεληδηφάγε, is the subject of a vehement epigram attributed to Euenus (*Anth. Pal.* 9. 251). Worms damaged papyrus extensively: for worm-holes on a piece of papyrus see E. G. Turner, *Greek Papyri: an Introduction*[2] (Oxford, 1980), pl. V (= P. Oxy. 1803 ed. Grenfell–Hunt = R. A. Pack, *The Greek and Latin Literary Texts from Graeco-Roman Egypt*[2] [Ann Arbor, Mich., 1965], 1826). The consumption of unfashionable literature by bookworms is a topos: cf. Hor. *Epist.* 1. 20. 12 'aut tineas pasces taciturnus inertis', Ov. *Pont.* 1. 1. 72 'conditus ut tineae carpitur ore liber', Mart. 6. 61. 7 'quam multi tineas pascunt blattasque diserti', 14. 37 (a threat levelled by a bookcase) 'selectos nisi das mihi libellos, / admittam tineas trucesque blattas'. Worms and rot are habitually named as sources of destruction for cloth (perhaps a satiric topos): cf. Var. *Men.* 227 Bücheler 'singulos lectos stratos ubi habuimus, amisimus propter cariem et tineam', Hor. *Sat.* 2. 3. 118 f. 'stragula uestis, / blattarum ac tinearum epulae, putrescat in arca'. Plin. *NH* 13. 86 quotes from the Republican historian, L. Cassius Hemina, describing the discovery of a box buried on the Janiculum which contained papyri from the reign of Numa (= Hem. *Hist.* fr. 37), 'in eo lapide insuper libros insitos fuisse, propterea arbitrarier, non conputuisse. et libros citratos fuisse, propterea arbitrarier, tineas non tetigisse'; for the application of cedar-oil as a preservative see Turner, *Greek Papyri*, 3.

11–13. *charta emporetica* was a cheap grade of papyrus, 'inutilis scribendo' (Plin. *NH* 13. 76), which was used for wrapping purchases: see N. Lewis, *Papyrus in Classical Antiquity* (Oxford, 1974), 46, 95. This becomes a topos for the fate of bad literature: cf. the story of the comedian Alexandrides who, if any of his plays failed to win, gave them to a merchant to cut up (Athen. 9. 374 A), and see P. Parsons, *PP* 23 (1968), 287–90 (but see on 13 below). In the Roman poets olives, spices, perfumes (not here), and fish are the most common commodities with which bad literature is threatened: cf. Cat. 95. 8, Hor. *Epist.* 2. 1. 269 f., Pers. 1. 43, Mart. 3. 2. 3–5, 50. 9, 4. 86. 8, 13. 1. 1, Sid. Apoll. *Carm.* 9. 318–28.

11. Libycis madent oliuis: olive plantations were encouraged in Africa under the Lex Manciana (*CIL* viii. 25902, 25943) and the import of their oil to Rome was particularly fostered by Trajan and Hadrian: cf. Juv. 5. 88 f. with Courtney's note, and see L. Foucher, *Hadrumetum* (Paris, 1964), 145. Clearly the berries themselves were also imported, and wrapped in paper for customers; hence the paper became soaked with brine (*madent*): cf. Mart. 13. 1. 1 ff. (combining the topoi of wrappings and bookworms) 'ne toga cordylis et paenula desit oliuis / aut inopem metuat sordida blatta famem, / perdite Niliacas, Musae, mea damna, papyros'.

12. tus Niliacum piperue: cf. Hor. *Epist.* 2. 1. 269 f. 'deferar in uicum uendentem tus et odores / et piper et quicquid chartis amicitur ineptis'. Pliny claims that frankincense (*Boswellia carterii*) came only from Arabia (*NH* 12. 51), but the Kew Index attests two species of *Boswellia* native to tropical Africa and one to tropical west Africa: see J. I. Miller, *The Spice Trade of the Roman Empire* (Oxford, 1969), 103. *tus Niliacum* must be incense imported down the Nile, either from the African interior or from Arabia: for the trade-routes see Miller, map 6 (facing p. 147), G. W. Van Beek, *The Biblical Archaeologist* 23 (1960), 70–95. Alexandria, on the Nile delta, was a major entrepôt (Miller, 173 ff.) and was renowned for corruption in the incense-trade (Plin. *NH* 12. 59) 'at Hercules! Alexandreae, ubi tura interpolantur, nulla satis custodit diligentia officinas'. Pepper came mainly from India: see Plin. *NH* 12. 29, Miller, 80 ff. For the *horrea piperataria* built by Domitian see on 4. 3. 107–13.

13. aut Byzantiacos cocunt lacertos: *lacertus* = κολίας = Spanish mackerel: see D'Arcy Thompson, *Fishes*, 120 f. *Byzantiacos . . . lacertos* must be fish imported via Byzantium (cf. *tus Niliacum*, 12): for their prevalence in the Bosphorus and the Sea of Marmara, and hence the importance of Byzantium in antiquity (and modern Istanbul) for processing and marketing *lacerti*, see id., *CR* 46 (1932), 247. They were suitable for salting (Cels. 2. 18. 7); salted fish were exported to Italy in amphorae: see André, *Alimentation*, 109 ff. They were soaked to remove the excess salt and then cooked. André, *Alimentation*, 112, notes that Apicius does not distinguish between recipes for dried and fresh fish. *colunt* (M) is meaningless. Although the paper is consigned to a fate of wrapping olives and pepper (both items sold in small quantities), St. cannot mean that it is used for wrapping fish (*pace* Parsons, art. cit. on 11–13 above) since they were carried in baskets (Apul. *Met.* 1. 24) or on a string (E. Pfuhl, *Malerei und Zeichnung der Griechen* [Munich, 1923], iii, figs. 705, 710). Cooks bought used paper: cf. Mart. 6. 61(60). 7 f. 'et redimunt soli carmina docta coci'. Spanish mackerel were cooked in it like criminals burnt alive wearing *tunicae molestae*: cf. Cat. 95. 8 'et laxas scombris saepe dabunt tunicas', Mart. 4. 86. 8 'nec scombris tunicas dabis molestas'. Hence it is suggested by D. F. S. Thomson, *Phoenix* 18 (1964), 30–6, 37–8 (two articles), that this culinary method became proverbial for the fate of bad literature (cf. Pers. 1. 43, Mart. 3. 2. 3 f.), and he emends St.'s passage to *cocunt. olent* is also attractive, since Spanish mackerel had a strong smell (D'Arcy Thompson, *Fishes*, 121), but *cocunt* is more pointed, implying that the paper is so worthless as to be dispensable.

14–16. For Grypus' career see intro. *trinum forum* designates the Fora Romanum, Iulium, and Augustum: see *TLL* vi. 1. 1203. 65 ff. These three fora represented the standard apprenticeship in oratory: cf. Ov. *Tr.* 3. 12. 23 f. 'scaena uiget studiisque fauor distantibus ardet, / proque tribus resonant terna theatra foris', Mart. 3. 38. 3 f. '"causas" inquis "agam

POEM NINE   229

Cicerone disertior ipso / atque erit in triplici par mihi nemo foro"'. For the centumviral court see on 4. 4. 43. St. seems to be suggesting a private copy of Grypus' speeches, comparable to the *libellus* he had copied for Grypus (9) and contrasting with the *libellus* purchased at a bookseller's (21), which Grypus had sent him. Copies of Grypus' speeches in public circulation do not seem to be implied.

17–19. For a detailed discussion of these lines see intro.

20. Bruti senis oscitationes: *oscito* ('gape', 'yawn') and its derivatives frequently denote boredom (like 'yawn' in English): cf. Pers. 3. 58 f. (the student's reaction to philosophy) 'stertis adhuc laxumque caput conpage soluta / oscitat hesternum dissutis undique malis', Sen. *Dial.* 10. 14. 4 (patrons greeting their clients) 'nomen oscitatione superbissima reddent', Mart. 2. 6. 2–4 'lectis uix tibi paginis duabus ... longas trahis oscitationes'; cf. also the metaphor for the proverbial jurisprudence of the Scaeuolae at Cic. *De Or.* 2. 144–5 'istam oscitantem et dormitantem sapientiam Scaeuolarum ... otio concedamus ... me tamen ista oscitans sapientia ... in libertatem uindicabit'. The contrast with Grypus' forensic oratory (14) suggests that the boring works by Brutus were probably speeches. E. M. Sanford, *CJ* 44 (1948), 57 f., assumes that St. deliberately underrates Brutus' writings, but if these were generally esteemed St. would have no grounds for criticizing Grypus' taste. Brutus, the assassin of Caesar, wrote speeches, philosophy, and poetry (Schanz–Hosius, i. 394 ff.). For the extant fragments of his speeches see Enrica Malcovati (ed.), *Oratorum Romanorum Fragmenta*[3] (Turin, 1967), 460–8. Cicero regarded his oratorical style as 'otiosum atque diiunctum' (Tac. *Dial.* 18. 5). It was marked by *grauitas* (Quint. 12. 10. 11, Tac. *Dial.* 25), monotony (Cic. *Orat.* 110), and predominantly iambic rhythms (Quint. 9. 4. 63, 76). His poetry, in Aper's judgement, passed unnoticed in its mediocrity: Tac. *Dial.* 21. 6 (Caesar and Brutus) 'fecerunt enim et carmina et in bibliothecas rettulerunt, non melius quam Cicero, sed felicius, quia fecisse pauciores sciunt'; his philosophical writings were generally considered more successful (Quint. 10. 1. 123, Tac. *Dial.* 21): see E. J. Filbey, *CPh* 6 (1911), 325–33, G. Kennedy, *The Art of Rhetoric in the Roman World* (Princeton, NJ, 1972), 244–6. But *senis* could not refer to this person's age, since he is recorded variously as having died between the ages of thirty-six and forty-three: see *RE* x. 973 f. (Gelzer). *senex* can, however, refer to a man who lived long ago: cf. *S.* 1. 1. 102 (Phidias) 'Atticus ... senior', 2. 253 'Callimachus ... senex', and see D. R. Shackleton Bailey, *Propertiana* (Cambridge, 1956), 132. An alternative identification is M. Iunius Brutus (*RE* x. 971 s.v. Iunius 49 [Münzer], Schanz–Hosius, i. 238 f.) who, with P. Mucius Scaevola (cos. 133) and M'. Manilius (cos. 149), belonged to the great trio of republican jurists and wrote three books on *ius ciuile* (Cic. *De Or.* 2. 224). But: oratory is more suitable than jurisprudence for contrasting with Grypus' speeches; no evidence has survived for the jurist's style; Caesar's assassin was arguably the most famous republican with the name Brutus, and the tedium of his style was still being cited by St.'s contemporaries.

21. de capsa miseri libellionis: the *capsa* and *scrinium* were large cylindrical containers which could hold between five and fifteen papyrus rolls each: see Birt, *Abriß*, 333. This was the standard method of storing papyrus rolls, both privately (Cic. *Caec.* 51) and commercially: cf. Cat. 14. 17 f. 'ad librariorum / curram scrinia'. *miser*, implying social inferiority (*TLL* viii. 1104. 61), is consonant with *libellio*, otherwise attested at Var. *Men.* 256 Bücheler and thus somewhat colloquial in tone. St. contrasts his own *libellus*, specially copied for Grypus (8–10), with Grypus' present which was not his own work and, in addition, was a hack copy picked up at an ordinary bookseller's.

22. plus minus: this idiom is attested both with and without asyndeton: cf. Enn. *Ann.* 154 Skutsch 'septingenti sunt paulo plus aut minus anni', Hirt. *BG* 8. 20. 1 'non longius ... abesse plus minus octo milibus dicebantur', Mart. 8. 71. 4 'plusue minusue duae [librae]'. Since an *as* was the lowest denomination of the Roman coinage, *minus* is *reductio ad absurdum*.

asse Gaiano: St.'s phrase suggests that by now *as Gaianum* was a byword for a worthless amount. Despite Vollmer, there is no evidence that Gaius devalued coinage. Hence St. seems to be referring to an aspect of the *damnatio memoriae* decreed after Gaius' death: cf. Suet. *Claud.* 11 'Gaii quoque etsi acta omnia rescidit, diem tamen necis, quamuis exordium principatus sui, uetuit inter festos referri'. Dio attests that the scope of the *damnatio* included Gaius' bronze coinage (60. 22. 3) τῆι δὲ δὴ τοῦ Γαίου μνήμηι ἀχθόμενοι τὸ νόμισμα τὸ χαλκοῦν πᾶν, ὅσον τὴν εἰκόνα αὐτοῦ ἐντετυπωμένην εἶχε, συγχωνευθῆναι ἔγνωσαν. There are two categories of evidence for the implementation of this *damnatio*, both from Lower Germany: asses on which Gaius' image has been defaced by chisels (see H. Chantraine, *Novaesium III: Die antike Fundmünzen der Ausgraben in Neuß*, Limesforschungen VIII [Berlin, 1968], 22) and others countermarked with the legend *CAC*, which is believed to denote Claudius' titulature (see D. W. MacDowall, *Schweizer Münzblätter* [= *Gazette numismatique suisse*] 20 [1970], 37–41). Hence it appears that *aes* coinage depicting Gaius' image was not legal tender after Claudius' accession. It has been suggested that *aes* coinage alone was affected because of its special link with senatorial authority, i.e. the senate did not want the legend *SC* associated with Gaius' portrait hereafter: see A. Bay, *JRS* 62 (1972), 22. According to Epictetus (*Diss.* 4. 5. 16–17), people refused coins which portrayed a 'bad' emperor (e.g. Nero).

23–45. St., asking Grypus whether the traditional Saturnalian gifts were unobtainable, insults him by listing gifts of inferior quality which would be expected from an *amicus* of inferior status: cf. the lists at Mart. 4. 46. 6 ff., where Sabellus is mocked for being proud of his clients' typical gifts, 7. 53. 3 ff., 72. 2 ff., and especially 4. 88. 3 ff. where Martial complains of receiving from a patron not even the gifts one could expect from a client. The connection between the annual market, Sigillaria, and the festival of the Saturnalia is somewhat obscure, but apparently by Ovid's day cheap clay statuettes (*sigilla*) and similar items were being replaced by much more expensive gifts for the Saturnalia: cf. Ov. *Ars* 1. 407 f. 'siue erit ornatus non, ut fuit ante, sigillis, / sed regum positas Circus habebit opes', with Hollis's note. Augustus was notorious for oscillating between sumptuous and trivial gifts (Suet. *Aug.* 75); Vespasian distributed *apophoreta* to men at the

Saturnalia, and to women at the Matronalia: cf. Mart. 14. 1, where *apophoreta* are specifically associated with the Saturnalia. For the festival see *RE* iiA. 201–11 (Nilsson), and for the exchange of gifts *RAC* x. 692 f. s.v. 'Geschenk' (Stuiber). Lists largely consisting of edible items are taken over from the comic poets into Greek epigram in such contexts as instructions and calculations for a shopping-expedition (*Anth. Pal.* 5. 181, 185) or preparations for a party (*Anth. Pal.* 11. 35): see N–H on Hor. *O.* 1. 38.

24. scissis pillea suta de lacernis: the *pilleum*, the conical cap slaves wore upon manumission, was worn by everyone during the Saturnalia as a symbol of equality: cf. Mart. 11. 6. 4 'pilleata Roma', 14. 1. 1 f. 'synthesibus dum gaudet eques dominusque senator / dumque decent nostrum pillea sumpta Iouem'. *lacernae* themselves were included among Saturnalian gifts (Mart. 14. 131, 133, 135), but St. suggests that Grypus could not even manage *pillea* made out of scraps of *lacernae*: cf. Mart. 14. 132 'si possem, totas cuperem misisse lacernas: / nunc tantum capiti munera mitto tuo'. Martial's expression *totas ... lacernas*, contrasted with the *pilleum*, also suggests that *pillea* were made out of pieces of *lacernae*. A *lacerna* which was worn out or damaged might be cut up to make *pillea*, much as worn-out sheets and pillowcases can be converted into garments for fancy-dress parties. *caesis* would refer to cloaks which had been cut up: cf. Quint. 11. 3. 139 'toga rotunda et apte caesa', i.e. 'well cut', 'cut to fit'. But this notion is too neutral in the context, whereas *scissis* (Heinsius) aptly suggests torn, second-hand clothing.

25–6. mantelia luridaeue mappae, / chartae: *mantelia* = cloths for wiping the hands: cf. Mart. 14. 139(138). *mappae*, table-napkins, and *chartae*, rolls of papyrus, are listed among Saturnalian gifts at Mart. 5. 18. 1 f. 'Decembri mense, quo uolant mappae / ... chartaeque': cf. Mart. 7. 72. 1 ff. 'gratus sic tibi, Paule, sit December / nec uani triplices breuesque mappae / nec turis ueniant leues selibrae', 10. 87. 6. Again St. implies second-hand items, *mappae* which were yellow (with age). Rolls of blank papyrus are listed as *apophoreta*: cf. Mart. 14. 10 *Chartae maiores*, 11 *Chartae epistolares*. The isolation of *chartae* is acceptable in a list.

26. Thebaicaeue Caricaeue: species of fruit are commonly known by their locality, e.g. *Damascena* (*pruna*), plums from Damascus (i.e. damsons): cf. Mart. 5. 18. 3 'acuta senibus testa cum Damascenis'. For *Thebaicae* (*palmae*) cf. Apic. 1. 2, and for *Caricae* (*fici*) cf. Cic. *Diu.* 2. 84, Plin. *NH* 13. 51, *Ed. Diocl.* 6. 85; they are paired at Plin. *NH* 15. 116 'placent crusta Thebaicae ... cute Caricae'.

27–8. The anaphora of *nusquam* (cf. 32) stresses the irony: St. pretends that Grypus must have searched high and low for a very ordinary present. *cottana* are a species of small fig from Syria: cf. Plin. *NH* 13. 51, *RE* vi. 2122 (Olck). The *pruna* which are frequently paired with *cottana* come from Damascus (see previous n.). Juvenal cites them together as typical Syrian imports (3. 83) 'aductus Romam quo pruna et cottana uento'. A *uas* of either variety was a suitable *xenion* (Mart. 13. 28, 29). They would have been dried for export, hence their popularity at Rome in mid-December. Jars of dried fruit, including *pruna* and *cottana*, are attested as Saturnalian gifts: cf. Mart. 4. 88. 5 f. 'Antipolitani nec quae de sanguine thynni / testa rubet, nec quae cottana parua gerit', 7. 53. 7 f. 'paruaque cum canis uenerunt cottana prunis / et Libycae fici pondere testa grauis'. *globus* suits a mass of dried fruit sticking together: cf. *Moretum* 114 f. (handling the *moretum* dough) 'tum demum digitis mortaria tota duobus / circuit inque globum distantia contrahit unum'. *condere* is the usual word for 'store' or 'pack': cf. Mart. 13. 28 *Vas cottanorum* 'haec tibi quae torta uenerunt condita meta, / si maiora forent cottana, ficus erat'. But what is a *turbo*? It is conventionally explained as a top-shaped jar, i.e. conical. Roman storage-jars, however, were not conical but bulbous, so that the aperture was narrower than the girth of the container and could be sealed easily. Only the bottom half of an ordinary *cadus* could be regarded as conical, and it is clearly these bases, broken off from the upper half, which Pliny recommends for planting seeds in (*NH* 27. 14) 'in turbinibus cadorum eam [aloen] serunt ut aizoum maius'. *ruo*, frequently used of collapsing buildings and other structures, suits the notion of 'falling to pieces': cf. Plin. *NH* 11. 23 '[apes] ruentes ceras fulciunt', *OLD* s.v. *ruo* 6. Hence St. apparently means fruit packed into the cracked bottom half of what had once been a storage-jar.

29. enlychnia sicca: wicks were commonly made from flax (Plin. *NH* 19. 17). See further R. J. Forbes, *Studies in Ancient Technology* vi² (Leiden, 1966), 156. Once soaked in oil or tallow they would ignite: cf. Vitr. 8. 1. 5 'si lucerna . . . postero die non erit exusta, sed habuerit reliquia olei et ellychnii', *Moretum* 11 'producit acu stuppas umore carentis', Plin. *NH* 23. 84, 28. 181, 35. 175. Since lamps are listed among *apophoreta* (Mart. 14. 61, 62), mere wicks represent a very meagre gift.

29–30. replictae / bulborum tunicae: *tunica*, like χιτών, is used of pods, rinds, skins etc.: cf. Theophr. *Hist. Plant.* 1. 12. 3 ἔχει δὲ αὐτὰ τὰ σπέρματα καὶ οἱ χιτῶνες οἱ περὶ αὐτὰ διαφορὰν τῶν χυλῶν, Plin. *NH* 18. 61 'tunicae frumento plures, hordeum maxime nudum'. Eating skins was a sign of extreme poverty: cf. Juv. 14. 153 'tunicam mihi malo lupini / quam si me toto laudet uicinia pago / exigui ruris paucissima farra secantem'. For the syncopated form of the past participle cf. Sen. *Epist.* 95. 2 'recitator historiam ingentem attulit minutissime scriptam, artissime plictam', N–W iii. 522 f. *bulbi* are cited as Saturnalian gifts (Mart. 4. 46. 11) and as *xenia* (Mart. 13. 34) and in the list of presents at Juv. 7. 120. For the different varieties and how to serve them to make them palatable see *RE* iii. 669 ff. (Olck).

30. nec oua †tantum†: *oua* are attested as *xenia* (Mart. 13. 40, cit. on ll. 32–3). *tantum* cannot be forced to bear the requisite meaning 'even' (nor does it mean this at Juv. 1. 131 'non tantum meiere fas est', where the elliptical use of *non tantum* conveys euphemism: see Courtney ad loc.). The only alternative would be an adjective (ascribing suitably banal properties to the *oua*) so that each noun in this list would have its own epithet.

31. nec lenes alicae, nec asperum far: two coarse grain-products which were staples of the everyday diet. *alica*, groats, was derived from hard emmers by pounding and sifting, and it was commonly made into *puls* (porridge): cf. Cato, *Agr.* 85, Plin. *NH* 18. 83–4, 109 ff., N. Jasny, *The Wheats of Classical Antiquity* (Baltimore, 1944), 130, L. A. Moritz, *Grain-*

POEM NINE 233

mills and Flour in Classical Antiquity (Oxford, 1958), 148. *far* was first crushed emmer and then a coarse flour (Moritz, 221), also originally prepared in liquid form as *puls* (Moritz, 149) and later in baked form as bread (Jasny, 130). Jars containing *puls* made from both these commodities are attested as *xenia*: cf. Mart. 13. 6 *Alica* 'nos alicam, poterit mulsum tibi mittere diues. / si tibi noluerit mittere diues, emes', 8 *Far* 'inbue plebeias Clusinis pultibus ollas, / ut satur in uacuis dulcia musta bibas'. *asper* frequently describes sharp-tasting food or drink: cf. Ter. *Hau.* 458 f. 'quid uini absumpsit "sic hoc" dicens, "asperum, pater, hoc est: aliud lenius sodes uide"', Cato, *Agr.* 109 'uinum, asperum quod erit, lene et suaue si uoles facere, sic facito', Virg. *G.* 4. 277 'asper in ore sapor', *TLL* ii. 810. 1 ff. In this sense its antonym is not *leuis* (smooth to the touch) but *lenis* (smooth to the taste): cf. the examples cited from Terence and Cato. Thus St. is referring to two types of *puls* with contrasting flavours.

The single stressed monosyllable ending the hendecasyllabic line creates a rough rhythm appropriate to the sense: cf. the effect achieved in a hexameter by a monosyllabic ending, e.g. Hor. *Ars* 139 'parturient montes, nascetur ridiculus mus', Virg. *A.* 5. 481 'sternitur exanimisque tremens procumbit humi bos'.

32–3. Hesiod refers to the snail by the denominative kenning φερέοικος (*Op.* 571): see I. Wærn, ΓΗΣ ΟΣΤΕΑ *The Kenning in Pre-Christian Greek Poetry* (Uppsala, 1951), 38 ff. St.'s couplet, an expansion of the motif expressed by the kenning, is similar to the periphrases which sometimes constitute an entire distich in the *Xenia* or *Apophoreta*: cf. Mart. 13. 40 *Oua* 'candida si croceos circumfluit unda uitellos, / Hesperius scombri temperet oua liquor'. Periphrases for the snail are parodied at Cic. *Diu.* 2. 133 'ut si quis medicus aegroto imperet, ut sumat "terrigenam herbigradam domiportam sanguine cassam" potius quam ... cocleam diceret'. The snail's nomadic existence is the subject of a fourth-century riddle (Symphosius, *Aenigmata* no. 18 *Coclea* = *Anth. Lat.* 281 Shackleton Bailey) 'porto domum mecum, semper migrare parata, / mutatoque solo non sum miserabilis exul, / sed †mihi concilium† de caelo nascitur ipso'. The African snail (Λιβυκός, *Africana*) was a well-known variety: cf. Diosc. 2. 9, Plin. *NH* 30. 45 'laudatissimae ... sunt Africanae', *RE* iiA. 594 (Gossen–Steier). St.'s phrase 'Cinyphiis uagata campis domus', suggesting the nomadic tribes of North Africa, aptly indicates the character of the snail's life: for *Cinyphiis* see on 4. 3. 90–1. *domus* regularly denotes the shell of invertebrates: see *TLL* v. 1. 1972. 49 ff. It is *uda* because of its slime (*saliua, spuma*), itself held to have medicinal properties: cf. Plin. *NH* 29. 116, 30. 72, 136. It is not even a whole snail (cf. Mart. 4. 46. 11) but merely its shell that St. assumes Grypus would have given him. For medicinal purposes the shell was usually consumed with its contents: Plin. *NH* 30. 44–5, *RE* iiA. 592. The shells alone were used as containers for olive-oil: cf. Xenocr. *De Al.* 49, Plin. *NH* 9. 174, 32. 147. Martial, adopting the same pose as St. here, feigns surprise at having received a cup of very thin metal from Paulus when he might have given him (amongst other things) a snail-shell instead (8. 33. 25 f.) 'cocleam cum mittere possis, / denique cum possis mittere, Paule, nihil?'

34–5. non lardum graue debilisue perna, / non Lucanica, non breues falisci: pork accounted for much of the meat eaten by the Romans: see André, *Alimentation*, 136 ff. It was variously preserved, usually by salting (cf. Cato, *Agr.* 162 'salsura pernarum') but also smoked (cf. Hor. *Sat.* 2. 2. 116 f. 'non ego ... temere edi luce profesta / quicquam praeter holus fumosae cum pede pernae'). For a gift of preserved pork cf. Juv. 7. 119 'siccus petasunculus'. Bacon, *lar(i)dum*, was the poor man's flavouring for vegetable dishes: cf. Hor. *Sat.* 2. 6. 63 f. 'o quando faba Pythagorae cognata simulque / uncta satis pingui ponentur holuscula lardo?', Mart. 5. 78. 10 'pallens faba cum rubente lardo'. It contributed to a very modest festive occasion: cf. Juv. 11. 84 'natalicium ... lardum'. The epithet *graue* is supported by the distinction drawn between 'light' and 'heavy' pork (attributed to the animal's diet) at Plin. *NH* 16. 25 'glans fagea ... facit carnem cocibilem ac leuem et utilem stomacho ... ponderosam querna, diffusam'. Hence *lardum graue* would be both a heavy lump and heavy to digest. But the repetition of the epithet with *falisci* is odd. *Lucanica* and *falisci* were regional specialities, sausages from Lucania and Falerii, commonly paired: cf. Var. *LL* 5. 111. 1 'quod fartum intestinum e crassundiis, Lucanicam dicunt, quod milites a Lucanis didicerint, ut quod Faleriis Faliscum uentrem', Mart. 4. 46. 8 'et Lucanica uentre cum Falisco'. Varro (*LL* 5. 111. 2–5) distinguishes these varieties and *fundolum* from the types called *farcimen*, *farticulum*, *hilla*, *apexabo* ('tenuissimum intestinum fartum') and from *longauo* ('quod longius quam duo illa'); hence sausages in the first category must have been short and fat: see Collart's notes ad loc. Thus perhaps we should consider *breues falisci* here rather than *lardum breue* (Markland) in the previous line. It is suitably disparaging in this list of presents to speak of 'short' sausages.

The remaining item, *perna*, is listed among Martial's *xenia* (13. 54). As in English 'ham', *perna* is properly the upper part of the leg. *debilis* is the word for describing weak limbs: cf. Juv. 10. 227 'ille umero, hic lumbis, hic coxa debilis', Maec. fr. 4. 1–2 Morel 'debilem facito manu, / debilem pede coxo'. But words descriptive of physical disability in human beings can also be applied metaphorically to limp or stale foodstuffs: cf. Mart. 7. 20. 11 f. (some of the pickings secreted in Santra's table-napkin) 'et excauatae pellis indecens uoluae / et lippa ficus debilisque boletus'. Hence St. here is playing on the literal and metaphorical meaning.

36. non sal oxyporumue caseusue: salt was recognized as an indispensable condiment and became proverbial for the essence of life: cf. Plin. *NH* 31. 88–9, Isid. *Orig.* 16. 2. 6, Otto, *Sprichwörter*, nos. 1569–70. For the production and harvesting of salt see R. J. Forbes, *Studies in Ancient Technology* iii (Leiden, 1955), 157–74. *oxypor(i)um* = ὀξύπορον/ὀξυπόριον (φάρμακον), a digestive agent, treated as both a medicine and a condiment. Apicius supplies a recipe for it consisting of cumin, ginger, rue, bicarbonate of soda, pepper, dates, honey, and vinegar (*De Re Coqu.* 1. 18) and includes it in a dressing for lettuce (3. 18. 2), itself believed to aid digestion: cf. Plin. *NH* 20. 65 '[lactucae] stomachis dissolutis utilissimae: adiuuantur in eos usus et oxypori obolis'. Spices and condiments are attested as *xenia*: cf. Mart. 13. 5 *Piper*, 101 *Oleum*, 102 *Garum sociorum*. Vollmer takes *sal* *oxyporum* together as digestive salts, but: (i) *oxyporum* seems to occur always in liquid form; (ii) *non* naturally governs the first element, *sal*, and the following pair of disjunctives (*-ue* ... *-ue*) replace repetitions of the negative: cf. *TLL* ix. 1212. 56 f. '[*oxyporum*] uix cum *sal* coniungendum'. Regional cheeses suitable for gifts are listed at Mart. 13. 30–3.

37. panes uiridantis aphronitri = ἀφρὸς νίτρου, ἀφρόνιτρον: cf. Mart. 14. 58 'rusticus es? nescis quid Graeco nomine dicar: / spuma uocor nitri. Graecus es? aphronitrum'. It was an efflorescence of sodium carbonate found in caves, and one variety could be compacted and exported in blocks: cf. Diosc. 5. 113. 1, Plin. *NH* 31. 113 'proxima aetas medicorum aphronitrum tradidit in Asia colligi in speluncis molibus destillans ... dein siccant sole, optimum putatur Lydium; probatio ut sit minime ponderosum et maxime friabile, colore paene purpureo. hoc in pastillis adfertur', Isid. *Orig.* 16. 2. 8. *panis* (dim. *pastillus*) denotes any substance formed into the shape of a loaf or cake: cf. Colum. 12. 30. 2 'sumito faecem uini boni et panes facito et in sole arefacito', *OLD* s.v. *panis* 3. The other variety was very powdery: for conflicting evidence for the names ἀφρόλιτρον and ἀφρόνιτρον for these two varieties see Galen *Simpl.* 9. 3. 18, Orib. *Collect. Med.* 15. 1. 27. 6 f. *nitrum*, including *aphronitrum*, was put to a variety of culinary, medical, and household uses, including laundry: see D–S iv. 86 (Alfred Jacob), R. J. Forbes, op. cit. (on l. 36), 174–9. A green variety is not elsewhere attested.

38. passum psithiis suis recoctum = *passum secundarium*. Grapes dried in the sun on the vine (Plin. *NH* 14. 81, Pallad. 11. 19) or on trays (Colum. 12. 27. 1, 39. 1) could be pressed without yielding all the sugar content in the pressing; *passum secundarium* could then be obtained by soaking the lees in rain water (Plin. *NH* 14. 82), or else in the must of a different grape or even in wine (Colum. 12. 39. 2–3), before they were pressed again. This information comes from J. André, *Ann. de la Fac. des Lettres d'Aix* 25 (1951), 58. ψίθιος was a type of vine from which *passum* was made: cf. Plin. *NH* 14. 80 'psithium [uinum] et melampsithium passi genera sunt suo sapore, non uini'; it was the grape particularly used for *passum* in Italy and adjacent provinces (Plin. *NH* 14. 81). St. is saying that the *passum secundarium* was boiled up out of the grapes which had yielded the first pressing.

39. dulci defruta uel lutosa caeno: *defrutum*, like *passum*, was a dessert wine, *dulce*, γλυκὺς οἶνος (André, art. cit. n. 51). To make it, the must was boiled down and reduced by half (Plin. *NH* 14. 80). The adjective *tenuis* could not be applied to these wines: cf. Plin. *NH* 14. 80 'uinum omne dulce minus odoratum, quo tenuius eo odoratius'. Hence *dulcia* were not 'light' wines, but thick and clouded (*lutosa*). *caeno* does not refer to sediment (as classified by *TLL* and *OLD*) since the liquid itself, not any sediment, would be sweet (*dulci* ... *caeno*), and it is cloudy (*lutosa*) not by reason of any sediment but because of the murky properties of the liquid. *defrutum* in Martial's list of Saturnalian gifts is specified as a dark wine (4. 46. 9) 'nigri Syra defruti lagona'. Hence *caeno* refers to the impurities in the wine (oxymoron with *dulci*).

40. quantum uel dare: *quantum* = *quantulum*. Between two questions (*usque adeone defuerunt*, 23, and *rogo, non licebat*, 42), *quantum* reads better as interrogative than exclamatory. *nec* (M) would imply that Grypus could congratulate himself on his self-restraint in having refrained from giving St. candles etc.; but *uel* matches this question to the other two, which both postulate difficulties that Grypus might have encountered in choosing a gift, i.e. 'weren't there any? were they too expensive? weren't you allowed to give them?'

cereos olentis: traditional presents at a midwinter festival: cf. *Anth. Pal.* 6. 249 (Antipater of Thessalonica) λαμπάδα κηροχίτωνα, Κρόνου τυφήρεα λύχνον, Mart. 10. 87. 5–7 'absit cereus aridi clientis, / et uani triplices breuesque mappae / expectent gelidi iocos Decembris', *RAC* vii. 164 (Gagé). Vollmer takes *cultellum* (41) with *olentis*, i.e. 'smelling of the knife' = freshlycut: cf. Theoc. 1. 27 ff. κισσύβιον κεκλυσμένον ἁδέι κηρῶι ... ἔτι γλυφάνοιο ποτόσδον. But Theocritus' context is not really parallel, since it is the carved wood which 'smells of the knife', not the wax overlay. Further, enjambment here would make *cultellum* unduly emphatic.

41. tenuis ... codicillos: one everyday writing-material consisted of wooden leaves characterized by their thinness: cf. Mart. 14. 3. 1 *Pugillares citrei* 'secta nisi in tenues essemus ligna tabellas'. These could be bent so that they folded up: cf. Herodian 1. 17. 1 (the emperor Commodus compiling his proscription-list) λαβὼν γραμματεῖον τούτων δὴ τῶν ἐκ φιλύρας ἐς λεπτότητα ἠσκημένων ἐπαλλήλωι τε ἀνακλάσει ἀμφοτέρωθεν ἐπτυγμένων γράφει, ὅσους χρὴ τῆς νηκτὸς φονευθῆναι. (Herodian may be elaborating a detail from Dio's account of the wooden diptych which Domitian used as a similar *aide-mémoire*: cf. Dio 67. 15. 3 καί σφων τὰ ὀνόματα ἐς σανίδιον φιλύρινον δίθυρον ἐσγράψας.) *pugillaria* described by Martial, notebooks small enough to be held in the fist (*pugnus*), can take two forms, either wax tablets or prototype *codices*: for *tabellae* cf. Mart. 14. 7 *Pugillares membranei* 'esse puta ceras, licet haec membrana uocetur: / delebis, quotiens scripta nouare uoles'; for *codicilli* cf. Cat. 42. 4 f., 11 'negat mihi nostra redditurum / pugillaria ... moecha putida, redde codicillos', [Suet.] ed. Roth (Leipzig, 1858), p. 311 'nec pugillaria nec pugillar dici potest aliter, quia proprium nomen est huius rei codices, inde per diminutionem codicilli, ut puta codicilli triplices'. A type of booklet consisting of thin wooden leaves, folded in half, tied together with thongs and bound with cords, was discovered at Vindolanda in 1973: see A. K. Bowman, *ZPE* 18 (1975), 237–52. They appear to have been bound together either in a 'concertina' arrangement so that they unfold in continuous sequence like a papyrus being unrolled, or else in diptychs arranged sequentially. The folded leaves are clearly a forerunner of the *codex*, which evolved into the modern book. These thin wooden leaves, designed to be written on in ink, were less durable than the heavier stylus tablets, and were used for ephemeral records, e.g. letters and accounts (as in the Vindolanda collection): see A. K. Bowman and J. D. Thomas, *Vindolanda: the Latin Writing-tablets* (*Britannia* Monograph Series 4) (London, 1983), 44. They were useful when (as at Vindolanda) papyrus was in short supply: see Bowman, art. cit. 246 f. For a description of further finds of leaf tablets at Vindolanda in 1985, including a letter inviting an officer's wife to a birthday party, see A. K. Bowman and J. D. Thomas, *JRS* 76 (1986), 120–3.

42. ollaris . . . uuas: the basic type of *olla* (*aula*) is a cooking-pot. Subsidiary types are the (preserving-)jar with a lid, and the funerary urn: see W. Hilgers, *Lateinische Gefäßnamen* (Düsseldorf, 1969), 39 f., 112 ff., K. D. White, *Farm Equipment of the Roman World* (Cambridge, 1975), 176 ff. The jars were especially used in a method for preserving grapes: cf. Cato, *Agr.* 7. 2 'uuae in olla in uinaceis conduntur', Hor. *Sat.* 2. 4. 71 'Venucula conuenit ollis', Hilgers, 114. Three or four bunches were placed in each *olla*, the lids sealed with pitch, the *ollae* arranged in a barrel with grapeskins packed between like straw, and the barrel finally covered and sealed (Colum. 12. 45. 2–3). Grapes preserved in this manner were known as *uuae ollares* (cf. Mart. 7. 20. 9).

rogo: the parenthetic use of a formula of request or persuasion is a feature of everyday speech: cf. Mart. 2. 80. 2 'hic, rogo, non furor est', 13. 58. 2 'hoc, rogo, creuit ubi?', L–H–S 472.

43. Cumano patinas uel orbe tortas: a *patina* is a flat, open dish used for cooking, baking, and serving, and frequently made of clay: see Hilgers, op. cit. (on 42 above), 72 f., 245 ff. esp. 247. For pottery from Cumae cf. Mart. 14. 114 *Patella Cumana* 'hanc tibi Cumano rubicundam puluere testam / municipem misit casta Sibylla suam'. Cumae was famous for pottery: cf. Plin. *NH* 35. 165 'nobilitantur his [patinis] quoque oppida, ut Regium et Cumae'. It produced, however, a common type which Tibullus cites together with Samian ware as an example of his modest aspirations (2. 3. 47 f.) 'at mihi laeta trahant Samiae conuiuia testae / fictaque Cumana lubrica terra rota'. The harsh asyndeton which *in orbe* involves is removed by *uel* (Heinsius): for the postponed position cf. 39. The instrumental ablative with *tortas* is also more natural: cf. *ficta . . . rota* (Tib. 2. 3. 48, cit. above).

44–5. *synthesis* was a set of either clothes or tableware. The outfit was worn at dinner-parties: cf. Mart. 5. 79. 1 f. 'undecies una surrexti, Zoile, cena, / et mutata tibi est synthesis undecies', *CIL* vi. 2068. 8 'cum synthesibus epulati sunt'. It was especially associated with the informality of the Saturnalia: cf. Mart. 14. 1. 1, 142(141). In the context of St.'s poem one expects a Saturnalian outfit, but his *synthesis* is the other variety: cf. Mart. 4. 46. 14 f. (also a Saturnalian gift) 'et crasso figuli polita caelo / septenaria synthesis Sagunti'. The parenthetic question *quid horres* delays the denouement: cf. Mart. 2. 46. 9 f. 'quantum erat, infelix, pannis fraudare duobus / (quid renuis?) non ne, Naeuole, sed tineas?' *calices*, in conjunction with *caccabi* (=pots), are probably also pots rather than wine-cups: for *calices* as a Saturnalian gift cf. Mart. 14. 94, 96, 102, 108, 109, 115. White pottery seems to have been rare: tin oxide, which can produce a milky-white glaze, is seldom used, and glazed items are in any case prestigious: see R. J. Charleston, *Roman Pottery* (London, 1955), 30. Hence *alborum* (M) has been suspected, but cannot be categorically disproved. Heinsius' *obbarum* is attractive: cf. Var. *Men.* 114 Bücheler 'dolia atque apothecas, tricliniaris, Melicas, Calenas obbas et Cumanos calices'. Alternatively *alborum* might conceal a different colour in the original text, red being the most common colour for pottery in the Roman period: see Charleston, 5. For *ruber* of pottery cf. Mart. 14. 106. 1 'hic tibi donatur panda ruber urceus ansa'.

46. statera = a weighing-machine, properly a steelyard: cf. Isid. *Orig.* 16. 25. 6 'haec duas lances non habet sed uirga est signata libris et unciis et uago pondere mensurata', T. Ibel, *Die Wage in Altertum und Mittelalter* (Erlangen, 1908), 65 f. But *statera* also = *trutina*, i.e. a pair of scales: cf. Vitr. 10. 3. 4 'id autem ex trutinis, quae staterae dicuntur, licet considerare', Petr. *Sat.* 35 'stateram in cuius altera parte scriblita erat, in altera placenta', Suet. *Vesp.* 25 'dicitur [Vespasianus] ... uidisse ... stateram ... positam examine aequo, cum in altera lance Claudius et Nero starent, in altera ipse ac filii', D–S iii. 1225 (E. Michon), Ibel, 56 ff. The context of the literary metaphor whereby the relative merits of two works are estimated 'by weight' (see next n.) suggests that St. has a pair of scales in mind.

47. idem mihi rependis: the metaphor of weighing is as old as the Homeric picture of Zeus measuring men's fates (*Il.* 8. 69 ff., 22. 209 ff.). With reference to comparative literary merits it is incongruous: cf. Aristoph. *Ran.* 797, 1364 ff. It is widely adopted by Roman writers, especially satirists, as a literary and rhetorical metaphor: cf. Var. *Men.* 419 Bücheler 'itaque uideas barbato rostro illum commentari et unum quodque uerbum statera auraria pendere', Cic. *De Or.* 2. 159 'haec enim nostra oratio multitudinis est auribus accommodanda ... ad eo probanda quae non aurificis statera sed populari quadam trutina examinantur', Hor. *Epist.* 2. 1. 29 f. 'Romani pensantur eadem / scriptores trutina', Pers. 1. 6 f. 'examen ... improbum in illa / castiges trutina', Juv. 6. 436 f. 'inde Maronem / atque alia parte in trutina suspendit Homerum'. In these examples it is quality which is being 'weighed', but St. is not using the metaphor in that sense since the point of his poem is that Grypus' book was far inferior to his own. In the context of St.'s list of alternative gifts (23–45) *idem* = 'the same thing', i.e. *libellus*. This equation prompts St.'s objections that courtesy does not always demand exact reciprocity (49–52) and his fear that this poem might elicit corresponding hendecasyllables from Grypus (54 f.).

48–52. St. argues that *amicitia* between social unequals precludes strictly reciprocal behaviour. He draws his illustrations from two fundamental institutions of Roman patronage, the *salutatio* (48–50) and the *cena* (51–2). The *salutatio* occupied the first two hours of the day (Mart. 4. 8. 1) and necessitated a very early start for the *cliens*: cf. Sall. *Cat.* 28, Mart. 1. 92. 5, 10. 70. 5, 12. 29(26). 1 ff., 68, Plin. *Epist.* 3. 12, Juv. 3. 127, 5. 19, *RE* iA. 2060 ff. (Hug), T. P. Wiseman in B. K. Gold (ed.), *Literary and Artistic Patronage in Ancient Rome* (Austin, 1982), 28 f. *ientaculum*, the first meal of the day (Isid. *Orig.* 20. 2. 10), appears usually to have been eaten at the third or fourth hour (as recommended by Galen 6. 332 f.): cf. Martial's retort to Caecilianus, who arrives for dinner before the fifth hour (8. 67. 9 f.) 'mane ueni potius; nam cur te quinta moretur? / ut iantes, sero, Caeciliane, uenis'. Since the *ientaculum* was a light and informal meal, it could be eaten early or late at whim: cf. Suet. *Vit.* 7. 3 'per ... stabula ac deuersoria mulionibus ac uiatoribus praeter modum comis ut mane singulos iamne iantassent sciscitaretur seque fecisse ructu quoque ostenderet'. Vitellius, a notorious glutton (Suet. *Vit.* 13), evidently ate abnormally large breakfasts: cf. Colum. 6. 6. 1 'cruditatis signa sunt crebri ructus ac uentris sonitus'. *semicrudus* suggests that St. got mild indigestion from gulping his *ientaculum* before the *salutatio*; a hangover might also contribute to discomfort at this ceremony (Sen. *Dial.* 10. 14. 4). On the *ientaculum* see Blümner, 381.

48. bene regularly intensifies *mane*: see *TLL* ii. 2126. 74 ff.

49. inflatam tibi dixero salutem: *inlatam* . . . *salutem* (M) would have to mean 'inflicted greeting': cf. the idiom *alicui inferre periculum / damna* (*TLL* vii. 1. 1384. 66 ff.), subtly hinting at the tedium of the *salutatio* from the *patronus*' point of view; this is very strained. But *inflatam* (Otto) fits perfectly with *semicrudus*: after his hurried breakfast, St. belches his greeting to Grypus.

51–2. dape ... opima, / ... similis ... cenas: *similis* conveys reciprocity, but the *uariatio* between *daps* and *cena* may hint that a meal at Grypus' house was naturally a more luxurious affair than whatever modest meal St. could offer. For the elevated tone of *daps* see *TLL* v. 1. 36. 41 ff. Axelson, 106 f., classified *cena* as a prosaic word with a common ring, but Gordon Williams has shown rather that it conveys a 'factual reality' and is hence appropriate to the realistic aspect of the *Odes* (and also to St.'s context): see *Tradition and Originality in Roman Poetry* (Oxford, 1968), 748. P. Watson, *CQ* NS 35 (1985), 436, adds the rider that this concept is sometimes in tension with considerations of genre; in our context both the realistic element and the light genre accommodate *cena*. A similar distinction between gastronomic simplicity and sophistication is expressed at Mart. 13. 14 *Lactucae* 'cludere quas cenas lactuca solebat auorum, / dic mihi, cur nostras inchoat illa dapes?' The plainness of a meal which the poet can offer is another theme reminiscent of Catullus: cf. his invitation to Fabullus (Cat. 13).

53. irascor tibi: Catullus' words to Cornificius (38. 6).

ualebis: a valedictory formula: cf. Cic. *Att.* 6. 2. 10, 5. 4, *Fam.* 15. 18. 2, Suet. *Gaius* 8. 4 (citing a letter of Augustus). After this formula, the parting shot which follows (54 f.) is in the nature of a postscript.

54–5. St. unexpectedly ends not with a command for reparation but a prohibition. This is a pastiche of motifs in Catullus: Asinius is threatened with *hendecasyllabos trecentos* unless he returns Catullus' napkin (12. 10 f.); when Caluus sends Catullus the works of *pessimi poetae*, Catullus threatens him with the same in return (14. 19 f.). *lepore* attributes to Grypus the urbanity and sophistication which were Catullus' criteria: cf. Cat. 1. 1 'cui dono lepidum nouum libellum', 12. 8 f. 'est enim leporum / differtus puer ac facetiarum ', 50. 7 f. 'atque illinc abii tuo lepore, / incensus, Licini, facetiisque'. For the hint of naughtiness conveyed by *lepos* cf. Sall. *Cat.* 25. 5 (of Sempronia) 'multae facetiae multusque lepos inerat'. St.'s choice of vocabulary which Catullus uses almost exclusively in the polymetric poems coheres with his choice of hendecasyllables as a vehicle for a witty experiment in occasional verse: see D. O. Ross, *Style and Tradition in Catullus* (Harvard, 1969), 109.

INDEX

ab urbe condita construction, 68, 145
Achilleid, xviii, xxi, 155, 203
adjectives: from names, 184; polar comparative, 215; quantitative, 89, 213
adynaton, 86, 118, 132, 135, 166, 186
Agaue, xvi
Alba Longa, xv, 101, 160
Alexander, 187–9; Domitian as, 79
alliterative pairs, 144, 160
amicitia, xxv, 170, 177, 191, 238
anacoluthon, 78
anaphora, 78, 88, 106, 124, 131, 161, 168, 170, 181, 193, 205, 231
anastrophe, 88
Apollo, 129–30, 156, 203, 214, 217
apostrophe, 112, 128
Arabia, 79, 166
Arco Felice, 128
art-collecting, 175
artistic vision, 184, 185
Augustalia, xv, xvi, 101; *see also* Games, Neapolitan
Augustus: consulships, 76–7; criticism of, 76–7

Bacchus, 93, 94, 98, 134, 211; *see also* Dionysus
'baroque', xxviii
bay, 79, 86, 130, 192, 214
Brutus, 229

Calderini, xxxiii
calendar, important days in, 180, 216
calque, 201, ?21
canon: of lyric poets, 199; of sculptors, 182
captator, 205–6
Caspian Gates, 149–50
castration, 107–8
Catullus, echoes of, 221, 224, 226, 239
ceilings, 89, 93, 109
cena, xx n., xxii n., 83, 85, 176, 177, 239
centumviral court, 146
Ceres, 93, 106, 217–18
Chatti, xvi, 74, 78, 101
China, 79
cinnamon, 166

clausulae, 56
codicilli, 236–7
colloquialism, 59, 60, 226
colours, 201–2, 213; *see also* purple
condiments, 234–5
consular inauguration, 62–4, 66, 73; oath at, 71–2
Crypta Neapolitana, 112
Cumae, 120, 129–30, 237
Cures, 171–2

Dalmatia, 195–6
damnatio memoriae, 196, 230
De Bello Germanico, xv, xvii n., xviii
deification, 100, 132
Dionysus, 188, 190; *see also* Bacchus
Dioscuri, 98, 165, 179–80, 207, 215, 218
dog-star, 140–1
Domitian: as *arbiter*, 125; building-programme, 100; castration-edict, 107–8; as censor, 107; as *conditor*, 123; consulships, 62–3, 73; deportment, 95–6, 97, 99; as *dominus*, 60, 85, 124; as εἰρηνοποιός, 71; as Germanicus, 66; and honorific months, 80; as *inuictus*, 207; as Jupiter, 72, 87, 88, 99, 207; and lictors, 68; power over nature, 90, 123, 124; *prouidentia*, 110; as *rex*, 81–2, 90; as second Romulus, 77, 123; titulature, xxix–xxx; as *uictor*, 125; vine-edict, 107
Domus Flavia, 67, 89
double entendre, 85, 109–10, 211

ecphrasis, xxii n., xxvi, 83, 88–9, 104, 175
encomium, xxvii, 139; astronomical imagery, 66–7, 75, 96, 215; of terrain, 103; topoi, 71, 75, 79, 165; *see also* λόγος βασιλικός, panegyric, parental example, physical resemblance, 'pre-eminence'
epic metaphors, 198, 200–1
epideixis, xxvi
epiphany, 81, 183–4
epistolary themes: author's œuvre, 155; 'if only you were here', 153; mutual friend, 142, 143; summer holidays, 141; weather, 140

INDEX

equites: offical designation, 75; rank, 136, 159, 168, 219, 221–2
Erato, 198–9
eucharisticon, xxx; *see also gratiarum actio*
exempla: triple, 132, 157, 185, 189, 191; *uirtutis*, 206

fallacy: 'artificial', 74; pathetic, 68
Flavian cult, 109
Forum Transitorium, 69–70, 74, 106
Fratres Aruales, 137

Games: Alban, xvii, xviii, xxi, 101, 164–5; Capitoline, xvii, 101; Neapolitan, xviii; *see also* Augustalia, Ludi Saeculares
garlands, 200, 210, 211
generic terms, xxx–xxxi
genethliacon, 197, 209
gestures, 69, 72, 212–13; *see also* posture
Geta: *see* Hosidius Geta
gomphi, 114–16
gourmets, 178–9
grain products, 232
gratiarum actio, 62–3, 82–3
Greek nouns, 92, 207
Grypus: *see* Plotius Grypus

Hannibal, 189–91
hendiadys, 170
Hercules, 98, 157; apotheosis, 186–7; and Auge, 186; birthplace, 180, 189; labours, 193–4; and Molorchus, 186; and Nemean lion, 143; *see also* statues
Horace, echoes of, xxiv, 138, 139, 146, 147, 155, 157, 159, 163, 164, 165, 166, 167, 169, 170, 174, 177, 199–200
Hosidius Geta, 136–7, 151–2
hymn, 72, 87–8, 124, 216–17; *see also* prayer-formulae, religious language
hyperbaton, 157
hyperbole, 86, 90, 94, 110

ientaculum, 238–9
imperatives joined by *nec*, 76
incense, 166, 228
internal accusative, 215
invitation-poem, 176
ius trium liberorum, 214
ivory, 94–5, 180

Janus, xxvii, 65, 69, 71, 72, 73, 76, 80–1, 106; Geminus, 69–71; Quadrifrons, 70–1

Julius Menecrates, 209, 221
Jupiter: *see* Domitian

kenning, 233

Lepcis Magna, 165, 166, 171
libellus, 54, 226
literary composition: *audacia*, xxvi n., 204; Callimachean ideal, 200; contrast with oratory, 146; fate of bad works, 227–8; lack of inspiration, 202; metaphors, 144, 172–3, 199, 203–4, 238; πόνος, 182, 185, 204; *quies* as a prerequisite, 170; *see also* epic metaphors
litotes, 215–16
Livy, 208
λόγος βασιλικός, 64, 86, 99, 100, 119, 132
longevity, 77, 78, 82, 100, 133–4, 214
Lucan, xxii, 54
Lucretius, echo of, 90
Ludi Saeculares, 72, 77–8
Lysippus, 173, 184, 185, 187

μακαρισμός, 77, 146
'mannerism', xxvii–xxviii
marble, 74–5, 91, 92–3, 128
Marcellus: *see* Vitorius Marcellus
marriage, age of girls at, 219–20
Mars, 97–8
Martial, 60, 173, 176; *see also* Statius
Menecrates: *see* Julius Menecrates
metonymy, 65, 68, 75, 91, 98, 100, 118, 129, 140–1, 146, 163, 168, 204, 205, 220
metre, xxii; alcaic, 160, 162, 166, 167; hendecasyllabic, 105, 108–9, 220–1, 239; sapphic, 197
Minerva, xvii, 74, 164–5
monosyllables, 233

names, play on, 160, 166, 200, 201, 204, 219, 221
Naples, xxii, 147, 202, 209–10, 211, 217–18, 219
neologism, 162
Nero, 67, 81, 83, 102, 106, 109, 118–19
Nouius Vindex, 173; *see also* Vestinus
numerals in poetry, 65

opening ceremonies, 104–5
opusculum, 55–6

INDEX

orbitas, 204–5
oxymoron, 67, 144, 165, 183, 194, 225
Ovid, xxvii, 69; echo of, 150

panegyric: of rulers, xxv, 63–4, 132; topos of distinctive height, 140; see also encomium, λόγος βασιλικός
papyrus roll, 54 n., 225–6, 227, 229–30, 231
paradox, xxvii, 60, 72, 88, 95, 97, 100, 110, 111, 124, 126, 138, 144, 145, 146, 161, 164, 183
parental example, 151, 206, 219
pars pro toto, 100, 112
Parthenope, 147, 209–10
pearls, 180
periphrasis, 84, 93, 94, 166
physical resemblance, 152, 212
Plotius Grypus, 220–4
poetic persona, 204, 216
Poggio, xxxii, xxxiii n.
Politian, xxxiii, 106
Polla, 95, 212–13
Pollius Felix, xxi, 95, 97, 151, 209, 211; son, 212
πολύπτωτον, 224
pork, 234
posture, 85, 88
praefectus uehiculorum, 221–3
prayer-formulae, 199; see also hymn, religious language
'pre-eminence', 91, 126, 212
prolepsis, 100
pronouns, declamatory use, 116
propaganda: building projects, 102, 104; formal vote of thanks, 110
propempticon, xxx
prose prefaces, 53–5
punctuation, 72, 75, 78, 81, 88, 90, 91, 132, 142, 148, 153
purple, 65, 152–3
Puteoli, 211

Quintilian, 58, 135

recusatio, 68, 78, 156, 197–8
religious language, 106, 131, 183–4, 213; see also hymn, prayer-formulae
respiratory system, 210
river-gods, 120–2, 123
rivers: Bagradas, 126; Cinyps, 126; Liris, 126; Orontes, 206–7; Tiber,

135, 139, 168; Timauus, 208; Volturnus, 120–6 passium
road-building, 105, 112–18, 127, 138
rubrum mare, 180

sacer, 56–7
Saepta Iulia, 177
Saguntum, 190–1
Sallust, 208
salutatio, 146, 238–9
salutatory formulae, 55, 72, 140, 160
Sarmatae, xvii, 78, 207
Saturnalian gifts, 230–1
sausages: see pork
Septimius Seuerus: emperor, 159, 169, 171; friend of Statius, 135, 158–9, 168, 169, 170–1
Sibyl of Cumae, 110, 130, 133
Siluae: characteristics, xxiv–xxviii; chronology of Book 4, xx–xxii; critics, 58–9, 61; and Domitian, 60; improvisation, xxvi, 58, 84; publication, xvi, xix, xxxi, 56, 59, 60; title, xxii–xxiv; see also tituli
spelling, 86–7, 114, 118, 143, 164, 166
sphaeromachia, 61
spokesman technique, 65, 104
Stagnum Nauale, 139
Statius: age, xix–xx, 151; father, xv, xvi, xviii–xix, xx, 160–1; and Juvenal, 59; and Martial, 59; wife, xvi, xvii; see also Achilleid, Agaue, De Bello Germanico, Siluae, Thebaid
statues: copies of, 174; ἐπιτραπέζιος position, 174; Hercules Epitrapezios from Alba Fucens, 173, 185; realism of, 181, 184; signatures on, 181; sweating of, 189; wax, 181
Sulla, 191, 194

tables, 94–5
Tarentum, 77–8
temple: of Capitoline Jupiter, 90, 108, 134; Gentis Flauiae, 109; of Peace, 69, 71, 108; see also Janus Geminus, Quadrifrons
Thebaid, xvi–xvii, xviii, 58, 155
'theme and variation', 117
tituli, xxviii–xxxii, 82
toga, 73–4
travelling speeds, xx, 129
Triptolemus, 93–4
triumphal arch, 127–8

uexillum, 97
umbones, 114, 115
urbanitas, 167, 224

valedictory formula, 157, 172, 239
vehicles, 110–11
Veii, 170–1
Vestinus, friend of Nouius Vindex, 173, 192
Via Domitiana, xix, 57, 102–5, 129, 138
Via Latina, 149
Vibius Maximus, 195–7
Vindex: *see* Nouius Vindex
Virgil: and Augustus, 60; echoes of, 89, 93, 116, 119, 121, 133, 134, 139, 142–3, 148, 150, 153; and Naples, 147; tomb, 148
Vitorius Marcellus, xix, 135, 155
vocative, reiterated, 225
volcanoes, xviii, 153, 154–5, 186, 210, 219

weighing-machine, 238
wine-making, 235
word-order, 76, 78, 93, 163, 202–3, 214; in names, 58; *see also* hyperbaton

Xerxes, 118–19

www.ingramcontent.com/pod-product-compliance
Lightning Source LLC
Chambersburg PA
CBHW052219300426
44115CB00011B/1757